ku797-090

D1609705

SPECIAL NEEDS IN ORDINARY SCHOOLS
General Editor: Peter Mittler

Improving Children's Reading in the Junior School:
Challenges and Responses

Special Needs in Ordinary Schools

General editor: Peter Mittler
Associate editors: James Hogg, Peter Pumfrey, Colin Robson
Honorary advisory board: Neville Bennett, Marion Blythman,
George Cooke, John Fish, Ken Jones, Sylvia Phillips, Klaus Wedell,
Phillip Williams

Titles in this series

Improving Children's Reading in the Junior School:
Challenges and Responses

Peter Pumfrey

CASSELL

Cassell Educational Limited
Villiers House, 41/47 Strand, London WC2N 5JE, England

First published 1991

British Library Cataloguing in Publication Data
Pumfrey, Peter D. (Peter David), *1930–*
    Improving children's reading in the junior school:
    challenges and responses.
    1. Great Britain. Primary schools. Curriculum subjects:
    reading teaching
    I. Title
    372.40941

ISBN 0–304–31723–3

Typeset by Fakenham Photosetting Limited, Fakenham, Norfolk
Printed and bound in Great Britain by Biddles Ltd, Guildford and King's Lynn

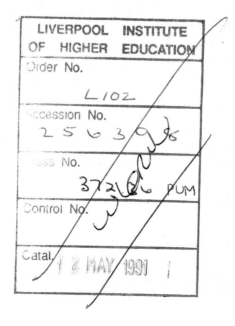

Contents

Acknowledgements

I am indebted to a vast range and number of individuals both in this country and overseas for what I have learned about the improvement of reading attainments and the nature, incidence, identification, alleviation and prevention of reading difficulties.

To Tom, the illiterate army conscript who, 42 years ago, asked me to read to him his letters from home;

to E. Mary Puddephat, then a lecturer at Dudley Training College, who so enthusiastically introduced me to the study of language development in general and reading development in particular; to the late Mia Kellmer-Pringle, to Charles Phillips and Ronald Gulliford who helped further that understanding during my period of study at the University of Birmingham Child Study Centre at Selly Wick House;

to Joseph MacNally and members of the City of Manchester Child Guidance Clinic, Schools Psychological and Remedial Education Services for giving me the opportunity of contributing towards the improvement of the reading attainments of schoolchildren in general and, in particular, those with severe and prolonged reading difficulties in a variety of mainstream schools in inner-city areas;

to the late Olive Sampson, one of the pioneer educational psychologists with a deep interest in children with all types of language difficulties, under whom I subsequently trained as an educational psychologist;

to Asher Cashdan and Margaret Skeffington with whom I worked with qualified and experienced teachers studying for the Diploma in the Education of Handicapped Children at the University of Manchester;

to Colin Elliott and Rea Reason, current colleagues with whom I have discussed many of the ideas in this book;

to Kenneth Cornwall and Robin Hedderley with whom I helped write a report entitled 'Specific Learning Difficulties: the Specific Reading Difficulties versus Specific Developmental Dyslexia Controversy Resolved?';

to the many qualified and experienced teachers who have attended, and contributed significantly to, in-service courses that I have organised on the improvement of children's reading attainments and on the identification, alleviation and prevention of reading difficulties;

to colleagues working in LEA Remedial Education and Support Services who have so readily shared their expertise;

to Mary, the 8-year-old who eventually learned to read despite having almost all imaginable odds stacked against her; and finally, to Larry who is still battling against illiteracy, but who will succeed.

In becoming a teacher, I was one of those fortunate individuals who managed to get paid for doing what I most wanted to do. From my colleagues in the profession, often in far from adequate material circumstances, I experienced characteristically wise advice, sound examples of professional practice concerning the teaching and learning of reading, and support in my own professional development. From pupils of all abilities and backgrounds attending mainstream junior schools, I learned the importance of recognising individual differences in physical, cognitive, emotional and social characteristics, the key roles of enthusiasm, motivation, pupil–teacher relationships and home–school liaison in education in general and in the improvement of reading attainments in particular.

More specifically, the late Tessa Roberts and the extant Peter Mittler have provided constructive editorial comment and encouragement. To them I express my sincere appreciation.

Finally, in common with many junior school pupils who have overcome severe reading difficulties, albeit for different but complementary reasons, I am deeply indebted to the ingenuity of Charles Babbage's followers.

Word processors are not only for the literate.

Foreword: Towards education for all

AIMS

This series aims to support teachers as they respond to the challenge they face in meeting the needs of all children in their school, particularly those identified as having special educational needs.

Although there have been many useful publications in the field of special educational needs during the last decade, the distinguishing feature of the present series of volumes lies in their concern with specific areas of the curriculum in primary and secondary schools. We have tried to produce a series of conceptually coherent and professionally relevant books, each of which is concerned with ways in which children with varying levels of ability and motivation can be taught together. The books draw on the experience of practising teachers, teacher trainers and researchers and seek to provide practical guidelines on ways in which specific areas of the curriculum can be made more accessible to all children. The volumes provide many examples of curriculum adaptation, classroom activities, teacher–child interactions, as well as the mobilisation of resources inside and outside the school.

The series is organised largely in terms of age and subject groupings, but three 'overview' volumes have been prepared in order to provide an account of some major current issues and developments. Seamus Hegarty's *Meeting Special Needs in Ordinary Schools* gives an introduction to the field of special needs as a whole, whilst Sheila Wolfendale's *Primary Schools and Special Needs* and John Sayer's *Secondary Schools for All?* address issues more specifically concerned with primary and secondary schools respectively. We hope that curriculum specialists will find essential background and contextual material in these overview volumes.

In addition, a section of this series will be concerned with examples of obstacles to learning. All of these specific special needs can be seen on a continuum ranging from mild to severe, or from temporary and transient to long-standing or permanent. These include difficulties in learning or in adjustment and behaviour, as well as problems resulting largely from sensory or physical impairments or from difficulties of communication from whatever cause. We hope that teachers will consult the volumes in this section for guidance on working with children with specific difficulties.

The series aims to make a modest 'distance learning' contribution to meeting the needs of teachers working with the whole range of pupils with special educational needs by offering a set of resource materials relating to specific areas of the primary and secondary curriculum and by suggesting ways in which learning obstacles, whatever their origin, can be identified and addressed.

We hope that these materials will not only be used for private study but be subjected to critical scrutiny by school-based inservice groups sharing common curricular interests and by staff of institutions of higher education concerned with both special needs teaching and specific curriculum areas. The series has been planned to provide a resource for Local Education Authority (LEA) advisers, specialist teachers from all sectors of the education service, educational psychologists, and teacher working parties. We hope that the books will provide a stimulus for dialogue and serve as catalysts for improved practice.

It is our hope that parents will also be encouraged to read about new ideas in teaching children with special needs so that they can be in a better position to work in partnership with teachers on the basis of an informed and critical understanding of current difficulties and developments. The goal of 'Education for All' can only be reached if we succeed in developing a working partnership between teachers, pupils, parents, and the community at large.

ELEMENTS OF A WHOLE-SCHOOL APPROACH

Meeting special educational needs in ordinary schools is much more than a process of opening school doors to admit children previously placed in special schools. It involves a radical re-examination of what all schools have to offer all children. Our efforts will be judged in the long term by our success with children who are already in ordinary schools but whose needs are not being met, for whatever reason.

The additional challenge of achieving full educational as well as social integration for children now in special schools needs to be seen in the wider context of a major reappraisal of what ordinary schools have to offer the pupils already in them. The debate about integration of handicapped and disabled children in ordinary schools should not be allowed to overshadow the movement for curriculum reform in the schools themselves. If successful, this could promote the fuller integration of the children already in the schools.

If this is the aim of current policy, as it is of this series of unit texts, we have to begin by examining ways in which schools and school policies can themselves be a major element in children's difficulties.

Can schools cause special needs?

Traditionally, we have looked for causes of learning difficulty in the child. Children have been subjected to tests and investigations by doctors, psychologists and teachers with the aim of pinpointing the nature of the problem and in the hope that this might lead to specific programmes of teaching and intervention. We less frequently ask ourselves whether what and how we teach and the way in which we organise and manage our schools could themselves be major causes of children's difficulties.

The shift of emphasis towards a whole-school policy is sometimes described in terms of a move away from the deficit or medical model of special education towards a more environmental or ecological model. Clearly, we are concerned here with an interaction between the two. No one would deny that the origins of some learning difficulties do lie in the child. But even where a clear cause can be established – for example, a child with severe brain damage, or one with a serious sensory or motor disorder – it would be simplistic to attribute all the child's learning difficulties to the basic impairment alone.

The ecological model starts from the position that the growth and development of children can be understood only in relation to the nature of their interactions with the various environments which impinge on them and with which they are constantly interacting. These environments include the home and each individual member of the immediate and extended family. Equally important are other children in the neighbourhood and at school, as well as people with whom the child comes into casual or closer contact. We also need to consider the local and wider community and its various institutions – not least, the powerful influence of television, which for some children represents more hours of information intake than is provided by teachers during eleven years of compulsory education. The ecological model thus describes a gradually widening series of concentric circles, each of which provides a powerful series of influences and possibilities for interaction – and therefore learning.

Schools and schooling are only one of many environmental influences affecting the development and learning of children. A great deal has been learned from other environments before the child enters school and much more will be learned after the child leaves full-time education. Schools represent a relatively powerful series of environments, not all concerned with formal learning. During the hours spent in school, it is hard to estimate the extent to which the number and nature of the interactions experienced by any one child are directly concerned with formal teaching and learning. Social interactions with other children also need to be considered.

Questions concerned with access to the curriculum lie at the heart of any whole-school policy. What factors limit the access of certain children to the curriculum? What modifications are necessary to ensure fuller curriculum access? Are there areas of the curriculum from which some children are excluded? Is this because they are thought 'unlikely to be able to benefit'? And even if they are physically present, are there particular lessons or activities which are inaccessible because textbooks or worksheets demand a level of literacy and comprehension which effectively prevents access? Are there tasks in which children partly or wholly fail to understand the language which the teacher is using? Are some teaching styles inappropriate for individual children?

Is it possible that some learning difficulties arise from the ways in which schools are organised and managed? For example, what messages are we conveying when we separate some children from others? How does the language we use to describe certain children reflect our own values and assumptions? How do schools transmit value judgements about children who succeed and those who do not? In the days when there was talk of comprehensive schools being 'grammar schools for all', what hope was there for children who were experiencing significant learning difficulties? And even today, what messages are we transmitting to children and their peers when we exclude them from participation in some school activities? How many children with special needs will be entered for the new General Certificate of Secondary Education (GCSE) examinations? How many have taken or will take part in Technical and Vocational Education Initiative (TVEI) schemes?

The argument here is not that all children should have access to all aspects of the curriculum. Rather it is a plea for the individualisation of learning opportunities for all children. This requires a broad curriculum with a rich choice of learning opportunities designed to suit the very wide range of individual needs.

Curriculum reform

The last decade has seen an increasingly interventionist approach by Her Majesty's Inspectors of Education (HMI), by officials of the

Department of Education and Science (DES) and by individual Secretaries of State. The 'Great Debate', allegedly beginning in 1976, led to a flood of curriculum guidelines from the centre. The garden is secret no longer. Whilst Britain is far from the centrally imposed curriculum found in some other countries, government is increasingly insisting that schools must reflect certain key areas of experience for all pupils, and in particular those concerned with the world of work (*sic*), with science and technology, and with economic awareness. These priorities are also reflected in the prescriptions for teacher education laid down with an increasing degree of firmness from the centre.

There are indications that a major reappraisal of curriculum content and access is already under way and seems to be well supported by teachers. Perhaps the best known and most recent examples can be found in the series of Inner London Education Authority (ILEA) reports concerned with secondary, primary and special education, known as the Hargreaves, Thomas and Fish Reports (ILEA, 1984, 1985a, 1985b). In particular, the Hargreaves Report envisaged a radical reform of the secondary curriculum, based to some extent on his book *Challenge for the Comprehensive School* (Hargreaves, 1982). This envisages a major shift of emphasis from the 'cognitive–academic' curriculum of many secondary schools towards one emphasising more personal involvement by pupils in electing their own patterns of study from a wider range of choice. If the proposals in these reports were to be even partially implemented, pupils with special needs would stand to benefit from such a wholesale review of the curriculum of the school as a whole.

Pupils with special needs also stand to benefit from other developments in mainstream education. These include new approaches to records of achievement, particularly 'profiling' and a greater emphasis on criterion-referenced assessment. Some caution has already been expressed about the extent to which the new GCSE examinations will reach less able children previously excluded from the Certificate of Secondary Education. Similar caution is justified in relation to the TVEI and the Certificate of Pre-Vocational Education (CPVE). And what about the new training initiatives for school leavers and the 14–19 age group in general? Certainly, the pronouncements of the Manpower Services Commission (MSC) emphasise a policy of provision for all, and have made specific arrangements for young people with special needs, including those with disabilities. In the last analysis, society and its institutions will be judged by their success in preparing the majority of young people to make an effective and valued contribution to the community as a whole.

A CLIMATE OF CHANGE

Despite the very real and sometimes overwhelming difficulties faced by schools and teachers as a result of underfunding and professional unrest, there are encouraging signs of change and reform which, if successful, could have a significant impact not only on children with special needs but on all children. Some of these are briefly mentioned below.

The campaign for equal opportunities

First, we are more aware of the need to confront issues concerned with civil rights and equal opportunities. All professionals concerned with human services are being asked to examine their own attitudes and practices and to question the extent to which these might unwittingly or even deliberately discriminate unfairly against some sections of the population.

We are more conscious than ever of the need to take positive steps to promote the full access of girls and women not only to full educational opportunities but also to the whole range of community resources and services, including employment, leisure, housing, social security and the right to property. We have a similar concern for members of ethnic and religious groups who have been and still are victims of discrimination and restricted opportunities for participation in society and its institutions. It is no accident that the title of the Swann Report on children from ethnic minorities was *Education for All* (Committee of Inquiry, 1985). This too is the theme of the present series and the underlying aim of the movement to meet the whole range of special needs in ordinary schools.

The equal opportunities movement has not itself always fully accepted people with disabilities and special needs. At national level, there is no legislation specifically concerned with discrimination against people with disabilities, though this does exist in some other countries. The Equal Opportunities Commission does not concern itself with disability issues. On the other hand, an increasing number of local authorities and large corporations claim to be 'Equal Opportunities Employers', specifically mentioning disability alongside gender, ethnicity and sexual orientation. Furthermore, the 1986 Disabled Persons Act, arising from a private member's Bill and now on the statute book, seeks to carry forward for adults some of the more positive features of the 1981 Education Act – for example it provides for the rights of all people with disabilities to take part or be represented in discussion and decision-making concerning services provided for them.

These developments, however, have been largely concerned with children or adults with disabilities, rather than with children already in ordinary schools. Powerful voluntary organisations such as MENCAP (the Royal Society for Mentally Handicapped Children and Adults) and the Spastics Society have helped to raise political and public awareness of the needs of children with disabilities and have fought hard and on the whole successfully to secure better services for them and for their families. Similarly, organisations of adults with disabilities, such as the British Council of Organisations for Disabled People, are pressing hard for better quality, integrated education, given their own personal experiences of segregated provision.

Special needs and social disadvantage

Even these developments have largely bypassed two of the largest groups now in special schools: those with moderate learning difficulties and those with emotional and behavioural difficulties. There are no powerful pressure groups to speak for them, for the same reason that no pressure groups speak for the needs of children with special needs already in ordinary schools. Many of these children come from families which do not readily form themselves into associations and pressure groups. Many of their parents are unemployed, on low incomes or dependent on social security; many live in overcrowded conditions in poor-quality housing or have long-standing health problems. Some members of these families have themselves experienced school failure and rejection as children.

Problems of poverty and disadvantage are common in families of children with special needs already in ordinary schools. Low achievement and social disadvantage are clearly associated, though it is important not to assume that there is a simple relation between them. Although most children from socially disadvantaged backgrounds have not been identified as low achieving, there is still a high correlation between social-class membership and educational achievement, with middle-class children distancing themselves increasingly in educational achievements and perhaps also socially from children from working-class backgrounds – another form of segregation within what purports to be the mainstream.

The probability of socially disadvantaged children being identified as having special needs is very much greater than in other children. An early estimate suggested that it was more than seven times as high, when social disadvantage was defined by the presence of all three of the following indices: overcrowding (more than 1.5 persons per room), low income (supplementary benefit or free school meals) and adverse family circumstances (coming from a single-parent home or a home with more than five children) (Wedge and Prosser, 1973). Since this study was published, the number of families coming into these categories has greatly increased as a result of deteriorating economic conditions and changing social circumstances.

In this wider sense, the problem of special needs is largely a problem of social disadvantage and poverty. Children with special needs are therefore doubly vulnerable to underestimation of their abilities: first, because of their family and social backgrounds, and second, because of their low achievements. A recent large-scale study of special needs provision in junior schools suggests that while teachers' attitudes to low-achieving children are broadly positive, they are pessimistic about the ability of such children to derive much benefit from increased special needs provision (Croll and Moses, 1985).

Partnership with parents

The Croll and Moses survey of junior school practice confirms that teachers still tend to attribute many children's difficulties to adverse home circumstances. How many times have we heard comments along the lines of 'What can you expect from a child from that kind of family?' Is this not a form of stereotyping at least as damaging as racist and sexist attitudes?

Partnership with parents of socially disadvantaged children thus presents a very different challenge from that portrayed in the many reports of successful practice in some special schools. Nevertheless, the challenge can be and is being met. Paul Widlake's books (1984, 1985) give the lie to the oft-expressed view that some parents are 'not interested in their child's education'. Widlake documents project after project in which teachers and parents have worked well together. Many of these projects have involved teachers visiting homes rather than parents attending school meetings. There is also now ample research to show that children whose parents listen to them reading at home tend to read better and to enjoy reading more than other children (Topping and Wolfendale, 1985; see also Sheila Wolfendale's *Primary Schools and Special Needs*, in the present series).

Support in the classroom

If teachers in ordinary schools are to identify and meet the whole range of special needs, including those of children currently in special schools, they are entitled to support. Above all, this must come from the headteacher and from the senior staff of the school;

from any special needs specialists or teams already in the school; from members of the new advisory and support services, as well as from educational psychologists, social workers and any health professionals who may be involved.

This support can take many forms. In the past, support meant removing the child for considerable periods of time into the care of remedial teachers either within the school or coming from outside. Withdrawal now tends to be discouraged, partly because it is thought to be another form of segregation within the ordinary school, and therefore in danger of isolating and stigmatising children, and partly because it deprives children of access to lessons and activities available to other children. In a major survey of special needs provision in middle and secondary schools, Clunies-Ross and Wimhurst (1983) showed that children with special needs were most often withdrawn from science and modern languages in order to find the time to give them extra help with literacy.

Many schools and LEAs are exploring ways in which both teachers and children can be supported without withdrawing children from ordinary classes. For example, special needs teachers increasingly are working alongside their colleagues in ordinary classrooms, not just with a small group of children with special needs but also with all children. Others are working as consultants to their colleagues in discussing the level of difficulty demanded of children following a particular course or specific lesson. An account of recent developments in consultancy is given in Hanko (1985), with particular reference to children with difficulties of behaviour or adjustment.

Although traditional remedial education is undergoing radical reform, major problems remain. Implementation of new approaches is uneven both between and within LEAs. Many schools still have a remedial department or are visited by peripatetic remedial teachers who withdraw children for extra tuition in reading with little time for consultation with school staff. Withdrawal is still the preferred mode of providing extra help in primary schools, as suggested in surveys of current practice (Clunies-Ross and Wimhurst, 1983; Hodgson, Clunies-Ross and Hegarty, 1984; Croll and Moses, 1985).

Nevertheless, an increasing number of schools now see withdrawal as only one of a widening range of options, only to be used where the child's individually assessed needs suggest that this is indeed the most appropriate form of provision. Other alternatives are now being considered. The overall aim of most of these involves the development of a working partnership between the mainstream class teacher and members of teams with particular responsibility for meeting special needs. This partnership can take a variety of forms, depending on particular circumstances and individual preferences. Much depends on the sheer credibility of special needs teachers, their perceived capacity to offer support and advice and, where necessary, direct, practical help.

We can think of the presence of the specialist teacher as being on a continuum of visibility. A 'high-profile' specialist may sit along-side a pupil with special needs, providing direct assistance and support in participating in activities being followed by the rest of the class. A 'low-profile' specialist may join with a colleague in what is in effect a team-teaching situation, perhaps spending a little more time with individuals or groups with special needs. An even lower profile is provided by teachers who may not set foot in the classroom at all but who may spend considerable periods of time in discussion with colleagues on ways in which the curriculum can be made more accessible to all children in the class, including the least able. Such discussions may involve an examination of textbooks and other reading assignments for readability, conceptual difficulty and relevance of content, as well as issues concerned with the presentation of the material, language modes and complexity used to explain what is required, and the use of different approaches to teacher–pupil dialogue.

IMPLICATIONS FOR TEACHER TRAINING

Issues of training are raised by the authors of the overview works in this series but permeate all the volumes concerned with specific areas of the curriculum or specific areas of special needs.

The scale and complexity of changes taking place in the field of special needs and the necessary transformation of the teacher-training curriculum imply an agenda for teacher training that is nothing less than retraining and supporting every teacher in the country in working with pupils with special needs.

Although teacher training represented one of the three major priorities identified by the Warnock Committee, the resources devoted to this priority have been meagre, despite a strong commitment to training from teachers, LEAs, staff of higher education, HMI and the DES itself. Nevertheless, some positive developments can be noted (for more detailed accounts of developments in teacher education see Sayer and Jones, 1985 and Robson, Sebba, Mittler and Davies, 1988).

Initial training

At the initial training level, we now find an insistence that all teachers in training must be exposed to a compulsory component concerned with meeting special needs in the ordinary school. The Council for the Accreditation of Teacher Education (CATE) and HMI seem set to enforce these criteria; institutions that do not meet them will not be accredited for teacher training.

Although this policy is welcome from a special needs perspective, many questions remain. Where will the staff to teach these courses come from? What happened to the Warnock recommendations for each teacher-training institution to have a small team of staff specifically concerned with this area? Even when a team exists, they can succeed in 'permeating' a special needs element into initial teacher training only to the extent that they influence all their fellow specialist tutors to widen their teaching perspectives to include children with special needs.

Special needs departments in higher education face similar problems to those confronting special needs teams in secondary schools. They need to gain access to and influence the work of the whole institution. They also need to avoid the situation where the very existence of an active special needs department results in colleagues regarding special needs as someone else's responsibility, not theirs.

Despite these problems, the outlook in the long term is favourable. More and more teachers in training are at least receiving an introduction to special needs; are being encouraged to seek out information on special needs policy and practice in the schools in which they are doing their teaching practice, and are being introduced to a variety of approaches to meeting these needs. Teaching materials are being prepared specifically for initial teacher-training students. Teacher trainers have also been greatly encouraged by the obvious interest and commitment of students to children with special needs; optional and elective courses on this subject have always been over-subscribed.

Inservice courses for designated teachers

Since 1983, the government has funded a series of one-term full-time courses in polytechnics and universities to provide intensive training for designated teachers with specific responsibility for pupils with special needs in ordinary schools (see *Meeting Special Needs in Ordinary Schools* by Seamus Hegarty in this series for information on research on evaluation of their effectiveness). These courses are innovative in a number of respects. They bring LEA and higher-education staff together in a productive working partnership. The seconded teacher, headteacher, LEA adviser and higher-education tutor enter into a commitment to train and support the teachers in becoming change agents in their own schools.

Students spend two days a week in their own schools initiating and implementing change. All teachers with designated responsibilities for pupils with special needs have the right to be considered for these one-term courses, which are now a national priority area for which central funding is available. However, not all teachers can gain access to these courses as the institutions are geographically very unevenly distributed.

Other inservice courses

The future of inservice education for teachers (INSET) in education in general and special needs in particular is in a state of transition. Since April 1987, the government has abolished the central pooling arrangements which previously funded courses and has replaced these by a system in which LEAs are required to identify their training requirements and to submit these to the DES for funding. LEAs are being asked to negotiate training needs with each school as part of a policy of staff development and appraisal. Special needs is one of nineteen national priority areas that will receive 70 per cent funding from the DES, as is training for further education (FE) staff with special needs responsibilities.

These new arrangements, known as Grant Related Inservice Training (GRIST), will change the face of inservice training for all teachers but time is needed to assess their impact on training opportunities and teacher effectiveness (see Mittler, 1986, for an interim account of the implications of the proposed changes). In the meantime, there is serious concern about the future of secondments for courses longer than one term. Additional staffing will also be needed in higher education to respond to the wider range of demand.

An increasing number of 'teaching packages' have become available for teachers working with pupils with special needs. Some (though not all) of these are well designed and evaluated. Most of them are school-based and can be used by small groups of teachers working under the supervision of a trained tutor.

The best known of these is the Special Needs Action Programme (SNAP) originally developed for Coventry primary schools (Muncey and Ainscow, 1982) but now being adapted for secondary schools. This is based on a form of pyramid training in which co-ordinators from each school are trained to train colleagues in their own school or sometimes in a consortium of local schools. Evaluation by a National Foundation for Educational Research (NFER) research team suggests that SNAP is potentially an effective approach to school-based inservice training, providing that strong management support is guaranteed by the headteacher and by senior LEA staff (see Hegarty, *Meeting Special Needs in Ordinary Schools*, this series, for a brief summary). Both GRIST and LEATGs have been replaced by Grants for Education Support and Training (GEST). Central government direction of priorities for expenditure has been further increased.

Does training work?

Many readers of this series of books are likely to have recent experience of training courses. How many of them led to changes in classroom practice? How often have teachers been frustrated by their inability to introduce and implement change in their schools on returning from a course? How many heads actively support their staff in becoming change agents? How many teachers returning from advanced one-year courses have experienced 'the re-entry phenomenon'? At worst, this is quite simply being ignored: neither the LEA adviser, nor the head nor any one else asks about special interests and skills developed on the course and how these could be most effectively put to good use in the school. Instead, the returning member of staff is put through various re-initiation rituals ('Enjoyed your holiday?'), or is given responsibilities bearing no relation to interests developed on the course. Not infrequently, colleagues with less experience and fewer qualifications are promoted over their heads during their absence.

At a time of major initiatives in training, it may seem churlish to raise questions about the effectiveness of staff training. It is necessary to do so because training resources are limited and because the morale and motivation of the teaching force depend on satisfaction with what is offered – indeed, on opportunities to negotiate what is available with course providers. Blind faith in training for training's sake soon leads to disillusionment and frustration.

For the last three years, a team of researchers at Manchester University and Huddersfield Polytechnic have been involved in a DES-funded project which aimed to assess the impact of a range of inservice courses on teachers working with pupils with special educational needs (see Robson, Sebba, Mittler and Davies, 1988, for a full account and Sebba and Robson, 1987, for a briefer interim report). A variety of courses was evaluated; some were held for one evening a week for a term; others were one-week full time; some were award-bearing, others were not. The former included the North-West regional diploma in special needs, the first example of a course developed in total partnership between a university and a polytechnic which allows students to take modules from either institution and also gives credit recognition to specific Open University and LEA courses. The research also evaluated the effectiveness of an already published and disseminated course on behavioural methods of teaching – the EDY course (Farrell, 1985).

Whether or not the readers of these books are or will be experiencing a training course, or whether their training consists only of the reading of one or more of the books in this series, it may be useful to conclude by highlighting a number of challenges facing teachers and teacher trainers in the coming decades.

1. We are all out of date in relation to the challenges that we face in our work.
2. Training in isolation achieves very little. Training must be seen as part of a wider programme of change and development of the institution as a whole.
3. Each LEA, each school and each agency needs to develop a strategic approach to staff development, involving detailed identification of training and development needs with the staff as a whole and with each individual member of staff.
4. There must be a commitment by management to enable the staff member to try to implement ideas and methods learned on the course.
5. This implies a corresponding commitment by the training institutions to prepare the student to become an agent of change.
6. There is more to training than attending courses. Much can be learned simply by visiting other schools, seeing teachers and other professionals at work in different settings and exchanging ideas and experiences. Many valuable training experiences can be arranged within a single school or agency, or by a group of teachers from different schools meeting regularly to carry out an agreed task.
7. There is now no shortage of books, periodicals, videos and audio-visual aids concerned with the field of special needs. Every school should therefore have a small staff library which can be used as a resource by staff and parents. We hope that the present series of unit texts will make a useful contribution to such a library.

The publishers and I would like to thank the many people – too numerous to mention – who have helped to create this series. In particular we would like to thank the Associate Editors, James Hogg, Peter Pumfrey, Tessa Roberts and Colin Robson, for their active advice and guidance; the Honorary Advisory Board, Neville Bennett, Marion Blythman, George Cooke, John Fish, Ken Jones, Sylvia Phillips, Klaus Wedell and Phillip Williams, for their comments and suggestions; and the teachers, teacher trainers and special needs advisers who took part in our information surveys.

SOME IMPLICATIONS OF THE EDUCATION REFORM ACT:
AN EDITORIAL POSTSCRIPT

Full access to the curriculum is the central theme of this series of
books and the fundamental challenge posed by the 1988 Education
Reform Act. What are the implications of this Act for children with
special educational needs? Will it help or hinder access to the
national curriculum? How will they fare under the proposed
assessment arrangements? What degree of priority will be given to
these children by the new governing bodies, by headteachers, by
LEAs and by the community? Will the voice of parents be heard
when priority decisions are being taken on how the schools'
resources will be used? What are the implications of local management, financial delegation and open enrolment? Is there a risk that
children in ordinary schools will be denied access to the national
curriculum? Will there be increased pressure to provide them with
the 'protection of a statement' and to press for them to be sent to
special schools? Will ordinary schools welcome children whose
needs call for additional resources and for a fully accessible curriculum? Will they be welcome in grant-maintained schools? What is
the future of the strong links which have been established between
special and ordinary schools during the last few years and which
are enabling an increasing number of special school pupils to be
timetabled to spend periods in a neighbouring ordinary school?
Will the Act make it harder for children in special schools to be
integrated into ordinary schools?

These and many other questions have been asked with growing
urgency ever since the publication of the first consultation paper
on the national curriculum. There was concern and anger that the
government appeared to have overlooked children with special
educational needs both in its consultation document and in the
early versions of the Bill and because it appeared to be ignoring the
strong representations on this subject which were being made
during the consultation process. The early Bill contained only one
special needs clause concerned with exclusion from the national
curriculum, accompanied by reiterated official references to the
need to be able to exempt children from a second language when
they had not yet mastered English.

There seemed to be little recognition of the risks to the principles
and practice of the 1981 Education Act, to the needs of the 18 per
cent of children in ordinary schools and to the dangers of inappropriate exclusion. For many months it was not clear whether grant-
maintained schools would be subject to the 1981 Act. At a general
level, there was concern over the reduced powers of LEAs, given
their key role in consultation with parents and their overview of

planning and monitoring of special needs provision over the authority as a whole. This last concern was most acutely reflected in relation to the abolition of the ILEA, which had not only developed good authority-wide provision but has published far-reaching plans for improved integrated provision in ordinary and special schools. Where are these reports today?

The extent to which these anxieties are justified will depend in part on the way in which the legislation is interpreted in the schools and LEAs, and on the kind of guidance issued from the centre. In this latter respect, there are grounds for optimism. Although it was only when the Bill was in its final parliamentary stages that there was evidence that special needs issues were beginning to be considered, there is increasing evidence that these special needs concerns are receiving a much higher degree of priority. New members with special needs interests were added to the National Curriculum Council and the School Examinations and Assessment Council. Clear statements of policy and principle from ministers, from the DES and from HMI are establishing the rights of all children to the national curriculum. Exceptions, exclusions, disapplications and modifications can only be made in individual cases for children with statements, with the full participation of parents and professionals and subject to appeal. There will be no blanket exemptions for groups of children, far less for types of school. Each modification will have to be fully justified by reference to the needs of the individual child, and against the background of a policy which is designed to ensure the fullest possible access to the curriculum. Exemptions for children not on statements can only be temporary. In all cases, schools have to indicate what kind of alternative provision is to be made. Modifications can be made in respect of single attainment targets, programmes of study or assessment arrangements. For example, it seems that children may be on programmes of study leading to attainment targets but might need a modified approach to assessment – e.g. oral instead of written, computer-aided rather than oral, etc. All these issues will need to be debated in relation to individual children rather than to 'categories' of pupils.

The national curriculum documents in science, maths and English as well as interim reports on design and technology and Welsh are all firmly committed to the principle of the fullest possible access for all children. The Report of the Task Group on Assessment and Testing (TGAT) went a long way towards meeting special needs concerns with its suggestion that attainment targets should be reported in terms of ten levels and that they should be formative, criterion-referenced and in profile form. These ten levels, which are linked to programmes of study, are designed to ensure progression and continuity and to avoid children being seen to 'fail the tests'. Children will be able to progress from one level to another for any of the attainment targets, even though they may be several years behind the attainments of other children of the same age. Finally, the specifications and terms of reference given to the development agencies charged with producing standard assessment tasks (SATs) – initially for key stage 1 at the age of about 7 – clearly specify that SATs must be suitable or adaptable for pupils with special educational needs.

Although the emphasis so far has been largely on children in ordinary schools, the challenge of implementing the national curriculum in all special schools will also need to be addressed. It is clear that special schools are without exception subject to the national curriculum and to the assessment arrangements but a great deal of work needs to be done to develop programmes of study and assessment arrangements which are suitable and age-appropriate for the whole range of pupils with special needs in special schools, without departing in principle from the framework provided by the national curriculum.

At the beginning of 1991, special needs provision is clearly at a highly critical stage. A pessimistic forecast would be that children with special needs, whether in ordinary or special schools, could be marginalised, isolated and excluded from developments in mainstream education. They might be less welcome because priorities may lie with children whose needs are easier and cheaper to meet and who will not adversely affect the school's public performance indicators. Such progress as has been made towards integration of special school pupils could be halted or reversed and an increasing number of children already in ordinary schools could become educationally and socially segregated in their own schools or inappropriately sent to special schools. The ethos of schools could become divisive and damaging to vulnerable children.

Because these remain real and potentially disastrous possibilities, it is essential to develop determined advocacy at all levels to ensure that the national curriculum and the new legislation are exploited to the full in the interests of all children, particularly those with special educational needs. Such advocacy will need to be well informed as well as determined and will be most effective if it is based on a partnership between professionals, parents and the pupils themselves.

Professor Peter Mittler
University of Manchester
January 1991

xxvi *Improving Children's Reading in the Junior School*

REFERENCES

Clunies-Ross, L. and Wimhurst, S. (1983) *The Right Balance: Provision for Slow Learners in Secondary Schools*. Windsor: NFER/Nelson.

Committee of Inquiry (1985) *Education for All*. London: HMSO (The Swann Report).

Croll, P. and Moses, D. (1985) *One in Five: The Assessment and Incidence of Special Educational Needs*. London: Routledge & Kegan Paul.

Farrell, P. (ed.) (1985) *EDY: Its Impact on Staff Training in Mental Handicap*. Manchester: Manchester University Press.

Hanko, G. (1985) *Special Needs in Ordinary Classrooms: An Approach to Teacher Support and Pupil Care in Primary and Secondary Schools*. Oxford: Blackwell.

Hargreaves, D. (1982) *Challenge for the Comprehensive School*. London: Routledge & Kegan Paul.

Hodgson, A., Clunies-Ross, L. and Hegarty, S. (1984) *Learning Together*. Windsor: NFER/Nelson.

Inner London Education Authority (1984) *Improving Secondary Education*. London: ILEA (The Hargreaves Report).

Inner London Education Authority (1985a) *Improving Primary Schools*. London: ILEA (The Thomas Report).

Inner London Education Authority (1985b) *Equal Opportunities for All?* London: ILEA (The Fish Report).

Mittler, P. (1986) The new look in inservice training. *British Journal of Special Education* 13, 50–1.

Muncey, J. and Ainscow, M. (1982) Launching SNAP in Coventry. *Special Education: Forward Trends* 10, 3–5.

Robson, C., Sebba, J., Mittler, P. and Davies, G. (1988) *Inservice Training and Special Needs: Running Short School-Focused Courses*. Manchester: Manchester University Press.

Sayer, J. and Jones, N. (eds) (1985) *Teacher Training and Special Educational Needs*. Beckenham: Croom Helm.

Sebba, J. and Robson, C. (1987) The development of short, school-focused INSET courses in special educational needs. *Research Papers in Education* 2, 1–29.

Topping, K. and Wolfendale, S. (eds) (1985) *Parental Involvement in Children's Reading*. Beckenham: Croom Helm.

Wedge, P. and Prosser, H. (1973) *Born to Fail?* London: National Children's Bureau.

Widlake, P. (1984) *How to Reach the Hard to Teach*. Milton Keynes: Open University Press.

Widlake, P. (1985) *Reducing Educational Disadvantage*. London: Routledge & Kegan Paul.

Introduction

Teachers always ask for very practical advice – even those who attend courses.

(Member of an inservice course, 1990)

He that loves reading has everything within his reach. He has but to desire and he may possess himself of every species of wisdom to judge and power to perform.

(William Godwin, 1756–1836)

The purposes of this book are to consider the nature of reading, including its difficulties, their identification, alleviation and prevention in junior schools, and to make practical suggestions that can contribute to the improvement of the standards of reading of all pupils. The Warnock Report, the 1981 Education Act, its associated Circulars and Regulations, the proposals in the DES publication *The National Curriculum 5–16: A Consultation Document*, and the 1988 Education Reform Act, provide the background (Committee of Enquiry, 1978; DES, 1981, 1987, 1988c).

Reading, the ability to comprehend the thoughts and feelings of another mind via the medium of text, is an amplifier of human abilities. Its acquisition empowers the pupil. Not to be able to read in our society is to be seriously and progressively disadvantaged. Illiteracy impoverishes the individual. Reading enriches.

To learn to read, to find that the skill is of utility in solving problems and can also provide affective and aesthetic satisfactions, are central objectives of education. We want our children to be able to read, to find it useful and to enjoy the activity. The number of adult illiterates in Britain who are currently seeking help in learning to read (and write) via the services of the Adult Literacy Basic Skills Unit suggests that all is far from well in schools. The 'Back to Basics' cry that echoes through some corridors of power reflects a concern that insufficient attention is being paid to literacy in our schools. The proposals for testing pupils' reading attainments at the ages of 7 and 11 represent a further indication of concern about what is achieved in state schools, as does the subsequent passing of the 1988 Education Reform Act. The Kingman Report on the

Teaching of English included a recommendation that pupils should be set a series of attainment targets at the ages of 7, 11 and 16 (DES, 1988a).

This is not to agree that such concerns are necessarily valid, but to recognise that they exist, and must be addressed by the teaching profession. They also include issues on which parents, pupils and professionals have important and, at times, divergent views. In this complex field, we must remain open-minded when considering how the related goals of improving junior school children's reading can be achieved.

In the interests of the pupils, parents and society that the educational system exists to serve, we cannot afford the absolute certainty of the second-rate mind. This is not to devalue the enthusiasm of the innovator, but to sound a warning. Beware the hawkers of snake oil, no matter how well packaged and presented their offerings. Any proposed educational panacea for all reading difficulties should be viewed with scepticism.

Communication is a portmanteau concept capable of holding almost all the junior school curriculum. In relation to language, it includes the expressive skills of speaking and writing and the receptive ones of listening and reading. All four are intimately related. A previously published book in this series by Alex Webster and Christine McConnell, *Children with Speech and Language Difficulties*, contains detailed information on the range of pupils' speech and language difficulties that the teacher will meet in the classroom. It also includes numerous suggestions for helping such pupils (Webster and McConnell, 1987).

The present book deliberately focuses on *one* aspect of communication: improving junior school pupils' reading abilities. This encompasses the identification, alleviation and prevention of junior school pupils' reading difficulties. The selection of ideas, methods and materials contained in it are drawn from three major sources.

The first is current research and practice in the field. This includes the range of books and articles written by a variety of experts interested in improving children's reading and, more specifically, the reading difficulties of children with special educational needs in ordinary schools. The second is the observation of junior pupils of all abilities, coupled with discussions with their class teachers, specialist teachers of reading, members of literacy support teams, advisers, educational psychologists and administrators. The third source is the author's professional experience as a primary school teacher, remedial teacher, educational psychologist and research worker with a long-standing involvement in the improvement of reading programmes and, in particular, the identification, alleviation and prevention of language and reading difficulties.

AN OVERVIEW

The nine chapters of this book are organised in four major sections.

Section A, 'Challenges: The Current Scene', provides a background to the issues discussed in the subsequent three sections. Chapter 1 sets the scene by looking at current thinking, policy and practice. In particular, how far has our system of education moved in improving pupils' attainments and progress in reading and in minimising reading difficulties? What can be done to achieve these ends within the reading curriculum in the mainstream junior school? It is suggested that the concept of special educational needs is a hindrance rather than a help. An alternative is suggested.

Chapter 2 outlines the nature of reading and its development in junior schools. Six major current controversies associated with the learning and teaching of reading are considered. The importance of a diagnostic–prescriptive approach to the learning and teaching of reading for all pupils is discussed.

Section B, 'Responses I: Assessment Issues', is concerned with the uses and limitations of differing types of observation procedures, tests and assessment techniques. The integration of assessment and teaching is considered in relation to the national curriculum. Chapter 3 provides a description of current identification practices. It includes a discussion of the strengths and weaknesses of normative, criterion-referenced and informal approaches in both formative and summative assessments. Chapter 4 identifies a number of promising practices, and discusses the assessment requirements of the national curriculum.

Section C, 'Responses II: Promising Practices', describes basic strategies and specialised interventions aimed at optimising progress in reading and alleviating reading difficulties. Chapter 5 outlines research findings and follows this with a selection of promising methods and techniques. Chapter 6 comprises accounts of ten specialised teaching approaches used mainly with dyslexic pupils. Chapter 7 describes a range of kits and Chapter 8 presents sources of information on current and prospective microcomputer applications, together with examples of some current applications.

The final section is 'Individual Differences in Reading in the Classroom: The Challenge of the National Curriculum'. Chapter 9 considers classroom-related reading curriculum development issues and practices. Sources of information on innovations in professional development in the teaching of reading are described.

Sources of information and advice are listed and described in Appendix 1. Appendix 2 contains the national curriculum (English) attainment targets and associated statements of attainment for key stages 1 and 2. Appendix 3 lists the information LEAs are required to tell parents of children with special educational needs.

CONCLUSION

By making explicit some of our often unvoiced assumptions and expectations about the nature of reading and reading difficulties it is anticipated that the reader will be in a better position to consider the efficacy of current practices.

The information on promising practices and available resources gives the teacher the opportunity of selecting, adapting and experimenting, with the aim of more effectively dealing with junior pupils' reading difficulties in the context of a 'whole-school' approach to meeting junior school pupils' special educational needs.

The objectives are to enable *all* children to discover that reading can be learned, is enjoyable and of utility. The miseries of prolonged reading difficulties must be minimised and the satisfactions of success and progress in reading maximised *for all children*. The improvement of professional practices and of reading standards is at the core.

These are challenging and continuing professional responsibilities. They are not new. They are of profound importance.

Personal Statement

Each statement that follows expresses the author's current views on the improvement of children's reading. The statements represent personal evaluations of studies, research and policies, seen in the light of experience in education. Each statement can be strongly supported by research findings.

Referring to the suggestions for the improvement of children's reading at a more pragmatic level, there is a useful touchstone against which to test any statement of policy or practice advocated by anyone: 'In what circumstances would I agree to this for my own child?'

Not to be able to read in our society is to be disempowered, impoverished, marginalised and frequently demeaned. Illiterates are cut off from major sources of knowledge, insights and speculations.

Helping all children both learn to read and find enjoyment in the activity are prime objectives of the junior school. Co-operation with the pupils' parents or guardians is necessary in achieving these objectives.

The two objectives of improving the standards of reading attainment of children in general and the identification and alleviation of reading difficulties of particular individuals, are complementary professional responsibilities.

The reading curriculum is an integral part of the language curriculum. A reading programme geared to minimising reading difficulties and optimising pupils' progress in reading will include the following two aspects of instruction:

adjustment of the instruction to meet individual differences; and systematic developmental programmes.

Learning to read is not the same as the teaching of reading. In the classroom, the two activities typically occur together. The aim of the latter is to foster the former.

All children can be taught to read and to obtain pleasure from reading. They will learn at different rates and in differing ways at different times.

Children of all abilities can be helped to make progress in learning to read. They will progress at different rates.

The assessment of differences in reading abilities *between* pupils (inter-individual differences), and also the pattern of an individual pupil's particular strengths and weaknesses (intra-individual differences) in reading skills, can provide the class teacher with valuable information, which can be used to improve the teaching of reading.

Although professionals' knowledge is very far from complete, teachers and psychologists understand a great deal about the learning and teaching of reading.

In junior schools there are significant numbers of children with reading difficulties, many of which can be prevented. Others, if noticed, can be corrected in their initial stages and prevented from being compounded by continuing failures and frustration. Some pupils will require greater support for much longer periods than are currently provided.

The causes of reading difficulties (and success) are typically complex and multiple. Many of the former are created by the situations in which we place children, the experiences we expose them to and the expectations we hold. Such reading difficulties are avoidable. Our ambivalence in *accepting* individual differences in reading attainments has great problem-creating potential for pupils, parents and professionals.

Difficulties in reading vary in type and degree. When minor difficulties are ignored, their adverse effects on the pupil's motivation and progress become cumulative and can lead to severe reading difficulties. Whatever causes a reading difficulty does not necessarily maintain that problem.

There are many different approaches to the teaching of reading. A vast range of methods and materials is available. No one combination will suit all children at all stages of reading development. Beware purveyors of pedagogic panaceas.

Each child is unique. In an important sense, *every* child is 'special'.

All junior school children have much in common. They typically share at least one spoken language and culture. They want to communicate with their peers, their teachers, their families and friends. They want to learn to read, to experience success in understanding and producing text.

Both the child's uniqueness and shared characteristics have implications for the teaching and learning of reading. Individual work and interactive group work each have important roles to play in the teaching and learning of reading.

Some approaches to the teaching of reading suit some children better than others. The search for such beneficial combinations (often called 'aptitude × instruction interactions') is a continuing professional responsibility.

The learner must be motivated and must be able to sense that his or her competence in reading is increasing.

The basis of a sound junior school reading programme is an acceptance by all the staff of a collective commitment to an agreed policy and programme. The policy and the programme must be evolving ones in which INSET and the development of community involvement are central. Systematic and regular evaluation of the policy and the reading programme is essential.

Although all individuals can learn to read, reading is *never* fully mastered by anyone. That is part of its continuing challenge.

Section A
Challenges: The Current Scene

Special educational needs and reading in the junior school

INTRODUCTION

What are 'special educational needs'? How are they characterised? What do we understand by 'special'? What are the responsibilities of the LEA, the school and the individual teacher?

The 'whole-school' approach requires schools to 'consume their own smoke'; to educate all pupils. If this objective is to become a reality, rather than remain rhetoric, every teacher in every school has to address the above issues and become involved in the development of policies and practices that facilitate the desired end (Hinson, 1987a; Hegarty, 1987; Wolfendale, 1987). The present book considers one deliberately limited but important aspect of the scene – the reading attainments of junior school children.

Are we entitled to argue that special educational needs may occur when children in junior schools in our society experience difficulties in learning to read?

After considering the background to these issues, an orientation towards coping with reading difficulties will be presented based on the central concept of individual differences rather than special educational needs.

SPECIAL EDUCATIONAL NEEDS

It can be argued that the concept of special educational needs has served its consciousness-raising purpose. In future, the interests of *all* the children that the system exists to serve can better be developed by concentrating on individual differences. By using explicit assessments of inter- and intra-individual differences as the key concepts, decisions about providing individuals with additional educational resources can be dealt with more openly. It will not make the related resource decisions any easier. It could make them clearer. Whilst this change is unlikely to come about in the short term, in an age when accountability and efficiency are increasingly demanded of educational institutions and procedures, it has much to commend it. It could improve both institutional and individual decision-making in education. Indeed, the importance of individual differences is recognised as of the essence in special education.

Despite this, the majority of junior school teachers (and others) have received little training in the uses and limitations of the considerable array of tests and assessment techniques available to make these differences explicit. To most parents, the information elicited about their child remains a professional mystery. This can and should be changed.

The issue is highlighted by asking teachers an apparently simple question. 'Should parents be told their child's reading test scores when discussing their child's reading attainments and progress with the class teacher?' Some teachers are in favour. Others have valid reservations. A further sizeable group of teachers has doubts concerning its ability to convey the reading test information adequately to parents. This is a pity. A school should have an agreed policy on such issues. Instead of having to refer to 'special educational needs because of poor reading attainments and/or progress', the child's attainments can be made explicit. This is a first step in deciding what to do. Teaching and testing can be mutually supportive in identifying, alleviating and preventing learning difficulties in general and reading difficulties in particular.

In my opinion, even when the value system underpinning both the Warnock Report and the Education Act 1981 is acknowledged and accepted, the term 'special educational needs' is of limited utility in either the theory or practice of education. Whilst there is general agreement on the purposes of education for *all* children, there is little agreement on the nature and incidence of special educational needs between the hundreds of professional and lay groups with interests in the field. Special educational needs is a relative and context-bound concept. For example, it is claimed that the frustrations sometimes experienced by a very able child educated in a junior school mixed-ability class represent special educational needs that are as worthy of additional resources as those of any other individual. An association exists to advance their interests (Welch, 1987). In 1987, 29 of the 104 LEAs in England and Wales had advisory teachers for exceptionally able children. One report estimates an incidence of 2 per cent for such pupils. Prior to the Education Act 1981, a similar proportion of pupils was deemed to be educationally sub-normal. Whilst these two groups may be considered as at the extremes of the ability range, their educational needs are likely to differ. But on what are the percentages based? Who decides on the cut-off lines? One suspects that somewhat arbitrary criteria have been used. In part, this is because the notion of special educational needs is a function of the educational aims, expectations, resourcing and competence of professionals and parents in a culture. Special educational needs are *not* solely a consequence of within-child characteristics; the context of education is often perceived as contributing to their creation and maintenance. Many children are moved either between classes within a junior school or between junior schools in order to meet what are sometimes construed as the pupil's special educational needs. Sometimes the moves are successful, sometimes they are not. The development of the special school system was based on the assumption that the special educational needs of many pupils could be more adequately met in separate and better-funded special schools, units or classes. Currently this idea is under attack. Evidence suggests that many special schools do not appear to be effective (Topping, 1983; Galloway, 1985).

The concept of needs is theoretically complex and currently imprecise. It is relative, characteristically subjective and open to many interpretations (Kavale and Forness, 1985; Salvia and Ysseldyke, 1985; Reason et al., 1989; Pumfrey and Elliott, 1990). Claims for the existence of special educational needs are sometimes the reason why groups and individuals covertly introduce moral imperatives based on vested interests into an educational system. How do we distinguish between 'My child needs extra help with his reading', 'My child wants extra help with his reading' and 'My child ought to have extra help with his reading'? There are, as yet, relatively few generally agreed means whereby special educational needs can be operationally defined. The term is sufficiently vague to mean all things to all people. Its major function is as a rallying cry uniting pressure groups. It has emotional connotations that appeal to community values. This is not in itself a serious criticism. In a continuing dialectic concerning the priorities in our society aspirations always exceed the availability of expertise and financial resources. Similar comments could be made about many other concepts used in educational theory and affecting educational practice. Education is a political battlefield. Special educational needs represent one of several fronts. Reading difficulties in junior schools constitute one very active sector on that front.

The current educational reality is that the concept of special educational needs is enshrined in law. This underpins a number of formal institutional and individual decision-making procedures and is used widely by professionals and parents. One of its major functions has been to generate additional resources for individuals and sub-sets of pupils, and for all teachers.

Every time someone talks of a child's special educational needs, it is almost inevitable that one is listening to a case of special pleading for either individuals or groups to receive extra resources from the limited pool available, or for expanding that pool. Decisions on the merits of a particular case are based on practice and custom in the LEA, on implicit value judgements concerning the educational priorities of a society and (increasingly) on the consequences of case law.

These may well be unavoidable, but we should be aware of what is taking place. Additional resources may be generated and lead to advances in our ability to conceptualise, predict and optimise the learning of *all* pupils. The concept of special educational needs and the current educational and administrative strategies based on it would then merit support. To date, the evidence on this issue is equivocal. The growth of special schools for the education of 'slow-learning children' apart from the ordinary school was an almost unstoppable tide at one time. Now the spirit of the times favours the education of as many pupils as possible in ordinary schools. Special schools are being closed in some LEAs. Their staff, and those of peripatetic remedial education and support services, are being redeployed as resource/support teachers in ordinary schools. It is appropriate for professionals to be cautious about such developments, but not reactionary. The unique combination of economy (normal school places are considerably less expensive than special school ones) and the manifest socio-educational virtues of current integrationist educational philosophy and practice is welcomed by all political parties. Note that this appears to be so *only* in the public sector of education. The combination of the cheap and the apparently good is almost irresistible, as many salespeople know. Although educational policies are typically determined more by ideological considerations than by a critical examination of evidence, one should not abandon the search for empirical evidence of effective policies and practices. Research is always needed.

The categories of handicap used to classify children prior to the Education Act 1981 have been officially discontinued. Despite this the voluntary bodies, whose formation and continuing existence are based on obtaining recognition of, and help for, children with certain characteristics in common, have continued and expanded. The British Dyslexia Association, the Dyslexia Institute and the Foundation for the Underachieving and Dyslexic *know* that the children who are their particular concern *are* covered under the provisions of the Act. Such groups' expertise is increasingly recognised by governments, the public and many professionals (Cornwall et al., 1984). Despite this, the current educational *Zeitgeist* condemns labelling children. The labelling process is seen as marginalising individuals, as failing to do justice to the complexity of their special educational needs and of introducing potentially unhelpful self-fulfilling prophecies into the educational process. Not all parents and professionals agree that the labelling of children is always disadvantageous. It can readily be argued that the use of labels is unavoidable in any aspect of human life. What matters are the *uses* and *consequences* of labelling pupils. On balance, these must be shown to be beneficial to the labelled. To be 'statemented' under the provisions of the Education Act 1981 is to be labelled. That labelling is intended to be helpful. To be designated as having special educational needs, but *not* to be statemented, is also to be labelled. Not to have special educational needs is to be labelled.

During the last decade, the term 'special educational needs' has permeated educational thinking and affected educational practices in this country. This permeation has, to a large extent, been a consequence of two major sets of events. The first was the 1978 Report of the Committee of Enquiry into the Education of Handicapped Children and Young People, chaired by the then Mrs H. M. Warnock, and entitled *Special Educational Needs* and the widespread discussion that this stimulated. The second set of events, evolving from the first, was the passing of the Education Act 1981, its implementation in 1983, and the associated circulars and regulations intended to clarify the intentions of the Act (DES, 1981). Every teacher requires a sound appreciation of the requirements of the Act. Every junior school teacher with an interest in reading difficulties operates within its context and needs to be informed of its provisions.

The Education Reform Act 1988, with its core subjects of mathematics, English and science, its other foundation subjects and nationwide testing of primary school pupils at about 7 and 11 years of age, is with us. Will such proposals help or hinder the identification and education of children with special educational needs in the junior school? The issues involved are controversial, although it is worth noting that the Warnock Report recommended that LEAs should monitor complete age groups of pupils at least three or four times during their school life. What is at issue are the purposes, modes and consequences of such assessments. There is considerable evidence that, in the field of reading, such authority-wide testing is already well developed at the junior school level (Gipps et al., 1983; Pumfrey, 1988a).

THE WARNOCK REPORT (Committee of Enquiry, 1978)

'Children are all the same: they are all different' was a well-known cry long before 1978. The recognition that both the common humanity of all pupils and the uniqueness of each individual pupil exist side by side is reflected in our educational provision. The Warnock Report stated that *all* children have two educational needs in common:

> first, to enlarge a child's knowledge, experience and imaginative understanding, and thus his [*sic*] awareness of moral values and capacity for enjoyment; and secondly, to enable him to enter the world after formal education is over as an active participant in society and a responsible contributor to it, capable of achieving as much independence as possible.
>
> (Ibid., para. 1.4)

Who could disagree with such broad educational aims? In theory, few; in practice, one notes reservations. Acceptance cannot be wholehearted as concerns other than education are also making their own cases for resources in our society. The National Health Service and defence are but two of many. In education, the fact that expenditure on books and equipment is well below recommended levels in many LEAs does not appear to have led to increases in resources from either local or central government (Publishers Association, 1986). Does such underfunding discourage literacy amongst junior school pupils? Does it help produce illiteracy? Is the educational system producing and maintaining special educational needs in this field? Without doubt, the provision of an adequate supply of books is a necessary if not sufficient condition for the encouragement of literacy and the improvement of reading attainments (Pumfrey, 1988b).

INCIDENCE OF SPECIAL EDUCATIONAL NEEDS

The Warnock Report recommended that the concept of special education should be extended and based on the assumption that: 'about one in six children at any time and up to one in five children at some time during their school career will require some form of special education'. Quite clearly, the vast majority of these pupils were already attending ordinary schools.

The report also recommended that the statutory categorisation of handicapped pupils be abolished. In future, the term 'children with learning difficulties' was to be used to describe children who, at the time, were categorised as educationally subnormal and those with learning difficulties who were the concern of LEA remedial services.

But the concept is far wider than the above suggests:

It extends beyond the idea of education provided in special schools, special classes or units for children with particular types of disability, and embraces the notion of any form of additional help, wherever it is provided and whenever it is provided, from birth to maturity, to overcome educational difficulty. It also embodies the idea that, although the difficulties which some children encounter may dictate *what* they have to be taught and the disabilities of some *how* they have to be taught, the point of their education is the same.

(Committee of Enquiry, 1978, pp. 6–7)

It was acknowledged that the interests of children having 'severe, complex and long-term' disabilities should be protected. The report recommended that a system of recording be established for those children who, after a detailed multi-professional assessment, were deemed by their LEA to be in need of special educational provision not generally available in the ordinary school.

Children differ in many, many ways. They differ physically, emotionally, socially, intellectually, motivationally and in their family circumstances. They differ in their learning styles and their attitudes to, and values concerning, education in general and reading in particular. The uniqueness of the individual can be construed as a pattern of different positions on a virtually unlimited number of dimensions. Some children differ so much from others on such dimensions, attainment in reading for example, that they are considered to have special educational needs. These needs were defined in the main by referring to the resources and facilities necessary to give such pupils access to the curriculum. Thus special educational needs are defined as requiring:

(i) the provision of special means of access to the curriculum through special equipment, facilities or resources, modification of the physical environment or specialist teaching techniques;
(ii) the provision of a special or modified curriculum;
(iii) particular attention to the social structure and emotional climate in which education takes place.

(Ibid., para. 3.19)

It was recommended that the law be amended to incorporate a wider view of special education and special educational treatment based on a child's individual needs as distinct from disability. This concept of special educational needs would include children with significant difficulties in learning, with emotional or behavioural disorders, as well as those with disabilities of mind or body. Special educational needs are to be considered as a continuum. This will range from pupils whose needs may be fairly easily met, to others (far fewer) who will require prolonged and intensive support in order for their needs to be met. Categories of handicap were replaced by a focus on educational needs. The scope of special education was extended and made a central concern of the entire educational system.

SPECIAL EDUCATIONAL NEEDS AND THE EDUCATION ACT 1981

Under the Education Act 1944, LEAs had the duty to provide sufficient schools offering such variety that children could be educated according to their age, ability and aptitude.

The Education Act 1981 (effective from 1 April 1983) was a landmark in educational legislation in this country. It changed the law on special education in the light of the Warnock Report and the consultations and discussions that ensued. Now LEAs must ensure that special provision is made for pupils who have special educational needs. Formerly, the provision of special educational treatment was based largely on a 'defect' model and LEAs were responsible for providing such treatment for pupils who 'suffer any disability of mind or body'. Ten different categories of handicap were officially recognised in England and Wales, and nine in Scotland. Approximately 2 per cent of children were identified as handicapped and were educated mainly in special schools, units or classes. In 1981 it was estimated that approximately 165,000 children were then receiving special educational treatment in England and Wales (DES, 1981).

The Education Act 1981 widened the scope of special education along the lines suggested in the Warnock Report, i.e. up to one in five pupils at some time during their school career. It recognised that most children with special educational needs would be attending ordinary schools. Whilst giving additional rights to parents and duties to LEAs, no extra resources were provided to implement the Act. These additional LEA responsibilities also involved further responsibilities for teachers in their schools, including that of organising the educational programmes designed to meet the pupils' special educational needs.

It is worth remembering that, as well as rights, parents/guardians have important responsibilities under the Education Act 1944. These have been expanded under the Education Act 1981. It is now their duty to ensure that their child receives efficient full-time education suitable to the child's age, ability, and aptitude and *to any special educational needs he or she may have*, either by regular attendance at school or otherwise.

The Education Act 1981 moved its focus in defining special educational needs from the necessary facilities for access to the curriculum that had characterised the Warnock Report. In the Act, a child is deemed to have a *special educational need* if he or she has a *learning difficulty* which requires *special educational provision*. *Special educational provision* is that which is additional to, or different from, the normal provision made in LEA schools for children of the same age.

A child is deemed to have a learning difficulty if:

(a) he has significantly greater difficulty in learning than the majority of children of his age; or
(b) he has a disability which either prevents or hinders him from making use of the educational facilities of a kind generally provided in schools, within the area of the local authority concerned, for children of his age.

(DES, 1981)

This definition has the clarity of pea soup. It represents an administrative nightmare and an educational embarrassment. The introduction of a system whereby the educational needs of individuals could be identified, formally acknowledged and met, led to a four-stage statementing procedure. The confusion surrounding this procedure is well illustrated by comparing the percentage of statemented children in all 104 LEAs in England and Wales. In 1986 these ranged from 0.04 per cent (N = 52) in Hereford–Worcester to 4.2 per cent (N = 6,454) in Avon. It is very difficult to understand why the effects of an Act should lead to a hundredfold difference between authorities in the proportion of children statemented. The proportions of statemented pupils in special and ordinary schools also show wide variations. The extremes in this were shown by Manchester LEA and Avon LEA. In the former, the ratio is 98 per cent (N = 1,824) in special schools : 2 per cent (N = 38) in ordinary schools compared with 42.6 per cent (N = 2,282) in special schools : 57.4 per cent (N = 3,071) in ordinary schools in the latter (Education, Science and Arts Committee, 1987). It is clear that whether children in the ordinary school are, or are not, statemented depends in part on *where* the child goes to school. This is a criterion that is difficult to defend. Other research highlighted many deficiencies in the working of the Education Act 1981 (Goacher et al., 1988).

The Act also established that all children, including those with special educational needs, can be educated in ordinary schools subject to certain conditions. These are:

• the parents have been consulted;
• the school is able to meet the child's special educational needs;

- the efficient education of other children in the school is not adversely affected; and
- the arrangement represents an efficient use of the LEA's resources.

It is the duty of the LEA to identify children who have special educational needs and, having identified them, to make appropriate provision. The emphasis in assessment is on looking at the whole child and ensuring that there is a partnership between the parents or guardians and the LEA in carrying out the assessment procedures. LEAs are required formally to notify parents/guardians that an assessment is to be made and also to provide them with information on the assessment procedures. Parents/guardians have the right to make representations and to offer written evidence within a prescribed period of being notified (29 days). The child's physical, emotional, social, intellectual, motivational characteristics and home circumstances may be assessed. The perspectives of parents, teachers, social workers, general practitioners, psychiatrists and psychologists can be incorporated in an assessment. (It is interesting that this multidisciplinary approach to assessment harks back to the early case study approach that characterised the clinical work of child guidance clinics.) Equally interesting, the effectiveness of this approach was called into question as being inefficient and ineffective (Pumfrey, 1980). The child's parents must be informed of the results of the assessment and must also be given the name of an officer of the LEA who will provide any further information required.

The purposes of the assessment are to obtain an understanding of the child's learning difficulties, to identify strengths and weaknesses, to provide a guide to an educational programme and a basis from which the child's subsequent progress can be monitored. The Act makes a clear distinction between the analysis of a child's learning difficulties, the specification of his or her special educational needs, the resources these will require and the programme that is specified in order for the identified needs to be met.

Statutory assessments (section 5 of the Act) are designed to help the LEA decide whether or not to make a statement under section 7 of the Act whereby a special educational programme is specified for the child. If the LEA decides to recommend a special educational programme, a draft statement of special educational needs must be made. This will include the parents' or guardians' views, the LEA's assessment of the child's needs and will specify the programme and resources that will enable the identified needs to be met. Parents/guardians have a right to receive a copy of the draft statement of special educational needs, together with details of the procedures to be followed should they disagree with this statement. If they do disagree, they have 15 days within which to inform the LEA of their objections and, if they so wish, to request a meeting with an officer of the LEA at which their objections can be discussed.

The LEA will consider any parental/guardian representations and then either make a statement in the original or modified form, or decide not to make a statement. The parents/guardians will be informed of the decision in writing. The LEA must, if it makes a statement, send a copy to the parents/guardians plus information concerning their right of appeal and the 'named person' in the LEA from whom any further information or advice may be sought.

Statemented children are subject to an annual review. All parents/guardians have the right to ask an LEA to carry out an assessment under section 9 of the Act. The LEA has a duty to do as requested unless it considers the request 'unreasonable'.

If the parents of a child attending a junior school class express concern about their child's progress in learning to read and request an assessment under the provisions of the Act, on what basis could the request be justifiably deemed 'unreasonable'? Increasingly, and at great expense, the courts are being asked to decide on this and other issues related to the provision of special educational programmes.

Under section 8 of the Act parents have a right of appeal against the special educational programme that is specified in the statement that is prepared as a consequence of either the initial or any subsequent assessment. These appeals are first heard by committees established under the Education Act 1980 (Schedule 2). However, the decisions by such committees on appeals made under the provisions of the Education Act 1981 are *not* binding on the LEA. This contrasts with the situation concerning other types of appeal.

If the above brief summary appears labyrinthine to readers, they are not alone. Many parents feel that the interests of their children are evaded by this bureaucratic procedure. Others are intimidated by its apparent complexity. Fortunately, help is at hand. The Advisory Centre for Education has produced a valuable guide to the Act that takes parents carefully through its provisions. This publication should also be in the staff library of every junior school (Newell, 1988b). Readers requiring a more detailed exposition will find that prepared by the Society of Education Officers of value (Adams, 1987).

Consider the Warnock Report's estimates that one in five children have special educational needs at some time during their school careers, and one in six at any one time. If these are valid, in a typical junior school class of 24 pupils there will be, on average, about five such pupils. It is likely that the special educational needs identified in pupils attending a school situated in the salubrious suburbs of a city are likely to be different in both type and degree from those found among pupils attending schools serving the decaying, socially deprived inner-city areas of any large conurbation. Interestingly, in *both* circumstances it is claimed by teachers that a number of their pupils have special educational needs because of serious reading difficulties.

The estimates of special educational needs given in the Warnock Report have been seriously criticised. To suggest that identifying such needs is the twentieth-century equivalent of medieval theological deliberations on the number of angels capable of being accommodated on the point of a pin, is too severe. However, there are some important reservations. Firstly, there is a serious danger that the Warnock Report's research-based estimate is being interpreted as referring to the least able/lowest-attaining 20 per cent in a given age group. Secondly, the general estimates can be misleading to junior class teachers, as will be demonstrated later. Thirdly, what had been an estimate for the population tended to become a 'target' for some schools.

THE 1988 EDUCATION REFORM ACT

The implications of the Act for pupils with special educational needs in general and for pupils experiencing difficulties in learning to read in particular, will have to be carefully monitored. It is possible that the spirit of the 1981 Education Act is not adequately represented in some of the requirements of the 1988 Education Reform Act. Whilst it will be many years before the full requirements of the Act are implemented, quite fundamental changes in the ways in which teachers and schools organise their work are already well in train.

The section of the 1988 legislation bearing on schools has four major objectives. The first is the development of a national curriculum within a clear framework of law that will be applicable to all pupils aged from 5 to 16 years in all maintained schools. The second purpose is to increase parental choice by abolishing restrictions on school admissions below the physical capacity of a school. The third is to secure a more devolved system of local financial management in which local education authorities, headteachers and governors have important new rights and responsibilities. The final purpose is to create new opportunities for the self-management of schools *outside* local education authority control. This will be achieved by establishing grant-maintained schools.

The Act is intended to result in the raising of educational standards for children of all abilities. The central position and role of literacy in the success, or otherwise, of the endeavour are self-evident.

The national curriculum is to be balanced, broadly based and designed to promote 'the spiritual, moral, cultural, mental and physical development of pupils at the school and of society'. Additionally, it will also 'prepare(s) such pupils for the opportunities, responsibilities and experiences of adult life'. None of this preamble will strike junior school teachers as particularly radical. What is radical is the degree of control of the curriculum and its assessment that central government has taken in order to achieve its stated objectives.

The curriculum of every maintained school must include religious education for all pupils. Additionally, all pupils of compulsory school age will follow what is called the national curriculum. This will be a basic curriculum consisting of core and foundation subjects. For each subject the following will be specified:

- attainment targets at key stages;
- programmes of study; and
- arrangements for assessing pupils at key stages.

Mathematics, English and science are designated 'core' subjects (the three jewels in the crown?). In Wales, Welsh is also a core subject in Welsh-speaking schools. The foundation subjects at all four stages are history, geography, technology, music, art and physical education. A modern foreign language is required as a foundation subject during the third and fourth key stages (at secondary school level).

It is clear that children's reading attainments and progress will form a key component in this endeavour. Consider the content of the national curriculum. Its delivery is virtually dependent upon pupils' ability to deal effectively with a variety of textual materials (Pumfrey, 1990b).

In June 1988, the Secretary of State for Education and Science stated that 'Primary schools will be centre stage when attainment targets and programmes of study are introduced'. The attainment targets and programmes of study are intended to help primary school teachers plan for both progression and more coherence in topic and project work.

> But just how the curriculum is organised; how it is structured in the classroom; how schemes of work are revised to take account of the

attainment targets and the programmes of study – these are all matters for the school and its head. . . . The National Curriculum is not a threat to an integrated approach. On the contrary, clear and challenging objectives will ensure proper breadth and balance in the integrated curriculum.

(Secretary of State, 1988)

He foresaw attainment targets and programmes of study being introduced according to the following timetable:

September 1989 – 5-year-old pupils in mathematics, science and English;
September 1989 – 12-year-old pupils in maths and science, with the introduction of English one year later; and
September 1990 – 8-year-old pupils in maths, science and English.

During the latter part of 1988 the Department tendered for the development of assessment and testing instruments. After these have been piloted in some primary schools from Autumn 1989, the first full-scale national assessments will be carried out in 1991 and the first results reported in 1992.

It is claimed by the Secretary of State for Education and Science that

The National Curriculum's assessment arrangements will provide a nationally coherent, systematic form of assessment. My talks to parents repeatedly remind me that this is one of the most promising and exciting parts of our reform of education . . . I have to say that I do not believe that assessing progress in a systematic way will confine or narrow the curriculum. On the contrary, it will reinforce teaching and learning, helping both teachers and pupils to plan their next steps. As to reporting the results, we have amended the Bill so that the Secretary of State cannot require the pupil's assessment results to be given to anyone other than his or her parents and, where they need to know in the child's interests, to the school's governors and the LEA. I also do not envisage the public reporting of aggregated results of a school's assessment results at the end of any key stages *until there has been one year's dry run.*

(Secretary of State for Education and Science, 1988; my italics)

The pilot studies by the three consortia involved in construction of standard assessment tasks and associated INSET materials, are discussed in more detail later.

THE KINGMAN REPORT

One of the Act's aims is the improvement of pupils' standards in the English language. In 1987 a Committee of Inquiry into the Teaching of English Language was set up under the chairmanship of Sir John Kingman. Its three terms of reference included recommending a model of the English language that could be used in teacher training and would enable teachers to understand how the language worked. The Committee was also asked for principles to guide teachers on how the model should be made explicit to pupils (what should be taught) and also to recommend broad attainment targets for pupils at 7, 11 and 16 years of age.

In the Report (DES, 1988a), teacher training is (inevitably) criticised. The recommendation of the 1975 Bullock Report that there be a substantial and compulsory course in language for all students in pre-service training is seen as not having been adequately acted upon, except by a few colleges. Initial inservice teacher training and all first-degree English courses should be redesigned to include more linguistics. In addition to reading and writing, school English lessons should incorporate speaking and listening. The Committee believes that there is a 'Standard English' and that the rules governing its use cannot be learned without rigour on the part of both teacher and pupils. Whilst there should not be separate classes to teach technical aspects of English language, grammar, punctuation, spelling and syntax should be systematically covered. The understanding of concepts such as verb, noun and sentence must be learned by pupils, preferably through the exploration of the language used by pupils.

The Kingman Report was published in May 1988 (DES, 1988a). Overall, it presents an understandable and almost inevitable compromise between the radical Right and Left schools of thought on the learning and teaching of the English language. As such, its initial reception by organisations such as the United Kingdom Reading Association, the National Association for the Teaching of English, certain teacher unions and the Labour Party, has been generally favourable. As with any report of this nature, it is open to legitimate criticisms. It was described by Kenneth Baker, the then Secretary of State, as 'an interesting report which will contribute to discussion about the teaching of English and about the importance of the grammatical structure of the language and of the correct use of the spoken word'.

The report made 18 recommendations. The most important is the proposal of a model (inevitably controversial) of written and spoken English language to provide a basis for teacher education. The proposed model of English language *in use* takes into account the forms and patterns of both speech and writing. It has four distinct yet interrelated components: forms of language; communication and comprehension; development and acquisition; and historical and geographical variation. Each part of the model is presented as a set of statements or lists that are examples only. Within these four categories, over 80 basic skills must be acquired by teachers if they are to be adequately prepared to teach all pupils. A summary of the model given in the Report is presented in Figures 1.1–1.5.

The report recommends that all intending primary school teachers should undertake a language course based on the model provided by the Committee. The courses should be evaluated at regular intervals by external assessors who have both pedagogic and linguistic expertise.

Whilst recognising that national assessments did not easily fit with the responsibility of schools to identify and meet pupils' individual needs, the Committee did not see the two requirements as incompatible. The report therefore recognised that diagnostic testing had an important role. Despite acknowledging the difficulties in setting specific and detailed attainment targets, the report strongly supports the setting of attainment tests in English language at the ages of 7, 11 and 16 years: 'Teachers need to be able to identify where children need help. At seven it is not too early; deferred, it may be too late' (DES, 1988a, p. 57). A combination of national testing and teacher assessment should be used to appraise pupils' progress. It is claimed that the detailed framework of criterion-referenced attainment targets, subject profiles and assessment arrangements proposed by the Task Group on Assessment and Testing has been taken into account in devising attainment targets.

Targets are sometimes divided into aspects that reflect pupils' performance (for example, at age 7 'Read passages of simple sentences – aloud as well as silently – with understanding') and aspects of language which the pupils should be expected to reflect and comment upon (for example, 'Understand main correspondences between letters and speech-sounds and know the alphabet'). The distinction is not necessarily one that has clear pedagogic implications. Fourteen targets are listed for the 7-year-old age group, 15 for the 11 and 14 for the 16-year-old age group.

The appointment in all primary schools of a member of staff designated as a language consultant, with a responsibility for advising on and co-ordinating language work, is recommended.

The implications of the report for inservice training of teachers are considerable. A three-year programme aimed at familiarising at least one teacher in every school in England with the model of language described in the Kingman Report was under consider-

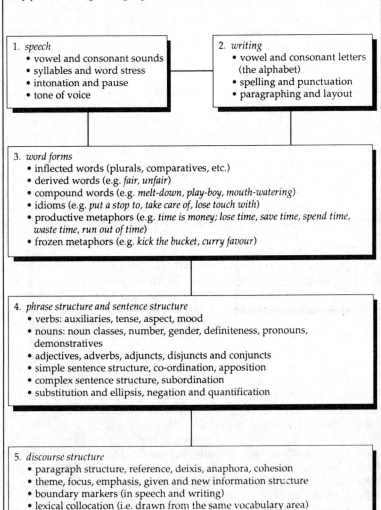

Part 1: The forms of the English language

The following boxes exemplify the range of forms found in English. If forms are combined in regular patterns, following the rules and conventions of English, they yield meaningful language.

1. *speech*
   - vowel and consonant sounds
   - syllables and word stress
   - intonation and pause
   - tone of voice

2. *writing*
   - vowel and consonant letters (the alphabet)
   - spelling and punctuation
   - paragraphing and layout

3. *word forms*
   - inflected words (plurals, comparatives, etc.)
   - derived words (e.g. *fair, unfair*)
   - compound words (e.g. *melt-down, play-boy, mouth-watering*)
   - idioms (e.g. *put a stop to, take care of, lose touch with*)
   - productive metaphors (e.g. *time is money; lose time, save time, spend time, waste time, run out of time*)
   - frozen metaphors (e.g. *kick the bucket, curry favour*)

4. *phrase structure and sentence structure*
   - verbs: auxiliaries, tense, aspect, mood
   - nouns: noun classes, number, gender, definiteness, pronouns, demonstratives
   - adjectives, adverbs, adjuncts, disjuncts and conjuncts
   - simple sentence structure, co-ordination, apposition
   - complex sentence structure, subordination
   - substitution and ellipsis, negation and quantification

5. *discourse structure*
   - paragraph structure, reference, deixis, anaphora, cohesion
   - theme, focus, emphasis, given and new information structure
   - boundary markers (in speech and writing)
   - lexical collocation (i.e. drawn from the same vocabulary area)

Figure 1.1

Figures 1.1–1.5 *The Kingman Committee model of English (DES, 1988a)*

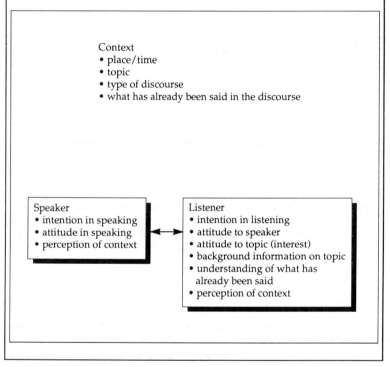

Part 2(i): Communication

Speakers and writers adapt their language to the context in which the language is being used. The boxes below indicate some of the main features of context which are relevant in conversations where the speaker and listener are talking face to face. In this section we shall also indicate how this model needs to be adapted to account for written language. (Note that in literature we often find *representations* of speech which rely on our experience of the spoken language.)

Context
- place/time
- topic
- type of discourse
- what has already been said in the discourse

Speaker
- intention in speaking
- attitude in speaking
- perception of context

Listener
- intention in listening
- attitude to speaker
- attitude to topic (interest)
- background information on topic
- understanding of what has already been said
- perception of context

Figure 1.2

ation by the Department of Education and Science in the middle of 1988. As yet, this has not been fully implemented by all LEAs because of other national curriculum implementation pressures on INSET work.

A critical, but informed and constructive set of six commentaries on aspects of the report and their implications for primary English was included in the proceedings of the 1989 conference of the United Kingdom Reading Association (Hunter-Carsch et al., 1990).

Part 2(ii): Comprehension – some processes of understanding

In Figure 1.2 we showed the context of communication which is of course the context in which comprehension takes place. We understand language in a context of use. Some of the processes involved in understanding are indicated in this figure which, like Figure 1.2, is orientated to the speaker/listener relationship.

1. interpreting speech sounds (Figure 1.1, Box 1) as words and phrases (Figure 1.1, Boxes 3 and 4), working out the relevant relations of these (Figure 1.4) and deriving a 'thin' meaning of the sort that a sentence might have out of context

2. working out what the speaker is using phrases *to refer to* in the world or in the previous discourse

3. working out from the form of the utterance what the speaker presupposes in making the utterance

4. inferring what the speaker means by making a particular utterance at a particular point in the discourse – the 'thick pragmatic meaning'

(All of these processes may apply simultaneously)

Figure 1.3

The report provided the foundation on which the National Curriculum Working Group on English subsequently built. It recommended that the English Working Group draw upon the proposed attainment targets in preparing components for the assessment of English in the national curriculum. The Group was

---

Part 3: Acquisition and development

1. Children gradually acquire the forms of language identified in the boxes of Figure 1.1. Whereas some aspects of acquisition are fairly rapid (most children have acquired a full range of vowels and consonants by the time they are 6 or 7), other aspects develop much later (for example, control of spelling patterns and conventions of punctuation).

2. Children gradually develop their ability to produce and to understand appropriate forms of language (both spoken and written) in a wide range of contexts (Figure 1.2). This development does not cease in the years of schooling but continues throughout life.

Figure 1.4

Part 4: Historical and geographical variation

1. Language changes over time – all forms of language are subject to change, to inception, modification and to decay, sometimes rapidly and sometimes immeasurably slowly. Changes continue to take place in our own time.

2. As populations are dispersed and separated, they typically develop regular regional changes in their language forms. These changes may mark different dialects (or eventually different languages). If one of these dialects is used for writing, that dialect may emerge as the standard language; it will, of course, share many characteristics with the other related dialects.

Figure 1.5

chaired by Professor Brian Cox of the University of Manchester, who had also been a member of the earlier Committee of Inquiry.

SPECIAL EDUCATIONAL NEEDS AND THE EDUCATION REFORM ACT 1988

Provisions in both the 1981 Education Act and the 1988 Education Act concern the education of children with special educational needs. Some incompatibilities exist between the two sets of legislation (Newell, 1988a). As children with reading difficulties comprise a sub-set of children with special educational needs, it is important for teachers to be aware of the implications of the 1988 Education Act for the education of such pupils. The following observations concern *all* pupils but have particular relevance to those who have special educational needs.

Under the 1988 Education Act, 'special cases' are specified in sections 17 to 19. For the purposes of development work or experiments, the Secretary of State may direct that the provisions of the national curriculum shall either not apply, or shall apply with modifications. This power can be exercised in two ways. The first concerns county, controlled or maintained special schools on an application submitted:

(i)   by the governing body with the agreement of the local education authority;
(ii) by the local education authority with the agreement of the governing body; or
(iii) by the Curriculum Council with the agreement of both the local education authority and the governing body.

The second concerns grant-maintained, aided or special agreement schools on the initiative of a school's governing body or by the Curriculum Council with the agreement of the school's governing body.

At first glance, it appears highly likely that the immediate effects of such provisions will be to *discourage* deviations from the national curriculum. Fortunately, the national curriculum is not necessarily a pedagogic straitjacket, unless the teaching profession allows it so to become. That proportion of the school curriculum not taken up with the national curriculum allows some flexibility. Of even greater practical importance, the integrated nature of the teaching methodologies characteristic of much junior school practice also allows considerable freedom. If a junior class teacher draws up a table with the subjects comprising the national curriculum of the junior school stage at the top and then puts a weekly teaching timetable down the side, entering ticks into the table would identify the wide range of national curriculum subjects involved in any *one* teaching session. The fact that the members of a class are unlikely to be engaged on identical aspects for the same periods of time also highlights the considerable flexibility inherent in the system. It is a virtue that may well allow suitable provisions to be made for children with special educational needs without recourse to the formal procedures outlined earlier. It will allow sensitive educational responses to both inter- and intra-individual differences in children's reading abilities and attainments to continue to be made.

In addition, the Secretary of State will have powers to make regulations which will provide that the national curriculum, or sections of it, 'shall not apply; or shall apply with such modifications as may be so specified'. Teachers and parents will be anxious to know how these provisions will be interpreted and applied in practice. The debate during the passage of the Bill has already indicated that the vagueness of this provision is causing concern.

Earlier the provision of statements under the 1981 Education Act was discussed. The 1988 Education Act allows special modifications of the national curriculum where pupils are subjects of statements:

> a statement under Section 7 of the 1981 Act of a pupil's special educational needs may include provision –
> (a) excluding the application of the provisions of the national curriculum;
> or
> (b) applying those provisions with such modifications as may be specified in the statement.

Critics of this proposal have argued that statements were intended as instruments of access and were regarded as safeguards for the individual pupil. The above proposal is seen as potentially making statements instruments of denial, rather than of access to the curriculum. It has been claimed that the provision will lead to an increasing number of legal appeals.

The Secretary of State has the power, after consultation, to make regulations enabling headteachers to modify the application of the national curriculum to a particular pupil for a period of up to six months. The headteacher is required to inform

> the school's governing body;
> the local education authority; and
> the pupil's parents.

The information that the headteacher is required to provide includes: (a) the fact of the action, its effects and his reasons for taking it; (b) the educational provision for the pupils to be taken during the specified period; and the headteacher must *either* describe the manner in which it is proposed to secure the full implementation of the national curriculum at the end of the period of variation; *or* indicate the view that the pupil has, or probably has, special educational needs which would require the local education authority to determine the provision to be made.

Parents are entitled to appeal to the school's governing body when the headteacher gives, revokes or varies a modification; refuses to give, revoke or vary a modification when requested by the parents; fails within a period to be prescribed to give, revoke or vary a modification at the request of the parent.

The powers of the governing body then enable it either to confirm the headteacher's action or to direct the head to take other actions deemed appropriate. The governors' decision will be given in writing to the parent and the headteacher, and the headteacher must comply with the lay governing body's decision. At present, the headteacher has no right of appeal against this.

The provisions whereby parts of the national curriculum and related assessment arrangements may be modified or disapplied are set out in Circular 22/89 (DES, 1989e). The Secretary of State for Education and Science may modify or disapply, in specified general cases and circumstances, under the provisions of sections 4 and 17 of the Education Reform Act 1988. These arrangements can apply to pupils with or without statements.

For individual pupils, under section 18 of the Act, a statement of special educational needs may modify or disapply any or all of the requirements of the national curriculum, if they are inappropriate to the individual pupil concerned. Under section 19, headteachers may give a general or special direction to modify the national curriculum for an individual pupil on a *temporary* basis for a period of no longer than six months in the first instance. General directions can apply to any pupil, including a pupil with a statement at an ordinary or special school, who develops temporary problems which it would not be appropriate to reflect in the statement. At the end of the specified period, the pupil can expect to return to the national curriculum as it applied to him or her before the general direction came into force. Special directions are more restricted. They can be used by the headteacher to modify or disapply the national curriculum for up to six months if the headteacher considers that an individual pupil has special educational needs which require the LEA to assess the pupil with a view to making a statement. Such a temporary exception is not always required when a headteacher refers a pupil for assessment. It remains the LEA's responsibility to determine whether there are sufficient grounds for assessment. One wonders *how* this can be known, unless an assessment of some sort is made?

The thrust of these arrangements appears to discourage rapid recourse by headteachers to the modification or disapplication of the national curriculum for individual pupils.

Voluntary and statutory bodies concerned with the interests of children with specific learning difficulties (dyslexia) are particularly interested in the effects of the legislation on educational policy and provision. If children are unable to read, no legislation will make the national curriculum available to them.

THE COX REPORT

The Cox Report (DES and Welsh Office, 1988a) covers the two key stages for the primary years of education, as defined in the 1988 Education Reform Act. It is concerned with (1) attainment targets and (2) programmes of study. Attainment targets are defined in the Act as: 'the knowledge, skills and understanding which pupils of different abilities and maturities are expected to have by the end of each key stage'. The same Act defines programmes of study as: 'the matters, skills and processes which are required to be taught to pupils of different abilities and maturities during each key stage'.

The attainment targets are themselves divided into statements of attainment. These are more precise and describe each of up to ten levels of attainment. These levels are designed to cover the complete range of attainment of *the majority* of pupils of different abilities during the period of compulsory education.

An appreciation of the place of reading within the field of English, set in the context of the Education Reform Act 1988, requires an understanding of certain key concepts. These are listed and defined in Table 1.1.

Extensive national consultation was carried out to obtain the reactions of the teaching profession to the proposed attainment targets and programmes of study contained in the Cox Report.

ENGLISH IN THE NATIONAL CURRICULUM

The consultation in relation to the Cox Report was completed in January 1989, and the findings published in March 1989. The results of this led to a report *English in the National Curriculum* (DES and Welsh Office, 1989b). In this report, five broad attainment targets in English were identified for pupils aged 5 to 11 years (DES and Welsh Office, 1989b). The subject of English was divided into three profile components: profile component 1 (attainment target 1) Speaking and Listening; profile component 2 (attainment target 2) Reading; and profile component 3 (attainment targets 3, 4 and 5) Writing, Spelling and Handwriting.

The profile components reflect the complex relationships between the various aspects of language. The five associated attain-

Table 1.1 *Key concepts*

1. *The whole curriculum* = The curriculum of a school, including the basic curriculum (see below) and all other curricular provision.

2. *The basic curriculum* = The national curriculum and religious education.

3. *The national curriculum* = The core subjects (see below) and other foundation subjects (see below), plus their attainment targets, programmes of study and assessment.

4. *The core subjects* = English, mathematics and science.

5. *The foundation subjects* = English, mathematics, science, technology (including design), history, geography, music, art and physical education plus, for secondary-age students, a modern foreign language.

6. *Programmes of study* = the matters, skills and processes which pupils must be taught during each key stage in order for them to achieve the objectives specified in the attainment targets.

7. *Attainment targets* = objectives for each foundation subject listing the knowledge, skills and understanding that pupils of different maturities will develop.

8. *Statements of attainment* = more precise objectives than the attainment targets. They are related to the ten levels of attainment on one continuous scale covering all four key stages.

9. *Profile components* = groups of attainment targets combined for use in assessment and reporting.

10. *Standard assessment tasks* = externally devised assessments intended to complement the teacher's assessments.

11. *Cross-curricular themes* = strands of provision running through many aspects of the curriculum.

ment targets are intended to be appropriate, at different levels, for children of different ages and abilities within the primary school. Levels of attainment within the targets and the statements of attainment at the various levels are intended to specify what each pupil '*should*' know, understand and be able to do at the reporting ages of 7 and 11 years. The assumption underpinning the *should* is a *normative* one based on what the majority of children have been observed to achieve in general. An overview of the five attainment targets comprising the three components of English is shown in the following pages.

Language attainment targets: an overview

1. Speaking and Listening

'Pupils should demonstrate their understanding of the spoken word and the capacity to express themselves effectively in a variety of speaking and listening activities, matching style and response to audience and purpose' (p. 24).

2. Reading

'The development of the ability to read, understand and respond to all types of writing, as well as the development of information-retrieval strategies for the purposes of study' (p. 28).

3. Writing

'A growing ability to construct and convey meaning in written language matching style to audience and purpose' (p. 33).

4. Spelling

Attainment target 4: Spelling is detailed on page 37 of the report. No comment is made on that page concerning the target. The following is taken from the 1988 report:

> The main line of development concerns children's increasing control not simply over the correct spelling of individual words, but also over the most frequent sound–letter correspondences and the other principles of English spelling. Despite the undeniable irregularities of English spelling, it is important that teaching and assessing focus on those areas that are systematic.
>
> (DES and Welsh Office, 1988a, para. 10.21)

5. Handwriting

Attainment target 5: Handwriting is listed on page 38 of the supplementary report, where no comment is made on the target (NCC, 1989f). The following is taken from the 1988 report:

> This target concerns children's increasing control over the physical and design aspects of writing. The development of handwriting should be seen as something meaningful and purposeful. When pupils move into secondary school, they will generally be expected to engage in various tasks which depend on fluent handwriting, so that they are not impeded in composing their own thoughts on paper and in note-taking.
>
> (para. 10.23)

Within the national curriculum, English has:

– Three profile components: Speaking and Listening; Reading and Writing.

– Five attainment targets: Speaking and Listening (1); Reading (1) and Writing (3) – Writing, Spelling and Handwriting.

At key stage 1, there are the following statements of attainment:

At level 1:

Speaking and Listening:	3
*Reading:	4
Writing:	1
Spelling:	3
Handwriting:	1

At level 2:

Speaking and Listening:	5
*Reading:	6
Writing:	4
Spelling:	4
Handwriting:	2

At level 3:

Speaking and Listening:	4
*Reading:	6
Writing:	5
Spelling:	4
Handwriting:	1

* Although this book focuses primarily on the improvement of reading attainments and attitudes to reading, the importance of the other aspects of language is acknowledged.

Attainment targets and associated statements of attainment for all profile components at key stages 1 (levels 1–3) and 2 (levels 3–5) in English are presented in Appendix 2. Standard assessment tasks plus teacher assessments will be used to determine pupils' standards and progress in reading.

Programmes of study associated with the attainment targets are described in the supplementary Report. The programmes of study are sufficiently broad to accommodate a variety of curricular paths leading towards the common objectives.

THE COX REPORT, SPECIAL EDUCATIONAL NEEDS AND THE ENGLISH CURRICULUM

Chapter 13 of the Cox Report contains a brief consideration of special educational needs in relation to the English curriculum. All of the attainment targets in the report can be assessed at various levels of attainment. It follows that children with special needs should be able to participate in the attainment targets, programmes of study and assessment arrangements. The point is made in the report that level 1 assessments are designed to identify children who may require special help in some form. From the subsequent accounts in Chapters 1 and 2, we know that children with reading difficulties will figure prominently.

'In many cases this will merely confirm what teachers already knew, and will strengthen their hands in taking appropriate action, for example in seeking a statement under the 1981 Act' (DES and Welsh Office, 1988a, para. 13.6). How, one asks, unless the requisite material and professional resources are readily available? At present, they are not. The working of the 1981 Education Act concerning the identification and alleviation of learning difficulties has received serious criticism from a Parliamentary Select Committee (Education, Science and Arts Committee, 1987).

The Cox Report continues:

> In others, it will come as something of a surprise, and there may then be a need for the child to undergo further diagnostic tests to establish the extent of the problem. A level 1 performance should always be a signal for further investigation. This might, for example, reveal that a child who appeared to be a slow learner, or inattentive, was in fact showing symptoms of specific learning difficulties (dyslexia) or a hearing impairment, possibly an intermittent one such as otitis media.
>
> (DES and Welsh Office, 1988a, para. 13.7)

Children with statements may have the requirements of the national curriculum modified. However, this will not be the case for the majority of children with special educational needs,

> either because the degree of special need is not considered severe enough to warrant it, or because their LEA's policy is to write statements only for children in special schools. Our suggestions will also be relevant to some of the unstatemented children with special educational needs, and hence to consideration of possible modifications, which the 1988 Act allows in respect of children falling within certain cases and circumstances, to Orders for attainment targets, programmes of study and assessment arrangements for English.
>
> (Ibid., para. 13.9)

It is stated that children with learning difficulties are likely to make only slow progress in reading and writing. In such cases, it is suggested that initially greater emphasis should be given to oral work, though the skills of reading and writing must not be neglected. This is hardly a dazzling insight.

The national curriculum assessment and record system, whereby some children will remain at level 1 Reading for several years, contains dangers. By 1992 when pupils' test scores are to be published, there is a danger that the term 'level 1' could become the new term of abuse replacing earlier playground pejoratives.

Enabling children with special educational needs to communicate their achievements is recognised as a major challenge. Additional help may be required from professionals in addition to teachers. For example, the services of speech therapists, occupational therapists or psychologists may be required: 'We recognise the resource implications, but feel the involvement of such experts to be essential if pupils with special educational needs are to be enabled to perform in English to their full potential' (ibid., para. 13.5).

It is interesting to see the word 'potential' being used in this report. If 'potential' is to be a criterion against which attainments in, for example, reading will be appraised, how will potential be assessed? The idea of 'potential' is partner to that of 'underachievement'. To date, the search for ways of measuring either has been beset with technical and ideological controversies. Interestingly, the still frequently found school report comment 'Could read better' and the parental opinion that 'He's not reading as well as he should' attest to the ubiquity of the notion that reading attainments should approximate potential. Though itself also a controversial issue, increasing resources is less so. It is to be hoped that the government will provide the additional funds necessary to help improve reading attainments. A draft circular has attempted to express the resource requirements of pupils with various learning difficulties in terms of the proportion of teacher time and special-support assistant time that is considered appropriate to meet a nebulous set of special educational needs. Non-statemented pupils with special educational needs attending ordinary schools are not mentioned (DES, 1990a). As each school becomes increasingly responsible for its own financial management under the scheme known as local management of schools (LMS), within-school competition for limited resources will increase (DES, 1988b). Will pupils with difficulties in learning to read suffer as a consequence of these pressures on resources? LMS looms large!

THE NATIONAL CURRICULUM AND SPECIAL EDUCATIONAL NEEDS

In February 1989, the Department of Education and Science issued advice in Circular 5/89 entitled *The Education Reform Act 1988: The*

School Curriculum and Assessment (DES, 1989a). The reaction of the NCC to this circular recommends strongly that minimal use should be made of the provisions whereby the national curriculum can be modified or disapplied for pupils with special educational needs.

The National Curriculum Council has consistently adopted a whole-school approach to the education of pupils with special educational needs. When the attainment targets and programmes of study in English were published in May 1989, they were accompanied by an NCC document providing 'Non-Statutory Guidance' for English key stage 1 (NCC, 1989a). These notes provided ideas on how the teaching of English in the national curriculum could be developed. The within-school development of schemes of work for English is considered. Suggestions for translating planning into practice; planning; organisation and resources; schemes of work; and the teacher's role were considered in relation to each of the three profile components in English.

Additionally, advice was given on how evidence of achievements could be collected (NCC, 1989a).

The suggestions are applicable to all pupils working at the prescribed levels.

The NCC also issued a further document in May 1989. Circular No. 5, dealing with the participation by pupils with special educational needs in the national curriculum (NCC, 1989c). The principle of access to the curriculum for *all* pupils is strongly stressed. The NCC sees this being achieved by

> encouraging good practice for all pupils. Special educational needs are not just a reflection of pupils' inherent difficulties or disabilities; they are often related to factors within schools which can prevent or exacerbate some problems. For example, schools that successfully meet the demands of a diverse range of individual needs through agreed policies on teaching and learning approaches are invariably effective in meeting special educational needs.

The research quoted later concerning the effective teaching of reading in the junior school supports this point (see pp. 62–9). The NCC advocates that, in principle, *all* pupils should receive 'a broad and balanced curriculum', and that there should be little need for 'detailed statutory modifications or exemptions to be written into statements' (NCC, 1989c).

A CURRICULUM FOR ALL

The NCC position is strongly reiterated in their subsequent report published in September. This document, the work of the Special

Educational Needs Task Group, was entitled *A Curriculum for All* (NCC, 1989d). It is a particularly important document. It reinforces the point that improving the reading of all pupils and identifying and alleviating the reading difficulties of a minority are not mutually exclusive professional activities. The advice moves from the principles stated in NCC Circular No. 5 to ways in which these can be put into practice. Of particular relevance to readers of this book will be the section dealing with 'English at Key Stage 1'. Advice on planning schemes of work, means of providing access to the English curriculum, support and resources, teaching resources and technological aids are discussed (NCC, 1989d, pp. 33–41).

ASSESSMENTS AND STATEMENTS OF SPECIAL EDUCATIONAL NEEDS (CIRCULAR 22/89)

This Circular (DES, 1989e) was a revision of an earlier one issued in connection with the Education Act 1981. The update was needed because of weaknesses that had been identified in the working of the Act (see pp. 18–19) and in the requirements of the Education Reform Act 1988. The document outlines the administrative procedures whereby assessments of a child's special educational needs are made and appropriate educational provision specified and provided. It covers all pupils who may have special educational needs, even though no operational definition of this category is provided. This can include children with either general or specific learning difficulties in reading. Annex 4 of Circular 22/89 (DES, 1989e) lists the information that LEAs need to tell the parents of children with special educational needs (see Appendix 3). Circulars are, however, only advisory. 'This Circular does not constitute an authoritative legal interpretation of the Act; that is a matter for the courts' (ibid., p. 4).

A SURVEY OF PUPILS WITH SPECIAL EDUCATIONAL NEEDS IN ORDINARY SCHOOLS

This HM Inspectorate report, published in December 1989 (DES, 1989f), is based on single-day visits to 55 primary and 42 secondary schools. Up to three pupils with special educational needs were followed for one day in either top junior or first-year secondary school groups. Because literacy in general and reading in particular permeates the whole curriculum, the Inspectorate's comments concerning the efficacy of the educational programmes are pertinent.

In the primary schools 165 pupils were seen in 269 lessons. None of the pupils was statemented under the provisions of the Education Act 1981. The quality of the work seen was deemed to be satisfactory or better in 55 per cent of the sessions, though there was considerable variation from one area of the curriculum to another: 'In about one-third of both primary and secondary schools there were pupils with special educational needs who were following curricula, which, when assessed in terms of breadth, balance, differentiation, continuity and progression, had obvious limitations' (DES, 1989f, para. 5).

- 50 per cent of the primary schools had a whole-school policy statement.
- In 25 per cent of the primary schools, pupils with special educational needs were taught by one class teacher in a mixed ability group.
- Half of the primary schools were providing support teaching within mainstream classes, albeit for limited periods.
- Only 2 per cent of schools had a designated remedial class.
- 9 per cent of schools had one or more pupils in off-site units.
- In 75 per cent of the primary schools pupils were withdrawn from their mainstream classes for small group work, usually on aspects of literacy. Groups varied in size from 1 to 15 pupils, with an average size of about 6. Extraction time ranged from 30 minutes to 2.5 days per week. There did not appear to be a clear rationale underpinning the varied arrangements.
- Two-thirds of the schools had a designated teacher with responsibility for special educational needs. Half of these had specialist training for this responsibility in half of the schools.
- 25 per cent of staff had attended INSET courses on special educational needs. One-third of the primary schools had involved all staff in school-based INSET concerning special educational needs.
- All the primary schools used the class teacher's judgement as a key means of identifying pupils with special educational needs. 80 per cent of schools also used standardised group attainment tests 'usually in reading and sometimes in mathematics'.
- 45 per cent of primary schools used diagnostic tests to help them in identifying where pupils with special educational needs might require further help.
- In about 50 per cent of the schools peripatetic support services assisted with identification procedures.
- Many of the schools involved parents in this work. Only a minority of schools did not consult the parents until the schools' identification processes had been completed.

The best identification procedures were those that:

- used a variety of information sources;
- involved results being co-ordinated systematically by one teacher;
- produced a written profile of information on each pupil;
- were part of a co-ordinated central record system;
- involved regular in-school reviews of progress of individuals;
- made the assessment profile available to the parents and all professionals who had contributed to its compilation; and
- were supported by an LEA guideline document which the teachers had helped to develop and in the uses of which they had been trained.

Successful sessions were characterised by the following:

- the learning tasks were matched to the pupil's achievement;
- project-based group work using a range of media and practical activities; and
- team-teaching (where agreement on joint roles and joint planning had taken place).

The use of both designated remedial classes and the placement of pupils in 'off-site' units was criticised. Both arrangements were seen as unsatisfactory: 'pupils were receiving a poorly balanced and unco-ordinated programme' (DES, 1989f, para. 32).

Unsatisfactory work was also associated with:

- insufficiently differentiated assignments –

This was *particularly evident* where a whole class or group were asked to use a worksheet or book which *had a readability level above the reading performance of pupils with special educational needs*. The use by teachers of an initial explanation of the contents of the text to the whole class or group seldom achieved the necessary differentiation for the range of ability and performance in the class or group.

(Ibid., para. 19; author's italics)

- pupils failing to understand the task they had been set;
- unstimulating exercises;
- lack of opportunities for discussion;
- withdrawal of pupils from the same mainstream activity each week for remedial tuition; and
- lack of integration between withdrawal group work and the rest of the programme.

The survey results clearly reveal that the issue of teaching pupils with special educational needs has been a priority in many schools and that the associated attention the issue has received has had positive benefits for these pupils and the standard of work they produce. However, about one-third of the primary and secondary schools will need to review their provision for pupils with special educational needs if they are to give them full and proper access to the National Curriculum.

(Ibid., para. 6)

PROVISION FOR PRIMARY AGED PUPILS WITH STATEMENTS OF SPECIAL EDUCATIONAL NEEDS IN MAINSTREAM SCHOOLS (DES, 1990b)

HM Inspectors visited 43 mainstream primary schools in 11 LEAs between January and July 1990. Their major purpose was to look at provision for pupils with statements prepared under the requirements of the Education Act 1981. Such statements apply to about 2 per cent of children. As noted earlier, the proportion of children in LEAs who are accorded statements varies greatly. The educational reasons for a variation of over a hundredfold between LEAs are unclear. Such apparently unjustified variation is worrying. The integration of pupils with special educational needs into mainstream education is currently seen as a desirable national policy that will benefit all pupils, subject to various caveats. Pupils with statements attending mainstream schools represent a vast and increasing variety of special educational needs. The arrangements for supporting such pupils are vital. Difficulties in reading may, or may not, be of particular concern in individual cases.

The recognition by the DES that children deemed to have dyslexia are included in those with specific learning difficulties and may qualify for statements is an important point. Most LEAs would prefer to develop services for such pupils within mainstream schools using their own appropriately trained teaching staff. Alternatives, such as attendance at a residential school, are seen by many LEAs as less suitable and are also vastly more expensive. Pupils with specific learning difficulties in literacy attending the mainstream schools may, or may not, be given the protection of a statement, with all the attendant resource implications that this can incur. There is a possibility that a statement will increasingly be seen by parents in particular as a promising legitimate means of securing the additional educational resources that such pupils can be seen as requiring. The implications of this HMI report (DES, 1990b) are therefore of considerable interest to voluntary bodies concerned with pupils with specific learning difficulties (dyslexia). These children are only a sub-set of the junior school pupils who experience difficulties in reading. LEAs are equally concerned, because of their legal responsibilities to all pupils and parents and the added responsibilities of balancing limited budgets and competing demands for priority. The advent of LMS will highlight such issues for schools to an extent previously unknown. On what rational basis can priorities in providing additional costed resources of professional expertise to particular individual pupils be determined?

Few of the mainstream primary schools visited by HMIs ensured that their curriculum met the needs of all pupils. Devising and adequately supervising individualised programmes for pupils with special educational needs presented great difficulties. Statements are intended to clarify the individual needs of pupils, yet it is reported that the quality of the statement was often inadequate for this purpose: 'As a result, the work of staff and pupils was adversely affected'. It is also stated that more effective use could be made of the assessment, statement and review procedures provided for under the Education Act 1981. Fortunately, the time to be taken for the completion of the prescribed consultations in preparing a statement has been reduced to a recommended maximum of six months, in Circular 22/89 (DES, 1989e).

HMI reported that few class teachers did individual teaching, or had made changes to meet the needs of statemented pupils in their classes. Despite this comment, work was considered 'satisfactory' in 70 per cent of classes, but 'excellent' in only 14 per cent and 'poor' in 16 per cent. The work done with children suffering from hearing or visual impairments was considered to be most effective. *'Pupils with speech and language disorders were less adequately helped'* (author's italics). Least successful of all was work with pupils who had severe learning difficulties.

Many schools had insufficient space for withdrawal teaching. Modifications to buildings were required if some pupils were to have access to an appropriate curriculum.

On the positive side, teachers who used a variety of teaching styles were considered more likely to meet the needs of pupils with statements. The best practice was observed in schools staffed with teachers and specialists who had undertaken appropriate inservice training. The quality of pupil–teacher relationships was generally considered good. Extensive evidence of warm and supportive relationships was observed between pupils with statements, peers and teachers. Designing programmes for children with learning difficulties requires detailed analysis, careful planning and management, and systematic evaluation and revision (Brennan, 1985, 1987; Branwhite, 1986; Dessent, 1987; Solity and Bull, 1987).

The role of LEA support services in helping statemented and non-statemented pupils with reading and other learning difficulties in the junior school is discussed in Chapter 9.

READING POLICY AND PRACTICE AT AGES 5–14

This report (DES, 1989g) also appeared in December 1989. It is based on observations by eight HM Inspectors who visited 17 schools, selected to be representative of different types of catchment area, for one or two days, either singly or in pairs. The focus was on reading policy and practice immediately prior to the introduction of the national curriculum English in August 1989. The work concentrated on years 1 and 2 (5–7 years), 6 (10–11 years) and 9 (13–14 years).

Particular attention was paid to:

- standards and attitudes;
- the formal provision for reading made by each school, including policy statements, staffing, resources and accommodation;
- the pedagogy used in the development of voluntary reading, reading for information, reading for purposes of study and critical reading.

All of the schools had policy statements for the reading programme. There was general agreement concerning the aims of teaching reading. Schools stressed that reading was more than decoding text to sound; meaning was of the essence. In addition, enjoyment of, and motivation to read, both fiction and non-fiction were seen as crucial if the aim of voluntary reading was to be attained. Whilst various advanced reading skills were also considered important, few schools gave coherent accounts of these or how they were taught. At the primary school stage, the focus was on various aspects of reading comprehension and information retrieval. Policies were more adequate for the initial teaching of reading than for the development of, for example, reference or retrieval skills. In summary, the policy documents were more informative when they dealt with aims and principles than when considering pedagogy. At the time most of the schools were reviewing their policy statements. This is likely to be a continuing task in all areas of the national curriculum.

The Inspectors reported that standards of reading fluency were at least satisfactory and that the skills of initial reading were taught successfully in all the classes visited. Attitudes towards reading for both enjoyment and information were retained in later years, as was the use of school and public libraries.

However, progress beyond the early stages was much less consistent. Extending beginning reading was not always effectively done. Pupils in years 1 and 2 who had achieved a fair degree of fluency were not sufficiently challenged. Those in year 6 often had insufficient opportunity to reflect upon and discuss the characteristics of the language met in their reading, for example the use of imagery.

The lower-attaining readers were the least keen and were also typically amongst those making very little use of either the school or the public libraries. The amount and variety of voluntary reading varied markedly between and within schools. Girls generally had more favourable attitudes towards reading than boys, particularly in relation to fiction. They also read more and borrowed more books from libraries. Schools that encouraged good library practices markedly reduced the sex difference in library usage. The importance of teachers' professional skills in improving pupils' involvement in reading, developing positive attitudes and higher attainments was also indicated: 'In general, pupils were enthusiastic but unchallenged readers. Many needed more guidance in choosing books and more encouragement to progress to increasingly demanding texts' (DES, 1989g, para. 8).

Part II of the report concerns observed practices. Graded reading schemes, supported by a variety of other books, represented the eclectic compromise combination of graded materials and 'real reading' referred to later. The 'apprenticeship' approach to reading, whereby pupils learn to read by reading with adults using a wide range of reading materials, was increasing.

> Where graded readers were well organised and their use supported both by sensitive intervention by the teacher and opportunities for pupils to discuss their reading, the materials provided a satisfactory framework for progression.
>
> (Ibid., para. 10)

A successful reading programme appeared to be related more to the existence of a coherent programme that was supported by the whole staff. Both the 'apprenticeship' approach that owes much to 'top-down' psycholinguistic theory and the use of a graded reading scheme based on 'bottom-up' behaviourist theory could be equally effective. Whilst this may be true for the majority of pupils, it is not the case for all. Under either approach, a number of children will experience great difficulties in learning to become literate. The report stresses the advantages of an eclectic approach to the teaching of reading. Only one of the schools had a detailed policy for reading across the curriculum which utilised the concept of text readabilities for various materials including books, documents and periodicals (see Chapter 4).

The value of silent reading for all pupils was increasingly recognised by practising teachers, but reservations were expressed by some teachers about whether this made too great a demand on certain pupils, presumably those with limited reading attainment.

Book provision in schools underpins such activities. The teaching of reading requires a wide range and variety of books and other reading materials. In this survey, the provision of books was less than adequate in two of the seven schools visited. Schools situated in socially advantaged catchment areas were better provided with books mainly because of the monies raised from parents. The more recent work by the Book Trust has clearly demonstrated that nationally there is a large gap between the 'desirable' and 'actual' amounts spent on books in primary schools (Book Trust, 1989). Once again, children attending schools in socially deprived areas of the large conurbations are likely to suffer unless the schools' financial difficulties are recognised by more favourable LEA funding.

In general, the impressionistic opinions expressed by the Inspectorate carry considerable weight in many quarters. The above two reports (DES, 1989f, 1989g) are based on data owing more to qualitative than to quantitative research methodology. Without doubt the experience of visiting and observing a wide variety of pupils, teachers and schools provides a valuable background from which to make judgements, but is this sufficient in an era when accountability is increasingly demanded by the consumers of education? Would these reports not be clearer and more convincing if a summative quantification of the reading abilities and attitudes being assessed were presented, based on instruments that would enable the Inspectors' findings to be replicated? A wide range of valid and reliable means of quantifying pupils' attitudes towards reading, their attainments in various aspects and their motivations is available.

THE INCIDENCE OF LEARNING DIFFICULTIES AND READING DIFFICULTIES

The three aims of a social science are to conceptualise the phenomena under consideration, to make predictions concerning the occurrence of the phenomena and to develop increasingly effective means of controlling the latter. This applies both to *special educational needs* and to *reading difficulties* as a sub-set of such needs. If colleagues are to communicate, they must be able to agree on what they are considering and the techniques whereby such phenomena can be observed: 'Whatever exists, exists in some quantity and can, in principle, be measured.'

So said Thorndike, one of the pioneers of applied psychology. Not all agree with his assertion. It is often claimed that the complexities of human behaviour, including thought processes, defy such an empirical approach. Some argue that, whilst measurement is possible, what can be measured is trivial. Writers referring to the 'intangibles' in education frequently adopt this position. Concepts such as special educational needs or reading difficulties cannot be directly measured. Operational definitions can be deduced from theory and instruments devised to measure aspects of the former. Thus what it measured has clear limitations *but has the great advantage of being explicit, public and replicable.*

One aim of the teaching profession is to obtain a progressively more adequate understanding of the development of reading attainments and of the causes and alleviation of reading difficulties. This involves the three related activities of conceptualising the processes involved, making predictions to test our theories about children's reading, and seeking to achieve greater control over our predictions. Each activity contributes to our ability to minimise children's reading difficulties and optimise their reading attainments. The classroom, the reading centre and the child guidance centre are crucibles in which both practice and theory are tested and developed. Theory, empirical research and practice are inextricably linked.

Parents and teachers can readily identify the tallest and the shortest pupils in a class. We tend *not* to describe the shortest as 'backward in height', 'retarded in height', 'having a height deficit' or 'in need of remedial growth'. We can accept individual differences between pupils. Whilst specialist hormone treatment may be prescribed for a *very* few cases, there is no cry for all pupils to be a standard height at a given age, or for all pupils to be 6 centimetres taller. Our expectations are governed by extensive exposure to visible evidence of variations in children's height. Our acceptance of this wide variation is an acceptance of individual differences. Some children are described as 'short for their age' or 'tall for their age', but irrespective of their children's heights or ages, parents and teachers do expect them to increase in stature with the passage of time.

Reading attainments, on the other hand, are not as visible to the general public as children's heights. Illiteracy is largely invisible. In this respect, teachers have a privileged perspective. The daily evidence of the classroom, of official reports and of research, emphasises the wide range of reading attainments to be found in any mixed-ability junior school class. Society is less tolerant of such individual differences than it is of differences in height. There are two major reasons for this. The first is that most people are only vaguely aware of the existence of such differences. The second, and more powerful, is because of the importance in which reading ability is held in our society. In every aspect of reading there is a considerable range of competence. Our definition of what constitutes a reading difficulty is almost always based on children's failure to achieve an *arbitrarily* selected level. On any normative measure, 50 per cent of children will be below average. How many of these have a reading difficulty? Irrespective of this, all children can improve their reading, given appropriate resources and motivation.

Children's reading attainments and attitudes towards reading are seen as aspects of individual differences over which the teaching profession, by virtue of its expertise, has some control. From the evidence presented in Chapter 2, this is certainly the case. Coupled with this comes a cry from society for ever rising standards of reading in junior schools. To encourage teachers in this endeavour, the government has proposed that 'bench-mark' tests of reading be established. The Education Act 1988 requires these to be administered nationally at the ages of 7 and 11 years, and the results published. If this issue is not handled with great sensitivity, a great deal of unnecessary suffering could be caused.

Beware of 'snake-oil'

Learning to read is an immensely complex and imperfectly understood process. The large number of theories that have been developed support this contention (Singer and Ruddell, 1985). When a situation is complicated, there is a tendency to oversimplify our descriptions, explanations and solutions. For example, take the question 'What can be done to raise junior school pupils' reading standards?' One group might cry 'Phonics for all'. Another will argue that a 'psycholinguistic approach' is the answer. A plethora of alternatives exist. History and comparative studies rapidly reveal the weaknesses in simple solutions to complex problems.

We can describe the behaviour that typifies the competent reader. We can provide objective indices of effective reading. Thus the goals of the reading curriculum can be operationally defined. The paths to the goal of competent reading are, however, not sufficiently well mapped for us to be certain that all children will become competent readers by following any single route. Different experts advocate different methods and materials, largely as a consequence of different theories concerning the nature of the reading process. Some teachers will argue that, because of their individual differences, children must find their own idiosyncratic way towards competence in reading (Snowling, 1985). Others will argue that a particular method will make it easier for all children of all abilities to read (Bradley, 1990; Bryant, 1990).

The history of the learning and teaching of reading, coupled with the many methods experiments that have been carried out to discover effective ways of improving reading, suggests that the proposals are not mutually exclusive. The idea that any one approach represents a royal road to reading that could, to advantage, be followed by all children, is suspect.

We would be suspicious of the physician who prescribed the same treatment for all patients seeking advice. Educational panaceas are as suspect in relation to helping children with reading difficulties, or with preventing them. Whilst a particular approach to helping children with reading difficulties may not be a royal road to competence in reading, it only becomes a cul-de-sac when the teacher becomes a prisoner of her own favoured approach. Teachers require a knowledge of different theories of reading and of differing approaches towards the alleviation of reading difficulties and the development of reading attainments.

Significant advances have taken place in many fields of scientific endeavour over the last century. These advances, which have enabled a greater control of our environment, have largely been based on the development and use of quantitative methods. The importance of quantification and measurement in the social sciences is not in its infancy. Members of all the 'helping' professions need to be aware of, and technically informed about, the uses and limitations of the variety of approaches to surveying, testing and assessment techniques that have been developed (Sumner, 1987).

Estimating the incidence of special educational needs is beset with difficulties. Such estimates depend on various considerations, many of which are never made explicit. They include the assumptions about the nature and distribution of special educational needs, the definitions employed, the instruments used and the population studied. In the applied social sciences, terminology is not used consistently. It is possible that this is because, as yet, the evidence in most fields does not command consensus. One extensive review of the literature quotes estimates of learning difficulties ranging from below 5 per cent to over 20 per cent (Tansley and Panckhurst, 1981). The estimate of special educational needs in the Warnock Report was of 16–17 per cent of pupils at any one time

and about 20 per cent during the course of education. These estimates were based largely on the epidemiological work carried out
on the Isle of Wight (Rutter et al., 1970).

More recent research on the incidence of special educational
needs in classrooms studied the views of 428 junior school class
teachers working in 61 schools (Croll and Moses, 1985). Teachers
were asked to make a note of any child in their class who they
considered had such needs. No definition was provided. Each
teacher was then individually interviewed concerning the nominated pupils by a member of the research team. The headteachers
and 37 remedial teachers in the schools were also interviewed.

The class teachers considered that 2,317 (18.8 per cent) of the
12,310 pupils in their classes had special educational needs. Pupils'
needs were roughly grouped into three categories: learning
problems; behaviour problems; and health problems including
sensory impairments and physical handicaps. 1,898 (15.4 per cent)
of the pupils were judged to have learning problems; 953 (7.7 per
cent) behaviour problems; and 540 (4.5 per cent) health, sensory
impairments and physical handicaps.

As any junior school teacher would expect, there is considerable
overlap between the three major categories. This is clearly shown
by summing the numbers for the three categories and comparing
the figure with the total number of pupils identified as having
special educational needs. The former figure is 3,391, the latter
2,317.

One of the values of this particular study is that the overlaps
between categories are quantified. The findings have been summarised in Figure 1.6.

One must always beware of the limitations in the broad generalisations implicit in such figures. There were considerable variations
between schools and classes in their estimates of the incidence of
children with special educational needs. At one end of the scale, 13
of the 61 schools (21.3 per cent) nominated up to 10 per cent of
their pupils; at the other end, 2 of the 61 (3.3 per cent) nominated
between 40 and 50 per cent of the pupils. As would be expected,
the disaggregated figures for class teachers show an even greater
range. At the lowest end, 92 of 428 class teachers (21.5 per cent)
nominated up to 10 per cent of their pupils, while at the highest
end of the range, 6 of the 428 teachers nominated 50 per cent or
more of their pupils.

These figures indicate that the general suggestions in the Warnock Report concerning the incidence of special educational needs
may be misleading. The sex, social class and age-linked differences
outlined on pp. 67–8 further underline this point.

Taking the overall picture, for these junior school teachers it was

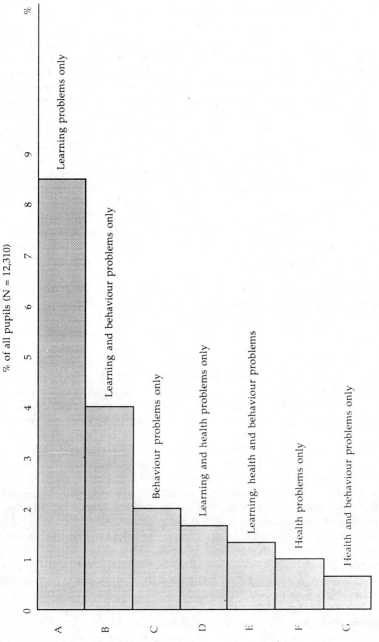

Figure 1.6 *Overlap of special educational needs (adapted from Croll and Moses, 1985)*

pupils' learning difficulties that formed the core of special educational needs in the classroom. The terms 'slow learner' (N = 1,493) and 'poor readers' (N = 1,661) were the most commonly used descriptions. These comprised 78.7 per cent and 87.5 per cent respectively of pupils with learning difficulties and 64.4 per cent and 71.7 per cent respectively of all pupils nominated as having special educational needs. Pupils' learning difficulties were seen as the major focus of special educational needs and *individual reading problems* comprised the largest area of concern within this group.

24.4 per cent of boys and 13.2 per cent of girls were seen as having special educational needs; 19.5 per cent of boys and 11.1 per cent of girls were considered to have learning difficulties and 17.5 per cent and 9.5 per cent were poor readers. This 2:1 sex ratio has frequently been found in other studies (Tansley and Panckhurst, 1981). The incidence of special educational needs was seen as decreasing between the first and fourth years in the junior school, from 21.1 per cent to 16.4 per cent. The reduction in learning difficulties was from 17.8 per cent to 13.2 per cent and in reading difficulties from 16.1 per cent to 10.7 per cent over the four years.

Britain is a multicultural society. British pupils of parents from many minority ethnic groups attend our schools. In one LEA it has been claimed that pupils are drawn from over 171 ethnic groups. In one study, 1,005 British children of parents of Asian (BA) and 277 of West Indian (BWI) origins were included in the total pupil sample of 12,286. A special needs by ethnic group analysis was carried out. Approximately 24 per cent of both BA and BWI pupils were considered to have special educational needs compared with 18 per cent for the white group. For boys the figures for the three groups were 24.4 per cent, 35 per cent and 23.4 per cent; for girls, 23.7 per cent, 13.1 per cent and 12.4 per cent respectively. In terms of learning difficulties the figures were BA 22 per cent, BWI 18.4 per cent and white 14.6 per cent. Analysing these figures by sex, the nominations for the BA boys were 22.2 per cent, BWI boys 25 per cent and white boys 18.9 per cent. For girls the equivalent figures were 21.7 per cent, 11.7 per cent and 10 per cent. In terms of concern about the pupils' reading attainments, 17.8 per cent BA, 14.8 per cent BWI and 12.9 per cent white pupils were seen as poor readers. The sex proportions were as follows: BA boys 18.5 per cent, BWI boys 20.7 per cent and white boys 18.5 per cent. For girls the figures were BA girls 17 per cent, BWI girls 8.9 per cent and white girls 8.9 per cent respectively.

For many BA pupils, English was not their first language. This may predispose them to reading difficulties. It is important to note that under the provisions of section 1 of the Education Act 1981, *language difficulties will not be regarded as learning difficulties without additional problems.*

A fuller consideration of the complex issues involved in providing an educational service appropriate to a multicultural society is presented in the Swann Report (Committee of Enquiry, 1985). The educational attainments of minority and majority groups are currently receiving much attention (Verma and Pumfrey, 1988).

It is worth noting that originally the provision of special schools, units and classes for children with learning difficulties was intended to help such pupils by providing a better-resourced, better-staffed facility. It was found that a disproportionately high number of British pupils of parents of West Indian origins were being sent to them. The effects on the pupils' attainments were minimal. West Indian communities have subsequently called into question the validity of such provision (Tomlinson, 1981).

PROVISION WITHIN THE JUNIOR SCHOOL FOR PUPILS WITH READING DIFFICULTIES

As noted earlier, the vast majority of children with special educational needs in the junior school are identified because of learning problems in general and *because of problems with reading in particular*. The most usual practice within schools is to withdraw pupils from the regular class for special help. A survey of LEAs carried out in 1983 revealed that 90 per cent had withdrawal services of some kind in operation at the primary school level. The majority of these were primarily concerned with helping pupils with their reading (Gipps et al., 1987; Gipps and Gross, 1987; Gross and Gipps, 1987b).

In looking in detail at the range of remedial provision in six LEAs, these workers found provision varying from off-site remedial centres to individual educational programmes that had been developed and delivered by class teachers. Discussions were held with the teachers involved and children receiving special help in different circumstances were observed. The findings were first reported in a paper presented at the annual conference of the British Educational Research Association in 1986 and subsequently published in the journal of the National Association for Remedial Education (Gipps and Gross, 1986, 1987). The observers reported that they never saw a child unwillingly go to a withdrawal lesson. This is not to say that all withdrawal work was without criticism. The practice is of value where it takes place:

- in regular sessions at a fixed time;

- in a small group;
- with a trained remedial teacher;
- using a carefully planned programme that was matched to the child's abilities; and is
- integrated with the child's classwork.

Not all withdrawal arrangements met these criteria and it is worth considering whether the arrangements in one's own school measure up to them. Additionally, the children's progress in reading and their attitudes towards it should be regularly assessed and discussed by the teachers involved with the pupil.

From other research on effective learning, it was concluded that the required learning environment can be described. These conditions apply to all pupils and *not* only to those who are experiencing difficulties in reading or any other field. Pupils who are experiencing failure in learning to read become caught in a vicious downward motivational spiral. The longer they remain in this situation, the poorer their chances of overcoming their difficulties. Pupils who are *not* experiencing difficulties do not have this problem. In learning to read, in overcoming reading difficulties, nothing succeeds like success. It is the teachers' responsibility to arrange situations in which all pupils will be able to experience such success, albeit at different levels. Such a strategy will optimise progress and minimise avoidable reading difficulties. Translating such an aspiration into a classroom reality is possible. Specific suggestions that can contribute toward this end are described in Chapters 5 to 9.

The desired learning environment is one that maximises pupils' concentration, ensures that the work undertaken is at an appropriate level, acknowledges and uses their interests and enthusiasms, maximises time on task and allows task-related pupil–teacher interactions. To achieve these ends, teachers must be involved in the development and uses of both teaching and assessment materials. The school must have an agreed and explicit language curriculum (including reading, listening, talking and writing). A large-scale inservice training programme is required. Co-operation between class teachers and remedial/support teachers is of the essence. The benefits of parental involvement in children's reading development should be encouraged.

In another study 56 per cent (N = 34/61) of schools provided a withdrawal service regularly. A further 8 per cent (N = 5/61) provided a partial service. Of the 1,898 pupils with learning difficulties in a total sample of 12,301, 57.3 per cent (N = 1,087) were withdrawn from their normal class for help and 42.7 per cent (N = 811) were not. The content of the help given to the 1,087 pupils showed that 97.7 per cent (N = 1,062) received help with reading, writing or spelling. Of those withdrawn, the time ranged from 30 minutes or less per week up to 10+ hours per week. The modal time was 1–2 hours per week (Croll and Moses, 1985). Work elsewhere has indicated that to produce significant changes in pupils' *relative* reading attainments, on average a period of at least two hours per week is required (Woods, 1979). The reality of the situation for junior school class teachers is that *they already bear the major professional responsibility for alleviating their pupils' reading difficulties.* This is not a new situation. It was the case long before the Education Act 1944. It will always remain the case because the individual differences between pupils in *any* teaching group, however constituted, cannot be ignored.

Unfortunately, the profession is not well equipped to deal with this continuing challenge. The absence of either initial or inservice training of the vast majority of class, head or remedial teachers in special needs or the teaching of reading has been commented on by HMI (DES, 1983a). Whilst the provision of one-term courses on meeting special educational needs in ordinary schools since then has helped somewhat, the focus of such courses has (understandably) been far wider than reading and language difficulties. Currently a number of initiatives by independent bodies have sought to rectify this deficiency.

The Royal Society of Arts and the British Dyslexia Association are two influential bodies active in this area. The tragedy is that changes in funding arrangements for teachers' professional development, the Grant Related In-Service Training (GRIST) and the subsequent Local Education Authority Training Grants (LEATGs) schemes, have dramatically reduced the likelihood of teachers being seconded to one-year courses at higher education establishments. A provisional survey carried out by Wragg indicated that, during 1986–87, 2,112 teachers were on full-time secondment. The comparative figure for 1987–88 was 673. The DES is reported as being surprised at this dramatic drop, despite having been informed well in advance that this would be one consequence of the GRIST proposals (Blackburn, 1988).

Opportunities for studying in depth children's language and reading difficulties have been reduced. One consequence already apparent in 1988 has been the closing of a number of such full-time courses. It has been argued that this will be to the long-term detriment of both children with reading difficulties and the teaching profession. That this should happen at a time when the government is introducing a national curriculum and emphasising the importance of language attainments in the Kingman Report, is difficult to understand (DES, 1988a).

The alleviation of reading difficulties and the improvement of reading attainments require an increase in motivated time-on-task by pupils. Ways of achieving these objectives are described in Sections B, C and D.

REMEDIAL EDUCATION SERVICES, SUPPORT SERVICES AND THE IMPROVEMENT OF READING

Gone is the remedial teacher, instead every teacher is a teacher of children with special needs.

(Gipps and Gross, 1986)

As Gipps and Gross admit, this statement is an oversimplification. LEAs still provide a range of services to help teachers in ordinary schools deal with their pupils' special educational needs. One of the most important has been LEA Remedial Services. Their development owed much to pioneer work carried out at the University of Birmingham Child Study Centre under the aegis of Schonell and his colleagues (Schonell and Wall, 1949). Historically remedial services concentrated mainly on helping able children with low reading attainments who were attending ordinary schools. Many became known as remedial reading services. Their focus of professional activity was clear. Typically, identification of their clients was based on LEA surveys of children's reading attainments and general intellectual ability. The existence of a large difference between, for example, a child's mental age or quotient (based on an intelligence test) and reading age or quotient (based on a reading test) was seen as an important diagnostic indicator. Where reading attainment was significantly lower than general ability, remedial teaching of reading might be provided. Such pupils were often known as *underachievers*. Teachers, parents and pupils are still very concerned when marked discrepancies of this nature are found. This group of children is recognised, in principle, under the provisions of the Education Act 1981.

As the value of remedial education services in improving children's reading attainments was recognised, their number increased. Their concerns expanded and developed over the years, the pattern of activities widened. The surveys continued as they were found of use to LEAs and schools. Increasingly attention was given to children with low reading attainments irrespective of their general ability (Sampson, 1975). The organisation, autonomy and objectives of these services currently vary considerably between LEAs.

Remedial services can claim considerable credit for the evaluations of their own efficacy that they carry out. It was demonstrated that the children they assisted by a variety of means made important progress in reading during the period of intervention. Children of similar initial reading attainments who had not received such additional help made significantly less progress. The short-term beneficial effects of the remedial teaching of reading are well established. This tradition of service evaluation of remedial education services is an important and continuing one (Simm, 1986). The National Association of Remedial Teachers, currently the National Association for Remedial Education, publishes a journal. Originally called *Remedial Education*, currently *Support for Learning*, it has carried many evaluative reports of the efficacy of the remedial teaching of reading by many services.

The staff of remedial education services have also been extremely active in developing and disseminating techniques and materials for use by classroom teachers. Examples of such services and the materials that they have developed will be given in Chapter 9.

Originally it was thought that underachievers who had received remedial help with reading would continue their enhanced progress when the intervention ended. One remedial teacher described his work as like 'lighting the blue touch paper on a firework and retiring to light some others'. This optimism about the long-term effects of the remedial teaching of reading was most frequently justified where the causes of reading difficulty were environmental. Remedial education services also carried out evaluations of the long-term efficacy of the remedial teaching of reading, which looked at pupils' progress after the end of the intervention. In general, the findings were somewhat disappointing. They showed that two years or so after the teaching had ended, no significant differences in reading attainments and attitudes towards reading existed between children who had, or had not, been helped. One group of professionals argued that this clearly demonstrated the long-term ineffectiveness of such teaching by remedial education service staff. Others argued that the additional support represented by the remedial teaching of reading had to be continued if the important short-term benefits to pupils were to be maintained and capitalised upon.

This controversy contributed to a reorientation of the work of a number of remedial education services. Many such services changed their names to 'support services' in order to signal this reorientation. Their brief was widened. Instead of providing a direct service to individuals or small groups of children with (typically) reading difficulties, the remedial teachers were asked to take on an advisory function. Their purpose was to help class teachers cope more effectively with *all* of the children in the class, which would reduce the number of pupils requiring to be withdrawn for help from visiting specialists. The class teacher was to be empowered, rather than devalued. Many remedial teachers were renamed advisory teachers. They carry out non-teaching work that includes offering advice and making suggestions concerning the reading curriculum, materials, methods, assessment and organisation.

One consequence of this change is that in future fewer children with reading difficulties will receive help within the school from peripatetic remedial reading specialists. It has recently been suggested that such remaining peripatetic teachers must concentrate on children who have been identified as having *specific reading difficulties*, rather than on those who are *slow learners*. Remedial services sometimes claim they can help the former group of pupils make significant improvements in reading attainments in a very short time. *This claim is highly suspect.*

Such assertions were also made many years ago, very early in the development of remedial reading services. Intelligent pupils with severe and prolonged difficulties in learning to read were called by one eminent research worker 'the most salvageable group'. Subsequent research showed that the difficulties of such pupils were *not* easily and rapidly overcome in the majority of cases (Cashdan et al., 1971). The parents and teachers of children currently identified as having specific developmental dyslexia need no research to prove this point. In general, it is true that bright children learn to read more readily and have fewer reading difficulties than slow-learning children. Able children who fail to learn to read are relatively rare. The inconsistency commands attention because it is not common. The speed with which such children respond to specialist help with their reading problems depends on the causes of their difficulties. If these are due to lack of educational opportunities, the prognosis is good when sensitive remedial teaching is provided. If the causes are endogenous, the likelihood of rapid progress is much less.

In one study of junior schools, out of the 1,898 children deemed by their class teachers to have learning difficulties, in only 163 (8.6 per cent) cases were there consultations with members of the remedial/support services. It is expected that the non-teaching functions of the remedial/support services and teachers will enable class teachers to deal more effectively with their pupils' learning difficulties within the classroom (Croll and Moses, 1985).

Manchester LEA has a proud tradition of educational innovation. Its School Psychological and Remedial Educational Service was one of the earliest in the country. Some years ago the Manchester LEA introduced a scheme whereby *all* primary school teachers were given additional training in the teaching of reading. The courses were run by members of the remedial education service. The effects of one phase of the scheme on pupils' reading attainments and attitudes to reading were assessed and shown to produce a beneficial result in respect of the former criterion (Brannen, 1971). A subsequent larger-scale study identified no significant improvement in *relative* reading attainments (Platt, 1975). More recently another LEA decided that all primary schools should have at least one member of staff who had attended a course on children's learning difficulties. They were then to have responsibility for the training of their colleagues. The first year of the scheme has been monitored. It was seen as both interesting and useful by participants. The effects on the pupils' reading attainments were not presented in that report. Since then similar training opportunities have been supported nationally via LEA training grants. The effects of such courses on the reading attainments and attitudes to reading of pupils with learning difficulties have not, to the best of the author's knowledge, been adequately evaluated.

In the 'Age of Accountability', it will be interesting to hear how and when the effects of the remedial/support services advisory functions on classroom practice, and on the incidence of junior school pupils' reading difficulties, will be evaluated. The author would be pleased to hear from readers who have been involved in such work in LEAs. Having been associated with the development of remedial education services and their replacement by support services, it would be encouraging if the evidence of efficacy regularly delivered by the former could be made available by the latter. Perhaps the impending national curriculum and the testing of pupils at the ages of 7 and 11 will produce this for the primary sector?

ILEA: SPECIAL EDUCATIONAL NEEDS, READING DIFFICULTIES AND FACILITIES USED BY ORDINARY SCHOOLS

The Inner London Education Authority (ILEA) no longer exists, but despite its demise it would be unwise to ignore the extensive and valuable research that the authority initiated.

In reviewing provision for special educational needs in the ILEA, a study was made of 1,342 pupils who remained on the roll of ordinary schools but attended four specialist facilities (ILEA, 1985). These facilities are known as tutorial classes (TC) (N = 793), educational guidance centres (EGC) (N = 115), remedial classes (RC)

(N = 302) and opportunity classes (OC) (N = 132), respectively. The first facility was attended part-time by pupils in small groups, and was particularly concerned with children showing emotional or behavioural disturbances. EGCs admitted mainly secondary school pupils, either full time or part time; they were intended for those whose anti-social behaviour was difficult to contain in ordinary schools. RCs provided specialised teaching on a part-time basis for pupils who were underachieving because of specific learning difficulties. (These classes have recently been renamed 'Classes for Specific Learning Difficulties'.) OCs served only the primary schools in which they were situated. OCs were used to help children who were slow learners and who might require continuing and concentrated support in many areas of the curriculum. Approximately 60 per cent (N = 1,342) of the pupils attending these facilities were deemed to have specific learning difficulties. In the RCs, 93 per cent (N = 281) had specific learning difficulties.

The most common problem in all types of class was difficulties in reading: 22.8 per cent in TCs; 18.3 per cent in EGCs; 59.9 per cent in RCs; and 35.6 per cent in OCs. The study also demonstrated that many of the pupils had multiple problems. When these pupils returned full time to the mainstream junior school, they were likely to require continuing support if they were to continue to make progress in reading.

THE ILEA JUNIOR SCHOOL PROJECT: THE EFFECTIVE JUNIOR SCHOOL

The ILEA also carried out a four-year longitudinal study of nearly 2,000 children attending 50 junior schools. The findings of this study are summarised in a 37-page report (ILEA, 1986a). Detailed results concerning 'Pupils' progress and development' (81 pp.), 'Differences between Junior schools' (228 pp.), 'Understanding school effectiveness' (122 pp.) and 'Technical appendices' (247 pp.) are also available (ILEA, 1986b, 1986c, 1986d, 1986e). The project reports have been summarised in a single publication (Mortimore et al., 1988).

The key questions asked will interest all junior school teachers:

(i)   Are some schools or classes more effective than others in terms of pupils' educational outcomes (both cognitive and non-cognitive), when variations in the intakes of pupils are taken into account?

(ii) Are some schools or classes more effective for particular groups of children?

(iii) If some schools or classes are more effective than others, what factors contribute to these positive effects? (ILEA, 1986a)

The answers are, encouragingly, 'Yes', 'Yes' and 'Here they are'.

The published documents are a major contribution to understanding the specific factors and processes related to junior school effectiveness. Effectiveness is considered at both the school and class level. The variables studied included measures of:

- pupils' background characteristics;
- cognitive and non-cognitive development and progress of pupils; and
- school and classroom policies and practices.

Data were also collected on variables over which the school and the class teacher can have little immediate control ('givens') and distinguished from those over which some control could be exercised ('policy' variables). At the school level the former included the nature of the building, status, size, resources, pupil intake and staff stability. At the class level, class size, pupil characteristics, the classroom, resources, guidelines, teacher characteristics and staff changes were used (designated 'givens'). From a mass of data and analyses, key factors consistently related to junior school effectiveness are identified. It is *not* claimed that these represent a blueprint for success. Not all aspects of junior school education were covered in the study. Schools change over time. School and classroom variables and processes are frequently related to a number of educational outcomes, both cognitive and non-cognitive. The validity of some of the measures used to test cognitive and non-cognitive outcomes can be questioned. Correlations between variables do not imply causality. Some would argue that what is possibly valid for junior schools in the ILEA is not necessarily so for junior schools in other LEAs. Despite such reservations, this research merits serious consideration. The major findings are summarised in Table 1.2.

Summary

The twelve points in Table 1.2 indicate a junior school in which the majority of teachers would be happy to work, would like their own children to attend, would recommend to colleagues and which would be perceived as effective and caring by pupils and parents.

Such a junior school would minimise children's reading difficulties. Individual difference between children in reading attainments and attitudes would still exist. These inter-individual differences

Table 1.2 *Key factors in effective junior schools*

A. *'Given' factors positively associated with effectiveness*
1. School includes the entire primary age range.
2. Voluntary-aided status.
3. Roll of under 160 children.
4. Classes with less than 24 children.
5. Good physical environment.
6. No disruptions by building contractors.
7. Established head (between 3 and 7 years' service) and deputy headteacher.
8. Continuity of class teacher.

B. *'Policy' factors positively associated with effectiveness*
1. Purposeful leadership of the staff by the headteacher particularly concerning curriculum development, teaching styles, record-keeping and inservice training of staff.
2. The deputy head is involved by the head in policy decisions, particularly in the allocation of teachers to classes.
3. The teachers are involved in curriculum planning and development. They are consulted concerning the classes they are to teach, matters of school policy and how capitation is to be spent.
4. Pupils benefit from consistency among teachers concerning the implementation of, and adherence to, agreed guidelines.
5. Structured teaching sessions provide pupils with a framework which allows them some freedom, but not unlimited responsibility.
6. The quality of teaching is very important in promoting the pupils' progress. It is intellectually challenging and teachers have high expectations of their pupils.
7. The school has a work-centred environment characterised by a high level of pupil industry. Movement around the classroom is not excessive, is typically work-related and the noise level is not excessive.
8. Pupils benefit when teachers concentrate on one particular aspect of the curriculum within a session. This does not imply that all pupils do the same work. The industry of pupils is less where mixed activities are taking place.
9. Interactions between teachers and pupils are high where pupils progress optimally. There is no undue concentration on teacher–individual interactions to the detriment of valuable teacher–class contacts.
10. The keeping of written records concerning pupils' work and their personal and social development is done by all teachers. The activities have a positive relationship with pupils' progress.
11. Parental involvement is a positive influence on the progress and development of pupils. An 'open door' policy beneficially encourages parents to help in classrooms and on school visits. Parental involvement in the child's educational development at home is also beneficial. Those who read to their children, listen to them read at home, and help them obtain books have a positive effect on their progress.
12. The effective school has a positive ethos. The emphasis is on praise rather than criticism, the pupils are valued as individuals, are happy and well behaved. Teachers, parents and pupils identify with the school and support it in a wide range of activities. Pupils are friendly to each other and to outsiders. Absence of graffiti reflects an ethos in which the members of the school community value and are involved in the work of the school.

---

would be explicitly identified, as would intra-individual differences in various aspects of reading. The school community's resources would be marshalled around an agreed reading curriculum as a key component of a larger agreed language curriculum. All pupils would know that they *were* making progress in their reading, albeit at different rates and at different levels. Teachers and parents would acknowledge this.

Since the concern of this book is with children's reading, sections of the ILEA's extensive report concerned with special educational needs and reading difficulties have been selected for comment. Almost all schools made extra provision for pupils with learning difficulties, 'most usually for reading and language' (ILEA, 1986a, p. 11).

The report makes the point that in looking at the effects of school membership, the pupils' background had systematically to be taken into account. It was demonstrated that the school can make a far larger contribution to the explanation of pupils' progress in reading than is accounted for by the pupils' background characteristics. It is estimated that 23.6 per cent of the variation in pupils' progress in reading is attributable to the school variable and *only* 6.1 per cent to the pupils' background. Important differences in effectiveness between junior schools in the teaching of reading were identified. In relation to an overall pupil average score on reading of 54, the most effective schools were 15 points above and the least effective 10 points below. This concerns *all* the junior pupils involved, not only those with reading difficulties.

The study clearly demonstrates that what is done in schools can make significant differences to pupils' reading attainments: 'it is the factors *within* the control of the head and teachers that are crucial. These are the factors that can be changed and improved' (ibid., p. 34). This is as true of the identification, alleviation and prevention of reading difficulties in the junior school as of any aspect of the curriculum. The clear message that schools, teachers and parents *can* make important contributions to pupils' progress in reading is welcome.

The study also clearly demonstrates that *relative* reading attainment at the start of junior school education is highly correlated with *relative* reading attainment three years later (r = 0.80). Thus early *relative* reading attainment is a good predictor of later *relative* reading attainment. Even with a correlation of 0.8, this still leaves 36 per cent of the variance in pupils' reading attainments three years later unaccounted for. Individuals do make relative changes in their reading skills over time. The point is made that lower reading attainment tends to result in *greater* learning difficulties *at a later age*.

The distinction between improving children's *absolute* reading attainments and improving their *relative* reading attainments merits comment. Assume that in your mixed-ability junior 1 class every pupil could read with understanding the leader in the *Guardian*. You would almost certainly be satisfied with this reading standard. However, some pupils would *still* read more rapidly, more accurately and with greater understanding than others. Individual differences would still exist, but the disabling and disempowering consequences of illiteracy would have been markedly reduced. If pupils can cope with textual material, they have greater control over many events than if they cannot. It is an acknowledged prime responsibility of the junior school to empower with literacy as many pupils as possible. The existence of *relative* individual differences must not distract us from that objective. Reading has both cognitive and affective aspects. Typically these are related. The competent reader, and the child who is making progress in learning to read, enjoy reading. Pupils experiencing difficulties do not enjoy reading. They tend to avoid the activity, thereby further decreasing their chances of making progress towards competence. They can become trapped in a self-defeating, vicious downward spiral. The challenge to the teaching profession is to help more children achieve competence and to experience success and satisfaction in dealing with textual materials. Children's attitudes towards reading can be changed from negative to positive by pedagogical means.

The ILEA study also examined differences in pupils' reading attainments, and in progress in reading, in relation to age and to a number of important background variables, including social class, sex and race. It is important for junior teachers to be aware of such relationships, as this knowledge can assist in identifying those individuals and groups most likely to require additional help.

Differences in reading attainments have frequently been reported in the literature for pupils of different ages within a year group, social class, sex, and ethnic group. The pattern of reading attainments is generally well known to teachers. Less attention has been paid to the relationships between these four variables and children's *progress* in reading over three years. The ILEA junior school research addresses both reading attainment and progress in relation to background variables.

Before presenting the results, a word of caution is necessary. The assessment of children's reading attainments at a given point in time can be done. A wide range of instruments and techniques is available (Levy and Goldstein, 1984; Pumfrey, 1985; Vincent, 1985; Hammill et al., 1989). The assessment of progress in reading, or in any other area of cognitive development, is much more difficult

(Cronbach and Furby, 1970). When allowances are systematically made for initial differences between groups of children, the difficulties in interpreting the adjusted relative reading attainments and progress in reading are compounded. In the ILEA research, age, sex, socioeconomic background, initial reading attainment, test reliability and the clustered nature of the sample were, wherever possible, allowed for in the analyses that were carried out. Despite the previous caveat, the findings of the ILEA junior school study are summarised here because of their importance.

Age within year group

On average, younger (summer-term born) children in an age group read less well than older (autumn-term born) children. This is hardly surprising. Whether extra help for children with reading difficulties should be given to those in an age group with the lowest *raw* scores on a reading test, or to children whose reading test scores are the lowest *having allowed for monthly chronological age differences*, is an important policy decision for the class teacher, the school and the LEA. Teachers are good at identifying the former pupils, but less so the latter. One weakness with the first policy is that by altering the (arbitrary) time at which the school year starts, the pupils identified as requiring additional help with reading change. If the school year starts in September, summer-term-born children will tend to be selected. If the school year starts in January, as it does in some countries, then children born during the Christmas term would tend to be identified as most in need of extra help (Pumfrey, 1971; Pumfrey and Ward, in press). Is such a policy justified? One might expect the policy to identify the *same* children irrespective of when the school year starts. The issue is complicated by the fact that, on average, the younger children in the year group have also experienced a much shorter period of infant school education. Does the current system attempt to compensate for this?

Allowing statistically for their initial differences in reading attainments, it is reported that the progress in reading over three years of children born at different times of the year is unrelated to age group. Thus the gap in attainments between older and younger pupils in an age group did not change during the three years.

Social class

Social-class differences were found in initial and final reading attainment and in progress in reading. Marked and increasing differences in attainments between social-class groups were found over time in the junior school. This is a well-documented relationship (Essen and Wedge, 1982). Children whose fathers were in non-manual work made significantly greater progress than children whose fathers were manual workers, even when allowances were made for initial differences in reading attainment and other background factors indicated earlier.

Sex

Girls showed higher reading attainments than boys in each of the three years. In year 1 there was, on average, five months of reading age superiority. Over the next three years this gap did not close, even when allowances had been made for the initial differences in reading attainment and other background variables. These findings agree with other major national studies (DES Assessment of Performance Unit, 1981, 1982). At the end of their junior school education 31 per cent of boys and 21 per cent of girls attending ILEA schools were recommended for special needs screening at secondary transfer because of their low scores (less than 35 points) on the London Reading Test. The sex difference in reading attainments is widely and well documented (Maccoby and Jacklin, 1980). Primary school girls are *not* superior in *all* aspects of language (Gorman et al., 1984). Girls were found to have more favourable self-concepts than boys in relation to school.

Fluency in English and minority ethnic group background

Understandably, pupils from minority ethnic groups who are not fluent in spoken English have markedly lower reading attainments than others. A brief visit to any country where one does not speak the language induces considerable sympathy with pupils in such circumstances. Ethnic background is a more complicated issue. Some minority ethnic groups score significantly lower than others even when fluency and background factors have been allowed for. It is reported that Gujerati speakers scored above average on the reading tests whereas pupils from Punjabi-speaking backgrounds scored below average. British children of Caribbean, Greek and Turkish family backgrounds scored lower on the reading tests than those from English, Scottish, Welsh and Irish backgrounds. A small group of pupils from Chinese backgrounds (N = 17) obtained higher scores than all other ethnic groups when allowance was made for background variables. It would have been interesting to see the scores of the children of the many other earlier immigrant groups to this country.

Both fluency in English and ethnic background affected progress in reading, even when differences in initial attainment were allowed for. Pupils from Caribbean and Asian backgrounds made much slower progress than other groups. These findings support those of other studies (Mabey, 1981; Scarr et al., 1983; Mackintosh et al., 1988; Pumfrey, 1990c). In the ILEA study the small number of Asian pupils precluded the analysis of the progress in reading of different language groups. The gap in reading attainment between British children from Caribbean and Asian backgrounds and those from the majority white population *increased* over time. The seriousness of this can hardly be overemphasised.

The causes of these social class, sex and ethnic group differences are far from clear. The nature–nurture debate is of little relevance to teachers who face the challenge of helping *all* their pupils become literate. Knowledge of the above relationships is neutral. If it leads to expectations concerning the reading attainments and reading progress of individuals and groups based on the unproven assumption that the relationships are causal, it can be harmful. All children can learn. The vast majority can learn to read. Given the necessary help, resources and motivation, they can be helped to read more competently. Difficulties can be minimised; attainment and attitudes to reading can be optimised. Teachers and schools can be effective.

SPECIAL EDUCATIONAL NEEDS VERSUS INDIVIDUAL DIFFERENCES

The author is suspicious of the educational utility of the concept of special educational needs. It has already been argued that the concept is virtually redundant and that emphasis should be placed on identifying and using pupils' individual differences in helping them learn to read.

In Circular 22/89 on *Assessments and Statements of Special Educational Needs: Procedures within the Education, Health and Social Services*, the 'specification of goals for change' is one of six issues to be considered when it is thought that a child may require special educational provision (DES, 1989e, para. 18). Taken in relation to pupils with either general and/or specific learning difficulties in aspects of literacy and the national curriculum (English) requirements, the specification of goals can be taken as a positive step. Operationally defined educational objectives are objective and observable guidelines for those involved in helping individual pupils improve their reading skills. It encourages the integration of assessment and teaching in the reading programme. In the author's view, this principle should apply to *all* pupils, irrespective of whether or not they are deemed to have special educational needs and are, or are not, accorded the protection of a statement.

There are very many dimensions to inter- and intra-individual differences between pupils, irrespective of how the classes in a junior school are formed. We know that no single method enables all pupils to learn to read satisfactorily. Hence the teacher must become aware of a wide range of methods and materials. Such knowledge facilitates the search for particular methods and materials that suit individuals at given stages. But the search must not be guided by a blind empiricism concerned only with what is effective: it must be firmly rooted in developmental theory. Then our understanding of why methodologies are, or are not, effective is likely to be increased.

It may be that every pupil must be helped, metaphorically, to find their own experiential ascent from the lowlands of illiteracy to the summits represented by competence in reading in various genres. With reference to the teaching and learning of reading by pupils, the professional development of the class teacher is also a continual series of challenges. The theoretical bases of reading as one aspect of language and of symbolic thinking, its normal development and anomalies of development, their prediction and control, are complex challenges to the individual class teacher and to the profession. Such theoretical and practical concerns are not new discoveries, but ones the teaching profession will continue to address. The crucible of the classroom is the most common place for developing and testing ideas about the improvement of reading.

Aptitude × interaction interactions (AIIs) are identified when methods match pupils' learning styles, and progress in reading occurs. Individual AIIs can be found. In practice, teachers are continually looking for methods and materials that are helpful to *more* than one unique, individual pupil. In searching for AIIs that will be beneficial to identifiable groups of pupils, class teachers aim at educational efficiency. Whether a pupil suffers from sensory impairments or from any other impediment to learning to read, the principle is the same. It is clear, for example, that the methods of teaching hearing-impaired pupils to read are not the same as those that are effective with visually impaired pupils. AIIs have also been identified for pupils without sensory impairments, as noted earlier.

Some research workers argue that pupils' cognitive abilities underpinning reading differ only quantitatively. If this is the case, the same methodology is likely to benefit all pupils, albeit in varying amounts and at varying times in their development. It is without doubt true that certain experiences in developing pupils' phonological awareness, both implicit and explicit, can be helpful to all pupils (Bryant, 1990; Bradley, 1990; Cashdan and Wright, 1990; Cataldo and Ellis, 1990; Snowling, 1990).

The author considers that, in addition to certain common quantitative differences between pupils, there are also important qualitative differences which can have implications for instruction (Snowling, 1985; Carbo et al., 1986; Gjessing and Karlsen, 1989; Tyler, 1990). Common quantitative differences and distinctive qualitative differences between pupils in cognitive abilities can coexist. An appreciation of both is important in understanding and improving the learning and teaching of reading for all pupils.

—2—

Reading and language: concerns and contemporary controversies

READING, LANGUAGE AND ACCOUNTABILITY

It is important to distinguish between the abilities of the competent adult reader and the child who is learning to read. An appreciation of the powers of the former demonstrates clearly the value of reading. The characteristics of the child learning to read differ from the adult reader in a number of important respects. These have implications for the teaching and learning of reading. Further, the ranges of inter-individual and intra-individual differences are extensive.

Symbols are the internal representation of objects and events external to ourselves. One of the distinguishing characteristics of our species is its widespread use of a vast range of symbols. These can be graphic, gestural, oral, spatial, mathematical or literary. Human thought is based on the ability to use such symbols. To think involves the creation, communication, manipulation and interpretation of symbol systems. To think is to reflect and hypothesise; to increase one's understanding of both past and present. It enables more adequate prediction of future events. The possibility of changes to, and control of, the environment are enhanced. To think is to be empowered.

The thinking abilities of the adult have developed from those of the child. The former are both qualitatively and quantitatively different from the latter. The same is true of the accomplished reader and the learner.

Thinking by either adult or child does not necessarily require reading skills. Conversely, to read requires and develops the ability to think. Not to be able to read is to be isolated from much of the mainstream of our culture. The emotional extension and satisfactions of literature remain (literally) a closed book. Accounts by literate individuals who have suddenly lost the ability to read make the point. Such accounts emphasise the distress, disorientation and disruption of life that ensues. Children with reading difficulties, and adult illiterates, who eventually learn to read testify to the enrichment of their lives that this achievement provides.

There are countless unanswered questions concerning the nature of reading and its development. Almost certainly many issues have not as yet been articulated. There are also important controversies over many aspects of learning to read. Despite these, enough is known for all *including the most severely handicapped* to learn to read. Deaf, blind, language-disordered, severely physically handicapped and children with severe learning difficulties (SLD) have been taught to read. Whether such an objective represents the highest priority for all children at a particular point in their lives is a different issue.

It is *not* claimed that the levels of competence in reading achieved, for example, by pupils with SLD are equivalent to those of the average child. Individual differences in speed, accuracy and comprehension will still exist. The satisfactions found by individuals in the mastery of reading and its potential rewards also differ. These are to some extent a function of the alternative modes of communication available to the individual, to their ease of access, the use made of them, and to the value a culture places on the ability to read.

Irrespective of the problems that a child is having, improvements in reading attainments can almost certainly be achieved. *The decision whether help should be provided is essentially a political and financial one.* Serious and prolonged difficulties in learning to read will almost certainly require intensive and long-term professional support. This is expensive. Society must face the issue 'How much are we willing to pay to achieve a literate society?' It is a matter of priorities. Competition for resources is considerable. In a democratic Western industrialised society that must compete in manufacturing and export to maintain the fabric of society, a highly trained, literate, numerate, creative and efficient workforce is essential. But what proportion of the population need that be?

It is current government economic policy to invest in success. Is this paralleled in education? Provisions in the Education Reform Act 1988 suggest that it is. Does this indicate that investing in the education of children with severe and prolonged reading difficulties is no more than a sop to alleviate some uncomfortably challenging moral and ethical issues? The use of the ambiguous, ill-defined and elusive term 'special educational needs' can be seen as a part of such a palliative strategy. The number of children with reading difficulties who *should* be given additional help is a political issue. The resource decisions are *not* the prime responsibility of teachers. They are the responsibility of the government in particular and of the whole community in general. Reading is but one of the language abilities. The four major elements of language are shown in Figure 2.1. The complexities of the relationships would

be better conveyed by a Venn diagram. In three dimensions it
would still be inadequate. Representation in multi-dimensional
space would almost certainly be required to represent very crudely
what is known about relationships between the various modes of
language.

| | | MODES | |
		Sound	Text
CHANNELS	Expressive	Speech	Writing
	Receptive	Listening	Reading

Figure 2.1 *Major language modes*

The junior school class teacher has many concerns. The development of pupils' reading attainments is a central responsibility
recognised by the profession and by society. The duties of identifying and alleviating pupils' difficulties in learning to read are an
important sub-set of those related to improving all pupils' reading
attainments. In a typical mixed-ability junior school, marked individual differences in pupils' reading attainments and attitudes to
reading will be apparent when the group first meets the teacher.
These differences will still exist, and may even be increased, when
the pupils move on at the end of the academic year. Yet it will be
anticipated that *all* pupils will have made some tangible progress in
reading. A range of indices will be used by the class teacher to
monitor this progress, including the number, variety and increasing difficulty of books and other textual materials read by the
individual during the year. Changes in scores on reading tests
measuring different aspects of reading over the year will provide
further indices of progress. The national tests of English proposed

in the Education Reform Act 1988 will provide information on the reading attainments of pupils arriving from the top infant school. The subsequent testing at the age of 11 will lead to some 'wash-back' effects on the junior school curriculum.

An integral component of the school's language curriculum will be its reading curriculum, which will comprise three major elements. The reading curriculum will specify the *objectives* of the programme, the *methods and materials* to be used and *tests and assessment techniques* whereby the efficacy of the programme will be both furthered (formative and diagnostic assessments) and evaluated (summative assessments). The reading curriculum is nested, in turn, within the language curriculum, the 'core' curriculum and the national curriculum, as shown in Figure 2.2. These three aspects are closely interrelated. Considerations that primarily affect any one will be seen to have implications for the others. For example, external examination of reading can affect both the objectives and the pedagogy of the reading curriculum.

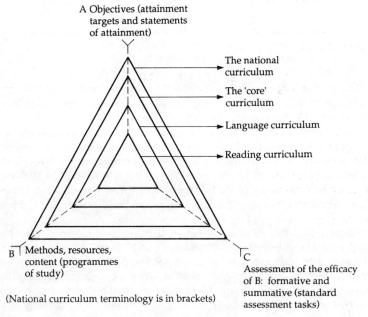

Figure 2.2 *Essential elements of a junior school curriculum*

This was shown in England during the period 1862–97 when a 'payment by results' system was in operation. A Royal Commission under the chairmanship of the Duke of Newcastle had been appointed to 'inquire into the present state of popular education in England, and to consider and report what measures, if any, are required for the extension of *sound and cheap* elementary instruction to all classes of the people' (my italics). The Commission's Report was published in 1861. Its focus was on increasing efficiency in education and on improving standards in the basic subjects:

> There is only one way of securing this result, which is to institute a searching examination by competent authority of every child in every school to which grants are paid, with a view to ascertaining whether these indispensable elements of knowledge are thoroughly acquired.

Thus spake the Reverend James Fraser, later Bishop of Manchester, who was an influential member of the Newcastle Commission. The subjects tested were reading, writing and arithmetic (and plain needlework for girls). The government grant to the school was made dependent on the pupils' average attendance at school and also on their performance in examinations conducted by HMIs. Each child could earn for the school a total grant of 12 shillings per year (60p). Four shillings (20p) were for general merit and attendance; 8 shillings (40p) were for passes in the three Rs. To fail in any one of the three Rs reduced the grant by 2s. 8d. (13.3p).

When Robert Lowe first presented the proposals in 1861 they included a scheme for the examination of infants. The proposals met with a storm of protest. The Revised Code was modified somewhat and given effect in 1862. When he again presented it in the House of Commons on 13 February 1862, Robert Lowe said

> I cannot promise the House that this system will be an economical one, and I cannot promise that it will be an efficient one, but I can promise that it will be one or the other. If it is not cheap, it shall be efficient; if it is not efficient, it shall be cheap.
>
> (Hansard, vol. 165, p. 229)

The whole tenor of this aspect of the Revised Code was in tune with the then dominant free market ethos. It did effect economies. One of the many powerful critics of the Revised Code was Kay-Shuttleworth. His critique, written in 1868, should be read by everyone concerned with the proposals for national testing contained in the Education Reform Act 1988 (Kay-Shuttleworth, 1873).

The American experience of 'performance contracting' is a contemporary descendant of 'payment by results'. The scheme allows agencies to teach, for example, children who have been identified as making little or no progress in reading. The agency contracts that the children will achieve clearly defined attainment targets in a specified time. In reading, payment to the agency is made only if the children reach the agreed attainment level. The efficacy of this system has been extensively studied. If either 'payment by results' or 'performance contracting' had been uniformly effective, the systems would have been far more rapidly and widely adopted than has been the case. A number of strengths and weaknesses have been clearly identified in both (Kay-Shuttleworth, 1873; Pumfrey, 1978). The major benefits and disadvantages of performance contracting in relation to the teaching of reading are summarised here:

Benefits

1. Performance contracting encourages the introduction of new techniques, materials, systems and concepts.
2. It emphasises the accountability of administrators, contractors and teachers in the improvement of pupils' reading attainments and attitudes towards reading.
3. Innovations that are found to be successful can be disseminated to local education systems.

Disadvantages

1. Some performance contracting programmes have been administratively too complex. This has increased unit costs and reduced the efficiency of schemes.
2. Reading objectives have to be operationally defined. Objective measures of pupil attainments are demanded. Both requirements operate to narrow the scope of the reading programme.
3. Unresolved legal issues concerning teacher status, problems of test selection, use and the administration of programmes have been raised. Cases of 'teaching to the test' have occurred (Pumfrey, 1978).

Under both the payment by results and performance contracting systems, certain pupils are likely to be neglected, unless protection of their interests is built into the financing of education. Already children with reading difficulties are at a great disadvantage in Western industrialised societies. The challenge of finding and funding a mechanism, seen as equitable by citizens in general, that can minimise the disadvantages of an as yet indeterminate group of pupils remains a challenge. The Education Reform Act 1988 can help or hinder the development of such a practice, depending on the values developed and resources made available for its implementation.

LISTENING, SPEAKING AND DISCUSSING: THE IMPORTANCE OF ORACY

Why is it that the reading attainments of average 16-year-old severely hearing-impaired pupils is at about the 8-year-old level? (There are, of course, individuals whose attainments are markedly higher than this.) In large measure, these pupils have been isolated from the continuing exposure to context-linked oral communication from which most children benefit. This sensory and social deprivation is severely limiting in certain respects. Its adverse consequences are all too often apparent in hearing-impaired pupils' speech, reading attainments and also in their writing skills. The commonly used grammatical constructions and wide vocabularies that hearing pupils readily acquire and use are not as easily available to the hearing-impaired pupil, despite the undoubted expertise, understanding and skills of specialist teachers in schools for the hearing-impaired and elsewhere.

The point is made both to emphasise the importance of oracy as a basis for literacy and to identify a key issue raised by moves to encourage the integration of hearing-impaired pupils into the normal school. It is clear that such developments require a considerable degree of within-class support for both the hearing-impaired pupil and the class teacher, coupled with INSET. The availability of suitably qualified and experienced specialist teachers and equipment is essential to satisfactory integration. It cannot be carried out 'on the cheap'.

The fact that some severely hearing-impaired pupils do learn to read competently is encouraging and challenging. The arguments between supporters of the oral tradition in the education of the hearing-impaired and others who seek a mixed educational economy involving manual signing (total communication) look set to continue. The mainstream junior school teacher into whose class a hearing-impaired pupil is to be integrated should be enabled to spend a period seconded to either a specialist school or unit, or a mainstream school at which an integration programme for the hearing-impaired has been successfully implemented. The work of Lane using his ARROW technique originated with pupils with hearing difficulties attending a special unit. The combination of sophisticated tape-recording technology with the psychological importance of the self-voice, appears to hold out considerable promise of improved reading attainments (Lane, 1990) (see Chapter 8 for further details).

The author has recently observed two hearing-impaired pupils who are, with support, being educated in a mainstream school. The most striking point was the great differences between the two pupils in terms of learning style, attainment and social adjustment. The common factor of their sensory disability underlined, rather than diminished, their marked differences. These were just as considerable as those between the extremes in the non-hearing-impaired pupils.

The national curriculum recognises the importance of speaking and listening as integral aspects of the English curriculum. Pupils will now be regularly assessed in order to foster and improve these skills. Their attainments and progress will also be measured using standard assessment tasks at the end of each key stage. The National Oracy Project (NOP) was established as a three-phase project in 1987. Phase 1 was completed in 1988; phase 2 will be completed in 1991 and phase 3 in 1993. The project's aims are:

- to enhance the role of speech in the learning process 5–16 by encouraging active learning
- to develop the teaching of oral communication skills
- to develop methods of assessment of and through speech, including assessment for public examinations at 16+
- to improve pupils' performance across the curriculum
- to enhance teachers' skills and practice
- to promote recognition of the value of oral work in school and increase its use as a means of improving learning

The NOP has led to the setting up of a wide variety of local initiatives. In January 1989, 13 individual LEAs were involved and a further 22 LEAs had formed consortia projects. The first edition of the NOP's journal, *TALK*, was published in early 1989 by the National Curriculum Council. The journal is a valuable forum for reports of current projects.

This first edition contains a helpful INSET activity, 'The Statement Game', which consists of a list of statements concerning the nature and uses of oracy in education. In groups, teachers are asked to place the cut-up statements into categories under headings such as 'Agree', 'Disagree' and 'It depends'. Statements found the most stimulating can be reported back to the whole group. Alternatives include groups creating their own statements.

It is clear that exactly this type of activity can be done in connection with various aspects of the teaching of reading. It is also clear that the creation, sorting and discussion of statements could be carried out by pupils as well as teachers. This would almost certainly be a useful way of developing the metacognitions on which effective reading is based.

THE NATURE OF READING

It is worthwhile reminding readers of the rich tradition to which we are heir (Mathews, 1966; Banton-Smith, 1970; Morris, 1973). Many cultures had been writing long before the pre-Christian Greeks, but these earlier systems were less flexible and failed to utilise all the speech sounds of the given language. The Greeks explicitly recognised that words were sounds, or combinations of sounds, and that writing should be a guide to sound. Their development of an alphabet which had Semitic–Greek origins provided a complete set of symbols (letters) by which every sound in their language could be represented. In its final form this alphabet set its letters in a fixed sequence and, as with earlier systems, each symbol (letter) had a name. Both these conditions facilitate the memorisation of the alphabet, thereby making learning to read and write easier. Anyone who understood the alphabet could write. All that was required was to sound out the word and then write down in sequence the letters representing the sounds. In Greek, a word has as many syllables as it has vowels and diphthongs. Syllables were basic speech units and had to be learned perfectly. Currently this would be described as 'mastery learning', 'learning to criterion' or 'automatisation'. Letters, syllables and then words comprised the instructional sequence. The direction of the writing from left to right was well established by the fifth century BC. For many years Greek writing did not separate text into words; writing was recorded as a continuous sequence. Their move towards separating the spoken words when recording them has been described as the last important step in the history of writing.

Gelb has described the Greek alphabet as

> the alphabet that subsequently conquered the world. Much as the hundreds of alphabets used throughout the world may differ from each other in appearance, they all have characteristics of outer form, inner structure, or both, which first originated in the small area surrounding the eastern Mediterranean.

With only minor exceptions, he claims, this is the dominant system of writing in current use (Mathews, 1966).

The issue of how pupils can best be taught to read is a perennial concern. To the pre-Christian Greeks, teaching pupils to read was seen as a monotonous, unimaginative, menial and not particularly difficult task. It called for neither learning nor aptitude and was therefore an occupation meriting no distinction or esteem. As such, the teaching of reading was frequently assigned to slaves.

So far as learning to read in English is concerned, the methodological issue is almost 500 years old, according to extant records. It may well be older. The history of the teaching of reading in English is a fascinating and rewarding field. Its exploration can yield many insights and surprises. The wheel is frequently rediscovered, in so far as the pedagogy of reading is concerned. In England it was recognised as early as the sixteenth century that reading might be made easier if every sound in the language was represented by one letter and if no letter represented more than one sound. Sir Thomas Smith's campaign demonstrated the inadequacy of the then 24-letter alphabet and he devised an augmented one of 34 letters (1568). John Hart's proposed 'new alphabet' (1570) and Richard Hodges's system of diacritical markings, developed whilst the latter was a schoolmaster in Southwark, failed to capture the allegiance of teachers, who remained devoted to the conventional alphabet.

In England, during the sixteenth and seventeenth centuries, the child was required to master the letters, to learn the alphabet forwards and backwards. Next syllables were learned, followed in turn by words and sentences. Practices, developed over the centuries by insightful teachers, to make the learning of letters easier were adopted. For example, pupils were given the medieval equivalent of 'M & Ms' or Smarties for each letter learned. The alphabet was set to music and children learned it by singing (Mathews, 1966). Despite their failure to be accepted during the sixteenth and seventeenth centuries, variants of the three pioneers' ideas re-emerge periodically. The Initial Teaching Alphabet and 'diacritical marking' have both received considerable attention during the last 20 years in the United Kingdom and elsewhere.

The social psychologist Lewin once made the point that there is nothing as practical as a good theory. Theories give us something to think about, and with. Recently there has been considerable interest in developing theoretical models of reading (Singer and Ruddell, 1985). Used in this way in connection with reading, the word 'model' means a tentative ideational construct used to develop and test predictions of children's reading behaviour. When predictions fail, the model is modified. Thus models of reading can be refined in the light of formal investigations and also on the basis of classroom experience.

As noted earlier, models of reading differ, depending on the theoretical background, training and assumptions of their creators.

Some models aspire to be comprehensive, to cover all aspects and stages of the development of reading, but the vast majority are limited to particular aspects or stages of reading. They may, for example, focus on pre-reading, on early reading or on mature reading from the educational viewpoint. The model can be one of reading accuracy, speed or comprehension. Other models are based on the assumption that reading is a cognitive process whereby information is extracted from textual materials. Others develop neuropsychological, sensory or perceptual models of reading. To understand any theory of reading requires a considerable investment of time and thought. The writings of the particular theorist must be studied, and reflected upon, in the light of one's own professional experience of how children make progress in reading. Three theories are outlined briefly here because of their contemporary importance.

It will readily be realised that the assumptions concerning the nature of the reading process that underpin these models differ markedly. Only to theoretical purists are the models mutually exclusive. Class teachers are characteristically pragmatists when it comes to the teaching of reading. They will draw from *any* source, theoretical or atheoretical, suggestions that they consider could be of value. They are too well aware of the gaps or chasms that exist between any *one* theory of reading and the teaching or learning of reading by children that it is their professional responsibility to foster. In the typical junior school classroom, eclecticism rules.

Reading as decoding from text to sound

Some workers from different professional orientations, such as teachers, psychologists, linguists, neurologists, audiologists and specialists in literature, consider that the core of reading is the ability to decode text into sound. So too do many parents. When faced with an unfamiliar word, many people fall back on such a strategy. (Try the following word taken from a report to the parents of a child with learning difficulties: 'dysdiadochokinesia'. Even a less technical but unfamiliar word such as 'floccinaucinihili-pilification' usually has a similar effect.) The key task for the child *beginning* to read is seen as mastering this particular decoding skill. Comprehension is not the first priority. That is not to say it is unimportant.

This orientation leads to instructional techniques involving discrimination of letters, their naming and the linking of letters' shapes and names with sounds. There is little agreement on the sequences in which these should be done. Whether one should work from individual letter–phoneme associations and blend these to pronounce whole words, or start from whole words and establish the associations, is another controversial issue.

Reading as extracting information from text

Mention has already been made of the work of the British psychologist Seymour. His work is aimed at testing the validity of a relatively simple information-processing model of children's reading and spelling skills (Seymour, 1986). His book is a gem. Rightly or wrongly, but unambiguously, he takes developmental dyslexia to be a disorder affecting the child's acquisition of basic reading and spelling skills. His assumption is that the intellectual system underlying the development of these two literacy skills can be conceptualised as a set of information processors. The operation of these hypothetical processors can be investigated using the experimental methods of cognitive psychology. The model he uses is based on interactions between hypothesised visual, semantic and phonological processors. Four major domains are identified: (1) visual-processor functions; (2) the morphemic route to phonology; (3) the grapheme–phoneme translation route to phonology and (4) the morphemic route to semantics. There is no assumption that any particular configuration will characterise competent readers.

Capitalising on the strengths of the microprocessor, Seymour was able to run, record and analyse a complex series of eleven tests on individual children. The tests comprised a systematic series of vocalisation and decision tasks to test the validity of the model. The child's responses to the vocalisation tasks were one focus of interest. Reaction time, accuracy and error type of the child's responses to the presented stimuli were recorded. In the decision-making tasks, judgements on visual, lexical or semantic characteristics of a stimulus were made and signalled non-verbally by the child. Yes/no reaction time and accuracy were recorded.

Seymour individually tested 13 competent readers, and 21 subjects deemed to be dyslexic. The latter group varied greatly in age, IQ, reading and spelling attainments. They were also divided into five smaller reading attainment groups ranging from extremely backward to less backward readers. The aim was to investigate the hypothesised information-processing system by looking at the changing patterns of pupils' objective performances on the given tasks. In providing a functional analysis of the reading of each pupil, the possibility of diagnostic and remedial applications was borne in mind.

The individual case studies are clinically fascinating. Each individual's performance is interpreted in relation to the information-processing model. The objective data highlight important processing differences between two groups of *competent* readers and also different patterns *within* competent readers. The five dyslexic groups also showed theoretically important differences in performance. Seymour's data point to the dangers inherent in *assuming the existence of a small number of sub-types of dyslexia* as suggested by some workers (Vernon, 1977; Boder and Jarrico, 1982). The uniqueness of the individual patterns of the pupils' performances was a striking characteristic of the data.

Whilst the model, the design of the tests, sampling of the pupils and the methods of analysis may have weaknesses, this work has one great strength and one major weakness from the class teacher's viewpoint. The strength is that Seymour has adhered firmly to a guideline all too frequently neglected in classroom practice. He followed the sound advice of the philosopher Jeremy Bentham: 'It is no matter if it be right or wrong so as it be explicit. If it is right, it will serve as a guide to direct; if wrong, as a beacon to warn.'

In capitalising on the promise of computer technology, what Seymour has done is imaginative, clearly described, objective and readily replicable. The microprocessor is to the teacher and the psychologist interested in understanding reading processes what the invention of the first telescope was to the astronomer. As with the telescope, the microcomputer system needs directing towards an appropriate target, if any insights into the learning and teaching of reading are to be obtained. What could be a more appropriate focus than the literacy skills of reading and spelling?

The major weakness of such work from the junior school class teacher's viewpoint is that it does not have an immediate classroom applicability. The work is experimental and concentrates on how the pupils extract information from single words only. Understandably, Seymour does not give clear guidelines to the practising teacher who wishes to identify pupils' difficulties in reading and alleviate them. Despite such reservations, the clinical descriptions of the individual pupils are of great value to anyone interested in the inter- and intra-individual differences of the pupils. They sensitise the reader to the nature of the complexities and, more positively, to the possibility of explicating them. Seymour's study demonstrates both the power of a basic research methodology based on information-processing technology and the promise of a model of one aspect of reading. Suggestions for the use of this technology in the assessment and improvement of reading difficulties are given in Chapter 8.

Although it is known that profoundly deaf pupils can be taught to read, it is accepted that they face severe difficulties. At the age of 16, the average reading age of the deaf pupil is about 8 years.

Special techniques are required in order to help them learn to read. A companion volume in the present series, *Children with Hearing Difficulties*, gives useful information and advice (Webster and Wood, 1989).

A number of cognitive psychologists are interested in trends in children's perceptual development and the implications of this development for understanding how children learn to read. Some also consider that learning to communicate by spoken language is a prerequisite for reading. One group has suggested that to move from the use of spoken language to reading involves three overlapping phases of learning. The first is essentially perceptual in nature. It involves learning to identify and differentiate graphic symbols. The second phase involves learning letter–sound relationships. Phase three is characterised by the use of progressively higher-order units of structure (Gibson and Levin, 1975). The differentiations involved in phase 1 are made on the basis of distinctive features of the graphic symbols, usually contrasting graphic characteristics. Examples include features such as tall v. short lines, straight v. curved lines, diagonal v. perpendicular and horizontal v. vertical lines.

When the letters can be distinguished from one another, decoding from print to sound can begin. This entails more than the simple one-to-one correspondences between graphemes and phonemes for single letters. Many groups of letters forming linguistic units that have consistent pronunciations, for example, 'ious', must be discriminated. There are numerous repetitive patterns in English orthography. These provide one means of helping pupils generalise and decode unfamiliar words. This technique is represented in classroom practice in the lists of words still used in connection with many graded reading schemes. Additionally, many letter–sound correspondences in English vary depending on context, for example, 'pear' and 'hear'. It is argued that awareness of this diversity, and the ability to cope with it in reading, can be encouraged by the simultaneous teaching of words exemplifying variable letter–sound correspondences. A helpful overview of this field, including the implications for the learning and teaching of reading, is available (Gibson and Levin, 1975).

The third phase involves the use of superordinate principles governing the formation of increasingly large and complex words. The detection of such structures in the text is considered by Gibson to be characteristic of efficient cognitive processing and thus of efficient reading.

If teachers are to help pupils attain this level, they must recognise that three types of structural principle exist in text. The first is the rules of correspondence between the phonological and graphical systems. The second is the rules of orthography whereby sounds are represented by spellings. The third is syntactic principles which restrict possibilities. Thus, in a 'cloze' test item such as 'John —— the pear' the omitted word is restricted to one particular type (a verb) and a limited set of these.

Gibson has advanced the view that there can be no single reading process. Therefore there is unlikely to be only one model of reading. She also acknowledges that there is no single 'best' way in which the various processes involved in reading can be taught (Gibson and Levin, 1975).

Reading: a guessing game

Goodman refutes the notion that reading is a precise process requiring, 'exact, detailed, sequential perception and identification of letters, words, spelling patterns and large language units' (Goodman, 1976b). In contrast, he considers reading a selective process, a psycholinguistic guessing game involving an interaction of thought and language. To read effectively involves the use of *minimal* language cues required to produce guesses that are right first time.

When children read, they strive after meaning. They bring to the reading task their entire experience, including their very considerable language and thinking abilities. The reader uses only the minimum of information necessary to get to the meaning of the text. This information is of three types: graphic, syntactic and semantic. The first is acquired visually whilst the other two are provided by the reader. By using previously acquired knowledge of language, the reader predicts the grammatical structure (syntax) and the content that will fit the structure. There is no need to attend to all the graphic information available. The more proficient the reader, the less conscious use is made of graphic information. There is no need to notice every letter or to read all the words in a passage.

Readers develop the following behaviour:

- strategies for sampling and selecting the most useful graphic cues;
- strategies for predicting the meaning (deep structure) of the text being read;
- strategies for predicting the ways in which this meaning will be manifest in the text (surface structure);
- strategies for confirming the correctness of the predictions; and
- strategies for correcting predictions that prove to be invalid.

Typically these require that further information from one or more of the three cue levels is sampled and processed.

The skilled reader perceives the graphic stimuli (text) and moves *directly* to meaning. This is the main goal of reading. Analysing the miscues that children make in oral reading provides a window on the reading process of that child's interaction with the particular piece of text.

Whether this is true of all reading is unclear. Reading can require both great attention to detail and high precision in situations where the consequences of a misreading could be disastrous. Accuracy to detail in reading papers on legal, medical, engineering, computer design and atomic engineering can be matters of life and death. The more homely instructions in the popular 'do-it-yourself' publications also require attention to detail.

Goodman has presented an 11-point psycholinguistic model of the process of reading English. He comments on the complexity of the model but asserts that it is still too simple to account for the actual behaviour of readers (Goodman, 1976a, 1976b). The implications of Goodman's model for the teaching of reading, which are pertinent to the current book, are summarised here:

- Reading instruction should begin, not with letters or sounds, but with the reader's relevant natural language.
- There is no hierarchy of skills in learning to read. The learner must use all skills simultaneously.
- Children who fail to learn to read do so because we have not built on their strengths as competent language users.
- To help children overcome reading difficulties, build up their confidence in their ability to predict meaning.
- Children learn to read largely by reading.
- Anyone who can learn oral language can learn to read and write.

These suggestions are controversial. They represent an important challenge to many traditional teaching practices, and their repercussions on the teaching of reading will be discussed later. Goodman does not discuss the ways whereby the child beginning to read develops the ability to recognise words. He does not attempt to explain how the reader processes graphic cues.

In reading, in trying to reconstruct from print the author's message, the reader uses information other than that contained in the text. Other workers have suggested that a balance is struck between the amount of non-visual information available to the reader and the use that is made of the textual information. The more non-visual information available to the reader, the less attention is given to the text. The less the non-visual information available to the reader, the more the attention that must be paid to the text (Smith, 1982). Reading is only partly visual.

The psycholinguistic position has been popularised under various labels. These include: 'Conceptually-driven' (Bobrow and Norman, 1975); 'Explorer' (Rozin and Gleitman, 1977); 'Top-down' (Kamil, 1978); 'Inside–outside' (Smith, 1979).

Because of its importance the 'top-down' versus 'bottom-up' issue is returned to in more detail later in this chapter (pp. 114–26) and a resolution indicated.

THE DEVELOPMENT OF LITERACY

Most children, long before they are able to read, have a well-established and functioning system of oral/aural communication based on spoken language. The importance of this system is indicated when one considers the difficulties in learning to read and the relatively low attainments in reading achieved by hearing-impaired children. It is generally acknowledged that children use the underlying spoken language system when they are learning to read (Foorman and Siegel, 1986). This is *not* to say that children without the advantage of normal language will be unable to learn to read. In England the Schools Council Communication Skills Project examined the role of young children's language and teachers' talk in education in general. It also considered their effects on children with moderate learning difficulties (Tough, 1981). A wealth of practical suggestions for increasing children's use of language is provided in Tough's book, and in other publications produced by the team. The suggestions and materials flowed directly from the school-based research that was the focus of the project.

It is accepted that the vast majority of junior school pupils will have few difficulties in using spoken language. An appreciation of how reading may build upon that base provides an essential background to understanding the development of reading skills. The processing system of children with normal hearing and speech, prior to the acquisition of reading, can be (and has been) schematically represented in many ways. One of these is shown in Figure 2.3.

The ideas derive from an information-processing model developed mainly by psychologists and neuropsychologists. The construction of a cognitive information-processing model requires that functionally defined systems are represented together with the channels of communication linking them. One of the earliest of these was the 'logogen' model developed by Morton (1969). This

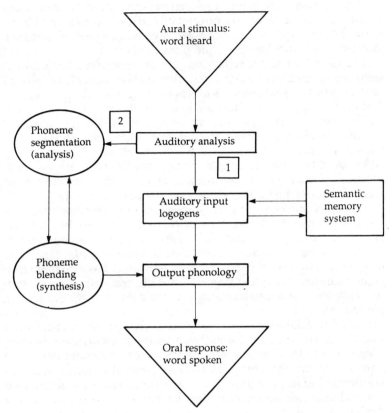

Figure 2.3 *The foundations of literacy (1): hearing, understanding and uttering a spoken word*

model provided an account of the effects of contextual influences on reading and listening. It also included the idea that interactions between incoming sensory information and centrally stored representations of meaning and speech might be mediated by a word (or morpheme) specific recognition and retrieval system. This was labelled by Morton as a 'logogen system'. Many variants of this model have been developed (Seymour, 1986). The model shown in Figure 2.3 concerns the processing of single words. One assumption is that the various functional components making up the information-processing system in humans are sensitive to different aspects of language. These will include the frequency with which

words are encountered and used, the regularity of their pronunciation and the concrete or abstract nature of their meaning.

At the pre-reading stage, children are able to hear, recognise,
use and understand a wide range of words. They are not able to
recognise the written forms of these words. The model indicates
that words comprising the child's spoken vocabulary are represented within an auditory lexicon which contains auditory input
logogens (in essence, recognition units). This auditory lexicon consists of the set of words and morphemes (the smallest linguistic
unit of meaning) known to the child. Word meanings are stored
within the semantic memory system, with which the auditory
lexicon is reciprocally linked. A complementary non-lexical system
is used for processing new words. Included in this system are
procedures for phoneme segmentation (analysis) and phoneme
synthesis (blending). These operate when new articulatory-motor
patterns have to be elaborated (see routes 1 and 2, Figure 2.3).

The exploitation by the developing child of the spoken language
system requires the integration of two systems (see Figure 2.4).
The first is the system that already exists for processing spoken
words. The second is one for processing written words. This integrative developmental process can be considered as a sequence of
phases during which text-processing skills gradually emerge and
slowly become independent and automatic (Frith, 1985; Snowling,
1990).

Typically, children's initial attempts at reading single words are
visually based. A sight vocabulary can be established using this
approach, particularly when the written words are ones that have
significance for the child. The classic book by Sylvia Ashton-
Warner on her work with deprived Maori and white pupils in New
Zealand bears eloquent testimony to this point (Ashton-Warner,
1963). Her subsequent work in the USA underlined the difficulties
in disseminating her ideas and practices in a different culture (Ashton-Warner, 1974).

Such a visually dominated approach often results in many oral
reading miscues. Thus the child might read the word *table* as 'blue'
because of the three letters that they have in common. The use by
children of the information contained in the first letter of a word
can also lead to incorrect miscues. For example, the word *horse* can
be read as 'heads', if attention focuses on the first letter, or as
'house' if more visual information is used. The general visual
shape of a word is also sometimes used as a guide to its meaning.
Some words have fairly distinct shapes. The utilisation of this
property has often been advocated as one means of helping pupils
memorise and read written words, but this has limitations (Spache
and Spache, 1986). The visual strategies used by children to recog-

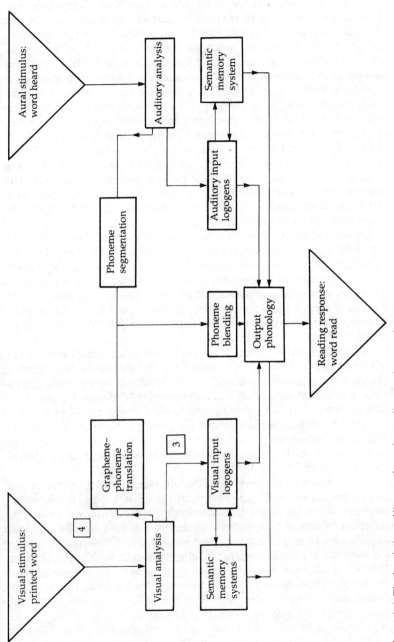

Figure 2.4 *The foundations of literacy (2): understanding a written word*

nise words are frequently crude and can include tangential information such as punctuation marks and even exclamation marks.
This initial phase of literacy acquisition in which a small number of
words can be recognised using partial information has been called
the 'logographic' phase (Frith, 1985). Quite clearly the limitations
that it places on children's reading are even greater in relation to
their spelling.

The first stage is followed by the *alphabetic* stage. To move from
the first to the second stage requires that the child be able to
segment the continuous stream of sounds into phonemic units.
This is often referred to in the literature as 'phonemic awareness'.
If children cannot do this, they will not be able to appreciate how
the units relate to writing and spelling patterns. The failure to
develop phonemic awareness frequently holds up the reading and
spelling development of children (Bryant, 1990; Moseley, 1990a).

In this second stage the child starts to abstract and utilise the
letter–sound relationships that exist in textual materials. The development of this skill enables the child to decode to sound unknown
words in print. These are read using a grapheme–phoneme translation system. Their spelling is now more adequately carried out
using rules relating sounds to letters in addition to the use of visual
information. In passing, the idiosyncracies and inconsistencies of
written English often create difficulties for the child learning to
read and spell. The experiments with the Initial Teaching Alphabet
in which each sound was given one symbol demonstrated that this
method did help children in both these areas. Many other ways of
simplifying the spelling of the English language have been, and are
being, advocated. These include Simplified Spelling (Wijk, 1959;
Haas, 1970). The language system shown in Figure 2.4 shows two
major channels whereby printed words can be read. One is the
direct visual or lexical route able to deal with visually familiar
words (3). The second is a non-lexical phonological route by which
new words can be read (4).

When readers have achieved the alphabetic stage, they can read
novel materials and also spell with phonetic accuracy. However,
the irregularities of the English writing system present problems.
A reader using the alphabetic mode only will have problems with
phonically irregular or inconsistent words. The English writing
system is not phonemic. The 26 letters (graphemes) in our alphabet
are used to represent 44 sounds (phonemes). The issue is highlighted in the following poem. How can anyone hope to read and
spell such a language?

I take it you already know
of tough and bough and cough and dough?
Others may stumble but not you,
On hiccough, thorough, laugh and through?
Well done! And now you wish, perhaps,
To learn of less familiar traps?

Beware of heard, a dreadful word
That looks like beard and sounds like bird,
And dead: it's said like bed, not bead –
For goodness sake don't call it 'deed'!
Watch out for meat and great and threat
(They rhyme with suite and straight and debt).

A moth is not a moth in mother
Nor both in bother, broth in brother,
And here is not a match for there,
Nor dear and fear for bear and pear,
And then there's dose and rose and lose –
Just look them up – and goose and choose,
And cork and work and card and ward,
And font and front and word and sword,
And do and go and thwart and cart. . . .

(Anon.)

There is a tendency for children learning to read to impose regularity on irregular words. Most qualified junior school teachers have used the Schonell Graded Word Reading Test. It is an individually administered test of a child's decoding skills comprising a list of 110 discrete words, graded by difficulty level, but not by grammatical form or content. The child is asked to read the words aloud to the teacher. In the early stages of learning to read, *island* is often decoded to sound as 'izland' (and spelled as 'iland'). Words containing identical groups of letters are often pronounced as if they rhymed, for example 'dear' and 'pear', as in the above poem.

One outstanding British advocate of the importance of helping children understand and use the patterned nature of English orthography is Morris. She has researched and written in the fields of the learning and teaching of reading for many years. One of her reading schemes, *Language in Action*, is based on the belief that English orthography is highly structured and that only a relatively small proportion of words in the language diverges completely from conventional patterns. Whilst such exceptions may have to be learnt as discrete items, the vast majority of words can be recognised and also spelt by: (1) applying the alphabetic principle of phoneme–grapheme correspondence; and (2) developing a knowledge of the statistical probability of the sound–symbol relationships that exist in English (Morris, 1984).

Frith calls the final stage in the development of literacy the *ortho-graphic* stage. It develops as a consequence of the integration of logographic and alphabetic strategies. It is entered initially in the field of reading and only subsequently in that of spelling. Children's ability to read words that they have difficulty in spelling at the early stages of learning to read supports this contention. At the orthographic stage, both reading and spelling are independent of conscious use of sounds. At this stage the reader recognises graphemic clusters that have become familiar, overlearned and automated. Examples include -ast, -est, -ing, -ove, -ust, -cian, -ead, and -tion. Effort and conscious attention in reading them is no longer required.

What had been somewhat unreliable word representations at the earlier logographic and alphabetic stages are now fully specified. Accurate reading and spelling can develop using these now largely automated learnings. This developed lexical system also allows the reader to elaborate a new strategy for dealing with unfamiliar words: the use of lexical analogies. With competent older readers, this is quite clear. For example, if it is unfamiliar to the reader, the word *faugh* can be read in at least two ways. By decoding, it can be read as 'faw'. Alternatively, it can be read as 'faff' using the analogy with 'laugh' (Snowling, 1990). According to Snowling, work by Marsh et al. (1980) has demonstrated the use of analogic strategies by college students. Recent work has suggested that even young children have a similar strategy available to some degree (Goswami, 1988). Despite such a finding, the extent of a reader's lexicon will be an important determinant of the degree to which such an analogic strategy can be used. It is likely that, by the time the orthographic stage has been reached, the use of lexical strategies will increasingly override the conscious use of grapho-phonic cues. The key point is that sound is required for the earlier establishment of orthographic representations. The use of alphabetic strategies emphasises the importance of individual letters by directing the reader's attention towards relationships between letter names, sounds and shapes. In contrast, at the orthographic stage of reading development, processing is claimed to be free from considerations of sound. Such suggestions are important in understanding why some children experience difficulties in learning to read. It also suggests strategies likely to alleviate these hold-ups.

Reading involves dealing with more than individual words. The ideas incorporated within sets of words, in phrases, sentences, paragraphs and so on, require a far more elaborate theory of reading. As already stated, there are many such theories (Singer and Ruddell, 1985). Increasing attention is currently being paid to variants of models of reading focused on the processing of single words. Such models appear to hold considerable promise both for understanding normal reading development and also for studying aspects of reading difficulties (Seymour, 1986). This avenue is seen by its proponents as opening up the possibility of an adequate theory of how continuous text is processed.

READING DEVELOPMENT

A longitudinal study of children's reading development can provide important lessons for the teacher. Children's changing uses over time of the grapho-phonic, syntactic and semantic cue systems in textual material merit comment. The achievement of competent reading is analogous to the successful ascent of a mountain. The non-readers are approaching the foothills. Eventually the vast majority will reach the peak. They will have learned to read with considerable skill. Unlike a mountain peak, reading is never completely conquered. Each summit achieved reveals further ranges, further challenges, if readers choose to see them.

Although pupils have much in common in physical, intellectual and social-emotional make-up, they also show considerable inter-individual differences in these or any other attribute that one specifies. Their individual paths to the peak represented by literacy are likely to vary markedly. There will be considerable inter-individual differences in the rates at which children progress and important differences in their individual learning styles. These will, in part, lead to their taking somewhat different routes from the foothills to the initial peak. Figure 2.5 illustrates the relationships between the conscious utilisation of the three cue systems as the child moves from being a non-reader to being a competent reader. The figure is used to help make four points.

Firstly, the importance of meaning is central at all stages in learning to read. Secondly, in the earliest stages, the use of grapho-phonic and syntactic cue systems can consciously be used by children to help access the meaning of the text. Thirdly, as the children's ability to use the grapho-phonic and syntactic cue systems become overlearned and virtually automated, conscious attention to these cue systems progressively diminishes. The competent reader goes immediately to the meaning of the text. Finally, when competent readers move metaphorically to conquer other peaks represented by more complex texts and different genres, they are likely to meet words, phrases, sentences and paragraphs that present them with difficulties of comprehension. When competent readers encounter an unfamiliar word, one whose pronunciation and meaning are unknown to them, one very commonly

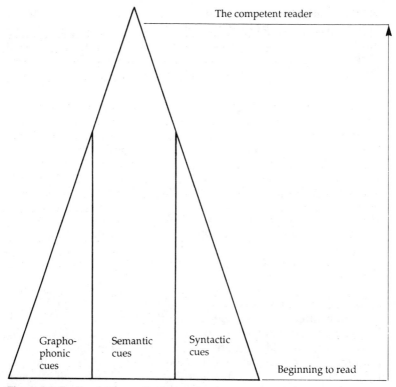

Figure 2.5 *Reading development and cue systems*

noted strategy is that the readers fall back on the use of grapho-phonic and syntactic cues. Whilst this is not necessarily an infall-ible strategy, its value cannot be ignored. Competent readers can call on a wider range of more proficient analytic strategies should they encounter 'difficult' text, than can the less competent reader.

'Developmental', 'corrective' and 'remedial reading' will be defined and discussed later (pp. 123–6). This tripartite classifi-cation of levels of responsibility is not of neatly definable and mutually exclusive categories, but it has an important message concerning professional involvement. It underlines the need for teachers to be aware of the commonly found productive and counterproductive interactions between readers and textual ma-terials. Teachers need to be aware of various circumstances that may temporarily (unless corrected) or permanently (unless re-mediated) impede their pupils' progress.

Stages of reading development

There are many differences between the reader–text interactions of the child learning to read and those of the accomplished reader. Models of the stages of reading involved can be of value in informing the developmental, corrective and remedial teaching of reading.

Many models have been developed. Each aims to describe, predict and improve control of reading development to the benefit of the individual reader. Different groups of professionals emphasise the importance of complementary, albeit contrasting, aspects of reading development. Neurologists are concerned with the development of the nervous system. Psychologists are frequently interested in profiles of children's cognitive abilities. Teachers of reading often focus on aspects of their pupils' reading-related behaviour and attainments. Other groups of professionals look at reading development from the perspective of their own specialisms. As their conceptual 'spectacles' are typically based on the specialism in which they have been educated, trained and practise, it is not surprising that a wide range of opinions exist.

One eminent educational research worker, who has spent a lifetime working in the field, has produced a tentative stage theory model of reading (Chall, 1983). The early stages in this particular model reflect the importance of the phonic aspects of initial reading identified in her earlier extensive research and reviews of the research literature. The model is linked to chronological age and is based on the assumption that later stages build on, integrate and elaborate the competencies developed during the preceding stages. In this respect, it reflects many of the ideas contained in the 'spiral' curriculum. The model does not assume that progression to the later stages of reading is impossible without mastery of the earlier ones, or that the earlier skills do not continue to develop. The model also accepts that the age spans for given stages will vary from culture to culture. An adaptation of this model is shown here.

AGE	STAGE
0–5 years	(1) *PRE-READING* The child develops spoken language and becomes aware of the use of symbols to represent objects and events. Metacognitions concerning the nature of literacy are developed. The child recognises that speech can be represented by letters, words, phrases, sentences, etc. Awareness of the concepts and labels used in connection with text is expanded.

AGE	STAGE
5–7 years	(2) *LEARNING TO READ* Learns to associate letters and sounds. Uses these skills to construct the meaning of textual material. Overlearning of skills ensues.
7–9 years	(3) *EXTENDING BEGINNING READING* Reading simple books and other textual materials centred on familiar themes continues. Earlier skills become overlearned and thus automated. Speed of reading increases and range of materials encountered extends.
9–13 years	(4) *READING TO GAIN NEW UNDERSTANDINGS* Access to new fields of knowledge is extended through reading.
13–18 years	(5) *APPRECIATION OF EVIDENCE AND ARGUMENTS* Can read and appraise the strengths and weaknesses of contrasting viewpoints on a range of issues.
18+ years	(6) *CONSTRUCTION AND RECONSTRUCTION OF UNDERSTANDINGS* Judgements concerning a widening range of literary genres and authors are made. The reader's knowledge, beliefs and values are challenged, revised and extended.

METACOGNITIONS: ATTRIBUTES UNDERPINNING PROGRESS IN READING FOR ALL PUPILS

Pupils require a number of attributes if they are to become effective readers. It is important that they have an understanding of what reading is about and why it is a valued skill. Notions such as the communicative functions of text should be appreciated and valued, even though the pupils may be capable of reading nothing. Work by Clay in New Zealand has resulted in the Concepts about Print (Sand and Stones) Tests (Clay, 1979). These are included in her book, *Early Detection of Reading Difficulties: A Diagnostic Survey with Recovery Procedures* (Clay, 1979 (1982)). Downing in Canada and England has produced the 'Linguistic Awareness in Reading Readiness (LARR)' test to measure how well pupils are prepared in the following fields: 'Recognising literacy behaviour', 'Understanding literacy functions' and the 'Technical language of literacy' (Downing et al., 1983). LARR is designed for children beginning to learn to read and also for older children with reading difficulties. Such knowledge about the nature and purposes of reading is important if the activities associated with reading and text are to have any significance to the pupil. Currently these types of understanding are referred to as 'metacognitions'.

Recent insights into the interactive and constructive nature of reading comprehension emphasise the importance of the active learner who, over time, directs an increasing range of cognitive resources to the comprehension of a variety of textual materials. A challenging review of research into metacognition and reading comprehension explores both concepts and their interrelationships (Garner, 1988). This summarises metacognitive performance differences in relation to chronological age and reading attainment. In the field of metacognitive research, the two most commonly used techniques are interview studies and error detection. Methodological issues are considered and their implications for furthering understanding of metacognitions discussed. For the practising teacher, the penultimate chapter in Garner's book presents summaries of research studies into approaches to training cognitive and metacognitive strategies that enhance reading comprehension. Text summarisation, reinspection, drawing inferences from texts and the 'Informed Strategies for Learning' (ISL) programme are described. The book concludes with an extension of such training studies to classroom settings. Six 'guidelines' are identified; they have much to commend them.

Metacognition and reading comprehension: guidelines

1. Teachers must care about the processes involved in reading and studying, and must be willing to devote instructional time to them.
2. Teachers must do task analyses of strategies to be taught.
3. Teachers must present strategies as applicable to texts and tasks in more than one content domain.
4. Teachers must teach strategies over an entire year, not just in a single lesson or unit.
5. Teachers must provide students with opportunities to practise strategies they have been taught.
6. Teachers must be prepared to let students teach each other about reading and studying processes.

(Garner, 1988)

READING COMPREHENSION AND COHESION IN TEXTS

Cohesiveness in text refers to the links or ties that connect text elements to provide unity or clarity, either within or between sentences, and contribute to the reader's impression of text coherence. The more coherence the reader perceives in a text, the more readily is it understood. Features which link component parts, for example, as back reference of pronouns to nouns, or the degree to which the parts of the text are related, are examples of cohesive ties (Harris and Hodges, 1981). Attention to this field is relatively recent, and owes much to the work of Halliday and Hasan (1976). They suggest that there are five major groups of cohesive ties in English text. Four of these are syntactic in nature; the fifth involves two aspects of vocabulary.

A. Cohesion and syntax

1. Reference cohesion can involve three varieties of cohesive tie: personal (e.g. he, she, him, her); demonstrative (e.g. here, there); and comparative (e.g. more, same, less). Within text (endophoric) cohesive ties can be backward acting (anaphoric) or forward acting (cataphoric). Ties that are outside the text are referred to as exophoric.
2. Substitutions can be nominal, verbal or causal.
3. Ellipsis is a form of substitution in which an implied meaning is omitted, but can be inferred.
4. Conjunctions, which may consist of one or more words, can be additive, adversative, temporal or causal.

B. Cohesion and vocabulary

(a) Reiteration involving repetition; synonym; superordinate and the use of general nouns.
(b) Collocation: utilises word associations.

If the above classification appears to lack cohesive ties, some excellent examples of each, drawn from Tolkien's *The Hobbit*, have recently been published (Beard, 1987).

Helping pupils become aware of the ways in which these ties function may improve their reading comprehension. A valuable review of the work by Halliday and Hasan has been published, together with an account of his own research into children's perception of personal references such as *he*, *him*, *her*, etc. in text cohesion (Chapman, 1983). Chapman's work involved 270 pupils in first, middle and upper schools. It demonstrated that children's awareness of personal cohesive ties was still developing within the upper school at a time when it is usually considered that the mechanics of reading have been mastered.

This finding is not surprising. I asserted earlier that reading is never mastered. By considering the nature of cohesion and cohesive ties, we begin to see why this might be. The 14,050 meanings that are shared by the 500 most common words in the English language, according to one distinguished linguist, give but one index of the complexities of text interpretation (Fries, 1962). Vocabulary, syntax and semantics are also constantly changing. Meanings multiply. Increased possibilities are generated for the interpretation of any text. An individual's use of language can be increasingly enriched. Whilst a particular genre, such as a legal document, may seek to reduce the possibility of more than one interpretation of the text, this is rarely achieved. The more competent the reader, the greater the number of different meanings that can be generated by a text and the greater variety of cohesive ties that can be perceived. Language lives; so too does reading.

Because of this, Chapman is probably correct in arguing that raising pupils' linguistic awareness enhances their ability to understand and construct the meanings of texts.

Many difficulties in text comprehension arise from grammatical structure. Readers typically tend to hold a clause in short-term memory when reading a passage. If the short-term memory is overloaded, the clause can be lost. Reading becomes more difficult when the grammatical structure is difficult to predict; the sentence does not readily divide into optimal segments; and short-term memory is overloaded (Perera, 1984). Anyone teaching pupils to read for understanding should be aware of the importance of promoting children's understanding of cohesive ties.

> How it is done will depend upon the age and reading ability of the child, but the fundamental basis of such teaching must lie in reading to the children so that they become familiar with the connections that are made across the boundaries of sentences and clauses. At first these will be relatively uncomplicated, nominal repetition will become obvious through stress and intonation, pronominal substitution may be clarified by the reader adding the actual noun, and the connection between ideas in the form of conjunctions can be reiterated in another form. The listeners will experience the links in the form of an understood story.
>
> (Roberts, 1989, p. 158)

A Book at Bedtime remains a popular programme for adults. Storytellers are valued in all cultures. Reading stories to pupils can help to improve their reading.

READING DIFFICULTIES: MAKING DECISIONS

When, as is almost inevitable, the class teacher finds that certain individuals are having difficulties in learning to read, or are apparently making no progress at all, what is to be done?

Many possibilities exist. For example, teachers could follow one or more of the following strategies:

- Decide that the materials and methods in use were inappropriate and try an alternative approach.
- Consult experienced colleagues on the staff and elicit suggestions.
- Consult specialist support teachers (formerly often known as remedial teachers of reading) and educational psychologists employed by School Psychological and Child Guidance Services.
- Reflect on what they had heard, seen, done and discussed during their own initial and (if they have been fortunate) INSET courses concerned with alleviating reading difficulties.
- Use their common sense.

Each option has its value. All have weaknesses. How can the teacher make an informed decision on the alternative methods and/or materials to be used? Hundreds of choices are possible. It is likely that different members of staff will make different suggestions. How can the teacher decide which to try? Similarly, experts in the teaching of reading frequently have contrasting views on the causes and alleviation of reading difficulties. How is the class teacher to make a decision? The fourth option has the weaknesses that the information gleaned will inevitably have been selective and the problems presented by the particular pupil under consideration may never have been considered. In the face of such uncertainties, and the pressures of time and work, the teacher may be driven back to what is frequently called common sense. This usually refers to intuitive hunches based on experience. The experience of teaching can, at times, limit one's thinking. The diagnosis of the causes of reading difficulties may be based on suspect assumptions about the nature of reading and the causes of reading difficulties.

All class teachers observe a vast range of reading behaviour. These include many differing aspects of reading accuracy, speed and comprehension. The pupils' behaviour is observed. On the basis of our assumptions about the nature of children's abilities, teachers infer processes. Predictions are made concerning the progress in reading that is anticipated. Where the predictions give cause for concern, programmes are modified.

The purpose of theories is to help us to understand, describe, predict and control phenomena. As professionals, class teachers aspire to understanding, describing, predicting and controlling the development of all children's reading attainments and attitudes. Theories help us deal more effectively with complex issues. It is difficult to think of anything more complex than the nature of reading, its development and the changing processes that underlie the performances we observe. The point is admirably expressed, albeit somewhat overstated, in the preface to the second edition of *Theoretical Models and Processes of Reading* (Singer and Ruddell, 1976).

> And so to completely analyze what we do when we read would almost be the acme of a psychologist's achievements, for it would be to describe very many of the most intricate workings of the human mind, as well as to unravel the tangled story of the most remarkable specific performance that civilisation has learned in all its history.
>
> (Huey, 1908)

Even if this were achieved, would it help the class teacher? It is a common mistake to assume that psychological theories will enable one to deduce definite programmes, schemes of work and methods of immediate classroom utility. William James made a valid point when he stated: 'Psychology is a science and teaching is an art, and sciences never generate arts directly out of themselves. An intermediary inventive mind must make the application, by using its originality' (James, 1899).

It is worth while to distinguish between the many theories on reading difficulties according to the level of investigation involved. Three major levels can be identified. These have been called 'competence' (level I), 'cognitive function' (level II) and 'physiological' (level III) (Seymour, 1986). The levels are not mutually exclusive. They are all potentially valuable.

The level at which research workers operate is largely determined by the specialism in which they have been trained. Typically, teachers and educational psychologists have been mainly interested in level I. Their central concerns are with pedagogy, with both the learning and teaching of reading. They well appreciate that the two are not the same. Neuropsychologists, audiologists, ophthalmologists and practitioners in other medically related disciplines are more involved with level III studies. They too may have something to say about the ways in which children can be helped to read. Level II represents approaches adopted by some experimental cognitive psychologists and educationalist psychologists.

Level I concentrates on the description of any publicly observed behaviour which defines the ability to read and to enjoy the activity. It also includes descriptions of reading behaviour that characterises pupils with reading difficulties. The aim of improving pupils' reading attainments goes hand-in-hand with the identification and alleviation of pupils' reading difficulties.

Level II involves functional analyses and explanations. These may be based on, for example, a psychological concept such as information processing. The central concept is operationalised in order to explore and understand the nature of both reading development and reading difficulties.

Level III provides an analysis based on the neurological and physiological structures and functions involved in reading.

Professional understanding of the theoretical bases of reading does not by itself teach children to read. Such knowledge has to be translated into learning and teaching activities.

If the teacher listens to a child reading aloud, a number of errors (miscues) will be noted. Children will frequently add, omit or substitute words without affecting the meaning of the text. These errors (miscues) will vary systematically with the complexity of the text. The knowledge that reading is one part of language and that this language background affects the way in which textual material is read, helps the teacher identify reasons for the pattern of errors or miscues. In this instance, it can help the teacher to understand that the errors (miscues) can be accepted. They almost certainly do not need to be corrected.

In this situation teachers have found the following strategy of utility.

Diagnostic–prescriptive teaching of reading

To be able to make sound decisions on the improvement of reading requires an awareness of the following:

- the differences and the overlap between the learning of reading and the teaching of reading;
- the characteristics of the pupil;
- the nature of the reading process;
- the goals of the reading programme;
- the instructional needs of the individual;
- the uses and limitations of a range of instructional material and methods;
- the strengths and limitations of the various types of information that can be provided by reading tests and assessment techniques;
- the distinction and overlap between information used for formative purposes and that used for summative aspects of the pupil's performance;
- the importance of keeping records; and
- an overall strategy that integrates the above considerations.

The suggested strategy is based on the diagnostic–prescriptive teaching of reading. It involves a six-stage, sequential hypothesis generation and testing approach. To describe the procedure as the educational equivalent of 'suck it and see', is to ignore the importance of teachers' theoretical knowledge that underpins their practice. The stages are shown in Figure 2.6.

Whether or not reading can be analysed into hierarchies of skills is, as yet, an unresolved issue. It is clear that a variety of reading tasks can be ordered in terms of their relative difficulty levels. This can be done both for groups and for individual pupils. Varying either the form or the content of such tasks will alter task difficulty. The tasks can be operationally defined and a pupil's strengths and weaknesses can be identified. Such information can help the teacher in devising instructional material and techniques that will enable pupils to master tasks at which they had previously failed. The principle is valid for *all* pupils, and particularly helpful to teachers working with pupils experiencing serious reading difficulties.

The diagnostic–prescriptive approach is most frequently associated with an objectives-based curriculum and the use of domain-referenced reading tests. It can, however, incorporate the somewhat different but often complementary information provided by normative testing. The teaching of reading can be both systematic and developmental. The diagnostic–prescriptive approach to the improvement of reading attainments fits well with many class teachers' beliefs concerning how assessment and teaching can be integrated.

TEACHING STYLES AND PROGRESS IN READING

Individual differences

At the Annual Convention of the International Reading Association there is always a huge display of teaching and learning materials and equipment. These range from the simplest to the most technologically advanced; from printed materials to interactive computer-assisted systems designed to identify children's reading difficulties and improve children's reading attainments. Similar, albeit smaller, displays are found at the annual conferences of the United Kingdom Reading Association, the National Association for Remedial Education and other organisations concerned with the overlapping issues of improving reading standards generally and, in particular, helping children with reading difficulties. A knowledge of what is available and what is being developed in this field is a professional responsibility. A school INSET day spent attending such an exhibition (in the UK) would be time well spent. A visit to one of the resource centres organised by the remedial/support

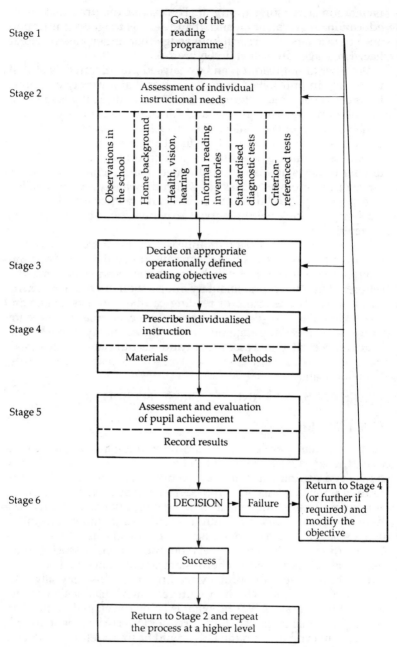

Figure 2.6 *Model of diagnostic–prescriptive teaching of reading (Pumfrey, 1985)*

services of many LEAs would also be valuable and considerably easier to arrange. In view of the vast range of methods and materials available, why do a significant number of children still experience difficulties in learning to read?

The Plowden Report suggests a major reason. It stresses the uniqueness of each pupil. Great variability exists in physical, intellectual and emotional characteristics between pupils of the same chronological age. There is no pedagogic panacea to the problems of learning to read and alleviating reading difficulties:

> Individual differences between children of the same age are so great that any class, however homogeneous it seems, must always be treated as a body of children needing individual and different attention.
>
> (Central Advisory Council for Education in England, 1967)

Official acknowledgement of this variability contributed to the abolition of streaming in primary schools. The pedagogic challenge presented by the unstreamed class was to translate into practice the principle of individual learning. The value of co-operative group work was recognised, as was whole-class instruction for certain limited purposes. The number of pupils in each class and the demands on the class teacher had to be borne in mind. But central to the report's recommendations were pupils' individual differences. Providing for these differences demands both great adaptability and flexibility by the class teacher.

This objective has never been fully realised. Other than in a 1:1 teacher–pupil situation, using programmed materials or computer-assisted learning systems, it appears a very difficult goal. Presumably, if it had been achieved, and the beneficial results anticipated had taken place, there would have been less concern that the educational system was failing to meet pupils' special educational needs. Concern about children's reading difficulties and about reading standards would have been less. The 'Great Debate', initiated by Prime Minister James Callaghan in the autumn of 1976 when he called for more attention to literacy and numeracy, would not have taken place.

The subsequent HMI survey, *Primary Education in England* (DES, 1978), showed that the fears were unfounded. The basics were *not* being neglected. If anything, there was a danger that too much time was being spent on them. Some critics argue that the objective of individualised work is itself suspect.

One of the most interesting, challenging and detailed analyses of both learning and teaching in the primary classroom is known by the acronym ORACLE. This stands for Observational Research and

Classroom Learning Evaluation (Galton et al., 1980; Galton and Simon, 1980). The major aim was to study the patterns of activity and instruction within the primary classroom and to examine the relative efficacy of different teaching approaches in the main areas of the primary school curriculum. The study is based on the observation of some 60 class teachers drawn from 19 schools in three LEAs. The numbers used in analyses vary somewhat for entirely legitimate reasons. It is reported that 48 classes were organised as a number of separate groups, usually between six or seven, each containing between three and seven pupils. Though the children spent most of their time in these groups, their work was characteristically individual. Teachers gave priority to working with individuals, rather than with small groups. Because there is usually only one teacher, the relationship is asymmetrical. Whilst the typical class teacher spends 78 per cent of the time interacting with individuals, groups and the whole class, the individual pupil only interacts with the teacher for about 16 per cent of the time *and most of this occurs when the teacher is interacting with the whole class*. The researchers suggest that a move towards class teaching and co-operative group work indicates that the individualisation advocated in the Plowden Report is inadequate as a base for primary school teaching in practice. They go further and suggest that in the typical classroom situation it is impossible. This may well be, but it does not remove the responsibility for recognising and responding to individual differences. The challenge is how best can the class teacher combine individual, group and class teaching?

This controversy will continue.

One of the most interesting aspects of the study was the identification of teaching styles and the relationships between these styles and children's academic progress. Firstly the teaching styles will be briefly described. These are based on the teacher–pupil interaction categories observed. Then the relationships between teaching styles and pupils' progress in reading will be outlined. Many junior school teachers are able to identify with one or more of the following teaching styles. Or are the sketches too broadly drawn and thereby failing to identify key aspects of professional practice?

Style 1: Individual monitors (22.4 per cent of the sample)

This group of teachers shows the highest level of individualised interaction with pupils, largely marking individual pupils' work. They do relatively little small group or class teaching. They have not the time. The teaching is largely didactic. Their questioning is factual rather than open-ended. Pupils are frequently given work-related instructions about their individual assignments. The teachers are under considerable pressure from individuals seeking information or clarification.

Style 2: Class enquirers (15.5 per cent of the sample)

These teachers spend the greatest proportion of time on class teaching. Though they spend 42.5 per cent of their time on individualised interactions, this is less than any other teaching style. This group emphasises class questioning related to task work, using the highest proportion of both closed and open questions. Much of the learning is teacher managed. New topics are introduced to the whole class. When not talking to the class, they move among pupils asking questions and giving feedback on the work in hand.

Style 3: Group instructors (12.1 per cent of the sample)

Involvement with the pupil groups is relatively high (three times that for the rest of the sample, but still accounting for only 20 per cent of the interactions). These teachers come closest to adopting the grouping strategy suggested by the Plowden Report. The incidence of individual attention is lower than style 1 teachers. They ask more questions and make more factual statements. A major emphasis is on providing information to groups.

Style 4: Style changers (50 per cent of the sample)

These teachers show the second-highest levels of individual, group and class interaction. They ask the most task supervision questions, make more statements of critical control and spend more time hearing children read than styles 1–3. They appear to utilise a mixture of the styles of the other three groups. They tend to adopt the characteristics of a particular teaching style as they change to its associated pattern of organisation.

Further analysis suggests that there are *three* distinctive subtypes of style changers.

Style 4a: Infrequent changers (10.3 per cent of the sample)

Members of this group had made a significant change in their style, albeit for a variety of reasons. For example, a different style was adopted as a response to changes in pupil behaviour. This group achieved the highest level of interaction of all styles (86 per cent). They also showed the highest level of questioning, provided high levels of feedback and introduced a high proportion of stimulating ideas.

Style 4b: Rotating changers (15.4 per cent of the sample)

The organisational form of the teaching strategy identifies this group. Different groups of pupils work simultaneously on different curricular areas. At given points in the day, the groups all move to different areas of work. The teachers show a high level of task supervision. They use critical comments to control the situation to a high degree.

Style 4c: Habitual changers (24.2 per cent of the sample)

These teachers made regular, but apparently unplanned, switches between individualised and class instruction. Often this was in response to changes in pupils' behaviour. Typically the change in style was a reaction to pupils who were causing difficulties. Questioning was used relatively little. Few open-ended or stimulating questions were asked and few ideas were introduced into interactions. The time spent in interactions with pupils was the lowest of all the styles (1.4 per cent).

(Readers wanting fuller details of these teaching styles are referred to Galton and Simon (1980) and Galton, Simon and Croll (1980).)

Progress in reading refers to changes that take place over time in the complexities of the interactions between the individual pupil and textual materials. It can also refer to average increases in reading attainments in a class. It is possible for the average reading attainments of a class to increase, but there to be no decrease in the number of pupils experiencing reading difficulties. This can occur when pupils have become differentially more spread out along the dimension of reading being measured: the better readers improve more rapidly than the slower readers. Norm-referenced reading tests capitalise on individual differences between pupils. Progress is measured in relative terms. In contrast, domain-referenced (often, and misleadingly, referred to as 'criterion-referenced') reading tests, stress changes in the individual pupil's mastery of a clearly defined set of tasks. Progress in reading is measured by an absolute index. (These issues are dealt with more fully in Chapter 3, pp. 171–3.)

There are many methods of measuring progress, from the simple to the statistically sophisticated. At first glance, the task of assessing pupils' progress in reading appears straightforward. A second look at the issues indicates that to do so rationally is often complex and controversial (Cronbach and Furby, 1970). The technical issues are not well appreciated by most classroom teachers, partly because such matters do not figure significantly in either initial or INSET training. This is already altering. The requirements for the national testing of primary school pupils at the ages of 7 years (or thereabouts) and 11 years contained in the Education Act 1988 has already increased professional interest in such matters.

At present, when the class teacher considers a child's progress in reading, readily available indices are used. These have what is currently called 'ecological validity'. Progress in the child's ability to read books and other textual materials of increasing complexity provide some of these indices. Hence, the valuable questions, 'Which book was he/she on at the start of term and which one now?' and 'Is the child reading with understanding and accuracy?' Estimations of progress can derive from both movement through the materials in a graded reading scheme, and through books not included in such a system. A growing reading vocabulary is also used as an index of increasing reading attainment. Changes in reading ages on valid reading tests provide a host of other indices of progress. These include reading accuracy, speed and comprehension.

The methods used to measure progress depend on whether one is concerned with the individual pupil or with a group. One expert has described five methods of assessing individual progress and three concerning groups (Davis, 1970). Each has strengths and weaknesses. The International Reading Association's book for teachers and research workers, *Reading: What Can Be Measured?* is particularly helpful concerning different ways of measuring progress in reading (Farr and Carey, 1986).

The method of measuring progress in reading used in the ORACLE research is based on the following reasoning. Given the reading test scores of a group of pupils in an initial and a subsequent occasion, the correlation between the pupils' scores on the two occasions can be calculated. Using this correlation and the pupil's initial reading test score, it is possible to *predict* the pupil's expected reading test score on occasion two. The higher the correlation between initial and final reading test scores, the more reliable the prediction. Some pupils will do better than expected; others will do worse. The differences in reading test scores between what was *predicted* and what was *actually achieved* are called the *residual-change* or *residual-gain* scores. Ways in which this method can be used by *the class teacher* were very well described many years ago (Tracey and Rankin, 1970). By comparing the effects over time of different teaching styles, it is possible to establish whether one or more of these styles leads to more pupils making greater progress in their reading attainments than other teaching styles. The technique was used in this country in a study of streaming in the primary school and subsequently in another study of teaching styles and pupil progress (Barker Lunn, 1970; Bennett, 1976).

The ORACLE findings are based on eight pupils observed in each of 58 junior classes. The relationships between teaching style and progress in reading over one year were explored. The major test battery used for this part of the study was the Richmond Tests of Basic Skills. This instrument includes vocabulary, reading comprehension, language skills, work-study skills and mathematics skills sub-scales (France and Fraser, 1975). Pupils' scores on the vocabulary and comprehension sub-scales were the criteria of progress in reading.

In the summary that follows, it must be remembered that the presentation is deliberately focused on language and reading. The authors make the point that *no* overall best style emerges for all the areas studied (Galton and Simon, 1980).

Allowing statistically for between-group differences on initial reading test scores, the relationships between teaching style and progress in reading attainments were as follows. Pupils whose teachers were classified as Infrequent changers had made the greatest progress during the year under study. Those of the Individual monitors, Group instructors and Class enquirers made the second most progress in reading. The pupils of Rotating changers and Habitual changers made least progress. Even when time-on-task was also allowed for, the pattern remained the same.

To avoid the possibility of this summary leading to an oversimplified view of the effects of teaching styles, the findings related to progress in language skills will also be outlined. Language skills, as tested, included recognising errors in punctuation and grammar in written English, and the ability to spell and punctuate, including the use of capitals. The analyses showed that the pupils of Class enquirers made most progress in language attainments over the year. The progress of pupils of Group instructors and Infrequent changers was slightly less, but not statistically significantly so. Pupils under Habitual changers made significantly less progress than those under Class enquirers. The pupils of Rotating changers and Individual monitors made the least progress. The relative success of the six teaching styles in promoting pupils' progress *using the specified test* is presented in Table 2.1.

Although Class enquirers appeared to be the most effective in developing pupils' language skills, the difference between their pupils' progress and those of the Group instructors and Infrequent changers was not significant. In reading and comprehension the most effective style was that of the Infrequent changers. Perhaps

Table 2.1 *Teaching styles and progress in language and reading over one year*

Progress	Language	Reading
A. Most progress	Class enquirers	Infrequent changers
B. Slightly less than A	Group instructors; Infrequent changers	
C. Significantly less than A	Habitual changers	Individual monitors; Class enquirers; Group instructors.
D. Very significantly less than A	Individual monitors; Rotating changers	Habitual changers; Rotating changers.

A–B differences non-significant statistically.
A–C differences statistically significant at the 0.05 level.
A–D differences statistically significant at the 0.01 level.

one of the key points is that the Infrequent changers interacted more frequently with their pupils than colleagues using other teaching styles.

The criticism is often heard that current junior school mixed-ability teaching holds back and bores the able child (Welch, 1987). The evidence from the ORACLE study suggests that, in terms of the teacher's attention, neither the able nor the slow learners are specially treated. Other studies have shown that class teachers spend more time with pupils who have reading difficulties (Croll and Moses, 1985). Are different teaching styles suited to pupils of different abilities?

Of particular relevance to the present book was the progress of pupils who had been classified as low achievers (LA) (the bottom 25 per cent), medium achievers (MA) (the middle 50 per cent) and high achievers (HA) (the top 25 per cent). The findings showed that, when initial differences in the pupils' achievements had been allowed for, there was a tendency for the more successful styles to be effective right across all three levels of achievement. There are, however, some important qualifications of this generalisation.

In promoting the development of *language* skills for HA and MA pupils, Class enquirers seemed to have the most effective teaching style. Group instructors came second. For HA pupils Infrequent changers came third but for MA pupils the third most effective teaching style was Habitual changers. For LA pupils, the Infrequent changers produced most progress. Group instructors came second. Class enquirers and Individual monitors came joint third.

In relation to *reading*, a different pattern emerged. For HA pupils the most effective teaching style was Individual monitors. Infrequent changers and Class enquirers came joint second. With

MA pupils and LA pupils, Infrequent changers produced the most progress. For both groups of pupils, Individual monitors came second. For MA pupils, Group instructors came third whereas for LA pupils it was the Habitual changers. The groups with the least success across all achievement levels tended to be the Rotating changers and the Infrequent changers.

It must be remembered that teaching style was defined in terms of the types of interaction taking place between the pupils and the teacher in the classroom situation. Both Individual monitors and Infrequent changers had the *highest* proportion of pupils either requesting or getting *individual attention*. The authors comment: 'for pupils of all levels of achievement individual instruction is important for success in reading with understanding' (Croll and Moses, 1985, p. 75). These finer analyses by achievement level provide qualified support for the view, expressed in the Plowden Report, that independent work by both individuals and groups provided the most appropriate context for effective instruction by the class teacher.

There is no teaching style blueprint for the junior school teacher to adopt, but there are important pointers.

The findings strongly suggest that class teachers must consider the organisation of the reading programme and the type of teacher–pupil interactions that they wish to foster. ORACLE indicates that teaching styles involving the greatest degree of class involvement produced most progress in developing pupils' mathematics and language skills. Teachers using the highest amount of individualised teaching were most successful in promoting the development of reading comprehension.

CURRENT CONTROVERSIES

'Bottom-up', 'top-down', and interactive models of reading

'Bottom-up'

Advocates of the 'bottom-up' model argue that complex skills such as competent reading are the result of the accumulation and integration of simpler ones. The potential pianist does not typically begin by attempting a piano concerto by Mozart. The skilled artist, craftsman or scientist serves an apprenticeship during which basic skills are developed and mastery acquired. In many spheres of human learning, breaking down complex skills into their component sub-skills and learning the latter first, is a commonly found teaching and learning strategy. With this approach, it is claimed that the likelihood of mastering more complex skills is enhanced.

Master the simple before tackling the complex, is the cry. Conquer conservation of number before trying integral calculus. The strategy is an extremely ancient and pervasive one, and is used in differing cultures throughout the world. Advocates of the 'bottom-up' theory see reading as no different in this respect from any other complex human behaviour. Witness to the long history of this approach can be found by looking at the system named 'Spell and read' devised in 1797 by Dr Andrew Bell and that published by the Edgeworths in 1798 entitled 'One letter – One sound' (Morris, 1973).

In its contemporary dress, the 'bottom-up' approach reflects a behaviourist view of learning and reading processes. It leads to detailed task analyses and emphasises the importance of so arranging reading tasks that the learner is virtually guaranteed success. The systematic reinforcement of the child's reading behaviour is designed to increase the probability of correct responses, increase the child's rate of responding and maintain the responding behaviour at a high level.

One leading behaviourist, B. F. Skinner, developed a system of linear programmed instruction. The major principles on which linear programmed learning materials were based derive from Skinner's theory of learning through operant conditioning:

1. Explicitly state the objectives of the programme in behavioural terms.
2. Arrange the materials to be learned in a logical sequence of small steps in which success by the learner is virtually guaranteed.
3. Active responding by the learner is required at each step.
4. Immediate feedback of results is given to the learner.
5. The learners proceed at their own individual rates.

During the 1960s many reading schemes were devised based on this approach. It has been claimed that such reading materials have been particularly helpful to socially disadvantaged pupils experiencing difficulties in learning to read. 'Precision teaching' and 'teaching by objectives' are current formulations of this approach (Ainscow and Tweddle, 1979, 1984).

One research worker has discussed what is involved in just one second of reading behaviour by a moderately skilled adult. He then considered what the young child coming to the task of learning to read brings with him or her in terms of abilities. He argued that to deal with the text requires, initially, the fixation of the pupil's eyes on the text. Only then can the visual pattern be projected on to the retina. Reading begins with print, attention, sensation and perception. The reader is not seen as a guesser. Whilst the reader may move from print to meaning as if by magic, this is only an illusion. The child 'plods through the sentence, letter by letter, word by word' (Gough, 1976). In his updated model of serial processing, Gough keeps lower-level letter-by-letter processing separate from the higher-order linguistic processing. Comprehension is seen as text-driven.

To have resurrected a nineteenth-century notion that reading involved a serial processing of letters comprising words and then a serial combination of words into sentences was audacious. After all, the serial (letter-by-letter) theory of word perception had been rejected in favour of the parallel (whole-word) approach on the basis of apparently unequivocal empirical studies carried out by James McKean Cattell in the mid-1880s. He had shown that words in prose passages could be read almost as rapidly as lists of letters; that the immediate visual apprehension span for random letters was much less than for letters in prose; that the delay between seeing and uttering words was shorter than that for letters; and that the visual recognition thresholds for letters were higher than for words.

A rebuttal of Cattell's parallel processing *interpretation* of his findings is based on recent work on visual information processing and in psycholinguistics. As one would expect, the controversy was lively, and continues (Brewer, 1976).

The implications of the 'bottom-up' model for the teaching of reading are as follows:

- Instruction in reading should begin with letters and their corresponding sounds.
- Decoding from letters to sounds is of the essence.
- The translation of print to speech is central to learning to read.
- Provided that the reader is a native speaker of the language, the meaning of the text will be self-evident when turned into speech.
- Decoding from text to speech is a skill distinct from general language and cognitive abilities.
- Decoding is an activity unique to reading in contrast to the many processes that reading shares in common with other thinking processes.

The author has been professionally involved with several native speakers of English who were able to decode to speech virtually any word, but who failed to comprehend the meaning of even the most simple of the words they had decoded. The distinction between decoding text to speech and comprehension is not one that can be ignored.

It must also be mentioned that some children learn to comprehend textual material without decoding text to sound. Profoundly deaf children may have learned to comprehend text without translating it into speech. With children who are not hearing-impaired it has also been argued, and demonstrated, that comprehending without decoding text to sound is both possible and to be welcomed in certain circumstances. James McDade, working in Chicago in the middle 1930s, developed a hypothesis of non-oral reading. He wanted to ensure that meaning was immediately fused with the printed word and not separated by a two-stage process beginning with decoding text to sound. A helpful summary of both McDade's work and Buswell's subsequent extended research into this hypothesis is available in Morris (1973).

According to a well-known English authority on the teaching of reading, the case for teachers having some knowledge of how to teach phonics is based on reasons that include the following:

1. Although English spelling has many irregularities, it is claimed that a high proportion of words in the English language (90–95 per cent) conform to regular patterns in their pronunciation and spelling (Wijk, 1959).
2. The learning of one phonic rule can help children recognise many others. Admittedly, only a very few of these rules have 100 per cent utility. One such is that for words beginning with 'kn', the 'k' is always silent. The decoding of a whole class of words is opened up by the rule.
3. A knowledge of phonics helps the pupil to decode unknown words. When such a word is in context, the grapho-phonic cues, coupled with the syntactic (grammatical) and semantic (meaning) cues, can be mutually supportive.
4. Children's ability to spell, write and read can be assisted by a knowledge of phonics.

(Southgate, 1986)

From the viewpoint of 'bottom-up' theory, instruction in reading would emphasise the development of skills, which would include many different aspects of both word identification and comprehension. The skills would be hierarchically arranged and the teaching would be aimed at ensuring they were mastered by each pupil.

There are many such hierarchies based on logical analyses of reading development. Empirical evidence supporting the existence of hierarchical structures is in relatively short supply, but is not entirely absent. Defenders of the 'new' serial processing approach to the teaching of reading are not unduly concerned. The advent and popularity of precision teaching, the objectives-based reading curriculum and mastery learning provide, albeit somewhat indirectly, a partial justification in practice. If, in the crucible of the classroom, the approach is found of value to children learning to read and to those experiencing difficulties, that is enough for many teachers. Teachers are interested in finding out which reading methods and materials work best for pupils at different levels of reading development and also for pupils with different intra-individual strengths and weaknesses at given levels.

In trying to establish why a pupil is having difficulties in learning to read, a diagnostic test can be administered. The test will enable a diagnostic profile of the pupil's individual strengths and weaknesses to be obtained. Having identified which skills had not been mastered, the teacher's challenge is clear. He or she will either use materials deemed likely to help the pupil master the skills, or develop appropriate ones.

'Top-down'

In contrast with the analytic approach to the learning and teaching of reading of the behaviourist psychologists, the Gestalt psychologists began from a very different set of assumptions concerning the nature of both animal and human abilities. Starting from their initial work in the field of perception, they explored learning. For them both perception and learning were seen holistically. The whole is more than the sum of its parts. The competent reader does not see letters, then words, then phrases and sentences. If presented with a passage in which a word has been omitted, the reader brings to bear all his or her knowledge in order to establish what has been omitted. Those who enjoy crossword puzzles are engaging in such a venture. It is interesting to find that the crossword enthusiast can get to know the mode of thinking characterising and underlying the compiler's cryptic clues.

This approach to reading contrasts markedly with the 'bottom-up' model. The major purpose of reading at all stages is the extraction, and *imposition*, of meaning on textual material. The 'top-down' model assumes that readers use all their experiences and expectations in trying to extract meaning from text. Comprehension is seen as reader-driven rather than text-driven. Instead of focusing on the sub-skills of reading, the 'top-down' theory adopts the view that the most effective way of learning to read is to read. If one wishes to learn to swim, getting into the water and splashing around is more productive than practising arm and leg movements on, for example, a bench at the side of the pool. If one wishes to learn to read, practising the sub-skills of decoding print to sound is of less value than attempting to read a text. Reading is seen as a 'psycholinguistic guessing game' (see pp. 86–8). Get on with the game and the sub-skills will look after themselves.

A text might say 'The boy enjoyed the meal very much'. The pupil reads aloud 'meat' instead of 'meal'. Further on the text says 'The dog ran down the road'. The pupil reads 'street' for 'road'. When faced with the sentence 'The boy swims every day in order to get into the team', the child reads aloud 'The boy swims every day to get into the team'. Such deviations from the text require an explanation. Merely to call them errors is to misconstrue and underestimate their significance in understanding the reading process.

The first example shows that the pupil substituted a similarly shaped, equal-length word with three letters in common. However, it was not just any word. It was both syntactically and semantically appropriate. The substitution made sense. In the second example the substituted word is not similar in length or in its constituent letters. Nonetheless, it is a syntactically and semantically acceptable synonym. The final example differs in that the reader has left out two words present in the text. Workers such as Goodman have argued that the discrepancies between text and oral reading should be called 'miscues' and not the more pejorative 'mistakes' or 'errors'.

An understanding of the nature of these miscues would give the teacher, listening to the child reading, an insight into the way in which the information was being processed. This enables the teacher to know whether or not the reader's attention should be drawn to a particular miscue. There are many ways of analysing children's oral miscues (Arnold, 1984). Further sources of information are given in Chapter 3.

Psycholinguistic theory indicates that the reading process does not necessarily begin with the text but starts with the language and experience of the reader. Reading involves the reader in making predictions about what is to come. The predictions that can be made are, in part, limited by the stored experiences of the reader. Whereas print is visible, the unique and idiosyncratic stored language experience of the child is not. This information includes the following:

- meaning based on the reader's experiences (semantics);
- grammatical knowledge based on the reader's use of language (syntax);
- knowledge of the relationships between letters in words (orthography);
- knowledge of the sound patterns and processes whereby words are pronounced and modified (phonological rules).

This invisible information, when applied to the visible information represented in the text, enables the reader to reconstruct the thoughts and feelings of the author to varying degrees. It has been argued that the greater the invisible information available to the reader, the less attention needs to be given to the text. Conversely, where the invisible information is limited, greater attention is paid to the text. With young children learning to read, or with children experiencing reading difficulties, the use made of the textual information can be very important.

If children read a passage *aloud* and then answer questions based on the passage, it is possible to estimate how adequately they have understood the text. When given a passage of parallel difficulty, asked to read it *silently* to themselves and then asked questions on the passage, children with reading difficulties frequently demonstrate reduced comprehension of the material. In many cases this is because, when reading silently, they rapidly skip material with which they cannot readily deal. They thereby extract a distorted version of what is being transmitted in the text. When a teacher is listening, the skipping of text is less likely to occur. The difficulty level of the textual material itself can either encourage or discourage skipping. The more difficult the text, the more likely is it that the reader will avoid the material.

Listening to children read aloud may have a number of disadvantages, but it also has many important pedagogical uses.

The implications of the 'top-down' approach to the teaching and learning of reading are as follows:

- Pupils must be encouraged to make maximal use of their internalised knowledge of language and life.
- Reading materials will avoid words in isolation and use only connected text.
- The reader will be encouraged to guess, to 'have a go', when unknown material appears in the text.
- The child's oral reading miscues should be carefully noted.
- Miscues must not be corrected if they do not distort the meaning of the passage.
- Reading is an integrated activity and is best learned as an indivisible whole.

The 'bottom-up' and 'top-down' models of reading are compared in Table 2.2.

Interactive reading

A combination of the 'bottom-up' and the 'top-down' models of reading development is required. *If either of the models alone had been adequate, it is likely that the other would have disappeared without trace.* Theoreticians and research workers will continue the studies that

Table 2.2 *The 'bottom-up' and 'top-down' models of reading compared*

Field	'Bottom-up' model	'Top-down' model
Key theorists	Gough (1976)	Goodman (1976b)
Cue emphasis	Use grapho-phonic cues to decode unknown words.	Use all cues available to determine unknown words, i.e. semantic, syntactic and grapho-phonic cues.
Word-recognition	Recognition of all words, via decoding to speech, is the key to comprehension.	Even though some words may remain unknown, text can be comprehended.
Comprehension	Text-driven.	Reader-driven.
Learning to read	Initially requires mastering and combining a range of word-recognition skills.	Occurs when pupils engage in meaningful activities involving all aspects of language.
Instructional emphases:		
(a) Units	Letters, letter–sound relationships and words.	Phrases, sentences, paragraphs, passages, stories.
(b) Focus	Accuracy in word recognition.	Predict, guess, get the gist.
(c) Books	Finely graded, vocabulary controlled books.	'Real' books.
(d) Diagnosis	Test on discrete skills. Identify strengths and weaknesses.	Miscue analysis.
(e) Intervention	Ensure skill is mastered.	Do not correct miscues if they do not distort the meaning of the passage.

are required to further understanding and control of the development of children's reading.

Such studies take place at different levels and from differing professional viewpoints. Disagreement is an entirely respectable condition: it is understandable and right that proponents of conflicting models should argue their cases. As yet it would be *wrong* to assume that either the 'top-down' or the 'bottom-up' model is the final word that should govern classroom practice.

Towards the end of his influential book *Psycholinguistics and Reading*, Frank Smith challengingly presents what he describes as 'Twelve easy ways to make learning to read difficult' (Smith, 1973). The rules are based on teaching activities considered counterproductive from a psycholinguistic viewpoint. No claim is made for originality in his selection. Most were gleaned from manuals for teachers and, in Smith's view, represent what was then part of the teaching profession's conventional wisdom concerning the teaching and learning of reading. Indeed, he suggests that the rules might not be out of place displayed on the wall of a staffroom as exemplifying sound practice. Smith warns that his 'Twelve rules for reading teachers' should not be taken too seriously, *but he doubts whether any teacher could follow these rules and teach effectively*. Like it or not, that is a very strong reservation. He takes each of the rules he presents and demonstrates that it has serious weaknesses. His purpose was to get teachers to *question* many of the practices that they have been trained to use in the teaching of reading. This is still a very useful objective.

Out of interest, Smith's 'rules' were recently presented to a group of 93 qualified and experienced teachers of reading. All were aware of Goodman's and Smith's psycholinguistic ideas and their implications for practice. They were asked to indicate anonymously whether they agreed, disagreed or were undecided about their use of each of the twelve rules in their own professional practice. The results are summarised here:

Use by 93 reading teachers of twelve rules considered *counterproductive* by Smith (based on 93 × 12 = 1,116 responses).

YES	45.1 per cent (N = 503 responses)
NO	35.8 per cent (N = 399 responses)
UNDECIDED	19.1 per cent (N = 214 responses)

No general claims can be made on the basis of such a small survey. Smith himself warned that the 'rules' should not be left lying around at meetings of reading specialists in case they were picked up, learned and applied. These findings indicate that the extensive practical experience in the teaching and learning of reading of this group of teachers had resulted in them being eclectic in their practice. For them, both 'top-down' and 'bottom-up' approaches are currently seen as of value to their pupils. There were also considerable differences between the teachers in their pattern of 'Yes', 'No' and 'Undecided' responses. In part, this pattern related to the age level of pupils taught and to whether or not the teacher was concerned with pupils with reading difficulties. The tendency was for teachers whose pupils had reading difficulties to be more eclectic than those whose experience was with children generally making satisfactory progress in reading development.

Smith also presents what he describes as 'One *difficult* rule for making learning to read easy'. This he sees as the antithesis of the twelve easy rules. It is 'Respond to what the child is trying to do'.

From his discussion, this can readily be interpreted as an interactive position. As he acknowledges, teachers of reading have been doing many things that are valid: most are not slaves to a particular pedagogic dogma.

Held rigidly, both the 'bottom-up' and the 'top-down' models have serious shortcomings. Young children, and some children with reading difficulties, have problems in understanding a sound–symbol system based on the alphabetic notation. Pupils can become frustrated at their inability to decode text to sound. Alternatively, they can become so attentive to the decoding process that they give little attention to the meaning of the message.

The 'top-down' orientation also has limitations. In the extreme, it could lead to children failing to give sufficient attention to the information contained in the text. Their own predictions, guesses and elaborations may create an idiosyncratic interpretation that does not give the reader access to the thoughts and feelings the author aims to convey. Attention to textual detail and accuracy is very important. Ignoring these can lead to avoidable difficulties and even to disasters for the reader and others: misreading instructions is one important example of this.

Summarising, the 'bottom-up' model underestimates the important effects of higher levels of linguistic processing, of the meaning of the text and the total experiences of the reader, on the lower-level decoding processes. The 'top-down' approach can lead to the sacrifice of accuracy and to failure in reconstructing the writer's message. Interactive models of reading processes and development represent promising syntheses of 'bottom-up' and 'top-down' models.

Developmental, corrective and remedial reading

All three of these adjectives qualifying 'reading' have more than one meaning. For the purposes of this book, developmental reading is taken to refer to the path followed by the great majority of pupils who learn to read by successfully completing the normal junior school reading programme. Such pupils are perceived as suffering from no outstanding inhibiting factors that will adversely affect their progress. The more adequately this programme accommodates pupils' individual differences, the higher the proportion of the class will successfully follow the programme. This is *not* to say that the individual pupils will progress at similar rates or in similar ways.

Corrective reading refers to the provision of supplementary instruction for relatively minor reading difficulties. These might be caused by absences, minor illnesses or difficulties with some aspect of the developmental reading programme. The difficulties are of a limited degree and scope, and most can be met by a junior school class teacher who can provide focused supplemental instruction. Typically the corrective instruction takes place within the ordinary classroom. 'Corrective reading instruction is more specific than developmental instruction, but less intensive than remedial reading instruction' (Harris and Hodges, 1981).

Remedial reading is a term that is currently causing some difficulties. The dilemma of the National Association for Remedial Education (NARE) bears on this issue. *What is being remedied?* There is suspicion that the term is frequently and incorrectly applied to children who are relatively slow in their progress in reading because they are slow learners. If this is the case, then nothing is being remedied when teaching reading to such pupils.

The term remedial reading is increasingly being used to refer to children who have *unexpectedly* severe, prolonged and complex difficulties in learning to read. For them progress under the developmental reading programme is extremely slow and typically very frustrating. In the junior school, such children may well be the subject of a 'statement' under the provisions of the 1981 Education Act, although practice between LEAs varies tremendously (see Chapter 1).

Many junior school class teachers are unlikely to have sufficient time to provide the extra help that such pupils may require. To prevent such pupils becoming progressively alienated from reading, additional help may be needed. This can be provided in various ways, including consultation with, advice and support from the following qualified colleagues employed by local authorities. The order of presentation represents the ease with which such help is likely to be obtained.

- colleagues working in the same junior school;
- an experienced colleague in the same junior school who has a specified school responsibility for 'special needs' provision;
- experienced colleagues working in the same junior school who have undertaken further courses of training concerned with reading difficulties;
- a peripatetic advisory teacher who has specialised in children's language and reading difficulties;
- a suitably qualified and experienced member of an adjacent linked special school for children with either moderate or severe learning difficulties;
- an educational psychologist employed by the LEA school psychological service;

- a child psychologist employed at a hospital-based clinic run by the area health authority.

It is important that the use of such expert advice does not lead to the junior school class teacher becoming distanced from the responsibility for alleviating the reading difficulties of a minority of pupils. That would be to marginalise class teachers and to undermine an important aspect of their own continuing professional development. Withdrawal from the classroom of children with severe and prolonged reading difficulties can be very helpful. In general, pupils welcome the experience. However, the practice has attendant dangers. If withdrawal is considered essential, whether for individual or small-group teaching, whether on the junior school's own premises, or elsewhere, it is essential that the following conditions be met:

- The help *cannot* be provided by the specialist within the pupil's normal classroom.
- Parents must be consulted and, where possible, their assistance obtained.
- The specialist providing the additional help must liaise closely with the class teacher and home.
- The content and methodology used in the withdrawal groups must be shared with the class teacher and, where helpful, with the parents.
- An explicit individualised programme based on a diagnostic–prescriptive approach must be devised.
- The work done during the withdrawal sessions must be reinforced during subsequent classroom periods and, if possible, at home.
- The timing, frequency and duration of withdrawal sessions must be carefully considered.
- The efficacy of the withdrawal programme on the individual pupil's reading attainments and attitudes to reading must be monitored.
- Evaluation of the pupil's progress must be both formative and summative.
- The progress in reading of pupils *after* the conclusion of the withdrawal programme must also be monitored by the school.

Teachers and psychologists are interested in identifying aptitude × instruction interactions (AIIs) for individual pupils and for groups of children who have some identifiable common characteristics (see pp. 70–1). Put baldly, one would not use a 'look–say' approach to teach blind pupils to read, nor a phonic-based system with a profoundly deaf pupil. There is evidence that less dramatic but equally important AIIs exist. AII is shorthand for an explicit, public and replicable productive link between learner characteristics and the methods and materials used in the reading programme. The identification of AIIs is a continuing professional imperative.

Expectancies of success and failure in reading: how valid are our assumptions?

What are the characteristics of junior school children who are likely to experience difficulties in learning to read? Collectively, any group of experienced junior school teachers would be able to draw up an educational/social/physical/emotional 'identikit' of this hypothetical population. There would be considerable disagreement between teachers about the relative importance of the characteristics identified. The lists, and the relative importance of the attributes identified, might also vary depending on the area in which the school was situated. The pressures and processes affecting children's progress in learning to read in a school in a salubrious city suburb are not necessarily identical to those operative in schools in severely deprived inner-city areas. There are, however, common themes characterising successful schools in *any* location. The major pedagogic problem with such generalised statements, even if they are valid, is that they may *not* be of great help to the teacher in enabling individual children to improve their reading or overcome difficulties. It is wise to remember that the utility of generalisations 'decays' as one moves from thinking about groups to considering individual children. This is a phenomenon to be welcomed! Where there is uncertainty, hope is not extinguished for the pupil, the parent and the teacher.

Many research workers have looked at groups of children and measured various aspects of their development *before* the children could read. The group is then followed up at the stage when the children are able to read. Such studies are concerned with the *predictive* validity of the initial measures. Thus early predictors of later success and failure in learning to read have been identified for many different *groups*. There are always individuals who will not conform to expectations based on statistics derived from groups.

As a general statement, there is a negative relationship between the degree of deprivation experienced by a child and progress in learning to read. This does not mean that all deprived children will fare worse in learning to read than those who are not deprived. The relationship is far from 'perfect' (i.e. allows prediction with no error). Some children from even the most deprived surroundings will learn to read more rapidly than others from more favoured backgrounds. One of the most outstanding young readers the author has taught in a junior school in a severely deprived inner-city area could not have had a more materially, socially, emotionally and physically disadvantaged background. The converse is also true. To come from a non-deprived background does not mean that success in learning to read is automatic. For most junior class teachers, the preceding statements will be blindingly obvious. They are made as a corrective to the often unconscious but damaging tendency to over-generalise expectations concerning progress in reading for *individuals* on the basis of *group* tendencies.

In their everyday work, teachers accumulate a considerable amount of information on the identification of children likely to succeed or fail in learning to read. It is important that such information be systematised and made explicit, rather than remaining private. Such 'public' knowledge is essential for the benefit of the clientele that the profession exists to serve. Knowing which pupils are highly likely to experience difficulties allows the possibility of avoiding or reducing problems.

Research workers have examined the relationships between various characteristics of children at different stages in learning to read. Here the concern is to trace the pattern of relationships between children's attributes and their *current* reading abilities. The focus is on the concurrent correlations between the attributes and children's reading.

Knowledge of the predictive and concurrent validity of pupils' characteristics can help improve educational decision-making, provided that the validities are sufficiently high.

Correlational analysis is typically involved. This enables quantification of the extent to which two attributes are related. When this procedure is used, the results are usually reported in terms of numbers called correlation coefficients. These range from zero (no relationship between the two variables) to ±1. Both correlations of +1 and −1 indicate that an individual's score on one attribute can be unambiguously determined from their score on the other attribute. The former (+1) indicates that there is a perfect positive correlation between the two variables. Pupils scoring high, average or low on the one attribute will score (relatively) equally high or low on the other. The latter correlation (−1) shows that pupils scoring high on the one attribute will score low on the other and vice versa. It will come as absolutely no surprise to readers to know that correlations of +1 or −1 are not found in practice when one looks at variables related to reading, or even in the relationships between different aspects of reading. The caution that *correlation does not imply causality* must also be noted.

Two American research workers have summarised studies reported in 25 major journals over a 30-year period; 322 reports containing 8,239 correlation coefficients were analysed (Hammill and McNutt, 1981). Their technique may be criticised, for example in the legitimacy of combining results from disparate groups and identifying 'median correlation coefficients'. Despite such reservations, their findings are of interest and value. To summarise the results from such varied studies, they defined 8 global and 34 specific constructs. The former were:

1. General academic achievement;
2. Emotion;
3. Intelligence;
4. General motor skills;
5. Perception;
6. Knowledge of phonics;
7. Readiness for reading;
8. Spoken language.

The latter 34 constructs focused on specific abilities. Alphabetically, these ranged from (1) alphabetic knowledge, (2) anxiety, (3) auditory memory . . . (18) oral rhyming . . . (22) self-concept . . . to (33) written rhyming and (34) written spelling. The total of 42 general and specific constructs defined the correlates of reading. The criteria of reading used were word recognition, reading comprehension and composite reading. The latter referred to reading tests that purported to include both of the other two types of reading.

In addition to analysing the research results by this approach, the workers also report the findings when reading is predicted from popular psychological and educational tests or sub-tests.

Typically, the relationships between attributes and the reading criteria fall with the passage of time. This is further evidence of both the stability and the changes that can take place in the development of children's reading. Concurrent correlations are characteristically higher than those obtained from follow-up data.

In terms of the global constructs, Hammill and McNutt report general academic achievement to have the highest relationship with reading. This will not surprise junior teachers or parents. Its predictive validity was represented by a correlation coefficient of 0.74 and a concurrent correlation of 0.85. Intelligence, measured in a variety of ways, was second with coefficients of 0.52 and 0.61 respectively. For phonics knowledge no longitudinal data were available, but the concurrent median correlation coefficient was 0.79.

Turning to specific constructs, written spelling had a longitudinal median correlation coefficient of 0.64 and a concurrent coefficient of 0.68. Mathematics skills came second with correlations of 0.57 and 0.68. This underlines the point made earlier in this chapter concerning the importance of *all* modes of symbolic thinking in understanding the development of reading. As a global construct measured in various ways, alphabet knowledge came third, with longitudinal and concurrent coefficients of 0.46 and 0.54 respectively.

If one is predicting reading from popular tests, the alphabet knowledge sub-test of the Metropolitan Readiness Test had the highest correlation with reading: it was 0.77. This does *not* necessarily mean that teaching alphabet knowledge is the most appropriate means of helping improve children's reading or of alleviating early reading difficulties. The interpretation of the extremely complex picture presented by Hammill and McNutt depends partly on one's assumptions concerning the nature of reading and its development. The 'top-down', 'bottom-up' and interactive models give somewhat different interpretations of the importance of alphabet knowledge in early reading.

In Britain the staff of the Barking and Dagenham LEA Schools' Psychological Service was funded by the Department of Education and Science to develop a screening test battery and supporting teaching materials for use by class teachers. The aims of the project included the early identification of each individual child's pattern of strengths and weaknesses, including attitude and motivation, and the provision of an individualised reading programme. The Barking Reading Project system was based on a continuous cycle of assessment and teaching. Whilst originally designed for top infant pupils, the materials are of value with junior school pupils experiencing difficulties in learning to read. Its orientation is 'bottom-up'. The principal educational psychologist presented evidence, and interpreted this as indicating that the teaching of letter names was important and could and should be taught (Barking and Dagenham LEA, 1982).

According to the earlier American findings, the following statements are popular generalisations that are only partially valid, i.e. they are *suspect*. This is *not* to say that the statements do not contain a degree of validity, merely to underline the danger of overstatement in this field. The reason for the qualification of each assertion is given in brackets.

- 'Spoken language is the base on which reading develops.' (Reading attainment correlates only marginally well with spoken language.)
- 'Reading develops out of a pupil's overall language ability.' (Reading is statistically related to a range of both language and mathematics skills, but it does not follow from correlational research that these influence the development of children's reading.)

- 'Phonics is the way to teach reading.' (We do not know whether the undoubted relationship between knowledge of phonics and reading attainments in the early stages is a cause or a consequence of success in learning to read.)
- 'Reading is a by-product of learning to write.' (The existence of high correlations between reading and writing variables is impressive, but by itself neither confirms nor refutes such an assertion.)

Perhaps the central message is that correlations of reading and reading-related variables can be helpful when thinking of *groups*, but less so when considering individual pupils. In either case, correlation coefficients should be treated with caution. Their existence should not be used to claim causality without much stronger supporting evidence. Well-designed methods experiments into the learning and teaching of reading are one such source. The help of colleagues competent in mental measurement and research design should be sought by any teacher interested in such evaluative work based on the reading programme in a school (Pumfrey and Elliott, 1990).

Teachers and psychologists are interested in identifying aptitude × instruction interactions (AIIs) for individual pupils and for groups of children who have some identifiable common characteristic. AIIs link learner characteristics, the objectives of the reading curriculum, the methods and materials used in the reading programme, and evaluation of pupils' progress in reading. The identification of AIIs is a continuing professional imperative. Recent work takes into account the individual learning styles of pupils (Carbo et al., 1986).

A rather different but equally important aspect of children's success or failure in learning to read concerns the reciprocal relationships between the teacher's, the parents' and the pupils' expectations. In the majority of cases, the teacher's expectations are the most potent. Parents' expectations come second and the children's third. This is no more than a reflection of the 'power structure' of the three parties involved. The junior school teacher *has* a wider and more extensive experience of children learning to read than the vast majority of parents. To some extent the increasing practice of systematically involving parents in helping their children learn to read appears likely to enhance the influence of parental expectations (see Chapter 5). It is far from clear that this *will* be the case. The systems of parental involvement are typically initiated and managed by the experts, namely the teachers. Where there are markedly different expectations between the parents and the teacher concerning a pupil's attainments and/or progress in reading, the child is often the sufferer. Such differences in expectations and their adverse effects are well known to teachers and to some parents, including many members of the British Dyslexia Association. Where such differences exist, it is important that they be made explicit and their validity explored by teachers and parents in the interests of the child. Not all such negotiations will resolve differences in expectations. Mutual involvement by teacher and parent in trying to help a child with reading difficulties is one way for expectations to be reappraised and made realistic. The consequences of a mutual contribution to the child's progress represents a beneficial educational spiral.

The importance of the effect of teacher *expectations* of pupils' reading attainments and progress on the pupil's *subsequent* attainments and progress was one starting point for research in this area. A teacher's expectations are based on often unconscious assumptions about the nature of children's learning abilities, the processes involved in reading development and the relative effects of nature and nurture in educational progress. The relationship that shows reading attainments typically to be lower in junior schools in socially deprived areas can often lead to an unwarranted expectation and acceptance of low reading standards. This is typified by the stereotypical statement 'What can you expect from children coming from that sort of background?'

Whilst the author was working as a senior remedial teacher in the most socially deprived area of a large city, the Remedial Education Service had a responsibility for supporting the improvement of reading in some 35 primary schools. There were severe staffing problems in the schools and resources, other than ingenuity and enthusiasm, were restricted. Reading attainments and progress in reading were regularly and systematically monitored. Two of the 35 schools consistently produced children whose reading attainments were significantly higher than the majority of the other schools. Most atypically, these attainments approximated to the national norms. This was not a 'one-off' event: it occurred regularly each year. What was achieved in these two schools demonstrated unequivocally that junior schools *can* make profound differences to pupils' reading attainments. The ILEA Junior School Project described earlier confirms the point (see pp. 62–4).

There are limits to the effects of teachers' and parents' expectations on pupils' progress in reading. Such expectations affect the methods and materials used and the morale and motivation of the teacher, the parent and the pupil. For teacher, parent and pupil the importance of expectations can hardly be overemphasised. Never let the children lose hope that they can learn to read. Once they have lost hope, they have lost everything. And so has the teacher.

Graded reading series versus 'real reading'

The development of ideas and practices in many fields progresses through the sequence of hypothesis, antithesis and synthesis. The 'graded reading series' and the 'real reading' approaches to the teaching and learning of reading represent a classic example. For many years the importance of well-graded series of reading books in both the initial and remedial teaching of reading was almost unquestioned. The value of texts in which the difficulty level of the words and the frequency of their repetition was carefully controlled and based on research findings had much to commend it. The approach was seen as using techniques that minimised the likelihood of failure and optimised steady progress in reading by the majority of pupils.

There is a vast and extensively used variety of these graded materials. They are well summarised in many compendia. Important British examples include the National Association for Remedial Education booklet, currently in its fifth edition, entitled *An A–Z List of Reading Books* (Atkinson et al., 1985). It includes 191 pages of information on reading books for infant, middle and secondary school pupils, providing titles, publisher, interest and reading level of books. Many local education authority psychological, remedial education and support services have developed their own compendia. Frequently such services also maintain resource centres at which teachers can inspect reading materials that they are considering using. The Child Psychology Service of the Metropolitan Borough of Sandwell provides details of 188 reading schemes and supplementary reading books in their publication *An Evaluation of Reading Books: A Teacher's Guide* (Kelly, 1981). The Leicester Schools' Psychological Service's *Reading and Remedial Reading Resources: Primary* and *Secondary* provide two similar sources (White, 1982a, 1982b). The work of these two services illustrates products valued by teachers.

Such compendia can never fully reflect the most recently published graded reading series and kits. Information on these is most readily obtainable at publishers' exhibitions mounted at the national and local conferences of professional organisations with particular interests in literacy.

Some educationalists argue that the use of graded reading materials makes invalid assumptions about the ways in which children learn to read. The alternative use of 'real' books, written by authors unrestricted by considerations of word difficulty and frequency of usage, are seen as having important pedagogical, literary and motivational advantages.

The work done in infant schools provides the basis on which

junior school teachers build. The 'graded reading' series versus 'real reading' represents one facet of the 'top-down' versus 'bottom-up' controversy considered earlier. Unfortunately, the controversy, as highlighted by recent events in one LEA, has generated more heat than light. At the time the LEA had no reading test that was used across all the primary schools in the borough to assess standards and progress in reading attainments.

In May 1987, 61 parents of pupils attending an infant school in the London borough of Bromley signed a petition protesting at the way in which reading was being taught in their children's school. The parents wanted the reintroduction of graded reading schemes which had been abandoned in favour of newer ways of teaching reading. These innovations included the use of a reading resource called PACT (PArents, Children and Teachers). This is a system designed to encourage children to choose, read and discuss 'real' books at school; the books the children have chosen at school can be taken home. As the acronym PACT suggests, at home parents are encouraged to help and talk with their children about the stories in the 'real' books. The books used were typically drawn from 'Story Chest', a collection comprising 'real stories', and from school library books. These 'real' reading materials were seen as more appropriate in helping children learn to read than the somewhat stilted stories frequently found in graded reading schemes.

In the latter, the vocabulary used is carefully controlled in terms of difficulty level and repetition. The idea has a long track history harking back to its origins in 1840 when Professor W. H. McGuffey presented the McGuffey Eclectic Readers to the educational world (Aukerman, 1981). Graded reading schemes include far more than graded books. In contemporary schemes there is a wide range of supplementary materials including well-documented manuals for the teacher. Such schemes are updated in terms of their form and content to reflect changes in society.

The contrasting idea of using 'real' books rather than graded reading schemes is also far from new. In part, it arose as a reaction against some of the extreme examples of graded reading schemes where any literary pretensions, and even sense, were virtually completely subjugated to the rigours of a strictly formula-controlled vocabulary. Indeed, almost 15 years ago in the United Kingdom, the Bullock Report commended the enterprise of schools in which the teaching of reading had been *successfully* achieved without the use of graded reading series (DES, 1975, para. 7.25). Had the system been used *successfully* in this particular infant school, parental concern would not have been aroused.

The LEA asked its inspectors to investigate. Their report, published in October 1987, showed that 18 out of 52 children in their final year were more than two years in reading age behind their chronological age. The findings illustrate how the use of standardised reading tests can help in evaluating the efficacy of particular reading curricula in schools. This is *not* to claim that the results of such tests are necessarily infallible.

The Director of Education is quoted as saying 'We want effective schemes which teach children to read. We do not want schemes at the end of which children are shown to be two years behind in their chronological reading age.'

The area's specialist language unit is on the same site as both the infant and junior schools. The unit is under the leadership of the two headteachers. The teacher in charge expressed concern that children 'statemented' under the 1981 Education Act, who were integrated into the infant school for part of the day, did not progress in their reading as expected. It was claimed that she was not allowed to buy test materials or to use specialist books and teaching materials that she considered necessary. Interestingly, it is claimed that no action was taken by the LEA until the parental petition appeared, despite the unit teacher's comments to the inspectorate.

The headteacher of the neighbouring junior school noted that three times the usual number of pupils had reading deficiencies when 52 top infants transferred to his school. The junior school class teachers considered that a significant proportion of the year group could not read at all, or had minimal reading attainments.

Prior to 1986, the junior school headteacher claimed that an average of 6 pupils per intake required extra help with reading. In 1986 this increased to 12 and in 1987 to 18. The Special Tuition Service subsequently tested 24 pupils using the Daniels and Diack Standard Reading Test 1 and found that 22 pupils had reading ages between 1 year 10 months and 2 years 10 months behind their chronological ages. The LEA was asked to provide extra help. A remedial system developed in the USA and known as DISTAR (Direct Instruction Systems for Teaching Arithmetic and Reading) was introduced (see Chapter 7 for further details of the DISTAR materials). Two extra part-time teachers were employed. It is claimed that the children subsequently made remarkable progress and are now showing an enthusiasm for reading that was hitherto missing. The headteacher of the junior school reports: 'after one term there is already a marked improvement in reading levels. The children have taken a step *forwards* not backwards with the help of ''mechanistic'' approaches.'

The controversy led to the 'blacklisting' of an inservice training course for primary teachers and to a major argument concerning how reading should be taught in Bromley's infant schools. A new headteacher took up post at the infant school in September 1987. The school was allocated extra money to purchase new books, reading materials and teaching time. Ninety per cent of the £2,500 windfall was spent on a range of reading schemes and the remainder on other types of reading books (Sutcliffe, 1988; Bayliss, 1988).

It is unfortunate that the situation polarised public and professional opinion. It was even more unfortunate that this took place, to some extent, along political lines. Reading from 'real' books was (incorrectly and unfortunately) castigated as an aberration of the 'loony left'. Graded reading schemes were equally incorrectly stereotyped as representative of unworthy traditional practice. The dangers of reading too much into a limited amount of evidence, where the cause of concern is less clear than simplified accounts suggest, should be avoided. This is not to say that the parents were wrong to express their concern. Unsurprisingly, a subsequent survey of the teaching of reading in *all* infant and junior schools in the borough showed that the schools were not typically extremist in their use of reading materials. The chief inspector stated that 'What appears to be coming through is a nice balance of real books and schemes' (Bayliss, 1988).

The arguments and evidence for and against both the graded reading schemes and the 'real' books approach need to be considered by junior school teachers. There are eminent individuals who champion one or the other position. What our children cannot afford is the absolute certainty that assumes only one approach to be valid. In fact, children can be helped to learn to read using either approach, or both. It is also true that poor teaching or staff morale can have adverse effects on children's reading attainments, irrespective of the materials or scheme in use.

The challenge to the teacher is the identification of that combination and phasing of graded and 'real' reading materials best suited to the individual pupil's characteristics, interests and stage of reading development. An awareness of the wide range of reading materials that are graded, 'real' or both is necessary to such professional expertise.

It is also clear that regular, systematic and explicit evaluation of pupils' attainments and progress in reading by schools and LEAs can alert those involved to deteriorating situations. On the positive side, the information that reading tests and assessment techniques can provide also enables promising practices to be more rapidly and clearly identified. The intention of the testing programme associated with the national curriculum is designed to address such issues.

Reading difficulties: does it matter what these are called?

Most teachers, parents and pupils accept the existence of both inter-individual and intra-individual differences in reading abilities and attainments. Some children read more readily, rapidly and with greater understanding than others. The pattern of individuals' cognitive strengths and weaknesses differs markedly. Plotting such differences by systematic observation, testing and assessment techniques helps to make explicit and public the characteristics of children as they develop differentially their reading attainments, attitudes and interests.

To function effectively in this particular field, the junior school teacher requires the following:

(1) an understanding of the reading process and its development;
(2) an understanding of the nature and extent of both inter- and intra-individual differences in children's reading abilities and attainments;
(3) the ability to predict the progress in reading that children with different characteristics will make under their current reading curriculum;
(4) the ability to identify, introduce and evaluate interventions designed to optimise children's progress in reading.

All of these include an appreciation of the limitations of professional knowledge and an awareness of the controversies in this field. One of the most temperature-raising of these is the use of labels to identify particular types of reading difficulty. For example, 'Do you believe in dyslexia?' Is the term the Unidentified Flying Object of education? Is it no more than a popular term for *any* difficulty in reading? Is it a technical definition of a neurological disorder? Is it of any utility?

The 1981 Education Act abolished the categories of handicap that had for many years provided the administrative basis for special education in Britain. Dyslexia and specific developmental dyslexia were not legally included as pre-1981 categories in Britain. Despite this, associations such as the Dyslexia Institute and the British Dyslexia Association were active and growing in their membership and influence. Under the provisions of the 1981 Education Act, instead of categories of handicap, children's 'Special Educational Needs' were to be identified and met. The concept was quickly adopted throughout the British educational system. Unfortunately, as discussed in Chapter 1, the inherent problems in identifying and providing the resources to meet special educational needs continue to present many problems. The label 'special educational needs' is virtually an all-embracing umbrella term. The wide range of voluntary organisations concerned with the interests of groups of children identified by specific labels has increased. In relation to severe and prolonged reading difficulties, Defining Dyslexia and the Foundation for the Underachieving and Dyslexic are two examples of such organisations. The provisions of the 1981 Education Act, its circulars and regulations offered the possibility of additional resources for these (and many other) interest groups.

There is a strong case for the appropriate use of labels in the continuing processes of understanding, predicting and controlling more adequately the development of children's reading abilities and attainments. One of the major purposes of concepts is to facilitate communication between interested individuals. Provided concepts can lead to testable predictions, knowledge can be advanced. With the accumulation of knowledge, concepts and labels found to be inadequate will be discarded. The rate at which labels used in education and psychology change suggests either rapid professional progress, or confusion in the face of immense complexities.

Are there different types of reading difficulty?

It can be shown that children differ both quantitatively and qualitatively in reading ability, attainment and progress. Differential programmes of intervention may be required by children exhibiting difficulties. In terms of educational efficacy, there is much to be said for finding particular combinations of methods and materials. This is no more than the continuing search for aptitude $\times$ instruction interactions referred to in Chapter 1.

The validity of a label identifying a distinctive condition requires that children to whom the label is applied should be differentiated from other children by one or more of the following:

- aetiology;
- presenting characteristics;
- prognosis;
- response to intervention.

It is worth noting that whilst distinctive aetiologies, presenting symptoms and prognoses may be identified, it does not follow that any effective intervention exists.

Rationally, and in the broadest terms, the causes of children's reading difficulties can be attributed to environmental conditions, to 'within-pupil' conditions, or to the interaction of environmental and 'within-pupil' conditions. In studying, and attempting to help, children experiencing reading difficulties, different professions often start from contrasting assumptions about causality. For example, the labels used by the medical profession in general and neurologists in particular contrast with those favoured by educational and child psychologists. Put baldly, the former groups frequently look for hereditary, congenital 'within-child' neurological causes. Many applied psychologists assume unspecified causes. They focus on the identification of the child's strengths and weaknesses and the manipulation of environmental circumstances likely to enhance the child's reading attainments and progress. The limited selection of labels presented in Table 2.3 underlines these contrasting, but not mutually exclusive, viewpoints. Agreements between professionals concerning the presenting characteristics of children with severe and prolonged reading difficulties is common. Disagreements arise concerning the aetiological, prognostic and intervention implications of these characteristics.

Table 2.3 *Terminology used in referring to severe and prolonged difficulties in reading*

Congenital symbol amblyopia	Disabled reading
Strephosymbolia	Word blindness
Congenital dyslexia	Backward reading
Congenital typholexia	Retarded reading
Amnesia visualis verbalis	Primary reading retardation
Analfabetsia partialis	Specific reading retardation
Bradylexia	Specific reading difficulty
Specific developmental dyslexia	Secondary reading retardation
Parietal dyslexia	Pure reading disorders
Acute dyslexia	Pure reading disability
Deep dyslexia	Defective reading
Surface dyslexia	Deficient reading

Currently many labels are used to designate reading difficulty. The purpose in presenting the definitions in Table 2.3 is to sensitise the reader to some key concepts found in the contemporary literature on reading difficulties. When using these concepts in professional exchanges, it is advisable to make explicit and elaborate one's definitions. This strategy can considerably reduce misunderstandings between colleagues, who may ascribe significantly different meanings to the same labels (see Table 2.4). Consequently communication collapses. It is also worthwhile considering the strengths and weaknesses of each definition in the light of empirical evidence.

It has been argued that, because of the differing assumptions about the nature and extent of reading difficulties, the term 'dyslexia' has come to have so many incompatible connotations that its value to teachers has become minimal. It functions only as a convenient shorthand for any reading problem, but has the 'advantage' of medical/neurological pseudo-respectability:

its use may create damaging cause and effect assumptions for student, family and teacher. Thus, in referring to a specific student, it is probably better that the teacher describe the actual reading difficulties, and make suggestions for teaching related to the specific difficulties, not apply a label which may create misleading assumptions by all involved.

(Harris and Hodges, 1981, p. 95)

Other experts would dispute this assertion. The mere fact that a particular label with a technical definition is used inappropriately by some individuals does not invalidate the label. At present in Britain the word 'dyslexia' has gained a popular currency with both politicians and the general public. In the process, the concept of dyslexia has been devalued. For example, increasingly it is used by parents to refer to virtually any type of reading difficulty, irrespective of its aetiology. The legislative procedures that have contributed to the situation are lengthy and labyrinthine.

In Britain the legislative process normally includes a Green (consultative) Paper, a White Paper followed by a Bill that is read three times each in both the House of Commons and the House of Lords. Modifications, additions and deletions are possible at any stage of the parliamentary process before the Bill is finally passed, receives the Royal Assent, and becomes an Act. One would imagine that this lengthy process would result in clear legislation. This was hardly the case in relation to many aspects of the 1981 Education Act. Successive circulars and regulations were issued clarifying the intentions of the legislation and its implementation. As will be seen from the quotation from the DES Circular 22/89 given in Chapter 1, p. 41, in the final analysis, where experts disagree, decisions are quite rightly in the hands of the courts. The current increase in cases where parents are seeking additional resources for children with severe and prolonged reading difficulties under the provisions of the 1981 Education Act underlines perfectly understandable and legitimate professional uncertainties.

Improving reading standards relates to junior school children's reading in general. The provisions in the 1988 Education Act for the national testing of children's language development, including reading, make the point. The short- and long-term effects of the proposals on children's reading attainments will be of considerable national interest.

This section began with the question 'Reading difficulties: does it matter what these are called?' In my opinion, the answer is an unequivocal '*yes*'. Because there are characteristically different types of reading difficulty, different labels are essential if we are to conceptualise, predict and control children's progress in reading more effectively.

Table 2.4 *Special educational needs: commonly used definitions*

1. *Learning difficulty*
'is defined to include not only physical and mental disabilities but any kind of learning difficulty experienced by a child provided that it is significantly greater than that of the majority of children of the same age' (DES, 1981, p. 2, para. 4).

2. *Learning disability*
'A disorder in one or more of the basic psychological processes involved in understanding or using language, spoken or written, which may manifest itself in an imperfect ability to listen, think, speak, read, write, spell or do mathematical calculations.' (The definition specifically *excludes* visual, hearing or motor handicaps, mental retardation, and the effects of environmental, cultural, or economic disadvantage.) (United States of America: Education for All Handicapped Children Act, 1975)

3. *Specific learning difficulties*
'Children with specific learning difficulties are those who in the absence of sensory defect or overt organic damage, have an intractable learning problem in one or more of reading, writing, spelling and mathematics, and who do not respond to normal teaching. For these children, early identification, sensitive encouragement and specific remedial arrangements are necessary' (Tansley and Panckhurst, 1981, p. 259).

4. *Specific learning difficulties*
These 'are defined as organising or learning deficiencies which restrict the student's competencies in information processing, in motor skills and working memory, so causing limitations in some or all of the skills of speech, reading, spelling, writing, essay writing, numeracy and behaviour' (Dyslexia Institute, 1989).

5. *Dyslexia*
(a) 'A disorder in children who, despite conventional classroom experience, fail to attain the language skills of reading, writing and spelling commensurate with their intellectual abilities' (World Federation of Neurology, 1968).
(b) 'is a rare but definable and diagnosable form of primary reading retardation with some form of central nervous system dysfunction. It is not attributable to environmental causes or other handicapping conditions' (Abrams, 1981, p. 95).
(c) 'We define dyslexia as a specific difficulty in learning, constitutional in origin, in one or more of reading, spelling and written language which may be accompanied by difficulty in number work. It is particularly related to mastering and using written language (alphabetic, numerical and musical notation) although often affecting oral language to some degree' (British Dyslexia Association, 1989).

6. *Specific developmental dyslexia*
'A disorder manifested by difficulty in learning to read despite conventional instruction, adequate intelligence, and socio-cultural opportunity. It depends on fundamental cognitive disabilities which are frequently of constitutional origin' (World Federation of Neurology, 1968).

7. *Specific reading difficulties*
A descriptive term used to indicate the problems of a relatively small proportion of pupils 'whose reading (and perhaps writing, spelling and number) abilities are significantly below the standards which their abilities in other spheres would lead one to expect' (DES, 1972, p. 3).

8. *Specific reading retardation*
'an attainment on either reading accuracy or reading comprehension which was 28 months or more below the level predicted on the basis of each child's age and short WISC [Wechsler Intelligence Scale for Children] I.Q.' (Rutter et al., 1970, p. 36).

Recently an extensive survey of the specific learning difficulties field has been carried out by a team of educational psychologists (Pumfrey et al., 1991). Historical and contemporary contexts concerning the nature of such difficulties are described. Legal and administrative definitions and procedures that compound the problems of identification, intervention and funding are examined. The viewpoints of the DES and of various voluntary organisations having interests in this area are reported. Theoretical and practical issues concerning the identification and alleviation of such learning difficulties are examined from psychological, psychoeducational and psychomedical perspectives in extensive reviews of the literature. The first of these includes emotional, social and cognitive factors. The second addresses educational interventions and their efficacy. This is followed by an examination of the strengths and weaknesses of support services in helping pupils with learning difficulties in general and those with specific learning difficulties in particular. Psychomedical considerations include neuropsychological, psycho-ophthalmological and psycho-pharmaceutical approaches to identification and treatment.

The policies of 89 LEAs are reported and the practices of 882 educational psychologists analysed and summarised. The policies and practices of examination boards in relation to applications and dispensations for both pupils with learning difficulties in general and specific learning difficulties in particular, are also considered. Associated with these various contributions are recommendations aimed at improving understanding of the nature, presenting symptoms and alleviation of specific learning difficulties.

An earlier helpful compendium by one of the founders of the charity Defining Dyslexia summarises the names and addresses of statutory and voluntary organisations and centres specialising in this field (Melck, 1986). Other well-known voluntary bodies such as the British Dyslexia Association and the Dyslexia Institute can provide similar information.

All definitions divide children into those included and those excluded. The ones above do this in the same way as the former definitions of the categories of handicap used before the 1981 Education Act came into force. The frequently heard claim that 'labels' had been done away with by the 1981 Education Act is spurious. Definitions frequently have legal implications for the responsibilities of a local education authority. These include the identification and alleviation of pupils' special educational needs in general and reading difficulties in particular (see Chapter 1).

In the case of the definitions in Table 2.4, only one (no. 8) provides an operational definition that is *relatively* explicit. Critics argue that its weaknesses are in both its conceptual basis and the specific instruments it employs. In the other definitions, the borderlines are even less clear and their conceptual bases equally controversial. Some definitions are seen only as *descriptive* of a child's characteristics at a given point in time. Thus the nature and extent of a pupil's reading attainments could be clearly specified. Other definitions additionally incorporate aetiological, causal and diagnostic implications. These could include reference to mental processes inferred from the pupil's performances. Descriptive definitions (labels) can be made explicit and unambiguous. One example might be the child's profile of attainments on a specified reading test battery. However, if a consideration of causality of reading difficulties ensues, professional disagreements immediately arise.

This problem is recognised by central government. In connection with the 1981 Education Act, circulars and regulations were issued to clarify definitions and procedures. The caveat added to one of these underlines the problems that remain and points to the only solution currently available: 'A Circular cannot be regarded as providing an authoritative legal interpretation of any of the provisions of the Act as this is exclusively a function of the Courts' (DES, 1983b, p. 1). This is why a number of parents, with the backing of voluntary organisations, have taken cases concerning local education authorities' legal responsibilities, provision and *decisions* about children with reading difficulties, to court. It is one means of obtaining further resources. The consequences of such case law can considerably affect local education authorities' policies and practices.

It is worth mentioning recent American experience concerning definition 2 in Table 2.4. The number of individuals included in the 'Learning Disabled' category in the United States of America has grown rapidly in recent years: currently it exceeds 1.8 million. (It is recognised that 'dyslexia' is the most common learning disability.) 'There is strong evidence that some of this growth reflects the tendency of some schools to place many students without physiologically-based learning problems in this category inappropriately.' One major study demonstrated that approximately 60 per cent of pupils identified as 'learning disabled' did not match the legal definitions or the definitions presented in the technical literature. It is suspected that individuals are categorised inappropriately in order to attract more central government funding. Suspicions of a form of educational gamesmanship have been expressed (Benderson, 1988).

Is there a tendency for something similar to take place in this country? The coupling of the terms 'specific learning difficulty' with 'dyslexia' and the assertion that these terms can be used interchangeably points to such a possibility. The tremendous variations between local education authorities in the proportion of pupils statemented under the provisions of the 1981 Education Act (see Chapter 1) underline the point.

Unless possible causes of reading difficulties are explicitly explored, none can be eliminated. Any intervention introduced is done so on a less than adequate professional basis. Parents are right to be concerned. Help can be provided. What is the value of a year's progress in reading attainment to a child? The key questions for citizens and society, rather than for professionals, concerning possible help with reading, are 'By whom?', 'To whom?', 'Why?' and 'Who pays?'

Reading difficulties: 'diagnosis' and 'treatment' versus 'identification' and 'intervention'

Reading difficulties are associated with a vast range of other characteristics of the pupil. So too is facility in learning to read. Aspects of children's physical, social, emotional, situational, cognitive and motivational characteristics are linked with both failure and success in reading. The danger is that, when an association is identified, a causal relationship may be assumed. It is salutary to remember that in the vast majority of cases of difficulties in reading, highly specific 'causes' cannot be found. Teachers and research workers are well aware that for almost every pupil who has a given pattern of strengths and weaknesses in the processes deemed to underpin reading development and failing to read, another pupil can be found with a similar pattern who has become a competent reader. The search for causal relationships is important. It is also difficult.

Which terms should we use to describe and communicate our work: diagnosis and treatment, or identification and alleviation? Diagnosis is defined as the act of identifying disorders from their symptoms. Technically it means only the identification and labelling of a disorder. Its medical connotations have brought both it and the associated term 'treatment' into disrepute with some, but far from all, teachers. The medical model of diagnosis and treatment is considered inappropriate to educational concerns by such disapproving individuals. The acknowledgement in 1980 by the British Medical Association that specific developmental dyslexia is the legitimate concern of educational psychologists and teachers, rather than a medical concern of general practitioners, was a related event. The disagreement of the World Federation of Neurology on this issue underlines a continuing controversy.

In education, the identification of a pupil's reading difficulties is

seen as an important first step towards constructive intervention to alleviate these. Based on an assessment of the nature and degree of a child's reading difficulties and consideration of their likely causes, an intervention is devised, implemented and its efficacy evaluated. The assumption that there is a 'disease' or 'condition' that can be identified through its symptoms, is seen as suspect by critics of the medical model. Such fine distinctions almost certainly do not impress the parents of children with reading difficulties. As many valid diagnostic reading tests have been developed and found of value by teachers, to discard the paired words 'diagnosis' and 'treatment' is perhaps unnecessary and premature.

In relation to children's reading difficulties, the terms 'identification' and 'intervention' may eventually supersede 'diagnosis' and 'treatment'. At present readers will find both sets of concepts in widespread use in the professional literature and in practice.

In some instances it is clear that a child's reading difficulties may well be a consequence of a medical abnormality of some kind. Children with visual or auditory impairments frequently experience severe and prolonged difficulties in learning to read. Whilst the grosser sensory impairments are readily identified, there are numerous less marked, sometimes overlooked, but none the less damaging sensory difficulties that can adversely affect the child's progress in learning to read. For example, conductive deafness is associated with deficiencies in middle-ear functions. One of the most common causes of these is otitis media, sometimes known as 'glue-ear', which can accompany a range of illnesses, but commonly results from colds, sinus infections and allergies. In some cases it can lead to intermittent hearing problems, which can have widespread effects on many aspects of a pupil's educational progress, including reading (Webster and Wood, 1989).

Broadly speaking, reading difficulties can arise as a consequence of two major groups of circumstances. Firstly, a wide range of environmental handicaps may militate against satisfactory progress. These can include a range of social deprivations typically, but not necessarily, related to poverty. Undernourished and poorly dressed children may be unable to take advantage of the learning opportunities provided by schools. The point is made, in part, on the basis of research findings but also as a result of the author having worked in a day school at which children were provided with breakfast, on both humanitarian and educational grounds.

Many surveys have been carried out in this country into the extent of deprivation in LEAs. The Department of Education and Science has stated that as there is 'some correlation between socio-economic disadvantage and educational need it seems reasonable to explore the groupings of LEAs that are formed by classifying LEAs by certain socio-economic indicators that are readily available' (DES, 1982). In that particular survey, the following indices of 'additional educational needs' were considered.

1. Children born outside the United Kingdom or belonging to non-white ethnic groups.
2. Children living in a household whose head is a semi-skilled or unskilled manual worker or farm worker.
3. Children living in households lacking exclusive use of one or more of the standard amenities, or living in a household at a density of occupation greater than 1.5 persons per room.
4. Children in one-parent families.
5. Children in families with four or more children.
6. Pupils receiving free school meals in maintained schools.

(DES, 1982)

The first indicator identifies additional needs for extra tuition in the English language whereas the other five indicators are traditionally associated with socioeconomic deprivation and several of them tend to be highly correlated. The analyses presented show with worrying clarity the immense differences between areas. The concentration of high levels of additional educational needs and of associated adverse environmental factors related to poor progress in reading in many inner-city areas cannot be ignored. Environmental factors that adversely affect children's learning can be changed, if society wishes and is willing to pay the price adequately to fund state education. If it does not so wish, it pays a different price later. Whether financial delegation and the local management of schools provided for in the 1988 Education Reform Act will benefit schools drawing their pupils from the most socially and economically deprived areas, is extremely doubtful.

Whilst the above six indicators are not necessarily the most informative from the viewpoint of identifying, understanding and predicting *individual* children's progress in reading, they are important at the level of policy-making. The earlier comment on interpreting to parents their children's standards and progress in reading, as is required under the provisions of the 1988 Education Reform Act, will require that the effects of the above and other environmental factors affecting individual schools be addressed publicly and annually. The consciousness-raising effects of such procedures could be dramatic, not necessarily on the lines currently anticipated by central government.

Any experienced junior school teacher who has taught in a school drawing pupils from homes characterised by socioeconomic deprivation will be well aware of the many individual children who are exceptions to the rule. Adverse socioeconomic situations do not necessarily result in low reading attainments and slow progress. Balancing this, individual children from socioeconomically advantaged families do not necessarily succeed in learning to read. The recent (1988) claim by a local councillor that children living in a house worth £100,000 were also guaranteed entry to the LEA's selective secondary schools, though containing an element of validity, was more populist than accurate. Pointing to a correlate does not necessarily identify a cause.

The second set of circumstances are within-pupil factors. A wide range of adverse genetic endowments can result in children being born with handicapping conditions that adversely affect their ability to learn. Some 150 illnesses or defects are carried by recessive genes. These can range from relatively mild sex-linked ones such as colour blindness to severely debilitating conditions such as haemophilia. Sickle-cell anaemia, Tay-Sachs disease (a degenerative disease of the central nervous system) and phenylketonuria (a metabolic disorder) are examples of other genetically transmitted conditions that can adversely affect the child's ability to learn to read. An awareness of such conditions and the use of medical labels in such cases can be of value in considering the child's educational needs.

Many normal traits and some abnormal ones appear to be inherited in more complex ways, through the combination of genes or the interaction of environmental factors and genetic predisposition. Spina bifida and cleft palate are considered examples of the latter (Quin and MacAuslan, 1986).

Each cell in the human body carries all our chromosomes. Each one reflects the individual's genetic constitution at birth. Chromosomes are stable over a lifetime. When something goes wrong with chromosomal development, serious abnormalities may develop. Some chromosomal defects are inherited; some are not. A Down's syndrome child is the consequence of a relatively common chromosomal defect, occurring once in about every 700 live births. The risk of having a Down's syndrome child rises rapidly with the age of the mother. Among 25-year-olds, the incidence is about 1 in 2,000; in 40-year-old mothers this rises to 1 in 100 and at the age of 45 is 1 in 40. With the younger mother's affected child, the likelihood is that the defect is hereditary. Over the age of 35, it is more likely to be a chromosomal accident.

The development of genetic counselling services for parents enables them to obtain information on possible risks of specific conditions, the implications of having a child with such a condition and the options open to the parents. The possibilities opening up in genetic engineering suggest that in future, much more is likely to be done to help parents and their children. It is even suggested that some abnormal genetic structures might be modified to cure inherited genetic defects. That is in the future.

The chances of survival of premature, very low birthweight babies have increased considerably with advances in medical expertise. The educational prognosis for many such children is exceedingly poor. Although the numbers of such children is relatively small, the challenge that their education presents is formidable (Quin, 1988).

Currently, LEA policies for integrating children with special educational needs into normal schools are being developed and implemented. The heterogeneity of pupils to be found in the junior school class is likely to increase. Teachers aware of the variety of children's individual differences will be better placed to provide the range of reading programmes that are likely to be required in meeting individual differences. This assumes that junior teachers also have a wide knowledge of reading methods and materials.

At any stage in development, from conception, gestation, birth, infancy onwards and throughout school life, adverse environmental influences can affect any child from any environment. However, socially and economically disadvantaged children are likely to suffer enhanced problems in learning to read. For example, they recover less quickly from the same illnesses, missing more school and typically experiencing less parental support and interest in their education. Schools can do little about the first two points. The third can be modified, but to do so requires considerable effort by teachers and parents willing to co-operate. Some of the advantages and support in learning to read experienced by children from advantaged backgrounds can be transmitted to disadvantaged children and their families (see Chapter 5).

For the junior school class teacher the messages are clear. Children's medical conditions and physical characteristics may affect their ability to read. So too can environmental factors. The interactions of environmental and within-child factors are also likely to affect differentially pupils' progress in reading. The possible effects of these variables and their interactions must always be considered when asking why a particular pupil is experiencing difficulties in learning to read.

Our understanding and control of reading processes and their development is far from complete. Caution is always needed when drawing conclusions from any diagnosis or identification of reading difficulties. To diagnose or identify accurately does not necessarily imply the ability to treat or intervene effectively. Despite this

note of warning, diagnostic procedures based on systematic observation and other assessment procedures provide a base from
which to advance our understanding of reading and our ability to
help pupils overcome their reading difficulties. These issues will be
returned to in Chapter 4.

Section B
Responses I: Assessment Issues

---3--

The uses and limitations of observation procedures, tests and assessment techniques

INTRODUCTION

A perennial public and professional concern with reading standards was yet again highlighted in 1990. Without the availability of reading tests and a regular testing programme, it is doubtful whether this could have occurred.

In April, a teacher who had formerly been in charge of one of north Kent's remedial advisory centres identified a cause for concern. He reported a marked increase in the number and proportion of first-year junior school pupils in the Gillingham area of north Kent who were underachieving in reading over the period 1983–84 to 1987–88 (Thomas, 1990).

Bright children typically learn to read more rapidly than less intelligent pupils. There are many ways of theoretically and operationally defining 'underachievement' in reading. Each has its particular strengths and weaknesses. All approaches to identifying 'underachievement' are as contentious as the concept itself. An understanding of language and reading development, test theory, research design and statistics is necessary if evidence about changes in the incidence of underachievement is to be appraised.

One way of identifying underachievement is to look at the gap between pupils' intelligence quotients and their reading quotients. For most pupils these quotients will be roughly similar. Underachievement can be construed as an unusually large gap between intelligence and reading attainment levels where, for some reason, the pupil does not read as well as might have been expected.

Intelligence and reading test scores were obtained for samples of between 1,202 and 1,361 first-year junior school pupils over each of five years. The percentage of pupils having a 20-point difference, or more, between intelligence quotient and reading quotient rose from 4.1 per cent (N = 49) in 1983–84 to 8.0 per cent (N = 109) in 1987–88. Earlier figures from 1980–81 gave an incidence of only 2 per cent (N = 25). A similar picture is reported as having been found in Medway with an increase from 30 cases in 1980–81 to 95 in 1987–88. The incidence of underfunctioning pupils was increasing in all schools, including those that had not previously experienced the problem. A meeting with the heads of the infant and junior schools that had shown the most change was called. It is reported that Thomas's findings came as no surprise to those present.

There have been changes. Apparently, in Kent, children with reading difficulties are now identified using different procedures and criteria. These capitalise on identification first by class teachers and then by special needs teams. These changes, coupled with the discontinuation of the administration of the Kent Reading Test, make comparisons with earlier data virtually impossible. The reasons for discontinuing the use of tests that teachers could easily administer and which, albeit crudely, ensured that children with relative reading difficulties could be readily identified, are themselves complex.

Thomas's article can be, and was, criticised on statistical and educational grounds. Despite such entirely legitimate reservations, it is worrying that there was no formal response to the detailed report of his research, and his meeting with the headteachers, that he submitted to the LEA.

Does Thomas's study represent an important 'straw' in an unsuspected and unwelcome 'wind of change'? Is it only a sampling fluctuation that could be expected by chance? Is it merely an artefact produced by a technical limitation of the tests and analyses used? On the assumption that the effect was real, it poses many challenges. Not least is the generality of the finding. This contrasts somewhat with the comments made in recent reports by HMI on reading in the primary school. In the absence of a detailed analysis of the full data, one must be cautious.

Only a few weeks later, senior educational psychologists from nine education authorities released to the *Times Educational Supplement* anonymous confidential data based on test scores of nearly 400,000 7-year-old pupils. A sample of this size is a substantial one. It was reported that, over a period of years, there had been a statistically and educationally significant decline in the pupils' mean reading test scores.

The psychologists met to discuss their concern on 22 June 1990, at the headquarters of the Croydon Psychological Service. 'Of nine authorities represented, eight seemed to show a decline. The ninth is a small authority which restandardises its test each year, but believes, nevertheless, that there is no decline. Another authority which does not consider its decline substantiated has the second smallest figure for decline ... It remains the case, though, that conclusive evidence of a *single* authority without such a decline has yet to appear' (Turner, 1990b).

Three of the LEAs have reading test data extending for ten or more years. These all show a decline over the last ten years. In particular, a marked decline has occurred since 1985, according to Turner. '... on a uniform basis of comparison (units of standard score), we have measured the average decline in population means across all eight authorities over these four years and found a drop of 3.12 points of standard score. The lowest decline in mean over the period is 2; the highest 4.7.

'This implies a rise overall of 50 per cent in the proportion of pupils with reading quotients below 80 (the lowest 10 per cent). However, in two large authorities, with means initially well above 100, the observed proportions of poor readers identified for screening purposes has in fact doubled' (ibid.).

The effects were found using a range of reading tests. The similarity of results across this range is reported as 'striking'. 'It does not appear to make much difference whether the test is old, new, group, individual, sentence completion or prose reading' (ibid.).

The groups of children involved were large. Three LEAs test annual groups of between 1,500 and 3,000. A further three tested groups of between 3,000 and 10,000. In the three largest authorities the groups were between 7,000 and 10,000. A total of over 400,000 pupils are represented by the test scores, which cover up to the past ten years.

> We felt bound by confidentiality to our LEAs (reports to the contrary notwithstanding) and have not declared their identities. After all, several LEAs are actively screening for poor readers and putting remedial resources where they are needed; some are reporting the data to their communities; and all are testing reading. What we have made public is the result of our own comparative analysis, information which did not exist until we held our meeting.
>
> (Turner, 1990b)

Commenting that 'The issue is too important for the facts to be locked away in a drawer', John MacGregor, the Secretary of State for Education, demanded to see the data.

The evidence from Croydon LEA was already in the public domain. On 6 July their Chief Inspector is reported as confirming that the mean reading scores of 7-year-old pupils in the Borough have declined since 1985.

A week later, four out of eleven education authorities contacted by the *Times Educational Supplement* were reported as having tests results '... which suggest a drop in reading standards among seven-year-olds' (Castle, 1990).

In September 1990, the Independent Primary and Secondary Education Trust, formerly the education unit at the Institute for Economic Affairs, published a book describing the findings (Turner, 1990c). The report says that there is clear evidence that hundreds of thousands of schoolchildren in nine LEAs south of a line from the Mersey to the Wash are subject to a sharply downward trend in reading attainment at the ages of seven or eight years. It is also claimed that there has been a 50 per cent increase in the number of pupils who can be described as very poor readers.

In the introduction to the report, Stuart Sexton, a former Conservative education adviser and director of the Trust publishing the report says 'This "reading failure" is a sponsored reading failure, attributed not to poor home conditions, or family breakdown, or too much television, or any other of the popular and totally unproven excuses; attributed to what goes on in our state schools, or rather what does not go on, namely teaching to read'.

The document is sharply critical of prominent sections of the educational establishment. The National Curriculum Council, LEA advisers and academics are charged with promoting an untested but ideologically appealing method of teaching reading. The 'real books' approach to the teaching of reading is claimed to be heavily implicated in the decline.

Critics argue that, if the decline in reading standards has taken place, Turner has not provided convincing evidence supporting his assertion. Having read the evidence, the current author is less sanguine. Turner's associated claim, that a major cause has been the adoption by schools of the 'real books' approach to enabling children to learn to read, is seen by some as even more suspect. Whether reading standards have declined and whether the formal teaching of reading has been neglected and this has contributed to the decline, are important questions. Evidence from Turner's work bears on this issue (Turner, 1990a, 1990b, 1990c). As is indicated in Chapter 2, pp. 132–5, and in Chapter 9, pp. 320–4, the arguments are complex and the evidence available almost certainly insufficient to support Turner's and Sexton's interpretations regarding a major cause of the apparent decline in reading attainments.

The report published in September was read by the Secretary of State for Education. He is reported as believing that the issue is about teaching methods and not about resources. Consequently, he has ordered an immediate enquiry by Her Majesty's Inspectorate into the teaching of reading in primary schools.

Turner has pointed to what he and a group of (anonymous)

experienced, competent, and informed professionals have identified as a reduction in children's reading standards. It is an important assertion and has not been made without serious consideration of the ethical, legal and technical implications. The ethics of publishing the results in the manner chosen by Turner and his colleagues have been questioned. Some see him as a martyr in the public interest; others question the morality and/or the legality of his actions and of those associated with the work. Were they, without permission, dealing with confidential data that remain the property of others?

The assertion that reading standards in a given number of LEAs are falling, touches the nation's quick. It is neither the first time that such assertions have been heard; nor will it be the last. Is it an accurate statement, or not? The nation has a right to be regularly informed of trends in children's reading attainments.

It is worth remembering that for many years this was done systematically, efficiently, regularly and cheaply by the Ministry of Education and then the Department of Education and Science. The sampling procedures adopted meant that no undue strains were imposed on LEAs, schools or individual pupils and their teachers. Whilst limited in certain respects, the sentence completion tests of reading comprehension used at the time provided valuable indices of standards and progress in reading at ages 11 and 15. It is a pity that this relatively simple system was abandoned, rather than extended and updated. In making this point I am aware of the important and innovative endeavours of the Assessment of Performance Unit of the DES in the whole field of language, and of their expertise in test construction, administration, sampling and data analysis (Gorman et al., 1988). Perhaps we would sooner rely on subjective impressions about reading standards, rather than be presented with somewhat harder data obtained through the use of objective tests of various types?

Turner points to a *reduction* over time in pupils' average reading attainments and an *increase* in the number and percentage of pupils underachieving in reading. It is worth remembering that it is also possible to have an *increase* in pupils' average reading attainments coupled with an *increase* in the numbers of children failing in reading. This apparent paradox is explained by the combination of an overall increase in children's mean scores on reading tests, coupled with an *increase* in the range of scores obtained by children. Precisely this latter pattern was identified in one of the many major studies of children's reading attainments undertaken by the ILEA.

Is there a problem? How widespread and severe is it, if it exists? *Without valid reading tests we cannot know.*

If there is a problem, what has caused it and what can be done to improve reading standards? *Without valid reading tests, we cannot know how effective our interventions have been.*

Identifying children with reading difficulties in a class is relatively easy. The teacher then casts around for an explanation. The causes are many and varied. The problem of disentangling associated factors from causal ones is often exceedingly difficult. In Chapter 2 reference was made to a review presenting the consensus of 30 years of correlational research into variables related to reading. 8,239 coefficients contained in 322 research reports testify to the ready availability of correlations between variables (Hammill and McNutt, 1981). Causes of reading difficulties are much harder to identify.

Difficulties can be caused by physical, social, emotional, cognitive, motivational and situational variables, and by any combination of these.

A more useful classification of possible causes of reading difficulties distinguishes between environmental factors external to the child that may be implicated, and 'within-child' factors. The complex interactions of these two major causes of reading difficulties can be crucial to progress or continuing failure.

IMPROVING READING: ASSESSMENT PROCEDURES

The improvement of reading attainments and attitudes involves the simultaneous consideration of three issues:

(a) the objectives of the reading programme;
(b) the curricula and resources whereby these objectives will be achieved;
(c) the assessment of pupils' progress towards the objectives (see Chapter 2).

The major objectives of the teaching and learning of reading in the junior school clearly cannot be achieved in isolation from the rest of the curriculum. In that context, the class teacher has the following professional responsibilities.

- appreciating that reading is but one aspect of the language curriculum;
- assessing the pupil's current reading attainments and attitudes;
- specifying reading objectives it is considered the pupil can achieve;

- arranging a programme of learning experiences designed to facilitate the pupil's achievement of these objectives;
- appraising systematically the extent to which the pupil has achieved the objectives of the reading programme;
- evaluating the results obtained;
- dependent on the results obtained, adapting the above cycle so as to facilitate further progress. (See diagnostic–prescriptive teaching of reading, Chapter 2, p. 106.)

Our concern here is with the contribution that assessments of various types can play in these activities. The importance of teachers being aware of inter- and intra-individual differences in their pupils' attainments, attitudes and progress in reading cannot be overemphasised. Only if these differences are made clear will teachers be able to improve standards generally and also to identify those pupils whose reading is a legitimate cause of concern.

An awareness by the class teacher of the uses and limitations of classroom observation procedures, tests and assessment techniques is essential. Knowledge of these and their availability is necessary for their effective use. Assessment procedures need to be built into the reading programme. Inservice training in their uses is essential.

There is sometimes a temptation for practising teachers to leave decisions on the selection of assessment methods and materials to other professionals who have a legitimate claim to expertise in the field of assessment. Educational psychologists form one such group. Experts working for publishing houses involved in the development of assessment instruments are another: NFER-Nelson, Macmillan and Hodder and Stoughton Educational are but three of many possible examples. The National Foundation for Educational Research in England and Wales, the Assessment of Performance Unit of the Department of Education and Science, the Godfrey Thomson Unit for Academic Assessment and Moray House College of Education are further well-known sources of expertise. There are very many others (Pumfrey, 1985). But despite the undoubted experience and expertise of such groups, the *decisions* on which assessment procedures to employ within a school should remain firmly within the control of the teaching profession. There is nothing that experts on testing know or do that is inaccessible to practising teachers willing to make the necessary investment of time and energy in coming to grips with the technicalities. In this respect, inservice training is vital if the teaching profession is to make informed choices in selecting assessment procedures and contribute to their development. Handing over these responsibilities to non-practising teachers diminishes the teaching profession.

USES OF ASSESSMENT PROCEDURES IN THE TEACHING OF READING

The three categories of assessment procedures listed earlier have various uses. Some of the most important are given in the following list. The ones shown are not necessarily mutually exclusive. Certain uses are closer to the interests of the class teacher than others; all impinge on the work of the junior school. The selection of approaches to assessment that are most likely efficiently to provide educationally useful information depends on judicious selection by the teacher.

Uses of assessment procedures in the teaching of reading

- finding a starting point for instruction;
- maintaining and improving attainments in, and attitudes towards, reading generally within the junior school class (hereafter any reference to reading includes consideration of *both* attainments and attitudes);
- comparing a class's reading with similar groups of pupils in other junior schools;
- comparing individual pupils' reading within a class;
- assessing and making explicit children's progress in reading;
- evaluating the effectiveness of particular materials and methods used in the teaching of reading;
- matching materials and methods to the pupil;
- research;
- identifying/diagnosing individual reading difficulties.

A survey of the testing of reading in the 141 Manchester primary schools was undertaken as part of an inservice course. Returns were received from 94 schools (66.7 per cent) (Tomkow, 1984). Only 4.3 per cent of responding schools reported that they did not use reading tests. (In passing, it would have been instructive to establish whether or not the reading attainments in these schools differed significantly from those where testing of reading did take place. Unfortunately this was not done.) The percentages of schools using 1, 2, 3, 4 and 5 reading tests were 32.9, 36.2, 15.9, 7.5 and 3.2 respectively.

As had been reported much earlier in an analysis of the reading tests used in 936 primary and middle schools in England and Wales in the Plowden Report (DES, 1967) and in the Schools Council research study *Record Keeping in Primary Schools* in which 192 schools were studied (1981), the variety of reading tests used was somewhat limited. The majority were norm-referenced. Individually administered tests of word recognition were the most popular in both studies. Many of the reading tests were dated.

The uses of the information provided by reading tests results in the Manchester survey were ranked by headteachers as follows:

1. Reading test results are discussed with parents when teachers are particularly concerned about progress: N = 81 (86.2 per cent).
2. Reading test results are discussed at parents' requests: N = 56 (59.6 per cent).
3. Reading test results are mainly for the use of teachers: N = 55 (58.5 per cent).
4. Reading test results are primarily used for record keeping: N = 26 (27.7 per cent).
5. All reading test results are discussed automatically with educational psychologists: N = 21 (22.3 per cent).
6. All reading test results are discussed automatically with all parents: N = 16 (17.0 per cent).
7. Reading test results are solely for the use of teachers: N = 3 (3.2 per cent).

(Adapted from Tomkow, 1984, p. 54)

There are many more valid uses to which reading test information is put by test users. The above limited list of restricted uses is mainly a reflection of the investigator's seven-item 'menu' presented to headteachers.

A greater awareness by teachers of the strengths and weakness of various types of reading tests and assessment techniques is essential. Only then can the important diagnostic information that such instruments and techniques can provide be used efficiently to improve children's reading attainments and attitudes to reading.

DEFINITIONS

Defining assessment techniques enables some of their most important common characteristics to be identified. A series of key concepts have been listed (nos 1–10 on p. 160). Each has then been given a sub-list of qualifying terms which can be used to elaborate the core concepts comprising the definition. The core concepts are in *ITALIC CAPITALS*.

A SHORT FORM definition and also an EXTENDED FORM are presented. Inevitably, the former definition is at a very general level.

The *SHORT FORM* definition includes lines on p. 160 containing any word in CAPITAL LETTERS.

The *EXTENDED FORM* includes a selection of important qualifying words. In practice, the particular combination of qualifying terms that will best meet your concerns will determine the type of assessment technique selected.

READING ASSESSMENT TECHNIQUES ARE:
1. **PROCEDURES* FOR
   systematic;
   public;
   replicable;
   efficient;
2. ELICITING **INFORMATION*
   reliable;
   valid;
3. OF A PARTICULAR *TYPE**
   norm-referenced;
   criterion-referenced;
   informal;
4. AT A SPECIFIED *LEVEL OF MEASUREMENT**
   nominal;
   ordinal;
   interval;
   ratio;
5. FROM WHICH *DESCRIPTIONS** CAN BE PRESENTED with or without specified confidence limits;
6. AND/OR *INFERENCES** CAN BE DRAWN with or without specified confidence limits;
7. FOR PARTICULAR **PURPOSES*
   pedagogic;
   formative;
   summative;
   descriptive;
   diagnostic;
8. CONCERNING *PUPILS'**
   individual;
   group;
9. *READING**
   attainments;
   attitudes;
   interests;
   activities;
10. AND LEADING TO *IMPROVED *CURRICULAR DECISION-MAKING*
    individual;
    institutional;

Reading tests and assessment techniques are efficient means of systematically eliciting valid information on a child's reading abilities and attainments. The information elicited can be used to improve individual and institutional decision-making for *all* pupils in schools.

ASSESSMENT ISSUES AND THE NATIONAL CURRICULUM

The national curriculum, with its programmes of study and assessment targets at key stages, sets the context within which work in schools will develop over the next decade. In large measure the success of the endeavour requires improved standards of literacy. Educational objectives, the curricula to achieve these and the evaluation of standards and progress in the subject areas will increasingly be highlighted in both public and professional debate.

Evaluating the efficacy of a school's language curriculum includes the assessment of children's attainments and progress in various aspects of reading (see Chapter 2). Professional concern that a national curriculum and national testing may lead to teaching to the test is valid. Worries are based on the precedents set by the 'payment by results' system used in this country during the nineteenth century and by the 'performance contracting' system developed in the USA after 1945 (see Chapter 2). The fears that the use of external tests could restrict teachers' own work, thereby limiting and devaluing their professional functions, were acknowledged. This danger still exists.

In developing proposals for the national curriculum, the Secretary of State for Education and Science set up a Task Group on Assessment and Testing (TGAT). Its brief was to give advice on the practical considerations that should govern all assessment within the national curriculum. This advice was to include a strategy for the testing and reporting of attainments at the ages of 7, 11, 14 and 16 years (or thereabouts). Table 3.1 shows the links between key stages and age groups.

In addition the TGAT was asked to advise on the following points:

- the marking scale or scales and kinds of assessment including testing to be used;
- means of differentiation so that the assessments can promote learning across a range of abilities;
- the relative roles of informative and of diagnostic assessment;
- the uses to which the results of assessment should be put;

Table 3.1 *The links between key stages, year groups and pupil age*

Key stage	New description of year group	Pupil age (majority at end of school year)	
*	R	5	} Infant school
1	Y1, Y2	6, 7	
2	Y3, Y4, Y5, Y6	8, 9, 10, 11	Junior school
3	Y7, Y8, Y9	12, 13, 14	
4	Y10, Y11	15, 16	} Secondary schools
–	Y12, Y13	17, 18	

* Key stage 1 also includes those pupils in reception classes (R) who have reached compulsory school age.
Note: Middle schools bridge the junior–secondary age groups.

The English curriculum will be introduced and assessed as follows.

			Key stage			
			1	2	3	4
English	Introduction	Autumn	1989	1990	1990	1992
	First reported assessment	Summer	1992	1995	1994	1994

- the moderation requirements needed to secure credibility for assessments;
- the publication and other services needed to support the system;
- means of securing efficient and effective assessment and testing arrangements.

These arrangements should be:

- simple to administer;
- understandable by all in and outside the education service;
- cost-effective;
- supportive of learning in schools.

It is worth asking whether the methods and materials that have been, and are being, developed in relation to children's standards and progress in reading have met these criteria.

The TGAT proposals were required *not* to increase demands on the time of teachers and pupils for activities not directly promoting learning. Costs also had to be limited. Advice was asked on the schedule for introducing the system. This had to take into account that an extensive national programme of training would be required for teachers in the methods of assessment and testing proposed.

Fortunately for the TGAT, it had not been charged with *finding* the educational equivalent of the Holy Grail within twelve months. Its less difficult but still challenging task was to point the direction(s?) that others should pursue. Many observers wondered whether any educationally worthwhile recommendations that could even approximate the requirements of the Secretary of State would be produced in the time allowed. The report of the TGAT was published in December 1987 (DES and Welsh Office, 1987). It contained complex proposals. These were generally supported ('broadly welcomed . . .') by the Secretary of State and by a number of professional organisations including some teachers' unions. In considering reactions to the TGAT Report, 'reading between the lines' is clearly an important literacy skill.

The TGAT proposals claim to be both 'evolutionary and radical' (para. 19). They are designed to build on existing good practice, but will be adopted on a national scale. The system will be criterion-referenced, formative, moderated and indicative of development. It should provide direct information about pupils' achievements in relation to clearly stated curricular objectives. The information obtained from the assessments (including tests) has to satisfy the following purposes. Their relevance to the teaching of reading is clear in theory; practical applications are more problematic. Information obtained must:

1. enable the positive achievements of individual pupils to be acknowledged explicitly and provide a basis for planning subsequent progress (formative assessment);
2. enable individual pupils' learning difficulties to be identified and appropriate remedial education provided (diagnostic assessment);
3. enable the overall achievement of a pupil to be recorded systematically at given points in time (summative assessment);
4. allow particular aspects of the work of a school, LEA or any other section of the educational service to be assessed and reported on (evaluative assessment).

In relation to attainments and progress in reading, quite clearly these four aspects of assessment are not mutually exclusive. Despite this, the thrust of the TGAT proposals is unambiguous:

> We recommend that the basis of the national assessment system be essentially formative, but designed to indicate where there is a need for more detailed diagnostic assessment . . .
>
> (para. 27)

We recommend that all assessment information about an individual be treated as confidential and thus confined to those who need to know in order to help that child.

(para. 28)

We recommend that for summative and evaluative purposes results should be aggregated across classes or schools so that no individual performances can be separated out.

(para. 29)

To realise the formative purpose of the national assessment system, pupil results in a subject should be presented as an attainment profile.

(para. 33)

The essential components in the reporting scheme are summarised in the following list:

National curriculum subjects (9, 10 or 11)
Profile components (from 4 to 6)
Attainment targets

    knowledge
    skills
    understanding

Standard assessment tasks
    Modes: Presentation
              Operation
              Response

The assessments proposed by the TGAT are intended to capitalise on the great strengths of the day-to-day teaching and assessments that are part of every teacher's work. Each pupil's progress is to be assessed in 'appropriate aspects'. Recognising that within each subject many different skills, ideas and activities are involved in the understandings and achievements that pupils show, the TGAT gives pointers towards making the assessment procedure manageable. It suggests that a balance between 'precision in detail' and 'overall comprehensibility' can be achieved if each subject working group identifies 'about four – never more than six – subdivisions of the subject for reporting to serve the purposes of the national curriculum' (DES and Welsh Office, 1988c, p. 8). The TGAT calls these subdivisions 'profile components'. It is anticipated that some of these will be common to a number of subject areas, thereby encouraging cross-curricular themes. The development with increasing age of profile components as shown in the main TGAT report is given in Figure 3.1.

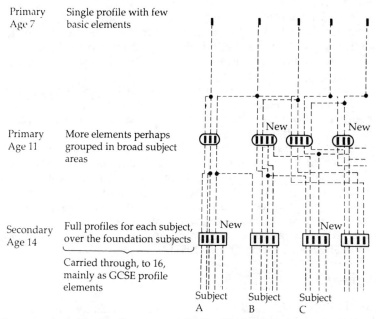

Primary Age 7	Single profile with few basic elements
Primary Age 11	More elements perhaps grouped in broad subject areas
Secondary Age 14	Full profiles for each subject, over the foundation subjects
	Carried through, to 16, mainly as GCSE profile elements

Figure 3.1 *Evolution of profile components (DES and Welsh Office, 1987, para. 121)*

Concern was expressed that a single class teacher of 7- or 11-year-old pupils might have to assess pupils in 'at least 20 and possibly 30 or more components' (ibid., para. 119). The suggestion that assessment at the primary stage be limited to the three core subjects was rejected as having a potentially narrowing effect on the primary curriculum.

In the event, pressures (detailed in Chapter 9) of the proposed assessments were recognised as putting too much of a burden on teachers and schools. On 9 April 1990, in a speech to the Assistant Masters and Mistresses Association Annual Conference, the Secretary of State for Education announced that 7-year-old pupils, and almost certainly 11-year-old pupils, will *not* have to take standard assessment tasks in six out of nine curriculum subjects. The core curriculum subjects of English, mathematics and science will be the only ones assessed using standard assessment tasks. For primary school pupils' attainments in the six non-core subjects teachers will use their own assessments.

Turning to the junior school English programme, there are five attainment targets (ATs). These are Speaking and Listening (AT1), Reading (AT2), Writing (AT3), Spelling (AT4) and Handwriting (AT5). These provide three profile components: Speaking and Listening (AT1); Reading (AT2) and Writing (ATs 3–5). At the ages of 7 and 11, within the profile component of Reading alone, an extensive array of statements of attainment must be addressed in the English curriculum. Further details are given in Appendix 2.

Linking 'attainment targets' to an equally wide range of modes of presentation, operation and pupil response in the standard assessment tasks (SATs) presents many further challenges. Each pupil is to be assessed on profile components using SATs. Pools ('banks') of those SATs have been developed, from which teachers will be able to draw. Across a balanced set of three SATs at age 7 and 3–4 SATs at age 11 years, '. . . it will be possible to appraise *all* of the profile components on several occasions and in several different contexts' (DES and Welsh Office, 1987, para. 149). Operationally defining instruments and procedures that will inform the process of 'formative assessment' will inevitably prove controversial. Examples of tasks comprised of discrete questions and of integrated tasks are presented in an appendix to the main TGAT Report (DES and Welsh Office, 1987).

LEVELS OF ACHIEVEMENT

The TGAT has proposed that the assessment and reporting system should utilise a scale from 1 to 10 to cover the complete range of progress made by children of different attainments between the ages of 5 and 16. Each number represents a level of achievement. Thus, level 1 will be the first level in a profile component, irrespective of the chronological age at which the component is introduced. A level is to be specified so that it will represent the average educational progress of children over a period of about two years. This is shown by the sloping line in Figure 3.2.

It is recognised that at any one chronological age, some children will be at higher levels than others. The vertical dashed lines in Figure 3.2 represent a (very) rough 'speculation' of the limits likely to include about 80 per cent of pupils at a given reporting stage. The spread of levels is smaller at the 7-year-old age level than at older ages by virtue of the differentiation that occurs as education proceeds.

Each of the subject working groups is required to define a sequence of ten levels in each of the profile components that it selects. Specific attainment targets will identify the levels.

The records of 7-year-old pupils will continue with them as they

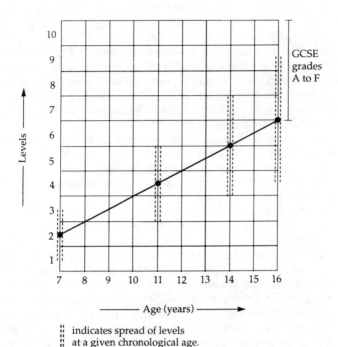

Figure 3.2 *Sequence of pupil achievement of levels between ages 7 and 16 (DES and Welsh Office, 1987, para. 104)*

progress through the educational system. Thus junior school teachers need to know the scope and purpose of the first stage in the national assessments. At the age of 7, assessment should comprise a selection of three prescribed standard assessment tasks for each child. The identification of children in need of help exceptional for a pupil of that age is central. Children making very little or very considerable progress in a profile component can be identified. A warning is given by the TGAT that 'Care should be taken at all reporting ages, but especially at this age, to avoid giving the impression that the assessment is a prediction of future performance' (DES and Welsh Office, 1987, para. 148).

Am I alone in wondering how this is to be done? As a parent of three children, this question has always been central to my concerns. As a junior school teacher, this question was frequently addressed to me by parents.

During the year in which the pupils reach the age of 7, their teachers will be asked to undertake the following duties:

1. Using continuous assessment linked to programmes of study and attainment targets, make judgements of all pupils across a number of profile components, using three levels of performance.
2. Select three standard tasks from within the range of work covered from the national item banks. At least one of the tasks should be selected in common with other local schools.
3. Incorporate the selected standard tasks into the teaching programme. Use standard task procedures and criteria for standard task administration.
   Record the performance of each pupil over three standard tasks in the profile components.
4. Attend a local group moderation meeting.
   Compare results and assessments across schools.
   Decide an overall distribution.
   Resolve discrepancies between schools.
   Adjust individual levels bearing in mind the agreed distribution.
5. Compile a confidential report, making comparisons with local and national distributions, for the consideration of the head-teacher and the governors.
6. Determine the levels for each pupil bearing in mind the general information on standards previously agreed at the moderation meeting. Report to parents.
7. Enter the pupils' results in the school records.

At the age of 11, similar procedures apply, with modifications. Thus the three or four standard tasks taken may be supplemented by other forms of externally provided tests. The profile components assessed will increase in number and complexity. The information on overall school attainments, set in context, will be included in published reports. The information concerning individual pupils will be made available to the secondary school to which the pupil will move. Details are currently being discussed. Decisions on the form and content of SATs will have a bearing on the nature of reports on individual pupils and institutions that will be adopted.

COMMENTS

Other groups were critical of the TGAT Report. The Centre for Policy Studies and certain members of the government, including the Prime Minister, were concerned that the arrangements proposed by the TGAT did not meet the four criteria listed on p. 162.

In essence, what was proposed was seen as unnecessarily complex, difficult to develop and implement, and likely to be expensive. Subsequently, the TGAT published three supplementary reports (DES and Welsh Office, 1988b). The first of these explains more fully the implications of some of the initial recommendations. The TGAT did not appreciably modify its original proposals. The second supplementary report concerns the application of the TGAT recommendations to the various foundation subjects, and the third develops recommendations for the type of support system that will be required. One part deals with the inservice training of teachers. An appendix presents a case study of a large LEA. This demonstrates how teacher training in the national curriculum and its testing arrangements could be accommodated in the LEA's INSET provision. It is clear that the endeavour will require an extensive INSET programme devoted to a particular national priority. As an initial step in the essential training programme for teachers on assessment of the national curriculum, a summary of the TGAT report *A Digest for Schools* was compiled and sent to every school in England and Wales (DES and Welsh Office, 1988c).

The TGAT proposals accept that assessment is central to the promotion of children's learning. It provides a framework within which educational objectives can be determined and pupils' attainments and progress made explicit. The fears that external tests could have adverse effects on pupils is addressed. In relation to pupils who do not succeed (for example, in learning to read adequately) the following position is adopted:

> Of course pupils do not always succeed, but poor performance against a target should not be seen as a prediction of personal inadequacy; it should be regarded as an indication of needs. Such needs must be met, perhaps first by the use of more detailed diagnostic assessments conducted usually by the school to identify specific difficulties, and then by further teaching help. It would be absurd if diagnosis of difficulty – and recognition by a pupil and parents and teachers of the need for help – were to be avoided because of fear of failure.
>
> (DES and Welsh Office, 1987, para. 14)

Anxiety that testing might damage relations between parents and the school is also seen as unjustified. Concern that the results would be published in league tables of scores leading to invidious, ill-informed and unjustified comparisons between schools, is acknowledged. The TGAT considers that the publication of assessment results for a school should occur only 'in the context of reports about that school as a whole . . . and take account so far as possible of socio-economic and other influences' (ibid., para. 18).

To the author, such a view exemplifies a utopian optimism concerning parental reactions. It is highly likely, but not inevitable, that pupils attending junior schools in severely socially deprived inner-city areas will, on average, have lower reading attainments than pupils attending schools in less difficult situations. How could this information be conveyed to the pupils' parents in a manner that would engender better home–school understanding and co-operation?

'Our pupils read less well than others because of the disadvantages of living in this area' or 'Our pupils are reading as well as can reasonably be expected in the circumstances' hardly meet the challenge. Doubtless more adequate 'forms of words' can and will be developed. It is extremely doubtful whether these will be sufficient for many parents. As information on the standards of reading in schools becomes more publicly available, whether or not parents understand and accept differences between schools will be revealed. There is considerable evidence that the majority of parents want their children to attend schools at which the standards of attainment in the basic subjects are high. In the USA, 'magnet' schools typically have high standards. In an educational 'market economy' where school income depends on attracting pupils, junior schools may be pressured to demonstrate high standards in pupils' literacy skills in order to attract parents, their children and income.

In October 1988, two years before the assessment of 7-year-olds was due to begin, the government had not decided what tasks it wished pupils to achieve. The School Examinations and Assessment Council (SEAC) invited contracts for the development of 'standard assessment tasks' in English, Welsh, mathematics and science. Contracts were planned to be finalised in December 1988.

The chairman and chief executive of SEAC, Mr Philip Halsey, was interviewed in October 1988. He is reported as stating that the system of SATs required is intended to provide 'a very much better way for teachers and parents to keep track of children's progress and as a result both would be better able to encourage and help children to learn'. At that time he was apparently unwilling or unable to give a specific example of *how* a child's achievement would be tested in any profile component of any field. Presumably this is the task of others. Nonetheless, one wonders whether the Secretary of State's reach will exceed the grasp of the professionals accepting SEAC's brief? The pilot work, now completed, is considered in Chapter 4.

NORMATIVE AND CRITERION-REFERENCED TESTS COMPARED

Teachers are familiar with ranking pupils within a class according to their *relative* attainments in reading. Observations such as 'John is a more accurate reader than Peter', 'Mary is the best reader in the class and Jean is the weakest' and 'David's comprehension is worse than his decoding ability' make the point. The first two observations focus on between-pupil comparisons; the third on within-pupil differences. Such observations are typically based on junior teachers' observations over time of pupils' responses to teaching. The comments are valuable. They are also subjective and specific to the particular classroom situation.

It is often asserted that much of the standardised assessment of reading carried out in junior schools is not closely related to what the children are being taught. For example, what links are there between a child's reading of isolated words out of context in an individually administered word reading test and reading as it is taught in the classroom? (Are 'flash cards' extinct?) This apparent unrelatedness of the content and format of some standardised tests to much of the educational experience of pupils is considered a criticism of standardised normative reading tests by some experts on reading. If this criticism is generalised, it is highly suspect and potentially harmful. The focus and format of standardised normative reading tests is extensive. Many have considerable ecological validity, for example 'cloze' tests of reading comprehension. Being clear about the purpose of a reading test determines whether or not the information it elicits will be of utility. The United Kingdom Reading Association has produced a guide to the selection of appropriate reading tests for various descriptive and diagnostic purposes at all stages of education (Pumfrey, 1985).

The focus in normative testing is on efficiently, systematically and validly assessing and comparing particular aspects of children's reading attainments with each other and with the larger group on whom the tests were developed. Inter- and intra-individual differences in attainments are of the essence in such testing. Thus a pupil's performance in relation to normative tables enables the teacher to relate reading attainments in a particular class in a given school to a wider group of similar pupils of the same age in other schools. Such tests are seen by some critics as providing the teacher with information of relatively little educational significance. For example, its instructional implications are considered minimal: 'It doesn't help me in planning my teaching.' Such criticism is fashionable, unwarranted and largely invalid. It is, in part, a consequence of the user failing to appreciate the type of information that a specified reading test can provide.

In contrast, 'criterion-referenced' testing is in serious danger of becoming 'criterion-reverenced', possibly sacrosanct. Normative reading test information gives a different but equally valuable perspective on what is being achieved by pupils. Normative profiles of reading attainments and abilities can provide valuable descriptive and diagnostic information on both attainments and progress in reading.

Norm-referenced testing does not appear to have a significant role in the TGAT proposals. Despite this crucial point, 'Diagnostic reports are [to be] confined to problems outside the normal range' (DES and Welsh Office, 1987, para. 27). How can this range be identified without information from normative tests? How can the very clear and substantial differences in reading attainments of children in the same class, but born in different months of the year, be openly, systematically and fairly considered in the absence of normative measures that incorporate monthly chronological age allowances? There is evidence, for example, that the absence of such information leads to the incorrect allocation of teaching resources to children with reading difficulties.

In contrast, the TGAT proposes the use of assessments centred on curriculum-related, criterion-referenced tests. These are to be based on a clear description of the performances required of pupils. Such tests involve setting explicit attainment targets that can be taught. They derive from the notion of 'mastery learning' and its value in motivating pupils and raising standards. It is claimed that such criterion-referenced tests will reveal the quality of each pupil's performance, irrespective of the performance of other pupils. If only things were that simple! From whence will the establishment of the 'performances required' derive if not intuitive normative considerations? The term 'criterion-referenced' test would be more adequately differentiated from 'normative' tests if the former had been designated and restricted to 'domain referenced' tests with clearly defined contents. Normative reading tests are criterion-referenced! Criterion-referenced reading tests inevitably contain a normative component.

It is essential for junior school teachers to understand the nature of, and relationships between, criterion-referenced reading tests and normative ones. Both types of test elicit complementary and valuable information. Some important characteristics of each are shown in Table 3.2. An awareness of the differences and similarities, the uses and limitations of both types of test, can be expected of any teacher.

Table 3.2 *Normative and criterion-referenced reading tests contrasted*

Issue	Norm-referenced	Criterion-referenced
Purpose	To assess inter- and intra-individual differences in reading attainments and attitudes to reading in a specified group of pupils.	To assess the extent to which specified operationally defined reading objectives have been achieved.
Focus	1 Generalised skills and reading abilities and attitudes. 2 Latent traits inferred from pupils' performances. 3 Problem may be 'within pupil'.	1 Specific and narrow reading skills and behaviours. 2 Detailed task analysis. 3 Problem may be contextual/ environmental.
Construction	1 Based on conventional test theory using item analyses with given limits to Facility and Discrimination indices of items. 2 Specification of the group to which the test is to be applied is of the essence. 3 Mathematical basis of measurement well developed and articulated.	1 Tests are based on items developed from an analysis of the objective to be mastered. 2 Explicit normative considerations are irrelevant because the successful mastery of the criterion by all pupils is the objective. 3 Mathematical basis of criterion-referenced measurement is still in the early stages of development.
Standards	Test results usually compared with children of the same age and from the same population.	Test results compared to an explicit criterion of mastery, e.g. number of items correct for a given objective.
Reporting results	Standard scores (e.g. deviation quotients, 'z' scores, T scores, stens, stanines), percentiles, and reading ages.	Percentage scores on number of items correct for a given objective. Number of items correct.
Teaching implications	1 Items must *not* be taught as doing so would invalidate the norms that have been obtained. It would also be impossible to interpret the scores of pupils after such teaching. 2 Does not provide a clear guide to required instructional content but can suggest *method*. 3 Focuses attention on normative standards.	1 The items have been selected as both desirable and able to be mastered by pupils. The content of the test *must* be taught. 2 Provides guidance concerning instructional materials. Tests can be directly linked to such resources. 3 Narrowness of objectives can restrict curriculum adversely.
Availability	Plenty.	An increasing number.

Details of 199 reading tests and assessment techniques classified to facilitate selection by age and purpose are available (Pumfrey, 1985).

—4——————————————

Integrating the assessment and teaching of reading

INTRODUCTION

This chapter gives a brief consideration of a selection of challenges that must be addressed in pursuing the goal of integrating assessment and the teaching of reading. Promising practices are identified and references provided so that interested readers can follow up these points.

The delivery of the national curriculum requires, and will encourage, high and rising standards of reading. This section focuses on improving integration of the assessment and teaching of reading. Some teachers claim that they never use reading tests or assessment techniques, yet their pupils learn to read satisfactorily. Others argue that to teach without an associated testing programme is unprofessional. This polarisation is, in part, a consequence of the first group having a narrow view of what is included in testing. Often it is incorrectly perceived as the administration of commercially purchased normative tests that may be of little direct relevance to the planning of the reading programme for the class or an individual with reading difficulties. The importance and wide variety of informal and criterion-referenced reading tests and assessment techniques as sources of instructionally important information is often overlooked. Observations by the writer in a considerable number of primary school classes have shown how both of these aspects of curriculum-related testing permeate the activities of the effective teacher.

The aims of educational theory and practice include conceptualising, predicting and modifying children's reading behaviour. In these the applications of test theory to the measurement of inter- and intra-individual differences are of central importance. One eminent psychologist, Guilford, commented that 'Whatever exists, exists in some quantity and can, in principle, be measured'. More importantly, reading tests and assessment techniques can provide valuable information. In relation to reading, assessment of attainments, interests, attitudes and motivations is vital. Imperfect though test theory, reading tests and assessment techniques may be, they have important merits. These include providing theoretical, explicit, communicable, replicable and testable reasoning about children's reading. They also provide a variety of means of making systematic observations of children's reading skills. They encourage and facilitate accountability.

DANGERS

The medical model of human functioning based on the concepts of diagnosis and treatment has received considerable criticism in educational and psychological literature: the work of teachers is typically seen as having more in common with psychology than medicine. Teachers are aware of the dangers in the slippery classificatory slope of:

- individual differences;
- deviations;
- difficulties;
- disabilities;
- deficits; and
- defects.

Pathologising the normal, rather than accepting the considerable range of individual differences, is an ever-present danger. Labelling can contribute to this process. Despite this, the uses of labels can be valuable and are essential in describing reading-related conditions, processes and performances.

The concepts of diagnosis/treatment and identification/intervention are not mutually exclusive; nor are they necessarily the property of any one profession. Both have developmental, corrective and remedial aspects. 'Fire prevention' and 'firefighting' are acknowledged responsibilities of different groups of professionals.

Diagnosis is the process of identifying disorders from their symptoms. Technically, diagnosis means only the identification and labelling of a disorder. In the Penguin *Dictionary of Psychology* this has been extended to 'Determination of the nature of an abnormality, disorder or disease' (Drever, 1964). However, in education, diagnosis typically includes the planning of interventions based on an evaluation of the child's characteristics and circumstances, a consideration of possible causes and the likely effects of pedagogic programmes aimed to improve the child's learning.

More specifically, the diagnosis of reading difficulties is intended to determine the nature of the processes involved in pupils' performances by carefully considering the functional relationships between their different aspects. This is the first step. For the teacher, diagnosis is a process whereby hypotheses concerning the nature of a reading difficulty can be investigated. The pupil's relative strengths and weaknesses can be identified. This assists in planning a reading programme that will capitalise on strengths and also help to improve skills found to be weak.

To some extent difficulties in reading are generated by society's desire for a conformity that may well be at variance with the nature of human beings. This should not be taken as indicating a belief that the improvement of reading and the identification of reading difficulties cannot be achieved. The complexities of the reading process mean that it is possible for a range of ineffective reading strategies and poor attitudes to be learned by the child. These can be modified, given the necessary resources. The issue is partly financial and political (Pumfrey, 1990a, 1990b).

One important concern is whether a pupil's reading difficulties are caused by environmental or by 'within-child' factors. The former can include poor educational opportunities, provision or lack of support; the second can include difficulties in sensory input, output or processing capacities. In general, it is easier to rectify environmental deficiencies. The teaching profession is continuously devising educational programmes that will alleviate all types of reading difficulty (Pumfrey and Elliott, 1990; Pumfrey et al., 1991).

The diagnosis or identification of reading difficulties is not an esoteric exercise carried out by specialists; it is performed at many levels. The class teacher is constantly engaged in informal diagnoses (or identification) and in making modifications to the child's educational experiences intended to facilitate reading progress, irrespective of the level of his/her relative skills. If this informal approach is unsuccessful, the teacher may initiate a more detailed examination, still within the classroom. If the difficulties continue, referral will probably be made to someone with more specialised knowledge or expertise. Professionals such as specialist support teachers, educational psychologists, audiologists, ophthalmologists, neurologists and psychotherapists may be involved.

At all levels, such diagnosis can be viewed as hypothesis generation followed by intervention. The result is further modification of the hypothesis and, if necessary, of the intervention. Put more prosaically, 'Tommy cannot synthesise short phonically regular words; why not? Perhaps it is because . . ., so I will arrange for him to . . . and see if it helps. If it doesn't, I'll have to think again.' The majority of teachers have not been adequately trained in the principles of educational diagnosis (Pumfrey, 1990a).

ASSESSMENT, TESTING AND TEACHING READING

The linking of reading tests and assessment techniques to the teaching and learning of reading is an important professional responsibility. It requires the teacher to be adequately versed in child development, pedagogy and the theory and practice of mental measurement. The last area is currently primary school teachers' Achilles' heel. Knowledge of the range of reading tests and assessment techniques available is very limited.

Virtually all educational psychologists employed by LEAs are qualified and experienced teachers who have undertaken further specialised training. Within an LEA, they are the professional group that has the greatest expertise in the uses and limitations of various types of test. Primary school teachers who wish to further their own knowledge and skills in this field would be well advised to capitalise on their services. It is essential that teachers have the technical 'know-how' to provide informed input into such deliberations.

The following section is concerned with a number of challenges. Users of reading tests and assessment techniques aspiring to link these with instruction need to be aware of such issues. I will then go on to indicate ways in which the testing and teaching of reading may be better integrated; both are highly pertinent to the effective delivery of the national curriculum.

CHALLENGES

Context: assessment, testing and the national curriculum

The introduction of the national curriculum with its specification of attainment targets, programmes of study and standard assessment tasks provides a new set of synonyms for the long-established notion that a language programme should have explicit objectives, content/methodology and evaluation (DES and Welsh Office, 1988a, 1989a; Pumfrey, 1990a).

One function of the national curriculum is to improve educational standards. The assumption is that monitoring and feedback motivates professionals, pupils and parents. The assessment system devised by the Task Group on Assessment and Testing is still being developed. Ten levels cover the full range of progress that children of different abilities should make between the ages of 5 and 16. The information that will be provided by SATs is unlikely to allow the 'fine-grain' analyses that are needed to help develop individual educational programmes for children with reading difficulties.

To the best of the author's knowledge, as yet no SATs include systematic age allowances. Is this unimportant in a year-group system where some pupils are almost a year younger than others? At the end of 1990 the first SATs had yet to be approved. Evidence must be provided that the instruments/procedures used to assess the various profile components in, for example, English attainment target 2, Reading, are valid and reliable. The concept of 'ecological' validity is likely to be utilised; it should be put under theoretical and technical scrutiny by disinterested professionals. In addition, the intercorrelations between the profile components should be reported. Without a quantified and simultaneous consideration of both the reliabilities and intercorrelations of profile components, the significance of differences between scores on profile components cannot be established. Put simply, the identification of strengths and weaknesses in reading skills depends on such procedures.

The Cox Report stated 'A level 1 performance should always be a signal for further investigation. This might, for example, reveal that a child who appeared to be a slow learner, or inattentive, was in fact showing symptoms of specific learning difficulties (dyslexia)' (DES and Welsh Office, 1988a, para. 13.6). The assessment of surface characteristics, such as reading attainments, is only part of what may be required. The importance of 'potential' is acknowledged in the Cox Report. In Circular 22/89, the subsequent revision of Circular 1/83, reference is also made to 'the child's *true learning potential*' (DES, 1989e, para. 88; author's italics). The primary school teacher is in a key position in the early identification of pupils who may require further investigation because of reading difficulties, whether these are general or specific. Such knowledge is a starting point for a developmental, corrective or remedial reading programme.

ISSUES INHIBITING INTEGRATING THE ASSESSMENT AND TEACHING OF READING

Integrating the assessment and teaching/learning of reading involves *all* primary pupils, not only those experiencing difficulties. What major difficulties inhibit the integration of the testing and teaching/learning of reading in primary schools?

Problematic theoretical considerations

What is your position in relation to each of the following issues?

(1) The natures of 'top-down' versus 'bottom-up' versus 'interactive' theories of reading development have to be clearly under-

stood by the teacher. What are the theoretical underpinnings of your own classroom practice? Awareness of such considerations is a professional responsibility. Teachers' theoretical assumptions affect the reading tests and the teaching/learning programmes that they adopt. As professionals, teachers can be expected to justify their pupils' reading programmes. To do this they must understand the theoretical basis of practice (May, 1986; Reason, 1990).

(2) The existence of qualitative and/or quantitative differences between pupils is an important issue. It affects the pedagogy that is adopted in order to maximise the progress that pupils make in their reading. Some workers consider that the development of pre-reading phonemic awareness in all pupils is an important way of reducing the chance of later failure (Bryant, 1990; Cataldo and Ellis, 1990; Snowling, 1990). There can also exist different types of specific learning difficulties (dyslexia), for example auditory and visual dyslexia. It is highly likely that somewhat different methods will be better suited to each group of pupils (Gjessing and Karlsen, 1989).

(3) Different workers place contrasting emphases on cognitive, affective and motivational (contextual) dimensions bearing on children's progress in reading (Johnston, 1983; Coltheart, 1987; Gentile and McMillan, 1987).

(4) The importance of the early identification and alleviation of reading difficulties has considerable appeal to parents and professionals. In theory, it might enable the prevention or reduction of later reading problems. In practice the strategy is not as straightforward as might appear. The earlier screening takes place, the more likely is it that errors will be made (Drillien and Drummond, 1983; Potton, 1983; Pearson and Lindsay, 1986). Despite this, screening has some uses when linked to a corrective or remedial programme (Clay, 1979).

(5) As yet no single pedagogic panacea is equally beneficial to all pupils. This suggests that there may well be qualitative differences in the learning styles of pupils (Carbo et al., 1986). Professional 'tunnel vision' should be avoided. Openness to the ideas of colleagues, coupled with critical acumen, is essential. The despairing cry 'I have tried *everything* with the child, but to no avail: the reading difficulties still persist' is not unknown in staffrooms or on INSET courses. The teacher who claims to have 'tried everything' to help a pupil with reading difficulties is almost certainly incorrect. There is a vast array of diagnostic/treatment or identification/intervention programmes available. Knowing about them and finding what suits which pupils at which stages in learning to read, and why, is a continuing challenge to the profession. The dilemma is keeping a balance between being a jack of many methods and materials and a master of none.

TEACHERS, READING TESTS AND ASSESSMENT TECHNIQUES

There are many limitations in reading tests and assessment techniques. Primary school teachers need to be able to make informed selections to suit their particular circumstances, so they must be aware of the variety (Vincent et al., 1983; Pumfrey, 1985; Farr and Carey, 1986; Glaser et al., 1988; Hammill et al., 1989).

Inter- and intra-individual differences in children's reading and reading-related abilities can be measured. Strengths and weaknesses can be identified. Individual profiles of reading and related abilities can be drawn up, and the information used to develop successful interventions (Pumfrey, 1977; Naylor and Pumfrey, 1983; Searls, 1985; Spache and Spache, 1986; Tyler, 1990).

Distinctions between the different types of information provided by normative and criterion-referenced tests should be clearly understood. The importance of these to the formative and summative evaluation of standards and progress in reading is crucial (Pumfrey, 1985, 1990a).

A knowledge of informal reading inventories enables the primary school teacher to initiate valuable diagnostic/prescriptive assessments of individual pupils. When linked to miscue analysis, important insights into the cues used, or not used, by pupils can be identified. Such knowledge enables more effective reader–text interactions to be developed (Arnold, 1982, 1984; Pumfrey, 1985; Johnson et al., 1987; Goodman et al., 1987; Pumfrey and Fletcher, 1989).

Inadequate understanding by teachers of the strengths and weaknesses of reading tests and assessment techniques (RTAT) is typically a consequence of lack of suitable opportunities in both initial training and INSET. These omissions can be rectified, if teachers consider the development of such professional skills necessary and make the necessary representations (Pumfrey, 1990a). The arrival of standard assessment tasks in connection with the national curriculum ensures that the relationships between teaching and assessment will figure prominently in 'Reading', in other profile components of English, and in the other subjects. The resolution of these key concerns will permeate professional practice for many years.

The testing and teaching of reading in the national curriculum of the primary school appear to be integrated, in principle. Until the standard assessment tasks are agreed in detail and have been tested in the crucible of the classroom, judgement on the educational utility of the integration must be deferred (DES and Welsh Office, 1988a; DES, 1989a, 1989d).

As noted earlier, professional controversies exist concerning the range of labels used in identifying pupils with learning difficulties in general and with specific learning difficulties and/or dyslexia in particular. From the viewpoint of the Department of Education and Science, administratively this is viewed as a class-inclusion relationship, specific learning difficulties forming the larger category. Scientifically, the situation is less clear. The requirements of the Education Act 1981 and the Education Reform Act 1988 bear heavily on the issue. Teachers already involved in assessment and statementing procedures for children with special educational needs for both groups will be sensitive to the controversies involved (DES, 1989b, 1989c, 1989e; Pumfrey and Mittler, 1989).

There are ambiguities and inconsistencies in the administrative procedures designed to facilitate the identification, provision and funding of additional resources for pupils experiencing learning difficulties (Education, Science and Arts Committee, 1987; DES, 1989a, 1989e). The resource implications of providing additional provision for individual pupils with, for example, specific reading difficulties or dyslexia are considerable. LMS will highlight such issues.

PROMISING PRACTICES

Primary school teachers have shown considerable ingenuity in integrating the assessment and teaching of reading. Innovative practices continue to be developed in both classroom and clinic. The identification and dissemination of continuing and, as yet, unsung promising practices and/or developments in this area would be of benefit to the profession and thus to pupils. In what ways have you seen this integration achieved in your work in schools? If so, how can the ideas be shared? Has your LEA a system whereby such knowledge can be evaluated and communicated effectively?

A short selection of six general strategies integrating the teaching and assessment of reading is listed here. Each can readily be adapted by any interested primary school teacher. Indeed, it is highly likely that most primary school teachers are already using variations on the themes presented. The extension of such activity has much to commend it. No expenditure of money is required. How many of these strategies are used in your primary school?

1. the diagnostic–prescriptive use of RTAT;
2. the development and evaluation of individual educational programmes (IEP);

3. the identification of aptitude × instruction interactions (AII);
4. the use of variations of 'cloze' procedure;
5. using word lists as a basis for criterion-referenced tests of vocabulary, reading and spelling;
6. informal reading inventories linked to miscue analysis.

Considerable work has been done in producing systems linking the assessment and teaching of reading. A short selection of developed materials and methods of value to primary school teachers is given in the following list. Each contains constructive ideas; consideration of their respective rationales and efficacies are matters for the user's professional judgement.

- Early detection of reading difficulties (Clay, 1979);
- Extending Beginning Reading (Southgate-Booth et al., 1981);
- Barking Reading Project (Barking and Dagenham LEA, 1982);
- Classroom Observation Procedure (ILEA, 1982);
- The Aston Index (revised) and Portfolio (Newton and Thomson, 1982; Aubrey et al., 1982);
- QUEST Screening, Diagnosis and Remediation Kit (Robertson et al., 1983);
- DATAPAC – Daily Teaching and Assessment for Primary Age Children (Akerman et al., 1983);
- Direct Instruction (Science Research Associates, 1985);
- SNAP – Special Needs Action Pack (Muncey, 1986);
- The Primary Language Record (Barrs et al., 1988);
- Assessment and Teaching of Dyslexic Children (Naidoo, 1988);
- Specific Learning Difficulties (Bushell and Cripps, 1988);
- Screening (Wiltshire County Council Education Department, 1988);
- Bromley Screening Pack (Bromley Local Education Authority, 1989);
- 'Touchstones' (6–7-year-olds national curriculum assessment materials) (NFER, 1989);
- ARROW Learning (Lane, 1990) (see Chapter 9).

LINKING TESTING AND ASSESSMENT OF READING: USES AND LIMITATIONS OF WORD LISTS

The Psychology and Pedagogy of Reading (Huey, 1908) was an early landmark in this field. In the introduction, the author recounts a story of how the explorer Livingstone aroused wonder and awe in an African tribe when he was observed each day looking at a book.

The book was eventually *eaten* by the natives, who wished to share the mysteries and the power they considered that Livingstone derived from this, to them, unfamiliar activity. Assimilation of the material certainly occurred, but led to little advantage in mastery of the skill of reading. Perhaps spaghetti letters, gingerbread letters and the many variants on edible forms of words that are possible represent a more effective mode of moving towards literacy. A valuable review of the way in which thinking about the nature of word recognition has developed from an emphasis on associative psychology to contemporary linguistic information processing is available. Inevitably, it raises as many questions as it answers (Henderson, 1987). Word recognition involves rather more than appears at first sight.

The importance of pupils' mastery of a relatively small number of words that comprise the majority of the textual materials they will either read or write is an important issue. Irrespective of theoretical complexities, word recognition appears to take place rapidly and easily for most pupils despite the complexity of the processes involved. But some pupils within a typical junior school class will experience considerable difficulties in establishing such a sight vocabulary, probably because their more effective learning style involves other modalities. The work described later (see pp. 185–7) refers to the reading and writing vocabularies of top infant class pupils. Much more widely known and readily available is the somewhat older vocabulary list, *Key Words to Literacy* (McNally and Murray, 1962). It is claimed that a mere twelve words account for about 25 per cent of reading materials; 100 words account for about 50 per cent of textual materials and 200 for about 70 per cent. The most frequently used twelve words are:

a	and	he	I	in	is
it	of	that	the	to	was

Mastery of these is essential to fluent reading. Building on previous experience in learning to recognise rapidly and correctly more immediately meaningful, personal, emotionally loaded and idiosyncratic words such as pupils' names and events about which they have strong feelings, the *key words* shown here can readily be similarly mastered, i.e., overlearned and automated. Then, when a text is encountered, the pupil's attention can be devoted to less frequently occurring words. In one sense, knowing a high proportion of a text increases the likelihood that unknown words can be either 'guessed at' using context cues or 'worked out' using grapho-phonic cues. The means whereby the essential overlearning is achieved are vital. Many approaches are open to teachers to ensure that this end is achieved without alienating readers (Southgate, 1986; Roberts, 1989).

Many lists have been made of the frequency with which particular words, and sequences of words, appear in textual materials of various types. One use for these lists is to control vocabulary in texts when this is considered necessary for producing reading materials graded by difficulty level. This is *not* to say that frequency consideration alone determines the form and content of such materials. *Key Words to Literacy* is one of the best-known word lists in use in the UK. It has been used in preparing a popular series of graded readers, the Ladybird reading scheme, written by W. Murray. In an analysis of the content of this series, presented by Murray, the following information is listed for each book. It shows the structured way in which the text was compiled, and demonstrates the importance given to providing practice in reading words several times in order for pupils to become fluent in reading these key words:

- number of new words per book;
- total of different words used;
- running total of words used;
- average repetition per word;
- carry-over to the succeeding book and to parallel books.

In addition, a number of suggestions for the use of *Key Words* in the teaching and testing of reading have also appeared (McNally and Murray, 1962, 1984). Their word list was based on a survey of other sources drawn up some time ago, and not necessarily having a UK provenance. An analysis of infant pupils' spontaneously written work was one of the earliest vocabulary lists based on British pupils (Edwards and Gibbon, 1964). Work carried out in Australia has presented lists of children's spoken language strings (Hart et al., 1977). This has been followed up in England, Canada and the USA, resulting in the production of graded reading series based on language strings.

Lists based on such materials provide valuable guidelines for authors and teachers. The content of a list identifies commonly used words that the reader will have to master in order to read effectively. Fluency in the recognition of words is essential to reading for meaning (Chall, 1983). The ability to recognise words out of context differentiates the skilled from the less skilled early reader (Ehri and Wilce, 1983; Ehri, 1985). Current thinking indicates that automaticity in word recognition is essential in order to free the young reader's attention from the mechanical task of decoding text and allowing it to be directed towards the meanings contained therein (Samuels and Laberge, 1983). The ability to recognise frequently occurring words, decode to sound, comprehend, spell, write and use them in compositions are related applications that also concern teachers. The means whereby pupils are enabled to acquire this facility are many and varied.

A major criticism of word-list approaches, such as the McNally and Murray one, to text construction is that patterns of language are not adequately represented in such contrived materials. More sophisticated analyses of children's language strings go some way to meeting this criticism. A strength of the word-list approach is that by controlling vocabulary, overlearning and mastery can be encouraged. The probability of success in reading can be increased. The motivational effects on pupils of this success, the sense of mastery and of progress that is engendered, are important in encouraging positive attitudes towards reading. The introduction of new materials is controlled so that children are not over-whelmed by the demands of a text. Successively more difficult texts build systematically on skills acquired by the mastery of ear-lier ones.

Fashions come and go in educational theory and practice. At one time graded reading books and materials dominated the reading curricula in junior schools. They still exert a strong and generally beneficial influence on the promotion of *all* pupils' reading. Many reading difficulties are a direct consequence of presenting pupils with texts that are too difficult for them to deal with satisfactorily. This is frustrating for the pupil and, if undetected by the teacher, likely to lead to alienation from reading. Failure to match the demands of a text to the attainments of a pupil can lead to unnecessary difficulties. Currently, the dominance of graded ma-terials is less marked. As noted in the earlier discussion of the 'real reading' versus 'graded reading series', a compromise combination is emerging in many schools. 'Real reading' materials are being graded, albeit in a somewhat different manner (see Chapter 9).

Word lists define a domain-referenced corpus of material, mas-tery of which can provide a legitimate and operationally defined educational objective for all pupils. If it is found that certain indi-viduals are having difficulty in reading important words in such a list, the teacher can select or develop a methodology and/or ma-terials that will enable the child to master the words. The over-learning of a relatively small number of key words can have a considerable effect on the textual material accessible to the reader. Automaticity in such activities is an essential prerequisite of fluent reading.

A study involving 350 top infant school pupils analysed the frequency of words encountered by these children in their reading and writing (Laskier, 1986). The main study was carried out in their last term of infant school education. Each child provided a piece of free writing. An equivalent sample of words was taken from their classroom reading material. The purpose of the study was to identify the corpus of words being encountered in their reading and writing by children at the end of what is now the first of the four key stages (i.e. at 7 years of age) specified in the Education Act 1988.

This sample of the children's reading and writing yielded a total of 55,610 words. Within the total there were 2,477 different words. The striking point is that 216 words accounted for 75 per cent of the 2,477 different words in the combined corpus on the basis of the sampling procedures used (Laskier, 1986).

A mere 8 words comprised 25 per cent of the specified corpus of writing and reading material; 45 words accounted for 50 per cent and 216 words accounted for 75 per cent of the words (excluding four proper nouns) encountered and used by our sample of children. The importance of the mastery of this core of words can hardly be overemphasised if the child is to become competent in reading and spelling.

The words can be used as a domain-referenced word recognition test. When this was tried with a sample of 71 7-year-old pupils, a mean score of 161 was obtained. There were significant sex differences in the scores obtained. Of more educational significance, the range of scores was from 31 to 215 of the 216 words correctly read. *Massive individual differences between pupils exist in their word reading attainments at this quite young age.* The explicit identification of such marked differences is of considerable pedagogic importance. If the teacher knows what words pupils can or cannot read, testing and teaching are well integrated.

Currently a domain-referenced battery of reading and spelling tests is being developed based on the 216 words identified. The battery will be called the Early Words Test Battery (EWTB) (Pumfrey and Laskier, in preparation). The aim will be to show that the group of 216 very frequently occurring words can be used in different ways for different purposes by the teacher. In part, the format and mode of administration of a particular sub-test in the EWTB will determine the purpose for which it can be used. It will also open up avenues for teacher ingenuity in teaching specific reading and spelling skills.

In the current work there is a significant positive correlation between the frequency with which these words are encountered by children and the children's ability to read them ($r = 0.53$; $N = 71$). It must be remembered that listing words in order of frequency of use does *not* necessarily list them in order of the ease with which they can be read or spelled.

Knowledge by teachers of various word lists is valuable. An appreciation of the educational implications of key words and word sequences in learning to read is even more so. The mastery, automaticity and sense of *independence* as readers that being able readily to read a relatively small number of such words and sequences encourages in pupils are not to be rejected lightly. There are many ways in which the mastery of key words in various modalities can be encouraged, even if graded reading materials are *not* used.

VOCABULARY DEVELOPMENT AND EXTENSION

A child's vocabulary development is both a contributor to, and a determinant of, progress in learning to read. There is a strong relationship between vocabulary and academic performance. Vocabulary knowledge has been shown to predict reading comprehension in a variety of countries, across various age groups and in different content areas of the national curriculum. As noted earlier, there are wide inter-individual differences between pupils in their attainments in various aspects of vocabulary knowledge. Nagy and Herman are reported as estimating that the difference in vocabulary size between low and high achieving students is between 4,500 and 5,400 words. In relation to socioeconomic status, at first grade level (entry to elementary school), pupils from middle-class backgrounds know 50 per cent more words than pupils from less advantaged backgrounds. There are diametrically opposed views on how such imbalances might be reduced; there are also suggestions for the synthesis of these positions (Marzano and Marzano, 1988).

Learning a new word is more than learning a label: it implies a rich understanding of word meaning. Once the phonological label (the sound) of a word and the orthographic label (the letters forming it) are learned, they support each other. Recognising one label provides cues to the recognition of the other. This provides the justification for teaching pupils to recognise, associate meaning, and spell a word simultaneously. The technique of simultaneous oral spelling is well known to teachers but wide reading and other language-rich activities are primary means for developing vocabulary. Unfortunately, not all pupils experience the opportunities and encouragement that facilitate vocabulary development.

The educational rationale and means of encouraging this development are controversial. An interesting approach to vocabulary instruction has recently been described by two research workers in collaboration with a group of 60 practising elementary school teachers (Marzano and Marzano, 1988). A corpus of 7,230 words used in elementary school textbooks was categorised into semantically related 'instructional clusters': 61 major clusters were identified, each with two levels of sub-clusters. In categorising phenomena such as words, the unfamiliar is rendered familiar. It has the added advantage that generalisation about a phenomenon based on knowledge of its category helps to extend knowledge about it.

In the light of current research and theorising concerning vocabulary, the authors identify the following guidelines from which effective practice can be derived.

> Wide reading and language rich activities should be the primary vehicles for vocabulary learning. Given the large number of words students encounter in written and oral language, general language development must be encouraged as one of the most important vocabulary development strategies.
>
> Direct vocabulary instruction should focus on words considered important to a given content area or to general background knowledge. Since effective direct vocabulary instruction requires a fair amount of time and complexity, teachers should select words for instruction that promise a high yield in student learning of general knowledge or of knowledge of a particular topic of instructional importance.
>
> Direct vocabulary instruction should include many ways of knowing a word and provide for the development of a complex level of word knowledge. Since word knowledge is stored in many forms (mental pictures, kinesthetic associations, smells, tastes, semantic distinctions, linguistic references) direct vocabulary instruction should take advantage of many of these forms and not emphasize one to the exclusion of others.
>
> Direct vocabulary instruction should include a structure by which new words not taught directly can be learned readily. Again, given the large number of words students encounter and the limited utility of direct instruction, some structure must be developed to allow the benefits of direct vocabulary instruction to go beyond the actual words taught.
>
> (Marzano and Marzano, 1988, pp. 11–12)

Making use of schema theory, the authors describe teaching strategies utilising semantic mapping (attribute comparison). The approach is seen as helping the teacher foster pupils' vocabulary knowledge and comprehension. The Marzanos' suggestions are interesting, practical and hold considerable promise.

ASSESSING TEXT READABILITIES

There are many other methods of calculating the readability of texts. Each has its particular strengths and weaknesses. Some are more appropriate to texts at particular difficulty levels. One advantage of trying out these formulae on texts being used in the classroom is that awareness of the aspects of language used can increase the teacher's sensitivity to specific aspects of language that affect text difficulty. Although these formulae have their uses, too much confidence should not be placed in the indices they provide. Readability scores can be useful, provided that the index is valid and the text being appraised is a suitable one in terms of content, structure and length. In many texts for young children, and for older pupils with reading difficulties, the text length is often too short and too contrived for a reliable assessment of difficulty to be made using certain of the available readability measures.

Even with suitable texts, readability scores provide only an approximation of text difficulty. Their accuracy is about plus or minus an American school grade, or year level in the English system. Children can, with assistance, or by dint of high interest in a topic, read texts whose difficulty levels may be above their reading ages. Pupils should not be denied access to texts they may wish to try to read because of a numerical mismatch between a readability measure and a child's measured reading attainments or estimated ability.

For example, consider the case of one junior school pupil who was carrying out a self-selected project on Louis Pasteur. After reading what was available in the school and in the local library, the boy wrote to the Pasteur Institute in Paris telling them of his work and asking for some information. The helpful letter he received in reply was in English. The informative materials that were enclosed were in French. Despite knowing very little French, the boy extracted a considerable amount of information from the French texts and illustrations that enriched his project. In theory, the readability level of the material in French vastly exceeded the boy's reading ability, but its content chimed with his particular enthusiasm at that stage. He learned a lot from the experience.

In general, the more the readability level of a text exceeds the reading level of the pupil, the greater the probability that the pupil will experience difficulties. The wider this gap, the more likely it is that the text will, in informal reading inventory terms, be at the *'frustration'* level. Such pupil–text interactions are particularly damaging to the motivation of pupils who experience difficulties in reading.

A valuable book on this topic discusses the nature of readability and the relationships between readability and comprehension (Harrison, 1980). The strengths of various measures, and particularly their limitations, are discussed. He also describes the use of 'cloze procedure' in text readability estimation. Guidelines are provided for the application of readability measures in the classroom at different age levels. The uses of readability information in writing texts is also considered.

Harrison presents, in tabular form, a summary of research data on nine popular measures of readability and ease of application. This is done using a variation on the *Which?* presentation technique. In addition, the reading age ranges over which six of the measures are most accurate has been incorporated. Information on the New Zealand Noun Count method has also been included (see Chapter 9). Table 4.1 is a modified version of Harrison's table.

Table 4.1 *Readability formulae*

	Validity	Age level accuracy (8–16 age-range)	Ease of application	Most reliable reading age range
Flesch formula (Grade score)	●●●●	●●●	●●	11–18
Fry graph	●●●●	●●●	●●●	5–18
Powers–Sumner–Kearl formula	●●●●	●	●●●	5.06–9.06
Mugford formula and chart	●●●●	●●●●	●●	5.06–13
FOG formula	●●●	●●	●●●●	
SMOG formula	●●●	●●	●●●●●	
Dale–Chall formula	●●●●●	●●●●	●	11–16
Spache formula	●●●●	●●	●●	5.06–13
FORCAST formula	●●	●●	●●●●	

Key: the more blobs the better.
Source: adapted from Harrison (1980).

Full details on the calculation of the above readability indices in Table 4.1 are given in Harrison (1980). In addition, details of a computer program to calculate text readability are presented in an appendix. The STAR program for readability estimation can produce the following range of information:

USA school grades level
- Dale Index (estimated)
- Flesch Grade Equivalent
- FOG (Frequency of gobbledegook) Index
- SMOG (Simple measure of gobbledegook)
- Powers–Sumner–Kearl
- FORCAST

- Reading ease scores
  These give a reading ease score out of 100. The higher the score, the easier the passage.

- Flesch index
- F–J–P index

- Fry graph co-ordinates
- Mugford difficulty index

The measurement of text readability has been in use for some 50 years. A recent publication presents an historical account of work in this area. It also describes measures that allow assignment of grade levels without using formulae (Zakaluk and Samuels, 1988). (In Chapter 9 of the present book, Southgate has suggested a means whereby this can be done using children of known reading attainments.) The final section outlines research aimed at developing more adequate ways of assessing text difficulty.

The Fry Readability Graph is one of the most widely used methods of assessing readability. It is now available in computerised format, but most teachers will find the version shown in Figure 4.1 (p. 192) of use.

Much more sophisticated means of textual analysis now exist than are represented in readability formulae such as those shown in Table 4.1, the list above, and Figure 4.1 (Blanchard et al., 1987). Their widespread use in schools gives them a currency that more complex recent developments have yet to achieve.

TEACHER ASSESSMENT

In December 1989, the School Examinations and Assessment Council (SEAC) published a package of INSET materials entitled *A Guide to Teacher Assessment*. It was distributed to all state schools in England and Wales early in 1990. From this brief description of the SEAC package it will be seen that some of it is central to teacher assessment in the classroom. The considerations apply to assessment in all curriculum subjects, of which reading is but one profile component in national curriculum English. The materials focus on key stages 1 and 2 for pupils aged from 5 to 11. The three major publications comprising the kit are listed here.

Pack A: *Teacher Assessment in the Classroom*

This is designed to assist class teachers of pupils in years 1 to 6 in developing strategies for the ongoing assessment of their pupils. It does this by capitalising on, clarifying and improving assessment skills within the context of existing schemes of work used in the classroom. The procedures suggested aim not to distort established

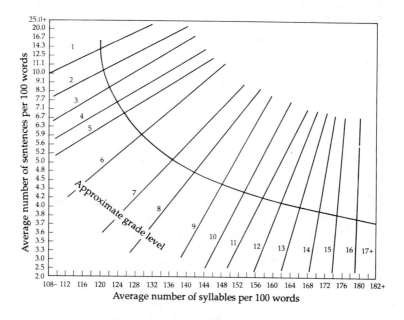

Expanded directions for working readability graph

1. Randomly select three (3) sample passages and count out exactly 100 words each, beginning with the beginning of a sentence. Do count proper nouns, initialisations, and numerals.

2. Count the number of sentences in the hundred words, estimating length of the fraction of the last sentence to the nearest one-tenth.

3. Count the total number of syllables in the 100-word passage. If you don't have a hand counter available, an easy way is simply to put a mark above every syllable over one in each word, then when you get to the end of the passage, count the number of marks and add 100. Small calculators can also be used as counters by pushing numeral 1, then push the + sign for each word or syllable when counting.

4. Enter graph with *average* sentence length and *average* number of syllables; plot dot where the two lines intersect. Area where dot is plotted will give you the approximate grade level.

5. If a great deal of variability is found in syllable count or sentence count, putting more samples into the average is desirable.

6. A word is defined as a group of symbols with a space on either side; thus, *Joe, IRA, 1945* and *&* are each one word.

7. A syllable is defined as a phonetic syllable. Generally, there are as many syllables as vowel sounds. For example, *stopped* is one syllable and *wanted* is two syllables. When counting syllables for numerals and initialisations, count one syllable for each symbol. For example, *1945* is four syllables, *IRA* is three syllables, and *&* is one syllable.

Figure 4.1 *Graph for estimating readability – extended (Fry, 1972)*

and continuing sound teaching and learning objectives. The acronym INFORM summarises the six steps whereby achievement in relation to attainment targets (ATs) and their component statements of attainments (SoA) can be used to assess and facilitate a pupil's progress through the national curriculum.

I = identify the SoA the lesson plan is designed to promote;

N = note situations in which the pupil can demonstrate achievement;

F = focus on the pupil's performance based on evidence of achievement;

O = offer the pupil opportunity to discuss the purpose of the activity and what was achieved;

R = record noteworthy aspects of the pupil's learnings;

M = modify the teaching programme for the individual, if required, in order to further progress.

'The guide has been designed to minimise demands on teachers' time over and above normal classroom practice, and Pack A taken with Pack C . . . is distinctive as a personal resource for the individual teacher.'

Pack B: *Teacher Assessment in the School*

Whilst this pack is intended particularly for headteachers and curriculum co-ordinators, it concerns the whole staff. The materials emphasise the development of a whole-school assessment policy through a programme of staff workshops. The six professional development activities from Pack A, plus a further two concerned with 'within-school' agreement trials, are included.

Pack C: *A Source Book of Teacher Assessment*

This consists of nine chapters each addressing systematically key assessment issues relating to the national curriculum. Pack C also includes case study materials that can be used in support of Packs A and B. Suggestions for the development of the essential recording, reporting and 'within-school' moderation of assessments are presented.

The SEAC overview of its assessment pack is reproduced in Figure 4.2.

Examples of trial development materials related to reading and writing set within a theme of 'Change' are included in the pack. The reading-related activity enables assessments of children to be made at national curriculum levels 1, 2 and 3. The particular extract included from the broader topic is aimed at pupils whom the teacher considers to be at, or nearing, level 3 in reading. Based on a

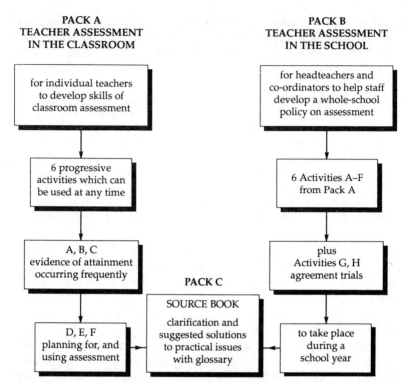

Figure 4.2 *A guide to teacher assessment: an overview (SEAC, 1989)*

specially written story, 'Supergoats', it builds on earlier opportunities that the pupils will have had of hearing and reading the story prior to this particular assessment. The sample material consists of instructions to the teacher, which involve discussions of the content by a group of four pupils with the teacher in attendance. Each pupil is then asked to read aloud a favourite part of the story. The pupil's fluency and expression when reading are assessed (not an easy thing to do reliably and validly). Comprehension is then assessed by asking each pupil at least *one* of six questions. If these instructions are carefully followed by teachers using the materials, it is claimed that assessment can be carried out consistently over a number of schools. The claim is important and will, in the fullness of time, be put to empirical test.

The SEAC assessment material has been developed by the Standard Tests and Assessment Implementation Research (STAIR) consortium which is based in the University of Manchester School of Education. This is a research group charged with developing standard assessment tasks in English, and other subjects, for key stage 1. In preparing the SEAC assessment pack, STAIR has drawn on its experience of early work on the development of standard assessment tasks for key stage 1.

STAIR is one of three consortia each developing somewhat differing approaches to standard assessment tasks (SATs). The other two are the Consortium for Assessment and Testing in Schools (CATS) and the National Foundation for Educational Research (NFER). SATs are intended to allow teachers to assess pupils' progress and attainments in relation to the attainment targets set in the national curriculum. SATs will be administered by class teachers. They will allow teachers to establish similar classroom activities and contexts within which the pupils' work can be assessed on a 'standard basis in the last term of each key stage' (SEAC, 1989).

As might have been expected in view of its importance, the SEAC INSET materials received a somewhat critical reception. The importance given to the principle of continuous, formative assessment of pupils' development as a means of planning and supporting learning is generally welcomed by teachers. The means whereby this is to be achieved in the national curriculum are considered more questionable. It has been argued that the statements of attainment (SoAs) are accorded too much importance in the scheme of assessment. The SoA-led approach in the packs contrasts with the teacher's formative assessment. The sheer amount of recording that might be required is also daunting. Taking the three core subjects of English, maths, and science and technology, at key stage 1 there are 39 attainment targets and 228 SoAs. To assess 30 pupils at key stage 1, the class teacher has to carry out 6,840 separate assessments. In English, at levels 1, 2 and 3, there are five attainment targets. At levels 1, 2 and 3 there are 12, 21 and 20 SoAs respectively. In relation to 'Reading' alone, there are 4, 6 and 7 SoAs at the three levels. HM Inspectorate has suggested that teachers are likely to need some 10 per cent of their time away from pupils for assessment and recording. For the many junior school teachers to whom the concept of 'free periods' is only theoretical, the resource implications for their schools are considerable. The subsequent reductions in assessment demands are specified below (pp. 201–2).

In summary, on the one hand these criticisms suggest that assessment using SoAs is insufficiently sensitive to map and facilitate a child's progress; on the other hand it is argued that the use of the available SoAs is too time-demanding. Perhaps even more worrying is the possibility that the 'wash-back' effect of an SoAs-based assessment procedure could lead to an impoverished curriculum and to the neglect of pupils who fared relatively poorly. This could well include pupils whose standards and progress in reading were low and/or slow respectively.

The first criticism might be countered by the argument that the problem can be resolved by the development of cross-curricular profile components. Further, as is described in Chapter 9, the Secretary of State is concerned about the high demands that assessment might make on teachers' time and energies. Clearly, he will not wish to see these become excessive. In relation to the second criticism, the director of the STAIR consortium considers that the progress of each pupil in a class on every one of the 39 current attainment targets can be carried out approximately once every two terms by devoting about five minutes to work with a child once a fortnight, based on continuing classroom activities. Even if one accepts these estimates, what will happen as the other subjects in the national curriculum come 'on stream' and have to be assessed, recorded and reported? It has also been pointed out that with 30 pupils in a mixed-ability primary school class, possibly spread over two or more year groups and allowing each pupil 5 minutes per week undivided attention, there are 1.25 hours per week when the remaining 29 pupils are unsupervised. This argument has been used to press for non-contact time for all primary school teachers to carry out the assessments required. The counter-argument is that the required observations, assessments and teaching are integrated. Even if this is accepted, the recording of observations and assessments, and the consideration of their curricular implications, represent an increased workload for teachers. Without reflection on what has been observed, the entire endeavour is suspect. These activities cannot all be done contiguous with class teaching. The third criticism remains unanswered. As noted earlier, the previous 'national curriculum' adopted in England and Wales, the system of 'payment by results' legally established in 1862, had an adverse effect on both the curriculum and on pupils who were the least likely to make progress in the subjects on which the school's standards, public esteem, funding and teachers' salaries depended. Interestingly, that system was also based on criterion-referenced testing. Why was it abandoned? History may well never repeat itself. It is to be hoped that we can learn from the past, but the advent of LMS suggests that a spiral political curriculum may be governing the educational agenda. It is vital that teachers ensure that the tail of assessment does not wag the curriculum dog. This is certainly *not* the intention of either the SEAC's or the NCC's philosophy and policies. Despite this, it could be a consequence of their proposals, unless teachers remain vigilant. For everyone who wishes the national curriculum to be a great success,

Kay-Shuttleworth's detailed comments on the consequences of introducing the Revised Code and its associated assessment procedures should be required reading (Kay-Shuttleworth, 1873).

Returning to the Education Reform Act 1988, concern has also been expressed that the equal opportunities assessment issues related to ethnic group and gender are not discussed in the SEAC pack. Bilingual children are identified as having special educational needs and some superficial advice given on what the teacher can do to ensure valid assessments (Kanji, 1990).

During spring 1990, regional conferences were organised by the SEAC on behalf of LEAs. These conferences were to help teachers consider the national curriculum assessment requirements and procedures up to the first unreported assessment of pupils that will be made in 1991 (see timetable given on p. 162).

The national curriculum involves many levels of decision-making, teaching plans, assessment recording and reporting. These are indicated in Table 4.2. The groups listed in column A are *all* concerned with columns B and C activities, but have different responsibilities.

Table 4.2 *The national curriculum: standard assessment tasks linking teaching and assessment*

A. Levels of decision-making	B. Teaching plans	C. Assessment, recording and reporting	

National bodies
  Department of Education and Science (DES)
  National Curriculum Council (NCC)
  School Examinations and Assessment Council (SEAC)
Local education authorities
Governors
Headteachers
Teachers
Parents
Pupils
	Curriculum policy document
	Programmes of study (PoS)
	Schemes of work
	Teaching plan
	Lesson plans
		Records of achievement
		Subjects
		Profile components (PC)
		Attainment targets (AT)
		Statements of attainment (SoA)
			Standard assessment tasks (SATs)

STANDARD ASSESSMENT TASKS (SATs): PILOT STUDIES

The three consortia that have developed standard assessment tasks (SATs) carried out a pilot study in the summer term, 1990. 23,000 7-year-old pupils attending 641 schools drawn from 51 LEAs were involved in these trials. This sample comprised over 2 per cent of the age group. On the basis of these pilot studies, decisions will be made by the SEAC on the nature of the SATs that will be used nationally in the summer term 1991. The SEAC is likely to report on the three pilot studies towards the end of 1990.

All three SAT developers accept that the assessments must be consonant with current primary school teaching styles and practices. The content is determined by the subject specifications in the national curriculum. The search is for a mode, or modes, of SAT that will satisfy the criteria specified by the SEAC when the contracts were issued. Together with teachers' own assessments of individual pupils, SATs are designed to cover all 32 attainment targets for pupils at the end of key stage 1 in the three core subjects. Administration of SATs will take place during the summer term and will take up to five weeks.

It must also be possible for the rest of the class to be taught whilst a particular pupil is being assessed. The challenge was to develop SATs that were meaningful to teachers, pupils and parents and did not make undue demands on the class teacher's time. If this point is accepted, it is unlikely that SATs can be based on statements of attainment in each profile component of each subject for each pupil. This will be a key policy decision for the SEAC when the approved SAT format is finalised. Doubtless the Secretary of State's comments on this issue made in March 1990 will have been noted by those who will be making decisions on the form that the finally approved SATs should take. There are justified fears that the combined effects of additional workloads on teachers, staff shortages, and low morale, exacerbated by the many uncertainties inherent in the early stages of LMS, could undermine the anticipated beneficial consequence of the national curriculum (see pp. 22–4 and Chapter 9). Given the combination of the severely restricted time scale within which the three consortia were working, together with differing views between the consortia on how *educationally* reliable and valid assessments can be achieved, it is almost inevitable that the SAT system eventually approved by the SEAC will be controversial.

Both the NFER and the Consortium for Assessment and Testing in Schools (CATS) saw SAT administration as forming part of the normal teaching programme. They are reported as stating that this would *not* mean 'lots of extra work for teachers' (Hofkins, 1990a). In contrast, the head of the Standard Test and Implementation Research (STAIR) reported that teachers who had been piloting STAIR SATs were spending between five and nine hours filling in the pupil reports required by government. It was believed that, as with *any* class work, teachers would have to work outside class time in order to prepare and mark the SATs to be used within their classes. An estimate of about an hour a day during the assessment period was considered likely by the STAIR project.

The NFER and the CATS consortia are reported as having concentrated on differentiation by educational outcome between pupils in relation to their standards and progress. Each pupil would complete the same SATs and the standard of the work they produced would demonstrate their level of attainment. In contrast, the STAIR system was deliberately devised so that it could be tailored by the teacher for each child. Despite this, pupils' performances still have to be assessed, recorded and reported against the ten levels of attainment approved by the SEAC.

The contrast appears, at this stage, between relatively simple assessment systems that *may* allow clearer inter-individual assessments (NFER and CATS) and one (STAIR) that deliberately reduces direct comparisons between pupils on educational grounds. The STAIR consortium considers that their proposed SATs will be more educationally motivating and informative to all parties involved. Contrasting approaches emphasising normative comparisons are seen as historically and inevitably demotivating to a considerable proportion of *any* group of pupils.

At present, the assumption is that the standardised national assessments will be teacher controlled, involving external moderation under specified conditions. Whatever decisions are made by the SEAC concerning the SATs to be adopted, the success of the system will depend on the class teacher. It is therefore essential that the SEAC's recommendations should be seen as educationally consistent with encouraging pupils in their learning, irrespective of relative attainments and progress. The very last thing that will improve reading standards in schools is to demotivate *any* pupils or teachers by virtue of the SATs adopted. By 21 May 1990, considerable disquiet had been expressed about the unrealistic demands on teachers' time and energies made by the pilot SATs. At least one LEA was reported as abandoning the procedure after four of the five weeks scheduled for the activity. The SEAC will have some difficult decisions to make in 1991.

Table 4.2 on p. 197 summarises seven levels of involvement in the development and implementation of the national curriculum, together with major concerns of various groups. The levels of decision-making interact. The content, form, recording and reporting of the standards and progress in reading (as one profile component in the English curriculum) at national, LEA, school and individual pupil levels, will be determined by the interactions alluded to. The situation is highly dynamic. The perfect is the enemy of the better. A timetable has been set. The teaching profession will

continue its accepted and vital role in improving standards of literacy.

At the 1990 Annual Conference of the National Association of Headteachers, the disquiet of members of the profession involved in the SAT trial work for key stage 1 assessments was clearly stated. Mrs Pat Moss, a headteacher from Rotherham LEA, expressed that concern by reference to her own school's experience. The letter subsequently sent by all the school staff and the governors to John MacGregor, the Secretary of State for Education, Margaret Thatcher, the Prime Minister, Jack Straw, MP, the Shadow Secretary of State for Education, and also to their local MP, summarised legitimate professional concerns. The letter, and reaction to it, received considerable publicity. The issues raised are central to the relationship between assessment and teaching in the improvement of standards of, and progress by, pupils in the subjects of the national curriculum.

Two teachers, each with 30 Year 2 pupils in their class, were required to make 176 assessments for each child. The time required for each assessment ranged from ten minutes to over an hour. The teachers had to work up to 30 hours per week out of school time on SAT-related work that was seen by them as educationally suspect and not providing an adequate return for the efforts, materials, time and resources it demanded. Over the almost five weeks spent on the pilot work, it is reported that the pupils' work and behaviour deteriorated. The time that the class teacher had to spend on the assessment of pupils often resulted in the other members of the class failing to receive the teaching they required. The letter referred to earlier said:

> ... SATs do not truly reflect the child's ability ... they simply confirm the teacher's own prior assessment ... SATs have not provided us with any new information about any child's ability or needs ... Schools simply do not have the money to provide the books, equipment and people to support such assessments ... In view of our serious concerns, we ask you to reconsider seriously the present proposals for the assessment and testing of year two pupils ...

The letter also contained constructive suggestions concerning how assessments could be carried out in educationally valid ways.

In her address to the Conference, Mrs Moss stated 'If next year's SATs in any way resemble the pilot ones, my conscience and my principles will not allow me to let them take place and I will be fully prepared to take any consequences for such action' (Moss, 1990, pp. 30–1).

The official response was that the SAT pilot studies were

intended to identify legitimate concerns about the uses of SATs. These could then be rectified in the procedures and materials developed for the final versions.

Even if confined to the assessments affecting the programme of study in English, or those concerned with reading attainments and progress, the criticisms were still valid.

As mentioned earlier, there were originally three consortia involved in developing SATs for key stage 1. Whilst the criticisms made of the pilot SATs at the NAHT conference were derived from experience with only one consortium, there were headteachers attending who were involved in pilot work with the other two. Professional support for any of these pilot schemes was less than enthusiastic.

Despite this lack of enthusiasm, SAT assessments can be made both educationally valid and useful. It will be interesting to see whether this is achieved in the ridiculously tight straitjacket of an implementation timetable that the government has imposed upon itself, its advisers and the teaching profession. There are times when the virtues of speed in implementing changes are offset by the vices of inadequately devised strategies.

In the event, the contract for developing the standard assessment tasks for key stage 1 was awarded to the NFER/Bishop Grosseteste College consortium. Their contract runs until March 1992 and will cost £909,000. It is anticipated that the new SATs will include elements from the three versions piloted in 1989–90. The major lesson that appears to have been learned is that the complexities of the pilot SATs demanded far too much teachers' time. An even more serious criticism was the questionable utility of the information elicited in relation to its costs.

The expense of this revelation exemplifies ineptitude of the highest order on the part of those responsible for the specifications of the initial contracts prepared by SEAC. By the time that this book is in print, the first unreported application of the approved SATs will have been carried out. It is to be hoped that what is produced and used avoids the criticisms mentioned above.

The SATs for key stage 1 have been dramatically cut. The number of attainment targets has been reduced from 32 across the core subjects of English, maths and science to only nine. Despite this reduction, teachers are still going to be very busy! They will be required to make up to 50 assessments for each pupil. For a class of 30 pupils, this involves 1,500 assessments. Each of these is approximately equivalent to a statement of attainment – the 'building bricks' from which the attainment targets are constructed. As the key stage 1 SATs cover three levels of attainment and include some 80 statements of attainment, the consortium developing the final versions will have to find means of capitalising on classroom work and teachers' knowledge of their pupils' attainments. In addition, they have been requested to provide guidance on classroom management, small schools, children who are not fluent in English, minimising stress amongst pupils and ways of reassuring those pupils who do not succeed on a task.

In relation to English, the attainment target 'Speaking and Listening' has been omitted, on the grounds that these aspects of language are difficult to assess in the context of a SAT. Pupils attending Welsh-speaking schools will be tested in Welsh, rather than English. Because the Welsh Office and SEAC consider that promoting the speaking and hearing of Welsh is an integral part of Welsh schools, speaking and listening will be tested rather than reading, which will be covered by teacher assessments.

The instructions to the consortium require that the SATs should be manageable by a teacher with a class of 30 pupils and neither additional help from adults nor extra equipment.

As in the pilot studies, the 1991 SATs will consist of activities which the pupils will carry out. Teachers will have greater flexibility in conducting the SATs than in the pilot studies. Whilst a programme of work will be suggested, teachers will be allowed to integrate these activities with ongoing classroom work. The SATs can be administered at any time during the first half of the summer term.

According to a recent report, the SATs will take 40 hours for a class of 30 pupils (Hofkins, 1990a, 1990b). Separate reading tests will have added 10 additional hours. Teachers will spend up to 20 minutes hearing each individual pupil read and discussing the reading with them.

The attainment targets in English that will be covered by the SAT have been reduced to the following four. They are linked to *examples* of the skills children will be required to demonstrate. The average seven-year-old pupil will be expected to achieve level 2, and the eleven-year-old, level 4.

ENGLISH

Reading

Level
1. Begin to recognise individual words or letters, such as shop signs or 'bus stop'; talk in simple terms about story content.
2. Use pictures, context and phonic cues in reading; read something without help from the teacher and talk with confidence about it.
3. Read familiar stories aloud with expression.

Writing

Level
1. Use pictures, symbols or isolated letters, words or phrases to communicate meaning.
2. Write stories with a beginning, characters and events.
3. Begin to revise and redraft work.

Spelling

Level
1. Use single letters or groups of letters to represent words.
2. Produce recognisable spelling of common words.
3. Make use of regular patterns for vowel sounds and strings of letters (ing, ion, ous).

Handwriting

Level
1. Begin to form letters with some control.
2. Produce capital and lower-case letters.
3. Begin joined-up writing.

In relation to the assessment of reading, teachers will be given a choice of texts to be read with the pupils. These texts will include currently available books and specially constructed materials. It was the view of SEAC that the administration of individual reading tests did not fit easily into the SAT timetable.

COMMENT

The assessment, teaching and learning of reading are three sides of the same triangle. Primary school teachers are more familiar and generally happier about the latter two than the first. Recently, there has been a move towards an increasing use of criterion-referenced reading tests. These are seen by teachers as having clearer educational implications for pupils' reading programmes than normative reading tests. The appreciation that every criterion-referenced reading test has a normative aspect, and vice versa, should moderate undue enthusiasm for one type only. Whilst in England and Wales the development of various standard assessment tasks related to the national curriculum is in hand, new systems for linking the testing and teaching of reading are constantly under development across the world.

Section C
Responses II: Promising Practices

5

Interventions: materials, methods and techniques

INTRODUCTION

The largest and most powerful organisation in the world of professionals concerned with the promotion of literacy is the International Reading Association. (This gives the initials 'IRA' a different significance for readers in the UK.) The headquarters of the Association is in Newark, Delaware, USA. In Britain, the United Kingdom Reading Association (UKRA) is an affiliated body. The services these two organisations offer their members are exceptional value for money, as members of either will concur. Those who are members of neither are missing out! Apart from the value of their activities to their members, the clients whom professionals serve are also beneficiaries of the professional development that both organisations foster.

At the respective annual conventions of the IRA and the UKRA, publishers vie to present their latest products to those attending. The sheer number and variety of offerings is breathtaking. These range from the most basic of materials to the most sophisticated uses of information technology. The impression is easily gained that somewhere in this cornucopia of materials, methodologies and technologies are the ingredients from which either the – or several – 'reading-difficulty-free diet(s)' could be blended. The professionals' ultimate goal of being able to ensure that every child becomes literate and that we can truly become a nation of readers, yearly appears a little nearer, albeit temporarily.

Attendance at the annual conferences of, for example, the United Kingdom Reading Association or The National Association for Remedial Education, a visit to an LEA language and literacy resource centre or the examination of the publishers' catalogues that are sent to all junior schools, underline this point. The plethora of methods, materials and techniques available is clear evidence that no single one or any 'cocktail' yet known, has demonstrated an efficacy that meets the objective of improving the reading attainments of *all* pupils. In view of the complexities of reading development outlined in Chapters 1 and 2, this is hardly surprising.

These annual offerings are, nonetheless, very important. They are more than a tribute to the ingenuity of research workers, practitioners and enthusiasts. Only a cynic would say that they represented the triumph of hope over experience. The aims of conceptualising, predicting and controlling reading development are advancing. What is *already* known could markedly increase children's reading skills, provided society was willing to accord that objective both the priority and the financial resources such a challenge demands. At present, the end is desired, but the means are denied.

Those interested in this endeavour need to be aware of both theoretical developments and their applications in reading centres, classrooms and the community. Whilst it is clear that there is no simple, single panacea, it is highly likely that the right 'mix' at the right time for a given individual could already be better identified than is typically done in practice. But how can these 'mixes', these effective aptitude × instruction interactions, be more clearly identified?

The research techniques involved in their identification are known: the pedagogic expertise is available. The psychological principles informing the identification of such 'mixes' have yet to be worked out in detail, though some promising lines have been identified. Being aware of developments in the pedagogy of teaching and learning reading is essential. Being aware of what is *already* available, in use and effective, is one of the necessary conditions for further progress.

The search for effective methods, materials and techniques continues. It requires that claims for efficacy be based on empirical evidence. This is easily said but less readily accomplished. Over 60 years ago, the editor of the (then) *Manchester Guardian* stated that 'Comment is free but facts are sacred'. In the context of reading, assertion is free: evidence is expensive (and rarely unequivocal). Despite this, it is important for junior school teachers to be aware of the variety of approaches and equally important that they bring to bear critical acumen in appraising materials and the evidence adduced in their support.

The following four chapters represent a personal overview and selection. The fields from which these selections have been made are vast. They are also continuously developing. The ideas presented have both considerable current utility and potential for improving children's reading, but the crux is finding which ones, combinations, or variations help which individuals at which stage in reading development. To solve a problem it is essential to know what resources we already have to hand.

WHAT WORKS: RESEARCH FINDINGS ABOUT READING, ITS TEACHING AND LEARNING – LESSONS FOR TEACHERS

Research-based advice on improving children's reading merits the consideration of professionals and parents. Two American publications are of particular interest. The first is *Becoming a Nation of Readers: The Report of the Commission on Reading* (Anderson et al., 1985). The Commission brought together findings from a vast amount of research into the development of reading and the conditions that encourage effective reading. To make these findings accessible to a wider audience, the results of the Commission's endeavours were condensed into two slim documents (28 pp. and 22 pp.). The first booklet identified the major implications of the report for teachers; the second summarises what parents can do to help their children become competent readers (Binkley, 1986, 1988: see below, pp. 227–40). Another valuable source is *What Works: Research about Teaching and Learning* (US Department of Education, 1986: see Chapter 9, pp. 312–16).

The booklet in which implications for teachers are described is divided into five sections, each dealing with instructional themes and providing examples of research-based pedagogy.

Five research-based key characteristics of effective reading are identified. These indicate the goals towards which teachers help all their pupils move and they have important pedagogic implications:

- Skilled reading is a constructive process in which information from the text and the knowledge possessed by the reader combine to produce meaning.
- Skilled reading is fluent. Decoding text should become automatic, rapid and accurate in order to enable the writer's meaning to be reconstructed by the reader.
- Skilled reading is strategic in that the nature of the text, the reader's familiarity with the topic and the reader's purpose in reading are all involved.
- Skilled reading is motivated by pupils appreciating both the utility and the enjoyment that the activity can bring.
- Skilled reading is a continuing endeavour for all. It is a skill that continues to develop and improve with practice.

Research has shown that early experience in talking and learning about activities and using written language is helpful in developing reading skills. Reading-readiness activities can build on children's oral language.

- The child who is unready for systematic instruction requires a wide range of opportunities to use and develop oral and printed language plus encouragement of and opportunities to write.

Activities that are suggested include the following:

- The children listen daily to the teacher read aloud and discuss stories.
- The teacher records on the blackboard collaborative stories dictated by a group of pupils.
- Ninety per cent of children entering kindergarten believe that they can write, but only 15 per cent believe that they can read. The encouragement of daily individual writing by pupils helps them learn about the relationships between expressive and receptive aspects of language.
- The classroom must be an environment rich in print in many forms, ranging from a plentiful and varied supply of reading books to the labelling of a variety of objects and pictures in order to strengthen the association between referents and their symbolic representation in print.
- Class discussion of events will help develop pupils' confidence in using oral language. Such discussion encourages reflection, hypothesising, and justifying adopted positions. The process can extend children's understanding of concepts and their associated vocabulary.

In the beginning stages of learning to read, the importance of implicit and explicit phonemic awareness is recognised. It should begin early (Bryant and Bradley, 1985; Bryant, 1990; Bradley, 1990; Cataldo and Ellis, 1990; Snowling, 1990). It can also be of value to somewhat older children who have been unsuccessful (Cashdan and Wright, 1990). The objective of such work is to help the child appreciate that there are systematic relationships between letters and sounds.

- Phonics instruction should focus on the most important and regular letter-to-sound relationships. By doing this, the teacher helps the child generate approximate pronunciations of words that can be checked against the child's own oral lexicon. Because meaning is always of the essence in any reading at any stage between the completely unskilled and the highly competent reader, phonics instruction must be done using meaningful materials. Children at the earliest stages of beginning reading can read meaningful materials provided the teacher uses some basic techniques. The importance of rhyme, rhythm and repetition are well recognised in the uses made of nursery rhymes and imaginative 'nonsense' rhymes.

- 'Assisted reading' comes in many forms (see pp. 233–42). The practice involves a more competent reader providing help to a less competent one. This helps the pupil to develop confidence in reading through successful practice. The pupil may be asked to repeat a word, phrase or sentence that the teacher has read. This is followed by both simultaneously reading the textual material. Then the pupil reads the material unaccompanied. Provided the text used is related to the phonetic skills that the teacher wishes the pupil to master, the pupil will have had three successful encounters with text during which the alphabetic principle will have been reinforced.
- Encouraging pupils to write using invented spellings facilitates the pupil's use of the alphabetic principle. Typically, initial and ending consonants begin to be used conventionally. The links between the development of reading and spelling in the development of literacy demonstrate that the two complex processes are not identical but have relationships that are pedagogically important, as shown in Figure 5.1 (Ehri, 1985; Frith, 1985): see also Chapter 2.

Planned reading lessons (known as 'directed reading lessons') represent the most frequently used lesson format. Such lessons typically have three stages, known as the preparation, reading and discussion stages. It is well established that the first of these is particularly helpful in improving children's reading comprehension yet classroom observations show that this stage is often given insufficient attention. Research suggests that when teachers give time to building up the background to a text, pupils are helped to focus on the important semantic aspects, with a consequent significant improvement in reading comprehension. Background development and direction-setting activities help pupils to think more clearly about textual materials. The principle that reading is a thinking process must never be neglected. The following strategies have been shown to be effective:

- Provide an advance organiser that gives in summary form an overview of the text content and themes.
- Get the pupils thinking about text by presenting questions, as in sequencing, predicting and justifying events described in the text.
- Where appropriate, encourage pupils to adopt the perspective of one of the actors (or elements) in a text.

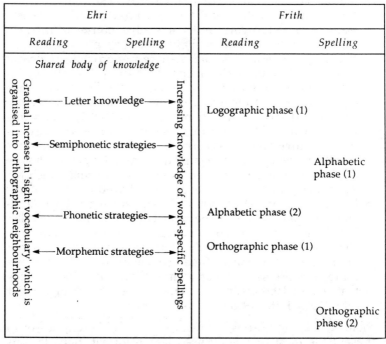

Figure 5.1 *Theories of the development of orthographic knowledge by Ehri (1985) and Frith (1985)*

- Ask, and stimulate pupils to ask, questions about important thematic aspects of a text.

Turning to the second stage, that of reading, the following strategies are supported by research as being helpful:

- Pupils should read a text silently before they read it aloud. This practice improves oral reading fluency.
- Oral reading by the pupil provides the teacher with important insights into the reader's strengths and weaknesses when interacting with a particular text. Ensuring that the pupil–text match is at either the instructional or independent level is one important piece of information. Additionally, an analysis of the pattern of the pupil's oral reading errors (miscue analysis) can help the teacher understand more adequately the strategies that the child brings to bear on the text.
- By the time that children are at junior 2 or 3 (national curricu-

lum years 4–6) they should be engaging in extended silent reading for a minimum of two hours weekly.

- In listening to children reading a text that is at the instructional level, miscues or 'mistakes' that do not disrupt the meaning of the text should, in the main, be ignored.

- If the miscue does adversely affect the meaning of what is being read, wait to see whether the child will correct this by him/herself. If they do not, the teacher should draw the child's attention to clues concerning the meaning of certain words, and/or the syntax of the passage, that will encourage the child to reread and rethink what he or she is reading aloud. This is where the art of the effective teacher is highlighted as the cues provided will be dependent on the nature of the miscue.

- After clarifying the miscue and, for example, correctly identifying a word, the child should reread the sentence to recover and reinforce its meaning.

Care must be taken to ensure that the time spent on oral reading is distributed effectively. How can this be done in a classroom? One advantage of the traditional and once very common 'round-robin' reading is that it allows each pupil an equal opportunity. It prevents the more assertive children from dominating the scene and the teacher's time. However, the 'round-robin' approach does not help fluency or comprehension. Nor does it resolve the perennial professional dilemma of what constitutes 'fair treatment' of pupils in a class whose individual pupils' reading attainments range from levels well above their chronological ages to markedly below. Evidence indicates that children who do not find reading easy, but have been encouraged and enabled to reread repeatedly and master a text, have markedly improved their speed, accuracy and expression during oral reading. Additionally, they have improved their comprehension during silent reading.

Repeated practice, until textual material has been mastered and an acceptable degree of fluency reached, can be accomplished by adopting techniques such as the following.

- Children practise silently and then read aloud to the teacher.
- Individuals can read accompanied by taped materials (e.g. ARROW; see Chapter 8).
- Pairs of pupils can take turns in reading aloud to one another.
- Small groups of pupils can read aloud together with an adult, or with a tape.
- Choral reading can be used to provide an experience of the importance of intonation, expression and pace.

The discussion stage of the directed reading lesson typically involves group discussion of the whole story, the development of ideas and knowledge, followed by further individual or group reading and/or writing tasks. Children starting to learn to read, and children of all ages who have reading difficulties, frequently fail to recognise connections between what they are reading and what they already know. It is activities that capitalise on what the pupils already know, whether it be content or 'how to do it' information, that are central to the development of their reading skills.

During the discussion stage, the teacher can further pupils' understanding and reading by a range of strategies:

- The use of judicious questions helps children identify and select information within the text and integrate this with that which they already 'own'. Such questions are usually open-ended ones to which there are no ready right or wrong answers. To deal with such questions, the pupil has to generate hypotheses and put together many pieces of information that test these hypotheses.
- Using direct instruction, it is possible to teach children how to think critically whilst they are reading. They can be taught to vary their style of reading dependent on the purposes of the reading and the demands of the text. Whereas good readers appear to discover such strategies with minimal assistance, beginning readers and slow readers typically require considerable help in developing such flexibility in reading style. When such instruction is provided, all readers make marked improvement.
- Teachers can 'model' how they set about making sense of written material. 'Reciprocal teaching' is a group strategy whereby the teacher shows the pupils how to monitor their understanding of a text. This is done by showing them how to devise questions about the passage, summarise the text, predict what will follow, identify inconsistencies and resolve them. Subsequently, in turn, each pupil adopts the role of teacher and asks the other members of the group questions about the text, identifies aspects of the text that appear confusing and gets the group to clarify these. In essence, the pupils adopt the role of teacher in monitoring each other's understanding of text.
- Informed strategies for learning involve teaching pupils different reading techniques for different reading tasks. They are taught why the strategies are useful, the circumstances when they can be employed and how to develop the skills. The importance of such approaches is reinforced by the use of

metaphors such as 'Be a Reading Detective' and 'Road Signs for Reading'.

Often it is not necessary to read every word in a text to obtain the information required. The use of a telephone book is one example. The ability rapidly to find one small piece of information is called scanning. Scanning is a skill that is picked up readily by most children but others, who perceive reading as a word-by-word sounding-out process, can find it difficult. The basic technique for teaching scanning is to set the pupils a limited time to find a specific piece of information in a suitable piece of text that all have read. Three types of scanning of increasing difficulty level are usually taught:

scanning for a piece of specific information that stands out clearly, such as a date in history, or the name of a city;

scanning for an answer that is worded similarly to the question; and

scanning for an answer worded differently from the question.

The skill of scanning is highly useful for finding specific facts rapidly.

- Skimming is a related technique whereby the reader tries to get the gist of a passage rather than finding a specific answer to a specific question; the strategy is often used when deciding whether a particular library book is one that the reader wishes to borrow. Skimming is often used to preview material before reading it carefully. In reading the initial paragraph of a book, the list of contents and the final paragraph, the reader is skimming.
- When teaching skimming, the teacher has to provide questions and tasks that encourage selective reading and not slow, careful reading. Questions such as 'What is the book about?', 'Is there any interesting information in it?' and 'Will it help you in your current project?' can be used to encourage skim reading.
- Children can be encouraged to form reading clubs. Teams can play competitive games that encourage reading. The author has seen such clubs operating successfully in Israel and in the UK.
- With training and support, junior school children are perfectly capable of running a school library efficiently. Such book-related activities should involve as many pupils as possible. *Children and Books* contains an excellent account of some early work carried out in this field in a large junior school (Cutforth and Battersby, 1962).

Many teachers also use a variety of workbooks and 'skill sheets' as follow-up or consolidation exercises forming part of the directed reading lesson. It is reported that 70 per cent of the time allocated to reading instruction is used in such activities. Workbooks and skill sheets have been used as a classroom management technique. Whilst the teacher works with one group, the other pupils are engaged in workbook activities. It is claimed that analyses of workbook materials show that many demand only a low level of reading. Readers are rarely required to draw conclusions or reason at more than the simplest level. Much of the content provides exercises that have little value in learning to read. Classroom research suggests that the amount of time spent on worksheets is unrelated to year-by-year gains in reading skills.

Alternative activities have been recommended. These should meet the following criteria:

The activity should allow either individual work or co-operative endeavour.

The reading activities should be based on meaningful units of text.

The associated writing activities should require the pupil to communicate a complete message. Reading and replying to letters and making enquiries for significant information that is in written form are examples.

- The provision of a rich reading environment, including a wide variety of books, at many levels of difficulty and interest, is associated with higher standards of reading. The value of children being encouraged and helped to keep a systematic record of their reading and their opinions concerning what they have read, provides a rich basis for discussion in the classroom. Work done during the Bradford Book Flood attests to the importance that the use of such records can have (Pumfrey, 1988b).

Clearly, writing and reading are mutually reinforcing activities. There is little doubt that the punctuation and syntax of a language are readily made explicit and more rapidly learned when pupils are engaged in writing (and reading) messages that have a psychological significance to the author. This means that the message must be addressed to an audience: even if the audience is the author and the writing a personal diary. The following activities have been found helpful in improving both reading and writing.

- As used in schools, dialogue journals are personal records of a dialogue between the pupil and the teacher. The teacher is required to respond to every entry but to make no correction, revision or evaluation of what the pupil has written. The pupil writes whatever he or she is interested in. The teacher's replies contain reactions including comments, questions and thoughts concerning the content of the pupil's notes. Suitably phrased comments, coupled with open-ended questions, encourage the pupil to expand and elaborate his or her ideas.

- Learning logs are a variation of the dialogue journal. Their purpose is to encourage pupils to reflect on their learning experiences and express these thoughts in words. The purpose is not to repeat what a book, the teacher, a peer or anyone else has said, but to consider how the reader/writer has linked new materials with existing knowledge and skills. The teacher can use specially formulated questions to help the pupil consider a particular instructional objective or learning experience.
- Getting children to write and publish their own journals and books is another valuable activity. The increasing availability of microcomputers and printers in schools helps greatly in such endeavours. Desktop publishing is a great stimulus to the development of literacy skills. The publishing process requires drafting and redrafting of materials and much consultation. The context ensures that a considerable amount of highly motivated reading, writing, rereading and redrafting is done.
- Some schools have formed centres where parent volunteers and teachers will help pupils clarify their ideas and see them through to publication.
- Handbooks can be prepared for use within a classroom by pupils either for themselves or for other children in other classes. Simple examples include a book giving colours and their verbal labels, number words, birthday books, scrapbooks and journals of school activities.

CO-OPERATIVE LEARNING IN SCHOOL

Working in small groups can benefit the social, language, cognitive and reading development of children of all abilities (Slavin et al., 1985; Bennett, 1987). Learning to read capitalises on children's oral language development. It has been demonstrated that the pragmatic aspects of language, the uses to which it is put, facilitate children's language and cognitive development (Wells, 1985; Reason et al., 1987). Small group reading-related activities that require children to negotiate shared meanings can help improve their reading (Walker, 1974; Beard, 1987; Roberts, 1989).

Teaching Reading as a Thinking Process was the title of a seminal book by an American, Stauffer, which was first published in 1969. In England this work stimulated interest in the use of group methods for encouraging reading development. These methods were seen as having the advantage of redressing an overemphasis on the individualisation of instruction in reading, and of being efficient, motivational and effective (Walker, 1974). A subsequent major research funded by the then Schools Council into ways of stimulating the effective use of reading used group discussions as a key strategy. This led to the development of Directed Activities Related to Texts (DARTS) (Lunzer and Gardner, 1979). Whether the groups should be of mixed or of similar reading attainments is a controversial issue.

These group approaches include:

- group cloze;
- group sequencing;
- group prediction;
- group SQ3R.

In 'group cloze' the teacher presents the children with a passage of text from which certain words have been deleted. The following example indicates the form of such material.

> When cloze procedure is . . . . to reading tasks the . . . . . . is asked to fill . . the gap, usually a . . . . . . word, which has been left . . . of the text. To . . this successfully the word . . . . conform to the rules of . . . ., have the correct meaning . . . be consistent with the . . . . and language patterns of . . . author. (adapted from Walker, 1974)

The teacher has many possible deletion policies. For example, every *n*th word may be deleted, or, as in this example, this may be varied. Particular categories of word may be deleted. Words in particular positions in a sentence may be deleted. Additional help in identifying the missing word can be given by presenting the initial and/or final letter of the deleted word. The length of deleted words can be indicated by presenting a dot for each missing letter or a line equivalent to the word length. The group's task is to come to an agreement on the missing words. Such an activity typically leads to a lot of discussion, reading and rereading of the text and exploration and justification of alternatives. Through an increasing awareness of synonyms, and a heightened sensitivity to the constraints imposed by both the grammatical structure of the passage and the rules of spelling, pupils' awareness of language is enhanced.

It is helpful to the teacher who wishes to devise cloze passages to know something about the frequency with which word classes occur and also the difficulty of prediction of different types of word. A more detailed exposition can be found in the work of Rye (1982).

The frequency of occurrence of word types in running text varies somewhat but tends to produce the following pattern ranging from the most commonly to the least commonly occurring: structure words; nouns and pronouns; main verbs; adjectives and adverbs. The analysis of the frequency of word usage typically found in text and presented on pp. 182–8 indicates instructional implications.

Word types: difficulty of prediction

EASY   STRUCTURE WORDS

   Articles
   Auxiliary verbs
   Prepositions
   Conjunctions

   Nouns   CONTENT WORDS
   Main verbs
   Adverbs
   Adjectives

HARD

'Group sequencing' involves presenting children with the segments of a continuous passage, or the frames from a comic strip with (or without) 'bubble' speech from the characters involved. The difficulty of this task can easily be modified by changing the number of elements into which the sequence is divided. The fewer the divisions, the less challenging the task.

The author has used the approach, based on comic strips, with children experiencing great difficulties in learning to read and to whom the prospect of being asked to read was anathema. Based on the cut-up review of a book on the teaching of reading, the author has used this approach with qualified and experienced teachers studying the teaching of reading on a post-experience course. In both situations the involvement of the groups with the materials was excellent.

'Group prediction' can be carried out using, for example, an overhead projector. The beginning of a story can be presented. The group is asked a number of prepared questions such as 'What is happening?' and, more interestingly because they are more open-ended, 'What led up to this?' and 'What will happen next?' Children offering opinions are asked to support their suggestions by reference to evidence in the material on the screen. Frequently different interpretations and different predictions will be made. These differences may, or may not, be resolved. The presentation of subsequent material on the screen typically provides additional information that enables the validity of the earlier interpretations to be checked. The author has used this technique using pictures only, then pictures with 'bubble' text, and then text only with children of all abilities. Provided the topic is one of interest to the group and the questions have been well prepared, the technique leads to a great deal of reading, re-reading, thinking and discussion of the presented material.

The SQ3R technique was pioneered by Robinson in 1946. This is a series of steps designed to help pupils when reading from a textbook for study purposes. S and Q stand for 'survey', 'question' (and anticipate), and the 3Rs are 'read', 'recite', and 'review'. The textual material is surveyed in order to identify and note key points pertinent to the assignment. Questions are posed concerning the successive sections identified; the text is then carefully read in order to answer these questions. The answer to each is recited. When several questions and answers have been dealt with, the material covered is reviewed (Robinson, 1961). Many variations have been developed. 'Group SQ3R' represents its adaptation to a group situation.

PRINCIPLES AND PRACTICES UNDERPINNING EFFECTIVE READING GROUP INSTRUCTION IN READING

'Why teach reading individually if it is possible to teach a group as effectively, or even more so?' It has been demonstrated by Southgate that certain individualised teaching practices are inefficient. Her advocacy of group work in reading instruction and of uninterrupted silent reading is well supported (Southgate, 1986).

From a survey of research findings, plus the workers' experiences as teachers, teacher trainers and researchers, Brophy and his colleagues identified key principles underpinning effective reading group instruction. From these principles, an instructional model was developed (Brophy, 1986). Twenty-seven teachers of 6-year-old pupils in nine schools took part in an experiment to test the effects of a training programme based on the principles.

Ten teachers were trained and then observed periodically during the school year. Seven were trained in the model but not observed. The remaining ten teachers were not trained in the model, but were observed periodically. The effects of the training programme on the teachers' pupils' scores on normative achievement tests were evaluated. Pupils were tested at the start and end of the programme. The effects on student learning showed that training teachers to use the model resulted in significantly higher pupil achievement. The pupils of teachers in both trained groups obtained higher achievement test scores than did those of teachers who had not been trained. Observation of classroom process–product relationships showed that certain processes were significantly associated with gains in achievement by the pupils. Put simply, what took place during learning affected the outcomes, the products. Many of these supported previous process–product research findings. Taken together, these data are interpreted as providing support for the model presented by Brophy. Critics may well argue that the sample of teachers was very small and that the design of the research used suspect analytic procedures.

Brophy and his colleagues revised the model, taking the empirical findings into account. The model now highlights the central ideas and provides a structure and a sequence that holds promise for 'most small group instruction in beginning reading' (ibid., p. 81).

Having worked for many years as a specialist teacher with small groups of junior school pupils who had been identified as in need of remedial help with their reading, I read Brophy's account with interest. From a considerable personal involvement and experience in the field of small-group work, the principles identified had the ring of truth. They characterise teaching that distinguishes effective small-group work from ineffective work. The list also underlines *why* there is a limit to the small-group size, if the principles are to be applied and the advantages gained. The list is valuable as a provisional checklist against which to consider the adequacy of small-group work in reading that may be carried out with pupils, and could form a useful topic for a within-school staff development session. The revised principles are summarised here:

Principles for small-group instruction in beginning reading

General

- Reading groups should be organised for efficient, sustained focus on content.
- Pupils' attention to, and active involvement in, the lesson should be obtained.

- Question and task difficulty levels should allow the pace of the lesson to be brisk and pupils to experience consistent success.
- Frequent opportunities should be provided for students to read, respond to questions and receive clear feedback concerning their performance.
- Overlearning of skills should be ensured and new skills introduced gradually whilst earlier ones are being mastered.
- Each individual in the group must be monitored and given the instruction, feedback and opportunities for practice that are required.
*• What is covered in small-group work should be an integral part of the class reading programme.
*• Records of what was attempted and achieved for each pupil during the small-group work should be kept.

Specific principles

(Each of the following items identifies important considerations in relation to small-group work in reading. Each is expanded in the original publication to indicate the precise strategies the class teacher should implement.)

Programming for continuous progress in relation to group work

1. time
2. academic focus
3. pace
4. error rate

Group organisation

5. seating
6. transition between activities during group teaching
7. getting started
* ending the session

Introducing lessons and activities

8. overviews of lesson
9. new words to be covered
10. work assignments

Ensuring participation

11. ask questions

12. ordered turns for pupil responses
13. minimise calling out by pupils
14. monitor individuals

Teacher questions and pupil answers

15. academic focus
16. word-attack questions
17. wait for answers
18. give help needed to ensure success
19. give answers when necessary, but focus the group's attention on the answer and *not* on their failure to respond
20. explain answers where necessary

When pupils respond correctly

21. acknowledge correct responses
22. even after correct answers, feedback on the means whereby the answer was obtained should be provided
23. follow-up questions

Praise and criticism

24. praise in moderation and specifically, rather than generally
25. specify what is praised
26. provide correction and *not* criticism

(Adapted from Brophy, 1986)

* Additional items suggested by the present author.

HOME–SCHOOL CO-OPERATION

Competent readers have two major attributes. Firstly, they have mastered the cognitive demands of reading and understand the intellectual aspects of a text. Secondly, they appreciate the emotions and feeling conveyed by the author. If we want to help our children become competent readers, as parents and teachers we need to be aware of both the cognitive and the emotional aspects of the exceedingly complex process of reading development. It is a prime responsibility of the teaching profession to capitalise on and utilise whatever resources are available in the community to achieve this end.

Children (and adults) often talk of activities in two ways. Firstly, the activity can be classified as either 'useful' or 'useless'. Secondly, it can be considered 'interesting' or 'boring'. Reading is an activity that can be classified in this way.

Reading activities permeate the whole of education. It is important that we help as many children as possible to experience reading as both 'interesting' and 'useful'. We must also recognise that some reading can be 'boring', but may be 'useful'. Other material may appear 'useless' from a utilitarian viewpoint but can still be very 'interesting'. The situation that must be avoided is for any child to reach the conclusion that the activity of reading is *both* 'useless' and 'boring'.

If a child is experiencing difficulties with reading, finding no success and seeing no evidence of progress, reading will rapidly be seen as both boring and useless. The child will enter a downward spiral in which both motivation to read and progress in reading will deteriorate.

This immediately brings out the importance of parents and teachers recognising the range of different interests that children have and the activities in which they voluntarily engage. The motivational consequences of these for children's learning to read particular materials is clear. If this range of interests and activities is *not* reflected in the reading materials available to them, children are less likely to become 'hooked on books'. But interest in the content is insufficient: the book, or other textual material, must be at a difficulty level appropriate to the child.

Our children are faced with many competing demands for their time and attention. When it comes to reading, teachers and parents have a *joint* responsibility for ensuring that children are given every opportunity and encouragement to become competent readers who find the activity rewarding both intellectually and emotionally.

One of the most interesting developments receiving increasing attention in the UK is that of Family Reading Groups (Obrist and Stuart, 1990). The UKRA has pioneered this work through a project supported by its Research Committee. In 1971 considerable professional concern was identified in two key areas: the absence of books in many pupils' homes, and the absence of home–school liaison. This led to the development of reading and reviewing groups in schools. The first of these was held in a junior mixed and infants school in North Bedfordshire.

FRGs have typically begun with a display of books provided by the schools' library service coupled with a talk on the value of literature. Pupils select books to take away with them. These books are either read alone, or read to and discussed with the child by parents. After a given time, all involved return and discuss the books that have been read.

There are many types of FRGs. Pre-school groups are run by parents in their own homes, in play groups, play schools or libraries. The schools' library service provides the books. It is reported that children as young as 2 years of age '... and even less' can become involved. Groups have been formed in nursery, infant and junior schools. Those held in infant and lower junior schools typically meet for the last period of the afternoon when parents come to collect their children from the classroom. FRGs with large numbers of members are usually split up into smaller groups of about eight to ten parents and children who sit in circles to discuss what they have been reading.

Subsequently the Department of Education and Science funded a two-year study of FRGs under the aegis of the UKRA Research Committee. FRGs are seen as valuable in bringing parents and children into schools to engage voluntarily in enjoyable and enriching language activities. A report is due in 1991.

The rationale underpinning FRGs owes much to the 'apprentice' and 'top-down' approach to reading development. The key characteristics of FRGs are:

- parental involvement;
- their voluntary nature;
- the availability of a wide variety of books;
- informal group discussions;
- their flexibility; and
- joint involvement by parents, professionals and pupils.

The overriding concerns of FRGs are to enrich, develop and extend reading habits and to encourage positive attitudes towards the many genres of texts available. Their aims include increasing children's and parents' enjoyment of books, and their awareness of the availability and richness of children's literature, and developing critical acumen.

FRGs have been instrumental in widening awareness of the best of modern children's literature. They have also encouraged constructive interactions between public librarians, parents and their children. Where local libraries support a school FRG, the benefits for all involved are enhanced. Pre-school children who are members of a FRG have increased opportunities of seeing books and reading as valued activities, and can become involved in listening to and discussing pictures and stories, thereby developing metacognitive abilities concerning the purposes of print. They also rapidly learn how to handle books effectively.

The unforced nature of the enterprise is important. Members grow in confidence largely because they have control over the extent to which they join in discussion, which books they read and indeed whether they attend or not. Books provided are not reading primers or the set books of the secondary literature syllabus, nor are they even 'junior classics'. Books are very often chosen because other children have recommended them. At FRG meetings younger children decide for themselves whether they will read a book, share it with a member of the family, or listen to the story being read. Parents report much more relaxed and enjoyable reading with their children when the story itself, rather than the child's reading performance, is the issue.... Virtually all FRGs rely heavily on the schools' library service for their supply of books and for the expertise of the librarian.

(Obrist and Stuart, 1990, p. 205)

The Bradford 'Book Flood' has demonstrated the value of a rich supply of books in developing the amount and variety of reading done by pupils in schools (Ingham, 1982). It also showed that the recording and discussion of what had been read was beneficial irrespective of whether or not a school had an enhanced supply of books. The availability of a rich and varied supply of books is a necessary but not sufficient condition for the development of sound reading habits. What is done with the books is of the essence (Pumfrey, 1988b).

In Israel many schools run reading clubs. These involve competitive activities between teams of pupils. For example, each team studies the same books for a given period. These books can include novels, any texts or reference books. The teams then meet and are asked questions about the books they have read. The books are available to both teams. The author has observed such competitive activities in Israel. They appeared to be greatly enjoyed by the participants, irrespective of whether or not their team obtained the higher score. Whilst this competitive activity contrasts somewhat with the ethos of FRGs, the Reading Clubs are considered very effective in getting pupils involved with books of various types and learning how to use them effectively.

HOME–SCHOOL CO-OPERATION IN THE TEACHING OF READING

A survey of a representative sample of 381 primary schools in England showed that 202 (53 per cent) reported that 'unpaid people assist with the teaching of reading on the school premises on a regular basis' (Stierer, 1985). The ILEA Junior School Project, outlined in Chapter 1, examined the extent and nature of parental involvement in the 50 junior schools studied. In approximately 50 per cent of the schools, parents worked in the classrooms with children; this type of parental involvement was more marked with the younger classes. In ten schools parents helped at all age levels (ILEA, 1986c). These findings underline the increasing use being made by schools of parents and other care-givers. Eleven schools experienced problems in identifying parents who were able to help. The class teachers in four schools did not favour the arrangement. On balance, all but two headteachers considered that the parental help was advantageous to the school. The judicious use of such parents can contribute towards improving children's attainments in and attitudes towards reading, but organisation, training and planning are required if parents are to be used effectively. This field of applied research is gaining increasing attention. There are many variants on this theme. One receiving considerable attention both here and overseas is known as 'paired reading' (see pp. 233–40 for further details).

Parental involvement in children's education is increasingly being recognised as a potent force. In the UK, the USA and certain other European countries, parents are asking for and being given increasing legal rights to be involved. Proponents of this move see it as representing an important and powerful addition to a school's resources. It can lead to increased reading attainments by pupils and also to more positive attitudes towards reading (Topping and Wolfendale, 1985; Wolfendale, 1987; Topping and Whitely, 1990). It can be particularly helpful to children with reading difficulties. It is not claimed that this idea is new; it has a long anecdotal track record. What *is* new is the attention being paid to it by teachers in the UK, largely as a direct consequence of action research based on the initiatives of school psychological services and remedial education services (Branston and Provis, 1986; Pryke, 1987; Waterland, 1985).

WHAT PARENTS CAN DO: RESEARCH FINDINGS ABOUT READING, ITS LEARNING AND TEACHING

The public financial and professional resources available to schools are never sufficient to meet the demands made by society. This says something about the nature, origins and changes in such demands that take place over time. A successful junior school does *not*, for example, satisfy demands for higher standards in all its pupils' reading attainments and attitudes, even if the pupils collectively demonstrate high standards in their performance. A school *creates* expectations and thus demands. The horizon of acceptable reading attainments for all pupils is recognised as an important, albeit somewhat nebulous, objective. It can readily be agreed in principle, but its operational definition in practice is not so easily agreed. By its very nature, that horizon can never be reached. It is not uncommon for the pupil unable to read, but who is subsequently helped to do so, to be found to have other literacy-related difficuties in, for example, spelling, writing and composition. As one goal is achieved, more is expected. The same is true of children who do not experience undue difficulties in learning to read. 'Satisfactory reading attainments' are a very movable feast. The wide range of inter- and intra-individual differences between children are systematically related to children's reading. These variables cannot be ignored, if one is concerned with individuals.

Many important and highly controversial theoretical and methodological issues remain unresolved concerning the nature of reading and its development (see Chapter 2). Despite this, *all* pupils can be helped to improve their various literacy skills. (The issue of whether or not this is a suitable priority for all pupils at a particular stage in their education is a separate one: it is also crucial, and should not be overlooked.) Literacy is but one facet of education; one may be more interested in other aspects of a child's development. There are well-documented cases of able students committing suicide when they have failed to achieve the socially highly valued success in public examinations because of specific learning difficulties in reading and writing that they thought they had overcome. There is more to life than being able to read; but if the skills can be learned or taught, their possession can prove enriching to the individual and society.

Recognising the need for soundly based guidance to both schools and parents, the US Department of Education issued a booklet, *Becoming a Nation of Readers: What Parents can Do* (Binkley, 1988) (see p. 209). This derives in large measure from an earlier report by the Commission on Reading (Anderson et al., 1985). The booklet summarises some of the major conclusions concerning ways in which parents can help their children to become literate. Its recommendations are predicated on the belief that: 'a parent is a child's first tutor in unravelling the fascinating problem of written language. A parent is a child's one enduring source of faith that somehow, sooner or later, he or she will become a good reader' (ibid., p. 28). The considerations listed earlier in this chapter, concerning the nature of reading and its development in relation to implications of the Commission's report for teachers are almost equally valid for parents. There is no hard and fast line between the role of the parent and that of the teacher in helping the majority of children learn to read. There are some children whose difficulties are severe and long-standing and who may require the help of specialists. Whilst parents are still an underutilised resource, the importance of an informed, qualified, disinterested (but *not* uninterested) third party, such as the teacher, can serve many important functions. In circumstances where a child may, for whatever reasons, not make the progress in reading that the parent anticipates, the emotional involvement between parents and children can become inhibiting to the child's progress.

In relation to the pre-school years, the following suggestions are included in Anderson et al. (1985). *Many of them still apply to junior school pupils who, for various reasons, are still not reading.* It is important that junior school teachers should be able to help parents help their children already attending school, and those who will be attending in the future, on the basis of research findings.

The importance of talking with children as a means of enriching and expanding their understanding of the world is a central contribution that parents can make. To make maximum use of their own and their children's experiences, parents should ensure the following.

- Because both children and adults are stimulated by new experiences, provide a variety of experience that will give the child wider horizons than the home. Many community resources can be used, including visits to zoos, museums, libraries, sites of local interest and beauty.
- This type of experience should be embedded in conversations with the child. Attention can be drawn by the parent to the variety of experiences being seen and shared.
- The child's vocabulary and conceptual framework can be elaborated and enriched. By drawing on their observations and also on their earlier experiences, parents can mediate their children's understanding of a range of activities. Encouraging the child to take an active part in such reflective activities is central. 'Language frames the world the child knows; the richer the language, the richer the child's world. Especially with a small child, it is better to say too much than too little' (Anderson et al., 1985, p. 5).
- Encourage the child to talk and to ask questions. This can be done by using open-ended questions (ones that do not have simple right or wrong answers and cannot be responded to by a mere 'yes' or 'no'). By getting children to focus on similarities and differences, on collecting, classifying and ordering materials, valuable experiences are made explicit in words and related to present actions.
- 'What if . . .' questions are important because they provide opportunities for conjecture and the exploration of possibilities by the child.
- The well-known 'why' questions should be valued by adults

and their potential realised. When one does not know the apparently requested answer (on reflection, *especially* if one does not), the opportunity of demonstrating how books and other sources of information can be used is invaluable.

- '. . . the single most important activity for building the knowledge required for eventual success in reading is reading aloud to children' (ibid., p. 6). Listening to adults reading should be associated by the child with pleasure, enjoyment, interest and excitement. There is much more to reading to children than saying the words. Stories, poems and rhymes that are not fully understood can be enjoyed by virtue of the cadences in the adult's voice and the rhythms of the language. Listening to such readings can lead to discussion, questions and explorations by the child that would never have taken place without the experience of listening to a reading.

- Children absorb the idea that reading is important if they see their parents enjoying and benefiting from reading. Letters from relatives and friends, newspapers, magazines, advertisements and books are all grist to this particular mill. The setting of such a powerful example to the child is an unobtrusive but positive and pervasive influence on how the child comes to construe the activity of reading.

- Most parents appreciate the importance of reading to their children. The challenges are more in deciding what to read, when to read and how to get the materials rather than whether to read to them or not. Fortunately, plenty of sources of help are available. These include the local school, libraries and bookshops. At the national level, the Book Trust (formerly the National Book League) can provide information describing suitable reading materials and sources. An even more readily available fund of information is the parents of children who have passed through this stage. If the local education authority has a pre-school service, it will have experts able and keen to assist.

- For parents unable to find the time to read sufficiently often to their children, other sources of help are available. These include other relatives, and local libraries that run 'Story time' sessions. Popular stories and rhymes on audio-cassette are also of value, provided the stories are discussed with the child.

  In passing, as a parent the fun of reading to one's children can be a shared pleasure that is priceless. Whilst this was being written, I asked my 22-year-old son if he could recall being read to as a very young child. His emphatic 'Yes', coupled with the comment that, although he could not remember the exact stories, he recalled where the reading took place and that it was 'a lot of fun', makes the point.

- In learning about reading, awareness of nature of text and writing is also picked up by many children. Their enjoyment of learning nursery rhymes and stories with a cumulative and repetitive pattern helps the child appreciate that the words in a particular written rhyme or story are always in the same order and on the same page. An understanding of the vocabulary of literacy begins. The meanings of letters, words, sentences, of books, rhymes and poems begin to be acquired. The organisation of textual materials begins to be appreciated. Many children enter school already knowing such things. They have a rudimentary but invaluable appreciation of what is involved in literacy, and (partially) already 'know the name of the game'. Research shows that such children make better progress in learning to read than those who have not acquired such metacognitions.

- Children enjoy dictating stories or journals to a parent. Descriptions of outings and activities that have been enjoyable and/or interesting, as well as imaginative stories, can be written down by the adult. The inclusion of mementos such as birthday cards, programmes, photographs or pictures cut from catalogues, can lead to a language-experience-based book that can give the young child much enjoyment.

- The following activities allow considerable scope for parents to help their children develop understandings that will help them learn to read:

  making lists, e.g., for shopping trips, parties
  using magnetic letters
  making scrapbooks

- Enjoyment is of the essence. Laughing about mistakes that the child makes is a vastly superior motivator to criticising the child for being wrong. Research suggests that children can learn as much or more from the types of informal activity described here than from the commercial workbooks that can be purchased.

Co-operation between home and school enables the parent to share many school activities with their child. Choosing books together, listening (without criticism) to their child read regularly at home are but two examples. Attending sessions at school for parents in which advice and instruction on how best to listen to and help their child is another. Procedures such as 'paired reading', 'relaxed reading' and 'pause, prompt and praise' are three of many systems that have been developed in this area (see pp. 233–42). Other approaches that hold promise include the following:

- Silent reading of self-selected material at the same time in a group at home provides the right model for the child. It also encourages motivated time on task by the child.
- Encourage all types of recording by the child in any medium. The use of a family message board, penpals and letters to friends and relatives can provide a range of opportunities. Each can lead to discussions concerning how words are spelled and how communication using writing can be a source of enjoyment and use to all members of the family.
- Parents often get concerned at the amount of time children spend watching television. Research has shown that more than 10 hours of television viewing per week has an adverse effect on children's learning. Restricting viewing makes available time for less passive activities – such as reading and writing. What the child watches is also important. Whenever possible, parents should watch programmes with their children and discuss what has been seen. There are many very valuable and informative programmes that enrich the child's background and that of the parents.
- Support by the parent for what the school is trying to do is vital. Promptness and application to homework by the child is one example. Children (and adults) typically work more effectively at reading (or any other activity) when they receive praise and encouragement for their successes rather than blame for errors. This is easily said, but less easy to apply to one's own child particularly if the parent's own education has been based on less positive experiences.

In striving to create a literate society, 'Parents, teachers, school personnel and policy-makers each have different but very complimentary [*sic*: presumably "complementary"] roles that will help us reach that goal. Parents, however, have what may be the most crucial role.'

Becoming a Nation of Readers calls upon parents to

> lay the foundations for learning to read ... [by] informally teaching pre-school children about reading and writing, by reading aloud to them, discussing stories and events, encouraging them to learn letters and words and teaching them about the world around them. ... In addition to laying a foundation, parents need to facilitate the growth of their children's reading by taking them to libraries, encouraging reading as a free time activity and supporting homework.
>
> (Anderson et al., 1985, p. 57)

The validity of these assertions is based on the critical evaluation of a massive body of research evidence. The dual purposes of encouraging high reading standards in all pupils and of identifying and alleviating the reading difficulties of others would be assisted if parents adopted such recommendations.

PAIRED READING

Hundreds of different methods, programmes, kits and schemes have been devised to help children learn to read (Aukerman, 1985). The present account describes *one* promising approach known as 'paired reading' (PR) and a number of variations on it that are receiving considerable attention in the UK. These approaches work best where co-operation between teachers and parents is good. They are of value to pupils at all levels of reading attainment. The ideas underpinning the suggestions have actually *encouraged* parent–teacher co-operation in school districts where such co-operation was largely unknown. Paired reading is just one aspect of the more general concept of paired learning (Paired Learning Project, 1989).

The variations of PR can also be of considerable value where a high level of parent–teacher co-operation cannot be obtained. The general strategy allows a wide range of applications. PR and its variants are neither straitjackets for parents, pupils and teachers nor panaceas for all reading difficulties. But the evidence available suggests that they *do* have considerable promise. The 'Paired Reading' project based in Kirklees LEA has stimulated both national and international interest (Topping, 1987a, 1988).

The theoretical reasons why PR is likely to be successful will be briefly outlined and the content of the two phases of PR will be described (see Table 5.1). Evidence concerning the effectiveness of PR will be considered, and some cautionary comments made. A description will be presented of a range of variations on the PR theme, with suggestions to help potential users of the PR and related strategies to avoid some of the pitfalls into which pioneers in this field stumbled.

PR is one of many strategies that utilise the educational resources of parents, their children and teachers. It does so in a specific way for sound theoretical reasons. The technique is geared to the notion that children best learn to read by reading, that the most helpful conditions for the child's involvement with text can be clearly stated, and that the method can be taught to parents.

There is little doubt that PR has caught the imagination of a growing number of members of the teaching profession, although in certain parts of the UK more than in others. Primary schools are more likely to be involved than other sectors of education. The strategy is being adopted in other spheres including special education and secondary schools, and with important variations. Of these, peer tutoring is one showing considerable promise and generating much enthusiasm amongst teachers (Topping, 1987b).

Fashions affect educational practice. Is PR a bandwagon that will, after a brief period of popularity, be overtaken by another innovation? Or is it a breakthrough in pedagogy?

The acceptance of educational ideas typically goes through five stages. In the first, the practice is of interest only to the initiators. Then, as others hear of it and sense its promise, the practice becomes increasingly known and used. In the third stage, reservations begin to appear as the promising findings of the pioneers are not always found by their followers: this is followed by a decline in the practice. Finally, the combined results of empirical investigations and the experience of teachers leads to a balanced appraisal of the educational validity of the innovation.

Rationale

The effectiveness of PR draws on several theoretical orientations. Collectively, these recognise the importance of the cognitive, affective and motivational aspects of learning to read. The 'whole' represented by the seven components is far more potentially potent than the sum of its parts (Pumfrey, 1986b). The seven key components are listed in Table 5.1.

Table 5.1 *Paired reading: key components*

---

1. an acceptance of the importance of the psycholinguistic basis of reading as a complex skill in which a 'top-down' approach is employed;
2. allowing the child to select the material to be read;
3. the involvement of 'significant others' in the reading activity;
4. modelling by the learner on a more proficient reader;
5. allowing the learner to control the provision of feedback of information about the text;
6. positive reinforcement of the learner's reading; and
7. increased 'time on task' by a well-motivated learner

The two phases

PR can be seen as a two-phase strategy. The content and relationships between the phases are summarised in Table 5.2.

Table 5.2 *Paired reading: content of the two phases*

Phase I (simultaneous reading: participant modelling)

---

1. Child chooses a book or other reading material.
2. Parent and child read the book aloud together.
3. The child makes an attempt at every word.
4. When the child makes an error, the parent allows time (3–4 sec) for the child to repeat the word correctly, without discussing it.

Phase II (independent reading)

---

1. When the child feels ready to read aloud alone, he or she indicates this by giving a previously agreed non-verbal signal.
2. The parent immediately stops reading aloud.
3. When the child makes an error, or is unable to read a word when reading alone, the parent gives the correct response. This is repeated by the child.
4. Revert to Phase I, simultaneous reading, until the child signals that the parent is to stop reading aloud.

In PR the child chooses the book or other material to be read. Some teachers argue that children must be allowed this freedom for motivational reasons, irrespective of the difficulty the child will face if the text selected is too complex. Experience shows that the children will rapidly learn to choose material at a suitable level (Topping and McKnight, 1984; Prentice, 1987). Others consider that, whilst the materials should respect the interests of the reader, the PR system works best where the reading materials are about two years below the child's tested reading age (Tyre and Young, 1984). In essence, the child finds a level at which he/she feels secure enough to cope with the challenge of reading aloud. It can be argued that the overlearning encouraged by such reading provides the child with the confidence and experience on which later progress to more advanced levels of reading can be built. The psychologist on whose original clinical work the PR strategy was developed has recently published a handbook providing details of how it can be applied (Morgan, 1986).

Results

The efficacy of PR can be examined by looking at the starting points and end products as measured by tests of the learner's reading attainments and attitudes to reading.

Research reports demonstrate a progression in the evaluation of PR from clinical studies of individuals, through methods experiments without control groups, to methods experiments with control groups and, finally, to more sophisticated methods experiments in which the effects of experimenter bias were countered by using a 'double-blind' research design. To date, these results show promise (Pumfrey, 1986b). The strategy appears to produce significant changes at least in the short term, and possibly longer. A comprehensive review of this field has been presented by the director of the Kirklees Paired Reading Project (Topping, 1990).

Notes of caution

The assumption that the 'pairing' adds anything of significance has been questioned by studies that demonstrate similar improvements in children's reading using other strategies that increase the pupil's 'time on task'.

The Hawthorne effect, whereby pupil and teacher involvement in any novel activity increases motivation and performance, has not been adequately controlled in many studies.

The measurement of pupils' 'improvement' in reading using tests is not as simple as appears at first sight.

Many of the recent results claiming to demonstrate improved reading in relation to comprehension and accuracy scores do so by using derived scores that purport to show the rates at which pupils were progressing before and after PR. Typically the latter is greater than the former. Such comparisons are frequently fallacious and based on a misunderstanding of the nature of the reading test scores from which they derive. For example, to be six months of reading age behind one's chronological age at the chronological age of 7 years is *not* the same degree of 'retardation' as being six months of reading age behind one's chronological age at 10 years of age on a given test. This is because the range of reading test scores, if quantified in months of reading age, increases with chronological age. Hence, six months' progress in two months at the two different levels gives *equivalent* rates of apparent progress of three months of reading age per month of PR when, in fact, the second represents a *lower* rate of progress.

The long-term effects of PR have not been adequately explored, as yet.

Some pairings can be counterproductive.

The reading difficulties of some pupils will require a more structured approach.

Variations

The PR technique is very flexible. This has led to the development of many variations on the original theme, some of which are listed in Table 5.3. One of the most promising of these variants is known as 'pause, prompt, praise' (PPP) (McNaughton et al., 1981). It makes explicit what is done by many teachers in a way that enables the technique to be taught to other tutors.

'PAUSE, PROMPT, PRAISE': HOW TO DO IT

When a child reads a text aloud to another person, the reader either reads correctly, or makes errors. Figure 5.2 shows what the tutor should do in either circumstance.

PPP: results

A number of studies of the effects of PPP when used by different groups of tutors has been reported in the professional literature. In general, these are positive. The technique holds promise and can be used to involve many individuals as tutors. Care is needed, however, when looking at the evidence brought forward in support of PPP. Many of the earlier strictures concerning the evaluation of PR also apply.

In addition to being studied to determine their effects on children's reading standards at the end of a period of treatment, both PR and PPP have led directly to a close examination of what happens when a child is reading to an adult. It has provided a window through which important aspects of the reading process can be glimpsed. It is to this fascinating field of research that we now turn. It contains important lessons for both teachers and parents.

Lessons for teachers and parents

To observe the interactions between someone reading aloud, the reading material and a second individual seeking to assist the reader appears easy. The observer can readily obtain a global impression of what is taking place by careful observation. To analyse *what* takes place with a view to identifying the processes taking place that are facilitative is infinitely more difficult. It is also potentially far more rewarding.

The use of audio- and video-recorders to capture the flow of interactions is the essential first step. Afterwards, it is possible, by using transcripts and rerunning the events, to explore the nature of the events taking place.

Explorations of this type are very time consuming, but of great promise in furthering our understanding of reader–text

Table 5.3 *Paired reading: variations*

Paired reading (Bryans et al., 1985)	The parent reads a passage. Then parent and child read the same passage together with the parent supplying words when the child makes an error. There is some control of book readability.
Paired reading (Young and Tyre, 1983)	Parent talks with the child about the passage, then parent and child read the passage. Parent and child read together with the parent delaying on easy words to encourage the child to say the word first. Child then reads the passage aloud. The readability level of the material used is controlled.
Paired reading (Gillham, 1986)	Parent and child talk about a short book. They then read it together. The parent corrects error words but the child does not repeat them. As the child becomes more confident, the parent lowers voice and 'fades out'. The parent joins in when the child encounters difficulties. Books used are read and reread (up to eight times). The text readability is controlled.
Shared reading (Greening and Spenceley, 1984)	Parent talks about the book with the child. Then parent and child read the book together. There is no correction procedure involved.
Relaxed reading (Lindsay et al., 1985)	Child reads aloud to parent. Parent supplies error words only. Advice to parents is individualised. The emphasis of the approach is on a relaxed and positive atmosphere.
Pause, prompt, praise (McNaughton et al., 1981; Glynn et al., 1987)	The child reads aloud to the parent or tutor. When an error occurs, the tutor gives a prompt dependent on the nature of the error. The child is given praise for successes. Tutors are trained. The readability of the text is controlled (further details on pp. 237–9).

interactions, and ability to control, for the benefit of readers, their acquisition of reading skills (Hannon et al., 1986).

It has been demonstrated that individuals can be trained to be more effective in the way in which they assist someone reading aloud. This applies to parents, or other adults, and to peers. Teachers can also learn important lessons from such research findings. The degree to which this increased competence in assisting the reader is translated into improved attainment and more positive attitudes is still under examination.

The time-consuming nature of the work described above means that such studies are typically small-scale. They are limited in the number of readers and helpers involved, the length of the PR or PPP programme and in the populations from which both readers and helpers are obtained. There is therefore considerable limitation to generalisations that can be drawn from the data currently avail-

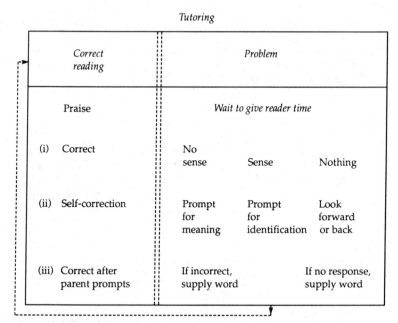

Figure 5.2 *Pause, prompt, praise (adapted from McNaughton et al., 1981)*

able. The temptation that has to be resisted is for enthusiasts to overgeneralise from restricted samples.

In looking at data from sets of dyads involved in PR and PPP, it is possible to mask particular dyadic interactions that are clearly counterproductive, insofar as both reader and helper are concerned. When looking at grouped data, the importance of interactions within dyads must not be overlooked.

Ways forward for parents, pupils and teachers

Products

Studies of the outcomes of PR programmes must be carefully designed. Knowledge of how to carry out such studies on data from both groups and individual dyads are readily available from educational psychologists, research workers and specialist teachers who have studied mental measurement, the uses and limitations of a wide range of tests and the design of experiments as an essential part of their professional training. Bear in mind the following points.

- Valid and sensitive observation schedules, measures, tests and techniques for assessing both cognitive and affective aspects of reading development must be carefully selected. A wide range of such measures is available (Pumfrey, 1985, 1986a).
- Be cautious when using 'improvement' scores.
- Be even more cautious when using 'rate of improvement' as an index of the efficacy of PR.
- If percentages are used, always specify the sizes of the samples to which they relate.
- Be aware of the importance of 'time on task' as a key variable that must not be overlooked in evaluating the products of any methods experiment.
- Consider 'output' or 'products' of PR from the viewpoints of readers, tutors and teachers (Ashton et al., 1986).

Processes

- Record PR or PPP sessions on audio- or video-tapes.
- Analyse processes so that the interactions between the reader, the text and the tutor are the focus of attention.
- Identify particular processes that are related to positive outcomes, for example the use of PPP (Wheldall and Metten, 1985).
- Sensitise tutors to these processes and increase the tutors' use of appropriately timed interventions.
- Identify processes related to negative outcomes, for example the use of negative comments and poor timing of interventions.
- Sensitise tutors to these processes and help them to decrease their use of them.
- Help tutors value the importance to the reader of 'overlearning' by a great deal of successful experience with material pitched at the independent level.
- Oral reading represents an important 'window' on the individual reader's reading strategies.

COMMENT

PR and PPP are related techniques. There are many other variants. All utilise combinations of most of the seven potent educational ingredients specified in Table 5.1 (p. 234).

Variations can occur in many ways that do not preclude this crucial combination. For example, the 'significant other', the tutor, may be a parent, some other relation or friend, male or female, an older student or a member of the peer group. Different means of identifying the texts with which the dyads will work are available. The timing and length of the joint sessions and their frequency can be varied. The involvement of the teacher as a consultant to the tutor can take many forms. The training and support given to the tutors can vary considerably. Despite such variations, the different forms of PR have much more in common from the pedagogic viewpoint than otherwise. The nature of the non-verbal signal used by the reader to control the tutor is probably the key feature distinguishing PR from many variants. The signal may vary.

The various reservations made earlier concerning the evaluation of the products and processes involved apply equally well to whatever variant of PR is under consideration.

It is still too early to state that the empirical evidence unequivocally supports the superiority of PR to other means of improving children's reading attainments and attitudes towards reading. Without doubt it is a technique that holds considerable promise. The *Paired Reading Bulletin* no. 3, edited by the director of the Paired Reading Project, makes the point forcibly. The accounts by teachers of a wide range of experiments in many situations understandably do not always meet the requirements of a formal evaluative study. Nonetheless, as 'action research' they indicate an important development.

In November 1986 I presented a paper at a symposium on PR attended by 27 delegates. Of these, 21 considered PR an effective means of improving reading; 6 indicated that they were uncertain. No one was convinced that PR did not work.

To draw any conclusions from such a straw poll would be completely invalid. The facts are reported as an index of the considered opinions of a small, involved but informed and critical group of professionals. Whether PR turns out to be a breakthrough of pedagogic importance, a bandwagon of educational fashion or something in between remains to be seen.

In attempting the very necessary but difficult tasks of assessing and analysing both the outcomes and the processes involved in PR, in PPP and other variations, the sage words of Metternich bear repetition: 'The fool learns by his own mistakes; the wise man learns by the mistakes of others'.

Of the five stages in the evaluation of an innovation described earlier (p. 234), groups in different parts of England are mainly at stages 2 and 3 in their use of PR and PPP. With a judicious balance of enthusiasm and explicit evaluation of both the products and processes of each, the 'drop-out' typical of stage 4 can be minimised. The attainment of stage 5 will thus have been expedited.

THE PREVENTION OF FAILURE IN READING

In the typical junior school classroom, even with the best possible management and the involvement of parental support, the amount of time that the teacher has to develop individualised programmes is severely limited. In practice, the majority of teachers use developmental, corrective and remedial strategies outlined earlier (see pp. 123–6). The development of individualised reading programmes is expensive in teacher time and expertise. In the classroom the teacher must be perceived as 'fair' in the allocation of her time. Typically, it is to pupils experiencing difficulties that additional help is given. But a balance between the needs of such pupils and those of the rest of the class must be achieved. Such a strategy contains the dilemmas of any compromise solution. The provision of additional help from specialist teachers employed by support services is one of many possible ways of addressing the issue. It is ironic that, at a time when the importance of improved standards of reading is recognised by central government, many such services are being disbanded.

Under the provisions of the Education Reform Act 1988 whereby schools will increasingly become responsible for their own financial management, it is likely that every educational activity will have an explicit price tag attached to it. 'How much will it cost to give John the three hours weekly of individualised instruction that it is considered he needs? Who will provide the expertise? From where will the money come?' Such questions will almost certainly become more prominent. Concern has been expressed that the needs of pupils experiencing reading difficulties may receive a lower priority, and hence resource allocation, than at present. Conflicts between the requirements of the Education Act 1981, and particularly the provisions recommended in Circular 22/89 whereby there is a statutory obligation to identify and provide help for pupils with learning difficulties, underline this point (DES, 1989e).

If our aim is to improve junior children's reading, the first objective should be to prevent avoidable failure in the initial stages. How can this be achieved?

Teachers need to be informed of the responses that the professional has made, historically and currently, and potentially can make, to the twin challenges of improving reading and minimising reading difficulties. This section outlines a further selection of what has been and is available and also provides readers with references for obtaining more detailed information.

Effective teaching of reading is one aspect of effective teaching. An appreciation of the historical background to research into effective teaching is valuable to teachers, because of the controversial issues involved. The International Reading Association has published a most helpful book reviewing research. It includes chapters on new directions in research, staff development programmes and effective compensatory reading instruction (Hoffman, 1986). Descriptions of a number of research-based and classroom-tested approaches to developing a cohesive 'total day' programme for both pupils with reading difficulties and their peers are also available (Gaskins, 1988).

Fashion in educational pedagogy is a powerful force that must be recognised. Techniques for the validation of particular methodologies have advanced markedly this century. These evaluative techniques provide hope that our ability to help improve children's reading can itself be improved. Explicit, replicable and public information on such issues is increasingly available (Pumfrey and Elliott, 1990).

Turning to our predecessors, it is worth noting the following contributions. It is not claimed that these are the earliest examples of particular approaches. They were used in the early stages of the expansion of the teaching of English reading to children and, under a variety of names, each has a number of 1990s versions.

1. *Spell and Read* (Bell, 1797)

This was based on a spelling approach to the teaching of reading using sand trays to learn the shapes and names of the letters of the alphabet with the assistance of monitors (peer tutors).

2. *One Letter, One Sound* (Edgeworth, 1798)

The use of diacritical marks was used to distinguish the different sounds of letters having more than one possible sound value.

3. *Sounds in Colour* (Dale, 1899)

Dale sought to combine 'phonic fun with phonic logic' by the use of oral work, carefully graded materials and coloured letters to highlight particular classes of sounds.

4. *Remember Me? The Little Red Hen* (L.R.H., 1899–1922)

This capitalises on the uses of rhyme, rhythm, repetition and memorisation in the teaching of reading.

5. *Parental Common Sense* (Martha's Father, 1918)

An account published in the *Journal of Applied Psychology* of how a parent helped a 2-year-old girl learn to read using a 'bottom-up' approach.

6. *The Moving Finger* (Fernald, 1921)

A strategy originally developed for children with severe difficulties in learning to read. It combined a language experience approach, multi-sensory input and cross-modal output with materials graded for complexity.

7. *The Living Sentence* (Jagger, 1929)

An approach based on the notion that 'Reading is thinking under the stimulus of the printed page'. This requires that children be taught using a non-oral approach using complete sentences.

8. *Words Have Shapes* (Davidson, 1932)

Starting with shape discrimination, this introduced recognition and discrimination of words by their shapes.

9. *Looking Without Saying* (Dale, 1936)

Dale aimed to develop non-oral reading whereby silent reading was the method adopted.

These brief notes do no more than indicate the orientation of the work to which reference is made. Detailed and interesting accounts of each approach are available (Morris, 1973). Of particular interest is the influence of research into the efficacy of these approaches. It should not be concluded that little has been learned by teachers and psychologists about the nature of reading, its pedagogy and the effectiveness of the latter in the intervening period. We now know much more about all three. The inevitable consequence is that we also know we need to know even more about more phenomena.

When thinking about the early stages of the teaching of reading, suspect dichotomies are often drawn between the rival merits of different approaches. The graded basal reading schemes versus 'real reading' is one contemporary example. An earlier one was 'look and say' versus 'phonics'. The nine approaches listed here provide a wide variety of paired alternatives.

To introduce greater rigour into this field, what is required is an integrative and more adequate theory of the development of reading as one of the products of symbolic thinking. There is nothing as practical as a good theory. Such a theoretical basis to pedagogy is a goal towards which teachers and psychologists are continuously working, and is a professional responsibility that cannot be jettisoned because it is a long-term objective.

THE EARLY STAGES

A valuable survey of approaches to beginning reading demonstrates that teachers have much from which to choose.

The 167 approaches described, summarised from Aukerman (1984) are grouped under six conceptually coherent headings. Aukerman has performed a valuable service in compiling his reviews. Class teachers can use the six headings as a checklist to establish the breadth and depth of their theoretical knowledge of the reading processes and of the instructional approaches to which these lead.

APPROACHES TO BEGINNING READING
Field (N = number of entries in a field).

Phonetic approaches
- Phonics workbooks and spirit masters (N = 39)
- Phonics workbooks with cassettes (N = 12)
- Phonics with games (N = 16)
- Linguistic-structured phonics approaches (N = 12)
- Phonics handbooks for teachers, parents and tutors (N = 8)
(Total N = 87)

Coded symbol–sound approaches
- Colour-coded approaches (N = 4)
- Mnemonic devices (N = 5)
- Alphabetic coded approaches (N = 3)
(Total N = 12)

Whole-word approaches
- The basal reader approach (N = 1) (for details of 15 basal reader series see Aukerman, 1981)
- Language-experience approaches (N = 3)

- Whole-word programmes (N = 18)
- Whole-word lists (N = 4)
- Individualised reading (N = 3)

(Total N = 29).

Natural reading approaches
- Learning-to-read-by-reading approaches (N = 9)
- Early reading strategies for infants and pre-school children (N = 9)

(Total N = 18)

Management systems
- Management systems for beginning reading (N = 12)

(Total N = 12)

Total language arts and eclectic
- Total language arts and eclectic approaches (N = 9)

(Total N = 9)

EFFECTIVE READING PROGRAMMES

The crucial practical questions asked by teachers when presented with a new method and materials are 'Does it work?', 'Why?' and 'What is the evidence?' In an attempt to answer such questions, the US Department of Education's Office of Educational Research and Improvement has established an organisation known as the National Diffusion Network (NDN). One cannot but be impressed by the scope and organisation of this initiative. It would be a great service to education in this country if we were to develop a similar system of identifying and disseminating information about effective educational programmes. NDN's brief is to provide educators and other interested parties with information that will help in improving the quality of the education provided in schools. The system was started in 1974 and has grown from 76 to over 440 programmes. NDN programmes have helped learners with many different needs including disabled pre-school children, disadvantaged inner-city children and those with learning difficulties in content areas including the basic skills of reading, mathematics, oral and written communication. The programmes described have 'demonstrated educational significance, transportability and cost-effectiveness' (National Diffusion Network, 1988, p. iv). They represent a national 'effort to share the excellent "harvest" of pre-

vious investment in the form of exemplary educational programmes' (ibid.).
   Information can be obtained from:

National Diffusion Network,
Recognition Division,
US Department of Education,
OER/PIP/Recognition Division,
555 New Jersey Avenue, NW,
Washington, DC 20208,
United States of America.

The NDN handbook, *Educational Programmes that Work* (16th edn,
1990) describes a range of valuable initiatives. It is divided into 15
sections, A to O. These include Section D: Basic Skills – Language
Arts/Writing (6 programmes), Section G: Basic Skills – Reading (28
programmes) and Section N: Special Education/Learning Disabilities (24 programmes). An indication of the type of programme
available and likely to be of particular importance to teachers interested in children's literacy is presented in the following list, which
summarises Section G. Information is provided in the NDN handbook on 8 aspects of each entry under the two major headings of
'Awareness' and 'Training'.

Section G: basic skills – reading

   AIRS: Andover's Individualized Reading System
   Alphaphonics: Integrated Reading Program
   BASIC – California Demonstration Program in Reading
   BAsic SKills in Reading (BASK)
  *Books and Beyond
   Conquest
  *Content Reading Including Study Skills (CRISS)
  *Cooperative Integrated Reading and Composition (CIRC) –
   Reading
   Cranston's Comprehensive Reading Program K-12
   Discovery Through Reading
  *Exemplary Center for Reading Instruction (ECRI)
   Futureprint
   HOSTS Reading: Help One Student To Succeed
   Intensive Reading Improvement Program (IRIP)
  *IPIMS Reading Center: Individualized Prescriptive Instructional
   Management System (for Underachievers in Reading)
  *Learning To Read Through The Arts Program
   Mount Vernon TV Reading and Communication
   PEGASUS-PACE: Continuous Progress Reading Program: Per-

sonalized Educational Growth And Selective Utilization of Staff
– Personalized Approach to Continuous Education
Programmed Tutorial Reading
RAM: Reading and Micro Management (formerly SIERRA
Reading Lab) G-24
Reading Achievement Program (RAP)
Reading and Content Area Resource Center (ReCaRe)
*Reading Education Accountability Design: Secondary (READ:S)
Reading Improvement by Teaching Effectively (RITE)
*Reading Power in the Content Areas (RP)
*Reading Recovery
SEAPORT: Student Education Assuring Positive Organized
Reading Techniques
Team Oriented Corrective Reading (TOCR)

* Projects currently funded by the NDN.

One of the most extensive and systematic searches for effective
reading programmes was earlier commissioned by the 'Right to
Read' Office of the US Department of Education. Using ten criteria
related to the value and efficacy of each programme, the American
Institutes for Research reviewed in depth 728 programmes out of
the 1,500 that were submitted for consideration; 27 programmes
were identified as meriting dissemination. A subsequent consideration of these 27 by the Office of Education Dissemination Review
panel resulted in the approval of 14 of the programmes. These
were then considered by the 'Right to Read' Office and 12 reading
programmes were approved for dissemination: 9 of these were for
elementary schools and 3 were for secondary schools and/or adult
reading (Rupley, 1976).

An examination of the nine primary reading schemes that were
approved reveals the vast range of approaches adopted in these
programmes, each of which had been shown empirically to be
effective. They range from traditional materials using a phonic
approach ('Alphaphonics') to innovative schemes such as the
'Learning to Read through the Arts' programme based on the
world-famous Guggenheim Museum in New York. This latter programme recognises the importance of self-expression through
artistic media as a means of enhancing both non-verbal and verbal
communication and leading to improved reading. The importance
of the affective, cognitive and motivational bases of reading development is clearly acknowledged. Summaries of 222 effective reading programmes were also published by the National Right to Read
Effort and are available through the Educational Resources Clearing House in Reading and Communication Skills.

It is not suggested that junior schools or individual teachers should adopt any of the approved programmes without a critical examination of its content and methodology in the light of their own situation, including the demands of the English profile components of the national curriculum. However, one would expect that the best 9 out of 1,500 programmes would have something to offer to many British schools and teachers. Benefits could accrue to pupils with, or without, reading difficulties.

EFFECTIVE COMPENSATORY READING PROGRAMMES

In 1977 a large-scale survey of compensatory reading programmes in grades 2, 4 and 6 (ages 7 to 11 years) was concluded in the USA. It involved more than 731 schools across the country. Of these, 232 were chosen for further study together with another 34 that specialists in reading had identified as having noteworthy compensatory reading programmes. The common characteristics of particularly effective reading programmes were identified. These findings had a considerable effect on the development of compensatory reading programmes (Trisman et al., 1976). A warning is given by the US Office of Education that 'The data from this study make it clear that current compensatory education programmes are no panacea'. The quest for effective reading programmes continues.

EFFECTIVE READING PROGRAMMES: 'BASIC SKILLS IMPROVEMENT'

The 'Right to Read' legislation was rescinded in 1979 and replaced by Title II Public Law 95–562 'Basic Skills Improvement', which continued the move towards identifying effective reading programmes. It is just one aspect of a demand for accountability increasingly apparent in both the USA and Britain. The National Diffusion Network first published *Educational Programmes that Work* in the early 1970s.

EFFECTIVE READING PROGRAMMES IN THE UK

In the UK efforts at identifying effective language and reading programmes were, and sadly remain, not as well funded, co-ordinated or disseminated as in the USA. Despite this, there have been a number of important and continuing contributions. Schonell and Kellmer-Pringle's pioneer work in the 1940s and 1950s at the University of Birmingham's Selly Wick Child Study Centre was an important stimulus to the identification and alleviation of children's reading (and other) difficulties (Sampson, 1975; Pumfrey, 1980). The work done by the then relatively few child guidance clinics, school psychological services and remedial educational services was influential. In the 1950s, as a newly qualified teacher, I was privileged to visit several such centres. In tandem with teaching pupils with reading difficulties, their staff developed resource centres at which teachers could inspect reading materials; they also ran courses on the teaching of reading and produced analyses of the books and materials available. The former West Bromwich Child Guidance Service (now Sandwell LEA) was a forerunner. Its work in this field is widely known and continues to this day. A wide range of LEAs have taken up the development of such services and have encouraged the staff involved to produce information, courses and materials. Work by a member of the Stockport LEA Schools Psychological Service and by the head of the Reading Service led to the publication of the nationally used *Learning Difficulties in Reading and Writing: A Teacher's Manual* (Reason and Boote, 1986). The ILEA had become a leader in this type of work up to its abolition in 1990. Such LEA services are key sources of information on reading materials, methods and techniques.

CITY OF MANCHESTER SPECIAL EDUCATION RESOURCES INFORMATION SERVICE (SERIS)

This is one promising local initiative in a progressive LEA. Manchester LEA's Special Education Resources Information Service aims to provide help, information and contact points on educational matters for all concerned with special educational needs at all ages. Its reference library includes a wealth of information on children with reading and related language difficulties. SERIS also keeps a register of research projects in the city's special schools and publishes lists of continuing and completed projects. Further information can be obtained from:

The Director,
SERIS,
11 Anson Road,
Rusholme,
Manchester M14 5BY.

KEY PROFESSIONAL ORGANISATIONS

Many organisations are concerned with the improvement of children's reading difficulties. Some are professional groups with particular interests in this field; others include both professionals and parents jointly seeking ways of helping children with unexpected and severe language difficulties.

One of the foremost professional groups in this country is the United Kingdom Reading Association. Its national and local conferences, periodicals such as *Reading* and *The British Journal of Research in Reading*, monographs and books provide a wealth of ideas. These are drawn from practising teachers, psychologists and research workers.

To assist its members, most of whom are practising teachers, the UKRA has produced two series of 'Reading and Language Development Flyers'. Each consists of a folded sheet of A4 paper devoted to the concerns of the practitioner and containing suggestions for classroom practice. Suggestions distilled from the daily experiences of practitioners have much to commend them, provided that potential users set them in a theoretical context. To give readers an indication of the topics covered in the first two series, their titles are listed below, with the author's name in brackets.

Series 1

No. 1 *Are You Going to Help Your Child Get Ready for Reading?* (Derek Thackray)
No. 2 *What Can Infants Write? – Using Drama as a Vehicle for Creative Writing* (Heather Cook)
No. 3 *'We Have a Problem . . .' – Improving Language and Learning through Problem Solving* (M. P. Yeats)
No. 4 *There's Some Interesting Work Being Done on . . . Summary Techniques and Skills* (I. M. Hunter)
No. 5 *Do We Give Them Time to Read?* (Heather Cook)
No. 6 *Close Encounters of the Print Kind: Using Environmental Print to Introduce Children to Written Language* (Nigel Hall)
No. 7 *Learn Better Handwriting – It's Still Important* (Valerie Yule)
No. 8 *Language is Needed to Think With* (Valerie Yule)
No. 9 *Bored Writing Bores: Good Reasons for Writing in the Primary School* (Valerie Yule)
No. 10 *Following Directions to Better Reading* (Margaret Bamber)

Series 2

No. 1 *How Can I Find the Time?* (Jenifer Walton)
No. 2 *Can Read but Don't* (Bill Dunn)
No. 3 *Preventing 'Dyslexia' in the Beginners' Class* (Valerie Yule)

No. 4 *Teaching Information Skills* (David Wray)
No. 5 *Paired Reading* (Robin Lane)
No. 6 *Parental Involvement in Reading* (Robin Lane)
No. 7 *Reading: A Shared Experience* (Wendy Dedicott)
No. 8 *From Pictures to Spelling: An Integrated Set of Games* (Tom McFarlane)
No. 9 *Remembering in Learning to Read* (Valerie Yule)
No. 10 *Using the Computer to Develop Reading and Language* (David Wray)

Another professional organisation that has a somewhat wider area of concern is the National Association for Remedial Education. One of its best known publications is *An A–Z List of Reading Books* (1st edn, 1973; 5th edn, 1985; Atkinson et al., 1985). It gives valuable advice on ensuring that the textual demands of materials match the reading attainment and interests of pupils. Details of a large number of reading schemes, games, kits and programmes are clearly and systematically described. Although it does not provide evidence on the efficacy of what is presented, it gives an overview of materials used widely in the UK. It is a book that should be in every school. The following summarises its major content:

1. The Reading Challenge: Motivation and frustration; assessing readability; where to start; the reading distribution; finding the right book; graded reading schemes; supplementary readers; listening to children read; requisitioning books and recording progress in reading.
2. Details of reading books: Infant and middle school levels; secondary and adult levels.
3. Materials, games and activities: Sight vocabulary; developing auditory and vocabulary skills.
4. Reading kits and programmes.
5. Teachers' books on reading and remedial education.
6. Publishers' addresses.
7. National Association for Remedial Education teachers' handbooks.

Appendix 1 contains a list of the names and addresses of other organisations with interests and expertise in the teaching of reading.

Specialised approaches

INTRODUCTION

The approaches described in this chapter have been selected because of their long-standing and widespread use. Nine of the approaches have been developed by professionals who accept that a syndrome of specific developmental dyslexia exists. In most cases, the individuals who developed the interventions have worked for considerable periods, or are still working, in centres, clinics or schools at which children who appear to have specific developmental dyslexia are assessed and taught. This is not to say that their approaches are all the same. The majority are based on variants of the verbal deficit hypothesis and tend to use highly structured, multisensory techniques. One, the Peabody Rebus Programme, was originally developed for use with pupils with severe learning difficulties, but has been found to have wider applications. The Icon Approach is a more recent development, representing a contrasting theoretical viewpoint on the nature of specific developmental dyslexia and the type of intervention that is indicated.

The above collection of approaches is selective. Certain of the materials describing systematic linkages between assessment and teaching listed in Chapter 3 have also been used to help pupils with specific learning difficulties: the Aston Index and Portfolio is one well-known example. The appropriateness and efficacy of these approaches is far from unequivocal. A selection of the better known ones is briefly described here because many teachers have heard of them, some use them and others may wish to investigate exactly what each has to offer.

ORTON–GILLINGHAM METHOD (Orton, 1967)

Orton, an American neurosurgeon and psychiatrist, was a pioneer in the study of dyslexia. Early in the 1920s he noted that an unusually high proportion of children with 'specific reading disability' showed marked reversal and orientation difficulties in reading and writing. Some showed a complete mirror reversal of words. The children also tended to be left-handed, or to have no established lateral preference. He hypothesised that, for some of these individuals, their reading difficulties were a consequence of the failure of one of the cerebral hemispheres to become the dominant control centre for speech, language and motor functions. Orton was convinced of the interrelatedness of all language functions. Developmental delays were considered responsible for the neurological difficulties underlying the symptoms (Orton, 1925, 1937).

Gillingham was an educational psychologist who worked under Orton's direction in the Language Research Project of the New York Neurological Institute from 1932 to 1936. She continued the work that Orton had started with Marion Monroe in 1925. The basic principles of the remedial approach that they developed required:

(a) multisensory techniques that developed simultaneous associations between visual, auditory and kinaesthetic language stimuli;
(b) identifying units of learning that could be easily assimilated by the child and then integrating these units into longer, more complex wholes.

The approach aims to establish efficient word-attack habits in reading, writing and spelling. It does this through 'systematic, well-planned sequences of repetitive drills'. Additionally, it aims to provide pupils with thinking patterns to assist them in dealing with the irregularities of the English language. The programme required that basic language units be mastered, and that their visual and auditory patterns be made clear to the pupil. The linkages between these were enhanced by simultaneously using the motor aspects of speaking and writing, culminating in the synthesis of sounds into words. The programme is based on a 'bottom-up' view of the nature of language development and has a heavy emphasis on phonics and other auditory skills (Orton, 1937). Successes using the method have been reported in the literature, but these studies tend to be limited in both scope and design. The method has been criticised as having a suspect theoretical basis, failing to take into account individual differences in modality preference and therefore not capitalising on the individual's pattern of strengths and weaknesses (Hicks, 1986).

Orton died in 1948. A group of his associates formed the Orton Society in order to continue and develop his work. The society remains active and has grown considerably since its formation. One of Orton's major contributions to education was that he inspired the development of teaching techniques by Fernald (1943), Gillingham and Stillman (1956) (see below).

THE GILLINGHAM–STILLMAN ALPHABETIC METHOD
(Gillingham and Stillman, 1956)

Stillman, herself 'wordblind', was a gifted and experienced remedial teacher who worked with Gillingham over many years developing their programme. It is a modification of Orton's multi-sensory ideas using a completely phonic approach. The fifth edition of Gillingham and Stillman's book appeared in 1969. The 344-page manual has been described as 'The first very detailed and fully comprehensive programme of teaching dyslexic children ... no other work has had such a monumental influence on the teaching of dyslexic children' (Naidoo, 1988, p. 56). Not all commentators would agree.

The manual was designed for those teaching children who have failed to learn to read by the traditional school methods. It is a phonic approach both to beginning reading and to the remedial teaching of reading. It uses a multisensory routine employing visual, auditory, kinaesthetic and tactile exercises. It can be described as a VAKT (visual, auditory, kinaesthetic and tactile) *synthetic* method. The training procedures are designed to establish decoding and encoding skills based on firmly established associations between sounds and symbols. These associations are referred to as 'linkages': the strength of recall of the weak is enhanced by linking it with the stronger modalities. The linkages are designed to clarify the visual, auditory and kinaesthetic modalities and associate them with each other. As this has to be done for all pupils, there is a three-stage programme of linkages, summarised as follows:

1. Eight linkage steps are required to establish and review the phonograms using letter cards;
2. Units seen in sequence are blended into sounds spoken in sequence, thereby constructing a larger recognisable unit; and
3. A four-point system of spelling provides practice in translating sounds, heard in sequence, into their letter names and written form.

It is claimed that the linkages are the essential component on which individualised programmes can then be developed for each pupil.

In addition to the tutor's manual, there are 170 drill cards, 610 word cards, diphthong cards, stories constructed to provide overlearning of particular phonic elements, syllabification exercises and instruction in a dictionary technique. The use of context to aid word identification is discouraged as the aim is to enable the pupils to use their phonic learning to decode text and not to have to rely on 'guessing' from context.

The manual contains a considerable number of helpful teaching points. According to one extremely experienced expert:

> The programme may appear to be dull and unattractive to the reader who has not taught in this structured, rather formal, and systematic manner. Such an impression is misleading. Children with learning disorders are delighted to succeed in tasks at which they have previously failed. Success itself becomes the motivating force. If there is boredom over drills and repetition, it is more often experienced by the teacher who has failed to understand a characteristic feature of the problem and whose presentation is probably dull.
>
> (Naidoo, 1988, p. 57)

The programme is time-consuming, extremely structured and lacking adequate individualisation (Hicks, 1986). On the other hand, any system that survives to its fifth edition, and is still in use today, is likely to have some merits. The Francis F. Parker School in Chicago adopted the Gillingham reading programme. The encouraging results of a seven-year study were presented at a meeting of the Gillingham Institute held on 26 January 1957. Films have been made of the use of the system in practice at Pine Ridge School in Massachusetts, where the work continues.

ALPHA TO OMEGA (Hornsby and Shear, 1975; Hornsby and Miles, 1980)

The authors of *Alpha to Omega* acknowledge their indebtedness to the earlier work of Orton and others such as Norrie (see pp. 259–62). Their approach comprises a highly structured, extremely detailed and sequential multisensory, three-stage phonics programme. It reflects the combined knowledge and skills of both teaching and speech therapy. The programme begins with individual letters, their sounds and alphabetical names. This leads into word building and the construction of sentences for reading and writing. Consonants are introduced according to the sequence in which they are developmentally acquired in spoken language: b, p, m, w, h; then d, t, n, g, k, m, g; f, s, z; v, th, sh, l, ch, a; y, qu, r, th, ks, or.

The teaching sequence is:

alphabet sounds
consonant digraphs
vowels
consonant blends
a variety of individual letter combinations, such as w, and associated rules
long vowels
rules of soft c and g
consonant trigrams; vowel digraphs
suffixing
syllabification

To quote from the programme:

Stage 1
This stage deals with monosyllabic words, except where the prefixes and suffixes can be added without changing the spelling of the 'root' word. The vowels are mostly short vowels, or one or two phoneme words ending in a vowel; open syllable words and the vowel will, therefore, be long. For example:

a	be	he	me	she	the	we
no	so	go	to	do		
I	by	my				

Also used are the 'lengthening *e*' vowels, which re-open the syllable:

cake	these	ripe	hope	tune

Stage 2
This stage also deals with monosyllabic words, but now we add prefixes and suffixes where the final spelling of the 'root' word does change. Here we also discover the other ways of getting long vowels.

Stage 3
This stage deals with polysyllabic words; the peculiarities of final syllables and open and closed syllables are gone into more thoroughly.

(Hornsby and Shear, 1975)

The sentences used also follow a developmental sequence, beginning with simple active affirmative declarative ones (SAAD). The importance of overlearning is emphasised. Lists of words for both reading and writing follow specific teaching points. Well planned sentences for dictation that illustrate and rehearse previously covered materials are provided. A spelling test is used at the end of each stage in order to establish whether the child is ready to progress to the next. There is a definite drill for presenting dictations. This includes the requirement that the pupil repeat a sentence with the aim of helping improve auditory memory performance.

A multisensory method is used to establish the various sound–symbol associations. Each letter, consonant digraph and consonant blend has a key picture used to 'unlock' the sound. A seven-step drill for learning these is clearly described. When the letters have been mastered, lists of phonically regular consonant–vowel–consonant (CVC) words are written and read. Reading and writing continue to be integrated by utilising multisensory methods capitalising on the combination of hearing, saying, seeing and feeling the symbols involved. Punctuation and literary skills are taught, including writing letters, précis, essays and stories.

The programme is set out in a 221-page spiral-bound book. It is well organised and enables teachers to identify the parts of the programme that may require revision. There is a set of 250 flashcards that provide the student with practice in single letters and sounds, consonant digraphs, consonant blends, vowel/consonant digraphs, 'Magic "e"', hard and soft 'c' and 'g', vowel digraphs, open and closed syllables and vocabulary. As mentioned earlier, mastery relies heavily on overlearning, formal structure and learning rules. The importance of automatisation of response is explicit. The aim is to eliminate failure and to ensure that errorless learning takes place: 'each step leads naturally and logically one into another, and at no time is the pupil required to read or write any spelling pattern or language structure which has not been specifically taught'.

The approach is open to criticisms similar to those levied at the previous two. It also has similar strengths. A study of three groups of children taught using *Alpha to Omega*, the Hickey Method and the Miles's Programme (three phonically based multisensory approaches) showed that all approaches produced significant gains in the pupils' literacy. The absence of control groups, the statistical analyses used and the very different settings of the three groups suggests the need for caution in interpreting the results (Hornsby and Miles, 1980). More recently, a follow-up study of 50 former students taught by the Alpha to Omega system indicates that those who had undergone the Alpha to Omega programme fared as well as the normative group in relation to certain examination successes and employment (Hornsby and Farrer, 1990). For reasons related to the design and analyses used, caution is also needed in interpreting these results.

EDITH NORRIE LETTER CASE (Norrie, 1960)

Edith Norrie, a Dane, was born in 1888. When she was 14 her parents were asked to remove her from school as she was making virtually no progress. She was unable to read, spell or write, yet she was not unintelligent. Subsequently Edith Norrie trained as a singer and then as a speech therapist. As a young woman she became engaged, but when her fiancé was posted to another part of Denmark she was unable either to read his letters or to write in reply. She determined that she would teach herself to read and spell. Motivation matters! This was a challenging, difficult and lengthy task, but she eventually succeeded. She began teaching others with reading difficulties in 1936 using the materials and method that she had developed for herself. It was at this time that she first heard of the term 'word blindness', which appeared to fit the symptoms that she herself had displayed. In 1939 she established the Word Blind Institute in Denmark and remained its principal for many years. Its work continues today and there is an English-language version of her system.

This system of teaching reading is primarily based on phonics, but also utilises Edith Norrie's professional knowledge of the perception and production of speech sounds, including the kinaesthetic sensations involved in sound production. Her materials, including a small mirror, are contained in a rectangular box called a 'Letter Case'. The mirror is deliberately kept small so that only the mouth can be observed.

The letters are arranged phonetically, not alphabetically. The letters of the alphabet, diagraphs and punctuation marks are colour coded according to how they are produced. Each is printed on a small rectangular card. There are plenty of cards for each letter/digraph and the capital of each letter is kept at the bottom of the appropriate pile. The vowels occupy five compartments at the bottom of the Letter Case. 'Y' is next to them and is colour coded with a red band to indicate that it can be used as a vowel. The importance of the vowels is emphasised. The child is helped to understand what syllables are and to realise that there is virtually no word, or even a single syllable, without at least one vowel or red letter in it. The two bottom right-hand compartments of the Letter Case contain the various punctuation marks. The colour code is as follows:

vowels	red
voiced consonants	green
unvoiced consonants	black

The consonants are further divided into three groups: labial, palatal and guttural. This arrangement helps the child narrow down the range of letters from which to select. The first group (the lip family) includes m, b, v, w and f. By using the mirror, the child can see that these sounds cannot be produced without closing the lips. The second (tip-of-the-tongue family) includes n, d, t, r, l, s, c, z, plus the digraphs th, ch and sh. Using the mirror reveals to the child that these sounds are produced by not closing the lips and by putting the tip of the tongue to the palate or teeth. The third group (back-of-the-tongue or throat family) includes k, g, q, x, h, y and ng. Whilst the mirror cannot reveal where these sounds are produced, it will show that the lips are not closed and the tip of the tongue is not used in producing them. Voiced letters (representing

Lips			Tip (tongue and teeth)			Back of throat		
2 M	2 B	2 N	2 D	2 T	1 Th	2 G		2 Q
							5 ng	
6 m	8 b	6 n	8 d	6 t	4 th	8 g		4 q
2 V	2 P	2 R	2 L	2 S	1 C	1 C	2 K	
								5 ck
3 v	6 p	12 r	8 l	6 s	5 c	6 c	3 k	
2 W	2 F	2 Z	2 J	1 Sh	1 Ch		2 H	
								4 , 1 ;
								1 ' 1 !
4 w	6 f	2 z	3 j	4 sh	4 ch	4 x	4 h	
1 Wh	2 A	2 E	2 I	2 O	2 U	2 Y		
								3 . 1 ?
							mirror	
3 wh	8 a	14 e	12 i	12 o	8 u	6 y		1 – 1 " "

A 'Clue card' accompanying the Letter Case presents the five vowels, each of which is illustrated by a picture.

Figure 6.1 *Edith Norrie Letter Case (Norrie, 1960)*

speech sounds requiring the vibration of the vocal chords) are in green: *m, b, v, w, n, d, r, l, z, j, g, ng*. Vowels are in red letters; Y has a red line through it to indicate its potential use as a vowel.

Each different group of cards is contained in a separate section of the box. The child is shown how each sound is produced and, by watching his/her mouth in the mirror, can establish the group into which each sound falls, and the place in which the letter equivalents are stored in the Letter Case. Thus, for example, the common developmental b–d confusion can be overcome because whilst the 'b' is labial, the 'd' is dental.

A sound, word or sentence may be dictated by the teacher. The child is required to repeat it and represent it using letters from the Letter Case. Recognition of sounds, represented by letters systematically arranged in a box, aids analysis. Recognition of letters is frequently easier than having to reconstitute them from memory. The aim is for the child to master the analysis of each uttered sound of a letter or word before writing anything down.

The system has been found particularly useful for children unable to follow their own speech sounds. It has been successfully used at the Helen Arkell Dyslexia Centre in London. In 1989–90 some 240 Letter Cases were sold, according to the head of the Centre. The development of information technology systems linking microcomputer, speech synthesiser and a video picture of the child's mouth can nowadays carry out similar procedures, albeit at greater expense.

Although the Edith Norrie Letter Case, and many other systems, have been of value to a number of pupils and adults with severe literacy difficulties, some individuals continue to have almost intractable problems. It is often said that specific learning difficulties/disabilities or dyslexia are not conditions that can be 'cured', even though many of their worst effects can be reduced with appropriate teaching: they are difficulties with which the individual learns to live. According to Kristin Illeborg of the Copenhagen Dyslexia Institute, in Denmark today the most severely disabled readers can obtain a small yellow card on which is written 'Jeg er ordblind' (I am wordblind). It is used in public offices and other places where an individual may be required to complete forms, and needs help so to do. Its purpose is to minimise the embarrassment dyslexics may feel in explaining their difficulties to strangers, and it makes it easier for others to be of assistance. The idea was originally developed by Bodil Holsting some years ago. Currently the card carries the logo of the Inter-European Dyslexia Association, with, on the back, the owner's name, address, telephone number and social security number. It is distributed in Denmark by the National Association for the Cause of Severely Disabled

Readers. The need for such a card points to the severe difficulties clients have in overcoming the many problems experienced in a wide range of language performances associated with dyslexia (Pumfrey et al., 1991). There are important arguments for and against the use of such a card. Should the idea be adopted in the UK? It could save a considerable number of individuals a great deal of difficulty.

THE BANGOR PROGRAMME: HELP FOR DYSLEXIC CHILDREN (Miles and Miles, 1983)

Dyslexia affects much more than learning to read, write and spell. The secondary emotional problems that can arise for the child, his or her parents and others involved, are considerable. The effects of a child's failure to read, write and spell can be emotionally devastating. In part, this is a consequence of the perceived importance of literacy in our culture. The dyslexic child's self-concept is often adversely affected, and the child loses confidence in his/her ability to learn. A diagnosis of 'specific learning difficulty' or 'specific developmental dyslexia' can have important beneficial motivational consequences for both pupil and parents. A valid diagnosis that the child's difficulties are the results of intellectual processes that differ somewhat from peers who experience no difficulties, can help the child with reading difficulties begin to accept and address these constructively. Under the current legislation outlined in Chapter 1 the diagnosis can also help in obtaining additional educational resources.

The Bangor programme has been developed on the basis of the verbal deficit hypothesis concerning specific learning difficulties (dyslexia). The teaching is based on the notion that the dyslexic child is able to understand ideas but has not mastered the coding system represented by, for example, textual materials. It integrates and develops the ideas contained in two earlier works, *On Helping the Dyslexic Child* (Miles, 1970) and *More Help for Dyslexic Children* (Miles and Miles, 1975). The programme is designed for use by both teachers and parents.

Chapters 1 to 3 outline the problems faced by dyslexic children and their families, and describe the patterns of difficulties that typify the dyslexic pupil. These include discrepancies between general intellectual ability and written language skills, letter reversals, letter transpositions, peculiar spellings, poor co-ordination, problems in rote learning and confusion concerning spatial and temporal concepts.

The teaching programme demonstrates how the pupil can be

progressively helped to understand and master the relationships between sounds and combinations of sounds and the letters and their combinations that comprise the English spelling system.

The programme is flexible. It recommends the use of various reading schemes based on phonic teaching methods, arguing that in general the 'look and say' approach is usually unsuitable for dyslexic pupils. Miles suggests that one starts with consonants and vowels, emphasising the structure of words to the child. A consideration of simple plurals, 'w' and 'l' words, single vowels, long vowels, vowel digraphs and the 'c' and 'g' rules ensues. Combinations of spelling patterns, irregular words, doubling silent letters, less usual combinations such as 'ch' and /k/ and suffixes follow.

To use the system teachers must be aware of the complexities of the written language system. It is recommended that the structure and spelling patterns of words are recorded by the child. Separate pages in an exercise book are reserved for exemplars of particular rules.

As a consequence of many years of work with children, generally of above-average intelligence, who have shown severe and prolonged difficulties in various aspects of literacy and numeracy, Miles has developed the Bangor Dyslexia Test (see Miles, 1983). This is *not* intended as a 'means of definitive diagnosis', but as a way of advancing understanding of the child's difficulties. This position is consonant with his view of dyslexia as a 'variable syndrome'. The test is designed for pupils of 7+ years, excluding children 'of limited ability'. The skills tested are:

- left–right (body parts)
- repeating polysyllabic words
- subtraction
- tables
- months forward
- months reversed
- digits forward
- digits reversed
- b–d confusions
- familial incidence

The scoring criteria for the test are only a guide. In interpreting the test results, 'you may prefer to rely on your overall impression rather than on the subject's precise score. Good sense is more important than numerical impression' (Miles, 1983, Manual, p. 1). The importance of 'incongruities' in a pupil's performances is considered central in deciding whether or not a child is, is not, or is partially dyslexic. The significance of the incongruities is determined by the particular case. The test is a clinical diagnostic instrument but is available to anyone in the 'helping' professions. It should be used with great caution bearing in mind the technical requirements of any valid diagnostic instrument. The Bangor Dyslexia Test has many weaknesses (Pumfrey, 1985).

FERNALD MULTISENSORY APPROACH (Fernald and Keller, 1921; Fernald, 1943)

Most readers will have heard of the magnificent triumph of determination, ability and sensitive teaching over the combined handicaps of blindness and deafness represented by the life of the late Helen Keller. Fernald developed a technique with Helen Keller utilising the kinaesthetic modality in teaching her to develop word recognition and writing skills (Fernald and Keller, 1921). The earlier 'breakthrough', by Helen Keller's teacher Anne Sullivan, had used the combination of finger spelling and tactile experience to establish communication with Helen.

At the time, tactile and kinaesthetic modalities were little used in the teaching of reading in mainstream education in the USA, other than in Montessori schools. (They had been used earlier when paper and pencils were less readily available, and are still used extensively in developing countries where resources are scarce but sand is plentiful.) At her clinic in Los Angeles, Fernald developed her auditory–kinaesthetic method for teaching wordblind pupils. In essence, it is a whole-word approach and provides no instruction as such in grapho-phonic associations. In contrast to the Gillingham–Stillman approach, it can be described as VAKT analytic.

Work begins with the child selecting any word he or she wants to learn. This is then written on a card measuring 12 in × 2.5 in (30.5 × 6.4 cm) with a wax crayon, or any other instrument that leaves a mark that can be traced by touch. Using the forefinger, the child traces the word, at the same time enunciating it. Intermodality associations (visual, auditory, kinaesthetic and tactile) (VAKT) are strengthened and a multisensory image is created by the child. The written word is then removed from sight and the child is asked to reproduce it from memory. If the child fails, the initial procedure is repeated until success is achieved on three consecutive trials. The child then extends his or her repertoire in the same manner based on self-selected words. The words learned are filed alphabetically. On the next day, the child is shown the word in typewritten form. If it is recognised from memory without any hesitation, no further writing trials are used with that word. If the child is not successful, the kinaesthetic exercises are repeated until the child can immediately recognise the word when presented in its typewritten form. After success with single words, the pupil goes on to continuous material including sentences dictated by the pupil to the teacher, who records what is said. The learner is then asked to read the dictated text and identify any unfamiliar words. These are then learned by the tracing method. The material dictated by a pupil and written by the teacher in a lesson is typed in time for the next lesson. Any unknown words in their typewritten format are then learned using the kinaesthetic technique.

Whilst acknowledging the very considerable individual differences in the number of repetitions required to master words in this manner, Fernald considered that in all cases a four-stage pattern of development could be identified:

Stage A

The learner can learn the words only by tracing them. Many repetitions may be required to master even very short words containing only two or three letters.

Stage B

Fewer repetitions are required to master words. The learner begins to drop tracing for some words, usually the shorter ones. The ability to read these shorter words has become 'automatised', i.e. mastered to the level where they can be read with no difficulty.

Stage C

At this stage a vocabulary of some 300–400 words will have been acquired. From the use of the dictated material approach, the pupil moves to printed text. The strategy taught is to scan a paragraph, passage or page quickly to identify words with which help might be needed. This is then given by the teacher. The pupil then settles down to read the text for comprehension. At this stage the learner can master the majority of new words after hearing the word pronounced and seeing it in writing. The use of tracing is used with only a minority of words.

Stage D

The learner can read text unaided.

The preface to Fernald's major book (Fernald, 1943) was written by the renowned psychologist Terman, co-author with Merrill of the

Stanford–Binet Intelligence Test. It is clear that Terman was deeply impressed by Fernald's ideas and results.

In summary, the success of the approach is not due solely to the kinaesthetic element in the programme. It has five major related strengths. It gives pupils who previously had never been able to cope with text, both a new method and an assurance that earlier difficulties were not due to personal inadequacy, but were a consequence of methods unsuited to his or her psychological constitution. This encourages the pupil to think positively about him/herself and is therefore highly motivational. Secondly, the material used initially is based on the learner's own language experience and personal selection. In contemporary terminology, the pupil psychologically 'owns' the material. Thirdly, the task involves associating a symbol with something that already has personal meaning for the learner, rather than looking at the symbol and deducing meaning. Fourthly, the kinaesthetic approach reinforces the left–right nature of reading, the sounding of the word as the learner's finger moves along the cursive script. Simultaneously, via the visual pattern of the script, sight and tracing are also linked in a feedback loop. The fifth strength is that the system allows for individual differences in the pace at which the work is covered.

Many of Fernald's ideas have been adopted by teachers and adapted for use in classrooms, particularly in early, corrective and remedial reading programmes.

BANNATYNE'S COLOUR PHONICS (Bannatyne, 1967, 1971)

Bannatyne, a psychologist, and his wife, a specialist in learning disabilities, developed this system over many years. The Bannatyne Learning Center has operated in Miami, USA, since 1969. Their system built on ideas derived, in part, from the Edith Norrie Letter Case (see pp. 259–62), using a multisensory technique, together with colour coding and phonics. It is based on the assumption that one of the major difficulties for dyslexic children lies in their inability to process auditory information efficiently. Bannatyne also considers that the required pedagogy should be deficit-oriented with a remedial approach concentrated mainly on phonics. The uses of a pupil's relative strengths and weaknesses is a continuing controversy in the remedial teaching of reading.

Early criticism of the Bannatynes' work concerned cost. When it was originally developed, colour printing was expensive. As the materials were largely expendable, the problem was exacerbated. Other criticisms were that the system encouraged 'barking at print' rather than understanding, and that colour-coding could well be only an additional processing problem for many children particularly when they transferred to normal texts. The latter criticism was one also levelled at the augmented Initial Teaching Alphabet (ITA). Some workers saw this as presenting unnecessary difficulties for pupils transferring to traditional orthography.

The Bannatynes' most developed colour phonics system was the Psycholinguistic Color System. More recently, they have developed a reading, writing, spelling and language programme that incorporates certain aspects of their colour system. This programme is highly structured. It is centred on a series of 13 workbooks grouped at three levels, and is built on a detailed task analysis of 1,200 steps of learned information. These steps are known as individualised educational prescriptions (IEPs). (British readers will note that the initials IEP in the UK refer to an individualised educational programme, a somewhat different concept.) There is a highly structured teaching routine aimed at ensuring that the 1,200 IEPs are taught in a step-by-step hierarchical order. The system is claimed to have 88 unique features. These include:

- systematic listening and articulation skills;
- eye movement tracking skills training;
- print of varying sizes for tracing over letter shapes and visual 'imprinting';
- systematic teaching of all initial, medial and consonant blends and digraphs. (Aukerman, 1984)

These are hardly unique features. Aukerman quotes Bannatyne as saying:

> Before a student reads a story for the first time, every word, every phoneme, every grapheme, every blend, every digraph, every bit of grammar, every word meaning etc., will *already* have been taught by the teacher and learned by the students in terms of reading, writing, spelling and language skills.
>
> (Ibid., p. 116)

The flavour of the programme can be gauged by considering the first part, which comprises five workbooks. Teaching the consonants and vowels is accomplished in a hierarchical series of 23 steps for each phonics element. With the 26-letter alphabet, a total of 598 learnings have to be mastered. The activities involve listening to the sound of a consonant (or vowel), and repeating it. Pictures of objects whose names have the consonant at the beginning, middle or end of the word are used. Throughout the 23 steps, ample pictures are provided to help pupils learn key words. The printed symbol is then presented in large 12 cm-high letters for tracing.

Subsequently the tracing of smaller letters is carried out. As the letter shapes are traced, the sound associated with each is spoken by the pupil. The letters are then used in consonant–vowel–consonant (CVC) word patterns, the pupils pronouncing the sounds as they print the letters. When these stages have been mastered, words of more than one syllable are studied. Short sentences are included in the reading programme. The first stage ends with the pupil *successfully* reading a short story composed of several sentences.

There has been a considerable amount of research into the efficacy of the Bannatyne Programme. Most of this has been carried out with classes of older pupils who were educationally retarded because of low intelligence, learning disabled, emotionally disturbed or of non-English backgrounds. There appears to be something effective in the programme for such groups of children (Aukerman, 1984, p. 119).

THE HICKEY METHOD (Hickey, 1977)

The Hickey approach draws on the work of Gillingham and Stillman, and also on the language training programmes developed by Waites and Cox at the Scottish Rite Hospital, Dallas, Texas. It can be used either with individual children or in a small group of up to four pupils. The method uses multisensory techniques and is based on the assumption that the child with dyslexia requires instruction in the structure of written language in order to master the decoding and encoding aspects of text processing. It is based on the idea that dyslexic children can use their stronger modalities for learning but must simultaneously improve areas of weakness.

Acknowledging that a considerable number of dyslexic pupils have weaknesses in auditory and/or visual perception and memory, Hickey includes suggestions for improving these functions. These are directly related to the accompanying reading and spelling work in hand. Such content has been shown to be essential if there is to be any transfer to the skills of reading and spelling. The self-correcting nature of many of the exercises facilitates independent work by the child, following initial input by the teacher.

The technique requires a considerable amount of drill and practice. The child has to be made aware of the grapheme/phoneme structure of text. Many dyslexic pupils find this task extremely difficult. If the child is to master the written language system, he or she must become conscious of its grapheme/phoneme structure. It is precisely this aspect that presents problems for most dyslexic pupils. The system can be made more 'ideographic' and less 'orthographic' if mediational clues are provided to assist the reader, for example by identifying a word pattern or a spelling that the child can immediately access. For example, Hickey advocates the use of cards with clue words. Table 6.1 shows some examples of the letters on cards, the clue word associated with it, the sound and examples of irregular words.

Table 6.1 *Clue words and word patterns*

Card	Clue word	Sound	Irregular word
or	stork	(or)	
ea	seat	(e)	
ar	car	(ar)	quarter, warm
ou	house	(ow)	could, should, would

The written language is, in part, syllabified. The child is helped to overcome short-term memory problems in combining letter sequences. If the child has immediate access to an overall sound–symbol pattern, there is no need to search for individual letter sounds.

The syllabus begins with letters, differentiates vowels and consonants, moves on to word building and then works towards phonetically regular and irregular polysyllabic words. Both the reading and spelling of these are considered simultaneously. The use of the Fernald auditory–kinaesthetic technique is recommended for learning phonetically irregular words. The approach does recognise the importance of mediational clues that can, for example, help pupils overcome short-term memory difficulties. Strategies to achieve this are described.

Because dyslexic pupils have not picked up the phoneme/grapheme aspect of text as readily as their peers, the written language has to be taught *very* thoroughly. There is a danger that lessons can become tedious. Considerable teaching ingenuity, plus good rapport with the pupil, are essential. By completing work successfully in small stages the pupil can appreciate that progress is being made in an area previously associated with utter failure and demoralisation. The quite formal training has to be interspersed with a variety of reading/language games and other activities.

For the teacher new to working with dyslexic children, it is advisable to work systematically through the scheme. One major advantage of doing so is that it helps the teacher clarify her understanding of the structure of written language and the basis for the teaching programme. With increasing familiarity, the materials can be used more flexibly.

THE PEABODY REBUS READING PROGRAM (Clark and Davies, 1979)

Long before the alphabet was invented, people communicated through pictures: some of the earliest are prehistoric cave paintings. At a later date, picture stories were engraved on the walls of palaces and temples. With the arrival of the alphabet, pictures were gradually replaced by less ambiguous text. Both pictures and text were combined in story puzzles produced for children during the nineteenth century. For example, in the nursery rhyme 'Little Jack Horner', a picture of a horn followed by the letters 'er' could be used. A sketch of a human eye was used to convey the meaning of the first person singular. Pictures used in this way are referred to as rebuses (from the Latin *rebus*, 'with things').

There are many uses of rebuses in everyday life today. Toilets are often indicated by stylised representations of male or female figures. International traffic and road signs are other examples of rebuses enabling effective communication in countries where the visitor may neither speak nor read the language.

The use of rebuses in the teaching of reading is defended by proponents who point to the use of pictures as aids to comprehension in graded reading series and other books for children. The early development of symbolic thinking for communicative purposes by children is clearly shown in the development of their drawings. Opponents argue that the absence of such pictures would make the learner concentrate on the actual form and meaning of the alphabetic representations of words. Where children have signally failed to learn to read using conventional materials and methods, the use of rebuses may well be helpful.

In 1964 Woodcock and Dunn at Peabody College for Teachers, Nashville, Tennessee, began developing a rebus approach to the teaching of reading to mentally retarded children. For experimental purposes, Woodcock devised the Rebus Reading Series in 1965. The major elements of the updated version are three programmed books, two readers (80 pp. and 72 pp.), a teacher's manual, and a considerable amount of supplementary material. Books 1 and 2 cover the reading-readiness stage. Book 3 and the 'Rebus Readers' are for the subsequent pre-primer level. Children are introduced to the system by the teacher, who initially shows the children four rebuses: cowboy, horse, dog, +. The + represents the word 'and'. The children are asked what they think the rebuses 'say' (mean). After reading this rebus vocabulary, the child is then presented with the rebuses symbolising 'cowboy and horse', 'cowboy and dog', and so on.

Using rebuses, the child who has reached page 8 of the pre-primer can read sentences such as: 'The little cowboy can see the big dog sitt/ing'. The 'ing' ending is presented in traditional orthography and can be linked to a rebus indicating an action. The identification of the rebus vocabulary involved many difficult decisions. Whereas many words can be presented by relatively unambiguous pictures, various structural words absolutely central to the meaning of consecutive text cannot. For these words (e.g. a, am, and, are, is) an acceptable symbol had to be devised. The rebus vocabulary comprises some 174 symbols and associated words. As the child works through the system, words are increasingly substituted for rebuses. The first time that any word in traditional orthography is presented it is accompanied by its rebus.

The pre-primer workbooks all have four rebus reading tasks on each page. Each requires the reader to interpret the rebus message and select the correct answer from up to three possible responses. To respond, the pupil has to underline the one rebus response using the dampened tip of a pencil rubber. If the response is correct, the ink in the response area turns green; if the response is incorrect, it turns red. This use of feedback of information on the accuracy of the pupil's response is intended to provide a high level of positive reinforcement. By virtue of the careful grading of the items, most pupils are correct for a high proportion of the time. The motivating effects of success are particularly valued by children who have known relatively little. The first two books each contain 384 frames and Book 3, 448.

Some small-scale studies suggest that rebuses can be more effective than traditional orthography in helping some pupils learn to read. The approach could well be of value to children who have difficulties in phonic analysis and synthesis and who have not responded satisfactorily to phonemic awareness programmes such as those advocated by Bradley (1990) and Snowling (1990).

THE ICON APPROACH (Neville-Brown, 1990)

Maple Hayes Dyslexia School and Research Centre at Lichfield in Staffordshire is closely associated with the Foundation for the Education of the Underachieving and Dyslexic (FEUD). The school is one of only a small number of private educational establishments officially recognised by the Department of Education and Science as providing a suitable education for pupils with specific learning difficulties.

Brown questions the current dominant phonics-*cum*-multisensory approach to the remediation of reading, spelling and writing difficulties. He is unconvinced by the assumption that the most effective methods are those 'focussed on the links between the ways letters and words look, sound and feel as they are produced in speech and simultaneous writing'. He suggests an alternative approach.

The somewhat simplistic assumption that phonetics is either necessary and/or sufficient to reading and spelling has been challenged by a number of research workers in addition to Brown. For example, he quotes Hynds' (1987) comment: 'I have not so far been able to find anyone, amongst even the most accomplished of readers, who has more than the vaguest notion of the twenty or so pure vowel sounds in English'. Goodman had earlier pointed out that any reader dependent solely on the conscious use of phonic/ phonetic strategies or cue systems for decoding text would be incapable of reading material of any length sufficiently rapidly to do so with understanding (see Chapter 2). The phonological route from print to meaning is just one of a number of channels that may be used independently, not necessarily at the same time, in learning to read and in efficient reading.

Brown also suggests that too much emphasis on the use of the phonological route, particularly with pupils experiencing great difficulties in that modality, could have an adverse effect upon other strategies of text processing. By analogy, if one has a damaged leg, to train for the high jump may be no more than a triumph of hope over experience. If the objective is to get one's body up to and over any particular height, alternative strategies could well stand a far greater chance of success. A promising alternative strategy in teaching dyslexic pupils, developed by Brown, is based on the importance of the morphemic structure of language.

The approach he advocates requires the pupils to proceed directly from the visual stimulus to meaning without phonological mediation. In the sense that the approach begins with the visual stimulus of text, he calls the technique a unisensory one. Many dyslexic pupils have great difficulty in segmenting semantically complex words into syllables, or into the discrete sounds that are attached to letters and certain blends. If pupils can be helped to segment such words morphemically by being provided with clues to the particles presented within such a word, their chances of being able to read and spell them will be enhanced.

A comparison of a phonic teaching programme with a morphographic programme based on visual mediators (called 'icons') devised by Brown demonstrated the superiority of the second approach in promoting the recognition, comprehension and spelling of long words that were used in the pupils' vocabularies but were not in their written lexicon. Letter or syllable sounding inhibited vocabulary recognition and spelling.

Recently Brown has presented a detailed case study of a boy called Alex. Alex had failed to respond to the multisensory phonic-based programme to which he had been directed by the school psychological service of his local education authority. As one reads Brown's account, in which writing and tactile senses were utilised, the term unisensory does not readily come to mind. What is clear is that the presenting symptoms of the child are carefully considered and that an effective individualised programme was devised. Whilst individual case studies are both important and interesting, it is hoped that the Maple Hayes Research Centre will produce further evidence of the nature, content and efficacy of its morphographic approach.

CONCLUSION

The existence of different dyslexias is a notion that has considerable research support (Tyler, 1990). This is probably why the term 'specific learning difficulties' is seen as synonymous with dyslexia by groups such as the British Dyslexia Association. It is also probably why the Department of Education and Science considers that the term specific learning difficulties includes dyslexia. The pluralities matter. The search for effective aptitude × instruction interactions suggests that different forms of educational intervention may benefit pupils differently, irrespective of whether or not they have specific learning difficulties or dyslexia. The twin objectives of improving junior school pupils' reading standards generally and alleviating reading difficulties represent the educational horizon. Let us ensure that we move in the right direction and do not dissipate scarce energies and resources in unproductive conflict between holders of polarised positions.

7

Kits

A selection of six popular kits of materials designed to develop literacy is presented. There are many others (Atkinson et al., 1985).

DISTAR

DISTAR is an acronym standing for Direct Instruction Systems for Teaching Arithmetic and Reading. The original materials were developed over several years of research in a programme conducted at the Institute for Research on Exceptional Children at the University of Illinois. The target group of children were those from socio-economically disadvantaged circumstances, a large group that also showed relatively low attainments in reading and other aspects of the curriculum.

Bereiter and Engelmann were the original director and assistant on the project. Bereiter later moved to the Ontario Institute for Studies in Education in Toronto, and Becker replaced him at Illinois. Following many years of try-outs and revisions, the first edition of DISTAR was published in 1969 by Science Research Associates who are still the publishers (Engelmann and Bruner, 1983).

Underpinning DISTAR is a set of assumptions including the following:

- Disadvantaged black children manifest a serious learning deficit. This must be remedied before they can successfully compete in middle-class, white-oriented schools.
- Prior to school, at the age of 4, they require a structured and concentrated programme to prepare them for education.
- Socioculturally disadvantaged pre-school children are typically non-communicative when addressed in the conventional classroom manner. This characteristic cognitive style must be changed so that habits of listening and responding are established.
- The objectives of the programme are based on what has to be learned, i.e. on a detailed task analysis. These objectives are *not* identified by individual assessment. Objectives must be

stated in terms of operationally defined aspects of knowledge to be learned, skills acquired and behaviour demonstrated.
- The system is teacher-dominated. It is the teacher's responsibility to ensure that the objectives of each session are attained.
- The teacher is required to use a clear, structured, step-by-step, fast, specific, absolute and direct instructional method using relevant materials.
- Direct instruction towards specific learning results in identifiable performances that can be readily tested. What is taught is learned. The aim is for it to be mastered.

The authors of the system have described their approach as 'an intensive, fast-paced, highly structured program of instruction . . .'.

As demonstrated by Engelmann, intensive drill sessions generate pupil involvement and enthusiasm. The pupils appear to enjoy the rhythmic, whole-group response mode. The sessions are speeded by the often repeated injunction 'Say it *fast*'. The programme insists on immediate and rapid responses by pupils. The sequences are highly structured. Word-by-word instructions are contained in spiral-bound books that the teachers use. Deviations from this straight (and narrow) path are discouraged. Creative teachers are instructed *not* to adopt a language-arts approach. Direct instruction does not allow for asides that might break the specified sequential steps in the instruction.

The system has been extended to cover several core attainment areas such as reading, spelling, handwriting, vocabulary and arithmetic (Carnine and Silbert, 1978). Different levels have been developed for various age groups. Project 'Follow Through' was the successor to 'Project Head-start'. When competing interventions were evaluated, DISTAR was by far the most consistently effective. In a number of cases, its use led to dramatic increases in the reading attainments of socioculturally disadvantaged children.

Three examples make the point; two are American and one British. In Flint, Michigan, it was reported that socioculturally disadvantaged children using DISTAR improved from having a pre-test median score at the 18th percentile to post-test scores at the 83rd percentile in reading and from the 8th percentile in language to the 50th percentile. Public School 137 in the Ocean Hill–Brownsville section in New York involved twelve classrooms, three at each age level from kindergarten to the third grade (8 years). In 1977 the US Department of Education funded a study to examine the efficacy of federally funded projects to improve educational attainments in New York and Philadelphia, two of the country's largest conurbations. The areas selected were characterised by sociocultural deprivation, teachers' strikes, high staff turnover in schools and generally adverse educational climates. There were 11 'Follow Through' projects in the two cities using a variety of approaches. Only the direct instruction model used in Public School 137 demonstrated consistent, significant positive effects. A subsequent analysis of the work done at this school suggested reasons for the success compared with other projects in similar ghetto urban schools:

- the involvement of the project manager from the University of Oregon who monitored teacher and pupil performances;
- the highly structured nature of the materials used;
- the detailed, structured teacher routines and behaviour;
- training programmes in the use of the materials and the method that had been provided for staff;
- 'time on task' was high; *three hours per day* were spent on the programme and materials with a teacher and a teacher aide;
- the division of each class into three groups of between 6 and 12 students for direct instruction: with small groups it is possible to ensure that all children are learning all the time;
- stress on the teaching of general cases: this helps children generalise to all members of a set after having mastered some exemplars;
- the use of positive reinforcement; the children are never told that they are wrong. This increases the involvement of the pupils and their motivation;
- monitoring progress using mastery tests built into the programme: children continue only when the teacher is completely certain that they have mastered the work covered.

Because of the extensive research studies confirming the effectiveness of the system, it has been used with large numbers of children of all ages. Its central ideas have also been developed for use with adults experiencing difficulties in literacy.

In England, a recent brief account of the use of the DISTAR corrective reading programme (modified to Direct Instructional System for Teaching and Remediation) has been presented (Turner, 1990a). The pupils involved had just completed their junior school education and were transferring to Sylvan High, a comprehensive school in Croydon. Twenty-five per cent of the entry were regularly found to have reading ages that were not considered functional, being up to four years below their chronological ages. At this stage the pupils were described as: 'often disaffected or demoralized after six years of primary education which have to all intents and purposes [been] wasted'. The formal 'statementing' procedures under the Education Act 1981 and Circular 22/89, whereby referral, formal assessment and statementing of individual pupils take place in order to secure additional resources, were seen as 'a meaningless and frustrating experience for all'.

The alternative policy was to adopt DISTAR for these 40 pupils. A similar group of 17 pupils attending another Croydon secondary school were using a different system known as 'Flying Start' to help with their low reading attainments. The results reported demonstrated significantly greater improvement in the DISTAR group's mean scores on independent measures of reading attainment. For example, starting with a mean reading age of 7.75 years on the Daniels and Diack Test 12, a sentence completion test of reading comprehension, by the end of the school year the group improved to a mean score of 9.25 years. The 'Flying Start' pupils improved from an average of 8.25 to 8.6 years: '87% of children on the Sylvan DISTAR made some absolute progress with reading. Further, 74% of the children made better than this, that is more than a year of reading age in a chronological year' (Turner, 1990a). Pupils, parents and teachers were delighted with the results. Clinical vignettes on the effects of success in learning to read on individual pupils' emotional problems and attitudes to school underline the value of the programme:

> DISTAR works. The 'corrective' reading programme is highly effective for most children in their early secondary years who have persistent reading problems. And such problems constitute the major factor in referral to school psychological services, in assessment for statemented extra support, in children's disaffections and problems of behaviour, and in parents' anxiety over their children and disappointment with school.
>
> (Turner, 1990a)

For many such pupils 'statementing' would appear to be a waste of time and resources (ibid.).

DISTAR Reading I is, in essence, a remedial and almost completely phonic approach. Pre-reading exercises lead on to reading, writing and spelling. DISTAR Reading II gives more emphasis to comprehension and advanced reading skills. Although phonics are still used, the aids used in I are gradually reduced. Materials for both I and II are provided in boxed kits.

'Schoolhouse Word Attack Skills (5–9)' comprises 170 sequenced work cards including sections on auditory discrimination, consonants, vowels, blends, digraphs, compounds, contractions, prefixes and suffixes. The subsequent 'Schoolhouse Word Attack Skills 7–10' includes 200 work cards in six colour-coded sections. These are phonics A and B, structural analysis, syllables, meanings and dictionary skills.

For middle junior to early secondary school levels, the relationships between sentence structures and comprehension are emphasised. 'Schoolhouse Comprehension Patterns (9–13)' contains 195 exercise cards designed to enable the relationships between sentence structure and comprehension to be taught.

The rigidity of the programme is such that it will not appeal to all teachers, or pupils. The author has visited a school district in the USA where an English primary school adviser had been brought in to moderate what some professionals saw as a suspect direct instruction educational 'bandwagon'. DISTAR is firmly bedded in task analysis and behavioural psychology. It has a 'bottom-up' theoretical emphasis and pedagogy. The balance of the evidence is that *it works* for many pupils. This is an important point that must not be overlooked.

SCIENCE RESEARCH ASSOCIATES (SRA) READING LABORATORIES (SRA, 1985)

Reading materials can be organised in such a way as to improve children's attainments through individualised skills development. Boxes of materials, often called reading laboratories, or kits, have been developed for this purpose.

The SRA Reading Laboratories is one of the most widely known, and used, of these approaches. Each laboratory comprises a carefully graded series of reading tasks aimed at encouraging individual and independent learning. The content covers listening, word-attack and comprehension skills. The laboratories consist of boxes of cards and booklets grouped by colour. The colour-coding represents different reading-age demands of the materials. An initial pre-test is taken by pupils in order to establish the level at which they should start. Pupils then work through the 12 or so cards at that level before moving up to the next one. Pupils keep records of their successes on criterion tests on a personal record sheet that is part of the system. If pupils achieve a series of very high scores at a given level, they are encouraged to discuss these with their teacher with a view to moving to a higher level of work. The uses of the various parts of the laboratory are carefully explained in the teacher's manual. The reading laboratory is intended to be used on a relatively intensive basis (several times weekly) for a term. This is followed by two terms when it is not used. The materials include 'power builders' and 'rate builders'. The first is designed to increase the pupils' reading comprehension; the second to increase speed of reading. Both sets of builders use the strategy based on the five activities: survey; questions; read; review and recite (SQ3R).

There are nine kits in all, covering reading-age levels from 6.2

years to 19.0 years. Within a large junior school, reading ages will range (at least) between 6.2 and 14.0 years. Details of the first six kits are presented here.

SRA Reading Laboratories

Series 1a, 1b and 1c
Skills covered include reading comprehension, word attack, vocabulary and listening.
Interest ages: 6.0 to 9.0 yrs.
The materials provide 12 levels of difficulty in each kit. Each includes:
144 power builders and answer key cards; 10 starter booklets.
Individual pupils' record books, teacher's handbook, an orientation tape and listening skills workbooks are also included.
Reading age levels in years:
1a: 6.2 to 8.5 (Chronological age range recommended 6:00 to 7:00 yrs)
1b: 6.4 to 9.5 (Chronological age range recommended 7:00 to 8:00 yrs)
1c: 6.6 to 10.5 (Chronological age range recommended 8:00 to 9:00 yrs)

Series 2a, 2b and 2c (Mark II)
Skills covered include comprehension (literal and inferential), study skills, sentence study, vocabulary, sentence analysis and phonics.
Interest ages: 9:0 to 12:0 yrs.
The materials provide 10 levels of difficulty in each kit.
Mark II series includes:
150 power builders and answer key cards;
150 skills development lesson cards designed 'to remedy diagnosed weaknesses';
150 rate builders and answer keys.
Individual pupils' record books, teacher's handbook, an orientation tape and a listening skills builder scriptbook are also included.
Reading age levels in years:
2a: 7.0 to 12.0 (Chronological age range recommended 9:00 to 10:00 yrs)
2b: 7.6 to 13.0 (Chronological age range recommended 10:00 to 11:00 yrs)
2c: 8.0 to 14.0 (Chronological age range recommended 11:00 to 12:00 yrs)

There is a supply of supplementary readers at the equivalent level of reading difficulty to accompany reading laboratories 1c, 2a, 2b, 2c and 3b by the 'Pilot Library Series'. Additionally, there are series of 32-page comic-like books at reading age levels of about 7.5, 8, 9 and 10 years.

It can be seen from this description and summary that the laboratories provide ample opportunities for reading at either the mastery or the instructional level. The importance of overlearning and of automaticity that is its conceptual Siamese twin, is integral to the system. Once set up with the pupils knowing what they are required to do, the system fits very easily into classroom organisation.

Does the system work? Does it improve children's reading attainments?

One of the major UK studies of the efficacy of reading laboratories was carried out with 530 11-, 12- and 15-year-old pupils as the experimental group using the SRA Laboratories and a control group of 488 pupils from the same age groups who did not. The pupils were tested on reading speed, accuracy and comprehension during the September and December of the term when the SRA Reading Laboratory was being used. They were tested again when six months had elapsed after the end of the Michaelmas term.

The results demonstrated clearly that the use of the SRA Reading Laboratory had important beneficial effects on some aspects of reading attainments. This was particularly the case with pupils whose earlier reading test scores had been below average. For pupils of above-average initial reading attainments, the subsequent scores on reading speed and accuracy were increased. Perhaps of greater note is the fact that the relative gains of the experimental group pupils were generally maintained, and in some instances further enhanced, when the group was retested on follow-up in June. The investigator summarised his conclusions with an unequivocal assertion unusual in the (usually justified) bet-hedging uncertainties that typify applied educational research: 'We therefore conclude that the SRA Reading Laboratories have been shown to be a valuable tool for promoting the effectiveness of reading across the ability range at all ages considered' (Fawcett, 1979).

As could be anticipated, this challenging assertion provoked a strong reaction from individuals and groups suspicious of the use of highly structured materials such as the SRA Reading Laboratories. Legitimate caveats were raised concerning the allocation of children to the control group and also to the similarity of the reading tests used to the SRA Reading Laboratory materials. This, it was asserted, could have given an unquantified and possibly unfair advantage to the experimental group. The Hawthorne effect was also invoked as having biased the results. Battle was joined. A balanced, succinct and constructive summary of the controversy is available (Beard, 1987).

In the present author's judgement, the case for the use of the SRA Laboratories established by Fawcett is a stronger one than that of his critics. In part, this weighing of the evidence is coloured by experience with the SRA Reading Laboratory with top juniors attending an inner-city school with low mean reading attainments in a North-West local education authority. Because of the promise of the laboratory and the seriousness of the problem faced by the school, a member of staff was trained in its use. The effects were most encouraging, in terms of both improvement in reading attainments and attitudes to school and also in school attendance. Being successful is something that most of us enjoy, unless lengthy experience of failure has so affected our perceptions that we cannot 'own' such successes as we experience and attribute them to 'luck', 'chance', or some other external agency. Sadly, some junior school children reach this condition in relation to reading. The pupils attending this particular school certainly developed different perceptions of themselves as a consequence of their successes. The laboratory encourages regular individualised reading, time-on-task behaviour, uninterrupted reading at an appropriate level and feedback of information on progress. Well done! Is this the panacea for which teachers strive? Sadly – or fortunately – 'No'.

The teacher who had been involved in this successful pilot curriculum development moved to another school. His replacement was asked to continue the programme with the next year group. On later visiting the class to observe the work, it was clear that the new teacher either did not know how to use the system or could not be bothered to ensure that the children used it properly. The management of the school was such that although this problem was known, the issue was not addressed. The Reading Laboratory was described by this teacher as 'useless'. There are important issues here for all teachers, for classroom organisation, staff development and school management that will be dealt with in subsequent chapters.

In addition to their Reading Laboratories, SRA produce a 'First Listening Laboratory', 'Researchlab' (for developing research and reference skills), 'Thinklab' (to develop problem-solving and creative, flexible reasoning strategies).

WARD LOCK READING WORKSHOP SERIES

This series of kits (published by Ward Lock Educational) covers three major phases of reading instruction. The first focuses on pre-reading skills, the second on reading from Y1 to Y5 and the third on remedial work for pupils in Y5 to Y9 (national curriculum terminology). All three kits contain a wide range of both fiction and non-fiction texts.

Pre-reading Workshops Stages 1 and 2
Listening and speaking skills, letter–sound activities and letter-matching activities (K to Y1).

Reading Workshop 6–10
150 graded work cards.
Readability levels from 6:06 to 9:06 years (Y1 to Y5).

Reading Workshop 9–13
100 work cards and 100 speed cards.
Readability levels 8:00 to 12:06 years (Y4 to Y9).

Remedial Reading Workshop
This is intended for pupils aged from about 10 to 14.
100 work cards graded in a colour-coded sequence.
Cloze procedure comprehension exercises are used extensively.
Multiple-choice questions are also used (Y5 to Y9).

The research by Fawcett quoted earlier included a comparison of the efficacy of the Ward Lock Remedial Reading Workshop. According to Fawcett, the SRA Reading Laboratory produced superior results. However, the sample using the Ward Lock material was relatively small. The findings require replication and extension before they can be accepted as convincing evidence of a differential relative efficacy.

Perhaps what is more important is that kits such as this should be seen as just *one* ingredient in a junior school's reading programme.

EFFECTIVE READING WORKSHOP

Published by Oliver and Boyd, this reading workshop differs somewhat from others. It is not a prescriptive sequence of graded and individualised reading assignments, but a variety of substantial and challenging texts that the publishers claim pupils find enjoyable in their own right. These include short stories, poems, non-fiction, jokes and extracts from plays and stories. The workshop is designed for pupils of the middle school age range who are 'reasonably competent readers'. The reading ages of the materials provided range from approximately the 9-year-old to the 13-year-old levels.

Table 7.1 *Effective Reading Workshop: contents*

Reading activity	Reading levels and number of items per level				Materials
	1 Red	2 Blue	3 Green	4 Tan	
Cloze completion	6	6	6	6 ⎫	Copymasters
Test sequencing	3	3	3	3 ⎬	
Projection/ prediction	2	2	2	2 ⎭	12 pp. booklets 2 texts, 3 copies at each level
Information retrieval	4	4	4	4	4 pp. cards and questions
Reflective reading tasks	6	6	6	6	4 pp. cards and questions
Teacher's manual plus pupil record sheet					

As a resource for the teacher, the workshop provides a carefully selected and well organised set of readings linked to a range of five reading comprehension activities for both groups and individuals. The structure of the workshops is shown in Table 7.1.

The individual pupil record sheet enables each pupil to keep a track of his/her own progress with the variety of reading tasks and levels of material. The criteria suggested for determining where pupils should start work are based on the teacher's professional judgement. It is recommended that this decision takes three points into account:

1. the teacher's knowledge of the pupil's attainments and the content of the workshop;
2. the pupil's results on a workshop card or sheet.

(The use of a workshop cloze task linked to the following criteria for competence taken from Harrison's work (1980) is given:

- 60 per cent and above – pupil is coping well and can probably attempt a higher level of work.
- 40–60 per cent – pupil coping adequately at the instructional level.
- Below 40 per cent – pupil faces a frustrating task. Move to a lower level of work.)

3. Results from recently administered reading tests.

Junior school teachers will wish to establish which of the national curriculum (English) profile components and attainment targets are represented in such materials. Having considered the attainment targets in some detail (see Appendix 2), it appears to the author that this can readily be done in relation to reading and to certain of the other attainment targets (English).

READING ROUTES

Published by Longman, Reading Routes is contained in two boxes, one blue and the other red. The materials were developed over a period of five years, and are designed for use by pupils at a (relatively) low reading level. Materials are written at between the 6:05 and 10+ reading age levels. The range of topics presented in the texts has been carefully selected for use with primary school pupils. Interest is intended to be extended by the inclusion of 'Things to do' on the answer cards that accompany the materials. The contents reflect the multicultural aspect of life in societies, both here and overseas.

The contents of Reading Routes are as follows:

Blue Box
120 colour-coded cards covering 80 topics designed to develop reading and comprehension skills.
96 answer cards (each suggesting three further activities).
16 story work cards containing cloze passages.
Audio cassette to accompany four of the story folders.
Content based on four themes: the natural world, homes, travel and people.
Reading age levels range from 6:06 to 10+ years (Y1 to Y5).

Red Box
144 colour-coded cards covering 120 topics.
144 answer cards which include additional suggested activities.
10 copies of the pupils' workbook.
10 target score sheets.
Project cards/folders.
Content based on six thematic 'routeways': 'Ordinary and remarkable', 'Transport and inventions', 'Nature', 'Famous people', 'Animals' and 'Story and fable'.
Readability levels range from 7:06 to 12+ years (Y2 to Y6).

The teacher's manual gives details of how the kit can be used, information on its vocabulary, structure and projects, and on how the scheme was developed and tested.

BREAKTHROUGH TO LITERACY (Mackay et al., 1979)

'Breakthrough to Literacy' is an initial reading and writing programme designed to enable young pupils learn to read, write and spell. The system was developed by four teachers involved in a research and development project known as the 'Programme in Linguistics and English Teaching'.

Central to the system is the construction by pupils of their own personal sentences using what is called a 'sentence maker' folder. The system has enjoyed considerable national and international success. It was initially designed for use with infant pupils, but has subsequently been successfully used with junior school pupils and adults with reading difficulties. The greatest strengths of the technique are its sound theoretical basis, its relative simplicity and its extreme flexibility.

Key pieces of equipment

Magnet board.

Teacher's sentence maker: 130 high-frequency words are printed on cards and visible in two large panels. A third blank panel is available for cards bearing personal words written by the teacher on spare blank cards that are provided.

Sentence maker folder: a triptych-like pocketed folder in which words on cards can be placed.

Project folder: a blank version of the individual pupil's sentence maker used to store children's words on particular topics that may arise regularly at given times in the year (e.g. Christmas and Easter) or because they are very popular topics and arise frequently in primary school work (e.g. animals, the family, transport).

Mini sentence maker: a small blank sentence maker designed for pupils who find the transfer from the teacher's sentence maker to the pupil's sentence maker too large a step.

First word book: a book in which children can record, in alphabetical order, the words they are able to use fluently when constructing phrases or sentences using the sentence maker.

Breakthrough 'blank books': pupils can transfer selected stories into these. They have a space for the title and author, just like the printed *Breakthrough to Literacy* books. There is also room for details 'about the author' and 'about this book'.

Breakthrough dictionary: designed to bridge the gap between picture dictionaries and conventional dictionaries, this is divided into thematic sections.

Breakthrough word makers: used initially by teachers with pupils to introduce phonics. Pupils are taught how to use their own 'word makers', used in conjunction with their sentence makers, to build up new words that they might require for a sentence.

Word card storage unit: a piece of equipment in which the teacher's central store/reserve of word cards is kept.

The first important piece of equipment is a magnet board. On it, figurine pictures can be held in place by small magnets. The pictures so constructed are used for discussion. Sentences stimulated by the materials are produced by the pupils. The teacher represents the sentence using words that have been printed on cards, a set of which is contained in the teacher's sentence maker which is supported in a plastic stand, and places these words on cards in the appropriate sequence underneath the picture.

In the next stage the teacher works with a small group of pupils using the teacher's sentence maker to construct a simple sentence. When a child can recognise about 10 to 20 words and can compose a simple sentence, the child is given a personal sentence maker containing only the words on cards that he/she knows. Sentences are constructed by the pupils using the words on cards and placing them on the plastic stands. The teacher is asked for any other words that may be required. When the sentence has been completed, it is read to the teacher. Next it is written by the teacher and then by the child into a personal reading book.

Phonics are introduced using the teacher's 'first word maker'. This contains symbol cards for vowels, kept on the right-hand side of the folder, and consonants and certain consonant blends kept on the left-hand side. These materials are used for word building and for examining the patterns of words and the identification of word families. Pupils are taught how to use their own 'word builder' to construct new words that they do not yet have in their 'sentence builder' collection but require to complete a sentence. More advanced phonic work is carried out using the 'second word maker'. This is a three-sided folder with symbols for initial consonant clusters on the left-hand side, vowel symbols in the centre and final consonant clusters on the right-hand side. This arrangement assists word analysis and synthesis.

The word cards contained in the sentence makers do not include any capital letters other than the singular pronoun 'I' together with any proper nouns written by the teacher. It is recommended that the formal use of capital letters is introduced later. Some teachers have developed their own capital-letter cards; others record each word with a capital letter on the *back* of the cards in the pupils' sentence builders.

Guidance for the teacher is provided on, and material available for, the systematic teaching of handwriting to pupils.

There is also a library of short 'Breakthrough Books' organised into four levels. Each book is based on stories or sentences written by children, thus capitalising on the psychological and motivational advantages of using the language of children. In providing such material for practice, overlearning and also the extension of the pupils' reading, the books have a considerable appeal. In certain respects the theoretical underpinnings are similar to those that led to the development in Queensland, Australia, of the Mount Gravatt reading series. This was based on the analysis of children's spoken language that had been electronically recorded. It is a developmental language-based reading programme that built on the research work of Hart, Walker and Gray (1977). Levels 1 to 3 of the materials were published in the same year.

A number of practical points must be borne in mind if the classroom floor is not to be inadvertently littered confetti-like with word and/or letter cards. The use of 'Breakthrough to Literacy' requires very careful organisation by the teacher and the full co-operation of the children if its benefits are to be maximised. The following practical hints will help those interested in adopting the system to do so more effectively:

- Read carefully and follow the advice given in the manual.
- Always ensure that pupils match back their word cards into their sentence makers.
- Ensure that the pupils can locate the correct place in their folders for a word. Marking word cards on the back with a number corresponding to that put on each line in the sentence maker can help.
- From the very beginning, train pupils to hold their sentence makers upright when either storing or retrieving them.
- Have an easily available container for 'unowned', 'spare' or 'lost' word cards.
- Train pupils to take turns in returning word cards from the container into the main word card storage unit.
- The word card storage unit should be readily available to the pupils before they begin working with their sentence builders.

Considerable research has been carried out into the efficacy of the 'Breakthrough to Literacy' method and materials. One interesting finding is that the method encourages exploration of the language and the production of novel and imaginative sentences.

The system was highly commended in the Bullock Committee's Report *A Language for Life* (DES, 1975), and has developed considerably since then. Currently, users continue to provide the authors and publishers with suggestions for its further improvement and extension. A videotape giving an overview and demonstration of the system is available on free loan from the publishers, Longman.

—8

Technological developments

INTRODUCTION

The potential of information technology (IT) in general and of microcomputer and microchip technology in particular for helping children learn is virtually unlimited. IT represents the third industrial revolution, in which the main commodity is information and the major activities are the storage, manipulation, analysis, retrieval, transmission and application of that information. Much of the information is still presented on visual display units (VDUs) in textual form. Reading has become an even more important skill as a consequence of these developments. A wide range of computer-assisted instruction and computer-assisted learning systems has been produced; their successors are under development. The assistance this technology can provide for all children cannot be overemphasised. To children with special educational needs it can be particularly valuable. For example, word processing helps make the production of legible script, the checking of spellings, the drafting and redrafting of material far quicker and easier for all pupils. It follows that the technology can contribute towards the reading progress of all pupils.

MICROCOMPUTERS

IT systems have been developed that can test aspects of children's reading, score their responses, analyse and record the results and provide teaching suggestions.

There is a wide and ever-expanding range of computer applications in reading (Ewing, 1985; Blanchard et al., 1987). A considerable variety of educational software ranging from drill and practice programmes, to simulations, interactive programmes and word processing is available. Speech synthesisers enable typed words to be electronically sounded out. The blind can read textual materials without using Braille. The profoundly deaf can be helped to hear by cochlear implants. Motor-impaired and language-disordered children can be helped develop expressive and receptive language skills. A useful article describing recent products of value in special needs teaching has been prepared by workers at the Oxford Centre (Aids to Communication in Education). This provides descriptions, critical comments and a list of 14 addresses from which further details can be obtained (Colven and Lysley, 1989). Other sources of information are described here.

During the 1980s some £16 million was provided by the Department of Trade and Industry to subsidise the purchase of microcomputers by schools (primary and secondary). The Department of Education and Science invested £23 million in the Microcomputers in Education Programme (MEP) which ran until 1986. Four regional special education microelectronics resource centres (SEMERCs) were established (see pp. 291–3). The Microelectronics Education Support Unit (MESU) initially was given £2.8 million per annum to develop parts of the MEP (DES, 1990c). In 1988 the Department of Education and Science injected £19 million in educational support grants for IT; £10.5 and £8.5 million were to be spent on appointing IT advisory teachers and on hardware respectively. The Technical and Vocational Education Initiative (TVEI) was used by a few fortunate schools to increase their IT resources.

In the 1990s the use of computers by pupils and staff in primary schools will be a statutory requirement. The national curriculum requires that in 1990 the design and technology programmes of study and attainment targets be introduced into the curricula of years 1, 3 and 7 (DES, 1989d). The National Curriculum Council is confident that there will be sufficient computers in schools by September 1990 for this to occur. It has also recommended that additional funds be provided through the educational support grant to provide training for teachers. A further grant of £750,000 was made in 1989 by the Department of Education and Science for the purchase of a considerable body of software suited to the demands of the national curriculum.

Despite this, the aspirations of the NCC may be somewhat optimistic. Many primary schools are not adequately provided with books. Some do not have enough teachers, let alone microcomputers and other IT devices. The pedagogic cornucopia represented by the increasingly sophisticated IT materials available is well beyond the financial reach of many primary schools. The capital costs, insurance, maintenance and rapid obsolescence of such IT systems and the purchase of software are expenses that few schools are likely to be able to meet (DES, 1989h). Despite such constraints, these technological developments have not been ignored by teachers. Reading about what is available and going on short INSET courses on IT is increasing. A considerable number of teachers are also involved in the development of both software and hardware for educational purposes.

One relatively simple drill, practice and feedback example of current work in the learning of reading is that developed by Terrell, head of research at the College of St Paul and St Mary, Cheltenham. It is reported that the system has been used mainly in teaching reading to infants and to children with dyslexia. The child sits in front of a screen and reads a particular sentence aloud. If the reader has difficulties, help can be obtained from the computer, which is programmed to 'talk' to the pupil under specified conditions. The child can work through the material at his or her own pace and the computer never gets impatient. Giving the pupil control is motivational. It reduces demands on teacher time, assuming the system is both reliable and understood by the pupil. It provides motivated practice for the pupil. In order to evaluate the system, five primary schools have been given five computers each to teach reading to 5–7-year-olds. The idea of linking text to talk through a machine is not new. The current technology is. (Some readers may recall the work of Omar Khayyam Moore and the 'talking typewriter' that was developed at the Responsive Environment Laboratory, Yale University, in pre-microcomputer days. The system was brought to the UK for trials in the late 1960s.) The following is an example of a current development that indicates the rate of progress in the IT field in relation to reading.

In 1989 the Department of Trade and Industry made an award of £50,000 to a company, Next Technology, based at the St John's Innovation Centre, Cambridge. The award was for the research and development of an electronic book that could be used by schoolchildren. Such a 'book' would be based on an interactive learning programme. It is anticipated that the 'book' will be A4 size, can be folded, and will run on rechargeable batteries. Pupils would operate it by either a keyboard or a touch-sensitive pad to obtain information displayed on a flat colour screen. Not only LMS-sensitive readers will be saying 'How much will it cost?' Time alone will tell. Next Technology already sells a system called 'Voyager' that accommodates up to 270 compact discs. It is claimed that this system, a unit the size of a large suitcase, can store all the textual and pictorial information available in a large public library.

Without considerable central government support over and above what is currently available, for most schools advanced IT applications will be as available as exotic foreign holidays to individuals on social security. A survey based on 921 responses from primary schools has revealed that the ratio of pupils per microcomputer was 107:1 in 1985, and in 1989 69:1 (Wellington and McDonald, 1989). Such averages hide a vast range of provision; one microcomputer to 300 pupils is not unknown. The modest educational goal of even one microcomputer per class is far from being achieved. Funding comes mainly from parent–teacher associations (71.4 per cent). School funds provide 7 per cent and industry about 1 per cent. It is highly likely that this pattern is not the same in schools in socially deprived and advantaged areas (ibid.). Shortage of funding, lack of adequate INSET and support, inadequate consideration of how the technology could be effectively integrated with the rest of the programme and other more immediately pressing activities such as implementing the national curriculum, were major concerns of primary school teachers. The same survey identified a large minority of primary schools who were markedly unenthusiastic about the value of educational computing. It is hoped that the survey will be repeated regularly in order that changing provision and practice and continuing problems in the educational applications of IT can be identified. The evaluation of the educational outcome of government investment in IT requires a more comprehensive monitoring than it has received to date. Does the use of specific IT materials with clearly identified groups of pupils enhance something as basic as reading skills? Is the investment cost-effective?

SOURCES OF INFORMATION

Special Educational Microelectronic Resource Centres (SEMERCs)

Four regional SEMERCs were originally established in London, Bristol, Manchester and Newcastle. Their purpose was to provide advice, information and courses on the uses of microcomputers with children having special educational needs. The value of these centres was demonstrated by LEA response to a consultative document issued by MESU in 1987: 78 per cent of LEAs wanted SEMERCs to be retained. The absence of any further central funding specifically for SEMERCs after March 1989 meant that consortia of LEAs could establish their own provision. Because the government was providing further funding for IT in schools over the next five years, joint SEMERCs represented one option open to LEAs.

In the event, regional centres supported by consortia of LEAs have been established at Oldham, Doncaster, Bristol, Newcastle and Redbridge (1990). They are a most valuable resource for teachers of all pupils. In late 1989 the Doncaster-based LEA consortium known as Resource, in conjunction with Learning and Training Systems, ran a conference on the educational issues in developing networks of computers. The National Council for Educational

Technology is also developing a national support structure for special needs teachers. These centres will act as regional focal points. Qualified and experienced teachers taking an advanced course leading to a Diploma in Advanced Studies in Specific Learning Difficulties at the University of Manchester have visited the Oldham Centre. The range of ideas pertinent to the teaching of reading as a thinking process was greatly appreciated, as were the details of 'free' programs available to schools and the technical advice and assistance that were available.

An excellent example of the type of information provided by SEMERCs is that contained in the Northwest SEMERC Software Survey (Littler, 1990). In the autumn of 1989 a survey was carried out in which key personnel in each local authority were asked to identify software that was of particular value to children with special needs; 183 teachers, advisory teachers and educational psychologists who had been nominated by 93 LEAs as delegates to the National Council for Educational Technology annual Micros for Special Needs course were contacted. In addition, the overlapping group of all NCET Special Needs Software contacts was consulted. The majority of the 62 respondents were advisory teachers with responsibility for computers and special needs. From the information supplied, a list of promising software was prepared. Whilst the concerns of Northwest SEMERC are far wider than the improvement of children's reading, their booklet contains many examples of both hardware and software that is, or could be, of value in this field. The publication lists the following:

- Ninety useful packages;
- Moderate learning difficulties list;
- List for severe learning difficulties, physical and sensory impairment;
- Program descriptions;
- The 21 top special needs software publishers;
- Details of the Survey;
- News from publishers; and
- 100 useful addresses.

Some children need alternatives to the QWERTY keyboard. The good old limited BBC B had a wealth of different sockets into which these devices could be plugged. Eleven of the packages mentioned give access to switch users, another eleven allow voice control through Micromike, fifteen packages support Touchscreen and almost forty support the Concept Keyboard (with almost 20,000 Concept Keyboards out there, so they should). Seven packages speak to help the child who cannot read the screen or who cannot see the screen.

(Ibid., p. 1)

It is then pointed out that the newer and more powerful micro-computers increasingly being used in schools unfortunately often required expensive additional ports and modules in order to support many of the above devices that are of value to pupils with special needs.

This group of children with a need for extra help cannot be ignored. It is not because they constitute one in six of the school population but because learning resources which allow access to some, but not all, children have no future. The National Curriculum gives all children the right to the same curriculum. This right cannot be delivered by media to which only a majority have access.

(Ibid., p. 1)

The development of a collection of software that could be freely copied began in the early days of the Microelectronic Education Programme. Because the materials were issued in blue plastic files, they were known as Blue File software. Teachers who wished to see the programmes that they had written more extensively used donated many to MEP, or received a small payment for the copyright. For teachers working with children having special educational needs, the system was particularly effective. Thus the programmes available for the relatively small market for switch, concept keyboard and touchscreen software, expanded considerably. SEMERCs and ACE Centres continuously reviewed the Blue File List.

Subsequently, the Special Needs Software Centre at Manchester SEMERC (currently Northwest SEMERC) developed a more powerful set of 'framework' programmes. These programmes were sufficiently flexible to enable any part of the curriculum to be incorporated at virtually any ability level. Touch Explorer Plus and List Explorer are examples of highly popular programmes.

Blue File software can be freely copied for educational purposes. Blue File is distributed on behalf of NCET by Northwest SEMERC.

Special Educational Needs Database (SEND)

SEND was established in 1986 and is supported by the Scottish Council for Educational Technology. Its aims include the provision of information on the use of microelectronics in meeting a range of special educational needs and the exchange of information by users of such materials. Subscribers to Prestel, Prestel Education and Campus 2000 can access the database.

The system is designed for users with little knowledge of, or experience with, microcomputer systems. A hardware selection menu offers three choices: the type of disability involved, the type of computer, or an alphabetical list of devices (for users who have a name already in mind). If the teacher identifies a particular disability, the child's level of physical control is requested. A list of potentially appropriate devices is then identified. For each device there is a description of what it does, from whom it can be obtained, its cost and the address of someone who has used the aid, or a comment by such a person. Users can add their own comments, but before these are introduced into the database they are edited by the SEND team.

In searching for software, the user selects from a number of 'learning/teaching' fields. Language and communication is one of these. This opens up a range of available programmes in various aspects of literacy. Additional information can be obtained from:

Anne Lavelle,
SEND Project Manager,
The Scottish Council for Educational Technology,
74 Victoria Crescent Road,
Glasgow G12 9JN.

National Educational Resources Information Service

Another source of information that is likely to increase in importance in the 1990s is the National Educational Resources Information Service (NERIS). NERIS is an electronic database directed mainly at schools, run by a non-profit-making trust and funded by the DTI through its Industry/Education Unit. It is also supported by DES, NCC, SEAC, CCW (Wales), NICC (Northern Ireland), SCCC (Scotland) and the Training Agency. Using commonly available educational computers, a modem and some specially written software, it allows users to locate learning materials and curriculum information. Equally important, it provides a means whereby adaptable materials can be delivered. It includes copyright-free materials that can be copied or adapted for use in schools. Schools subscribing to NERIS have to pay only for telephone calls, which are charged at local rate irrespective of distance. Institutions using Prestel, Prestel Education and Campus 2000 (the successor to the Times Network System) can access the NERIS database. At present both the network charges and overheads are subsidised; NERIS is grant-aided by the DTI, but it is expected that the system will be self-supporting by 1992.

NERIS was established in 1987 to help the many teachers who were having difficulties in finding information about available teaching materials and other resources. The aim was to establish a single source for users, mainly educationalists. Its original brief was to focus on sciences, mathematics, social and personal education and geography, but this is now being extended. Information on the national curriculum is being incorporated. This will allow users to search the database for study programmes and attainment targets in a particular curricular area and to identify published materials that address these. The materials can then be ordered using the system.

In June 1990 the database was still relatively small (33,000 records) but growing. Some 5,750 schools are reported as using the service. Primary schools can obtain the discs containing information relevant to that stage of education, rather than subscribing to the complete on-line system. Further information can be obtained from:

The Director,
NERIS,
Maryland College,
Leighton Street,
Woburn,
Milton Keynes,
Buckinghamshire.

Aids for Communication in Education

In 1984, the Aids for Communication in Education (ACE) Centre was established at the Ormerod School for Delicate and Physically Handicapped Children, Wainflete Road, Oxford. The Centre acted as a focus for information on applications of microelectronics and information technology in the education of children with communication problems. It provides facilities for those who wish to see equipment in use and to try it out. Workshops and open days are organised, and the staff will also give advice on equipment. The Centre also surveys and evaluates new products and co-ordinates research and development projects. The Centre receives visits from parents with their children and from teachers and other professionals.

ARROW (AURAL, READ, RESPOND, ORAL, WRITTEN)

Teaching methods in which children listen to their own recorded voices as a means of improving their reading, writing, memory, oral language and spelling skills have been developed over ten years by the head of the Special Unit at the Hugh Sexey Middle School, Blackford, Somerset. The work originally began in the 1970s as a means of improving the speech and listening skills of hearing-impaired children. ARROW is based on the hypothesis that most individuals internalise the principles of language by sounding out individual words and phrases to themselves. ARROW is designed to help children who appear to be unable to do this by themselves. The key to the system is the psychological significance of the child's own voice.

In summary, the technique requires that the child listen to the teacher's voice through a headset, copy this by speaking and then listen to his/her own recorded voice on replay. Instant recording and playback facilities based on advanced recording techniques ensure that the child using the equipment does not lose concentration. During this 'echo' phase, the child may be asked to carry out related learning tasks such as reading, writing, dictation or auditory discrimination.

The system has been extended and used with both children and adults with or without specific learning difficulties, and to other language performances including reading and spelling. Its effectiveness has been empirically demonstrated (Lane, 1990), and it has also been shown to be effective across the ability range. Following trials in some 60 schools in Somerset, the LEA has plans to install equipment in every school. Other LEAs have shown considerable interest, and the system has also been introduced into Sweden.

ARROW capitalises on enabling the child to listen to his/her own voice using a two-track tape recorder and a technique called the 'self-voice echo'. Whilst several of the ARROW strategies can be carried out using an ordinary tape recorder, not all can be followed without more sophisticated hardware. The ARROW equipment comprises a special two-track machine that does not erase the teacher's pre-recorded material. In addition it has a rapid rewind facility not commonly found on ordinary tape recorders. The headset and boom microphone configuration used has much higher-quality voice recording characteristics than ordinary machines. The equipment is marketed by The Cambridge System Ltd, based in Buckden, Huntingdon.

ARROW is not a rigid learning system; it is a flexible procedure which can be used to enhance a variety of language performances, including reading. ARROW can be supervised by teachers, welfare assistants or volunteer helpers. The training sessions for children are only 5–10 minutes a day for three to five sessions a week. Except for the very young or less able, many pupils in ordinary schools can operate the system themselves. The material used can be based on curricular demands, such as programmes of study in English, or on the particular concerns of any given child.

Children using the system are involved in at least one, and typically several, of the ARROW components:

Aural: The child listens to speech on a headset. The speech can be from either a live or recorded voice, and is usually provided by a teacher, assistant, parent or volunteer helper.

Read: Whilst listening to the recorded voice, the child refers to the written format of the message. If the child is a non-reader, pictorial material can be used to represent the oral message visually.

Respond: When the child has listened and read the material visually presented, the child imitates the message heard on the tape (or given live by the teacher).

Oral: The child repeats the utterance presented by the teacher and listens to his/her own recorded speech on replay.

Written: Whilst the child's own voice is being replayed, he/she may be asked to write down what he/she has heard. Non-readers would be asked to arrange or order the pictorial visual support material, such as pictures or picture sequences.

The ARROW manual explains the management of the equipment. Training a teacher in the principles involved requires no more than 5–10 minutes, plus a few daily 10-minute sessions to become familiar with the working of the equipment. Tapes and a book describe the techniques and present suggestions on how these can be implemented. The technique appears to have considerable potential for further development.

MICROCOMPUTERS, SYNTHESISED SPEECH AND READING DEVELOPMENT

The value of using computers to improve children's reading, spelling and writing skills is receiving increasing emphasis as the versatility and availability of equipment increases (Moseley, 1990a; 1990b). The national curriculum proposals for English indicate the value of such approaches, emphasising their uses in group work: 'Since the information on a word-processor or computer screen is visible to several children at once, it can be a vehicle for group discussion and exploration of the language' (DES and Welsh Office, 1989b). The report also urges teachers to make full use of word processing, redrafting, spell-checking and the use of databases.

No mention is made of the very considerable possibilities opened up by the increasing availability of speech synthesisers. Computer speech is currently at a high level of sophistication and developments continue apace. The new system being produced for use with the BBC 'Archimedes' system is just one promising contender. The potential of such systems to deal at high speed with print, colour, graphics and speech opens up immense teaching and learning possibilities. Their use makes it easier for the relationships between sounds and symbols to be made explicit and appreciated by learners. Current technology enables text and speech to be linked. Words, phrases and sentences presenting reading difficulties can be checked immediately by the pupils. After developing oral reading fluency with synthesised speech support, the transition to sustained silent reading can be achieved. The presentation of the combination of symbol and sound is now more amenable to control and selection by teacher and pupil than ever before. The importance of pronunciation, stress, cadence, intonation and cohesion can be given explicit consideration in the context of active learning.

In passing, the importance of the 'self-voice' that is capitalised on in the work of Lane's ARROW technique provides one comparator against which the value and efficacy of systems utilising speech synthesis can be considered (see pp. 296–7). Do the undoubted psychological significance and motivational effects of 'self-voice' outweigh that of a synthesied voice? It appears that both approaches have differing strengths and weaknesses, but they remain complementary. ARROW uses less sophisticated and less expensive equipment than computerised systems. Such apparently mundane considerations usually determine a school's purchasing policy unless the cost/benefit ratio of the more expensive equipment is considered superior.

Relatively few individuals are experts in both language development and computer applications. One of these considers that computer systems 'are capable (with teacher support) of increasing every child's level of literacy at least to the level of his/her spoken language' (Moseley, 1990b). This is a challenging assertion. It comes from an established authority with an outstanding record of teaching, research, innovation and publication in this field.

Moseley has described research-based arguments for the use of computers in the improvement of reading, spelling and writing. He considers that such programs should:

- teach pupils to categorise words by their sounds;
- develop fluency in word recognition;
- highlight linguistic patterns in the relationships between speech and text;
- use the versatility of the system to provide dynamic displays of text; and
- avoid visual, auditory and linguistic 'overload'.

For a number of years, Moseley has been developing systems towards such ends. Using the BBC microcomputer and the word-processing package 'Wordwise Plus', text can readily be translated into a phonetic code which can then be spoken by the computer. On this basis, a 'Read and Speak' program has been developed by Moseley. This can be used in any of the following formats:

Using a 'central window' screen presentation, single words or phrases can be shown. Using the speech synthesiser, clauses and sentences can be spoken to give contextual support to the word presented.

A page of text can be presented cumulatively, word by word, phrase by phrase, or sentence by sentence, accompanied by speech-synthesised clauses and sentences providing contextual support.

Within each of these formats, the text and synthesised speech are linked in one of three modes: word, phrase or sentence.

Automatic presentation allows the word, phrase or sentence to appear long enough for the pupil to read it either aloud or silently. The computer then speaks the text, which remains visible for practice or examination. To build fluency, the speed of presentation can be increased from slow to medium to fast. If desired, the user can elect to retain keyboard control of timing and speech. Synthesised speech can be used either all the time or only when required. Repetition of the synthesised speech is also available.

There are, therefore, 25 different ways in which the text may be presented (45 ways if choice of print size is added into the equation). This provides for individual differences and for repetition. Pilot experience with the program shows that sustained attention and mastery learning are possible even in children who have previously failed to respond to skilled support teaching.

(Moseley, 1990b)

The following indicates some applications that Moseley has developed. Using a language-experience approach, pupils have tape-recorded their own material. This has then been presented using the 'read and speak' system outlined earlier. Other pupils have worked with lists of subject- or topic-related vocabularies that they wish to learn and use in their school work. It is claimed that this raises the level of work the pupils are able to address. Longer words can be broken up into their constituent syllables, and these can be presented on the screen accompanied by synthesised speech. Another format enables grapheme–phoneme correspondences to be highlighted and rhyme and context to be used in helping the pupil understand and master the grapheme–phoneme relationships presented.

It is highly likely that respective proponents of the 'top-down' and 'bottom-up' approaches to the learning and teaching of reading will have theoretical arguments concerning the validity of Moseley's work. In the meantime, the pupils should not be forgotten. If such systems prove effective in improving children's literacy skills and in alleviating their reading difficulties, they cannot be ignored. Effective applications can modify inevitably imperfect theories.

Advantages of the system are that, whilst requiring the pupil to remain alert to the emerging meaning of the text, it allows each pupil sufficient time to see, hear, repeat and master each word, phrase or sentence. Moseley considers that this is likely to be of particular value to poorer readers and quotes recent research evidence in support (Beveridge and Edmundson, 1989). He could easily have cited much more (e.g. Anderson et al., 1985). When the meaning of the text has been established, the emphasis moves towards fluency building (automaticity). The tremendous value of automaticity is something which most competent readers have virtually forgotten: we take it for granted. Only when faced with unfamiliar and complex texts are competent readers brought up against the daunting challenges that much everyday text can present to junior children with reading difficulties. The unfortunately common overexposure of children in their school work to texts that are at the frustration level can be obviated by automatic individualisation of instruction.

Section D
Individual Differences in Reading in the Classroom: The Challenge of the National Curriculum

Classroom-related reading curriculum development issues and ideas

INTRODUCTION

A major aim of the Education Reform Act 1988 is to raise levels of pupils' achievements. In this endeavour, the class teacher is the linchpin on whose commitment, caring and competence all will depend. Because policies and practices in the classroom must be based on a school's considered and agreed curriculum, it is possible that a somewhat more cohesive educational programme will now take place in connection with the teaching and learning of reading (and of other subjects).

Earlier it was argued that the success or failure of the national curriculum is largely dependent on the extent to which children's standards of literacy in general, and reading in particular, are improved. To say this is not to ignore the importance of other aspects of language and thinking. For example, making and doing things, creating and controlling objects and systems, rather than being able only to read about or describe verbally how and why to make, do, create or control them, is important. Having someone competent at any task is probably more valuable to the individual and society than having pupils able to describe fluently, but unable to perform, the skills in applied situations. Both fields of activity require symbolic thinking and are not mutually exclusive. Communication by demonstration can be as important as communication by symbolic representations using text. However, at the more advanced levels of generalised problem-solving, the latter mode is vital. This is one of the major reasons why reading is so highly valued in our society.

In our educational system pupils are expected, and required, to access the meanings embedded in texts of varying types and complexities in most of the subjects comprising the national curriculum. Dependent on the purposes for reading a text – for example, poetry or prose, fiction or non-fiction – different activities are required of the reader. These can include instructions that must be followed precisely, text from which particular items must be identified or the content paraphrased or summarised. Pupils are expected to have a repertoire of different reading skills to bring to such varied tasks across the range of subjects in the curriculum. Section 1 of the Education Reform Act 1988 requires that all pupils have access to 'a balanced and broadly based curriculum'. Imagine what a national curriculum would look like if pupils were unable to read.

Again, it must be emphasised that concentrating on the centrality of literacy in general, and of reading in particular, is not arguing for either a 'back to basics' or a solely academic-oriented curriculum. It is emphasising the empowering and enriching consequences to all pupils of being literate.

CONTEXT

How can the challenges of the national curriculum be managed by the class teacher? The English curriculum has now been determined by central government. Associated programmes of study, attainment targets and the more detailed statements of attainment have been specified. An approach to assessment generally, in the school and in the classroom, has been devised and disseminated (SEAC, 1989). Standard assessment tasks designed to help class teachers assess pupils' progress and standards have been piloted. Legal responsibilities on schools to assess, record and report to their pupils' parents have been enacted.

It is essential that the class teacher has a full appreciation of what has been proposed, and is aware of the problems and opportunities these proposals present and how they can be constructively addressed. A quite detailed plan of the structure and content of the curriculum has, apparently, been laid down but its implementation involves much more than the mechanical following of a prescribed recipe. For one thing, the ambiguities inherent in the technical terms used represent a Pandora's box of valid but differing interpretations of what precisely is entailed. This is, in fact, a strength rather than a weakness from an educational viewpoint. A million curricular flowers can continue to flourish, and new ones be propagated, in the junior school curriculum.

The advent of the Education Reform Act 1988 must have contributed considerably to the greenhouse effect. The flood of publications from the National Curriculum Council, Department of Education and Science, Her Majesty's Inspectorate and the School

Examinations and Assessment Council is, sadly, a classic example of quantity before quality in many respects. If readers have the time, and wish to check that their school has the pertinent publications, Circular No. 7 by the NCC lists what had been published by these bodies in connection with the national curriculum up to December 1989 (NCC, 1989e). Publications concerned only with English and with pupils with special educational needs comprise a substantial number of documents. The sheer volume is either awe- or anger-inspiring, or both. How teachers can be expected to read, discuss, reflect upon and implement what has been published, and also continue to teach full time, shows at best an unawareness by the national curriculum industry of the pressures of class teaching; at worst, an indifference to the additional demands being made on teachers' time and energies. Fortunately, there are signs that the minister is becoming aware of such dangers. For example, at the Conservative Party's 1990 Local Government conference, John MacGregor publicly commented on the need to avoid overloading teachers with impossible national curriculum assessment demands.

Currently, in addition to English, junior school teachers are involved in introducing national curriculum mathematics, science and, soon, design and technology. The total number of statements of attainment involved at key stages 1 and 2 are legion. The system will be made to work by virtue of the dedication of teachers, but there will be many unexpected difficulties to be identified and resolved before it can be expected to run efficiently. That is why the concept of the school development plan is essential (see pp. 306–10). In 1990 one already hears voices calling for a *new* Education Act to replace the Education Reform Act 1988.

Reverting to the demands on class teachers of the national curriculum, for each subject they need to know the following elements and to understand the pedagogic implications of their interrelationships:

- Programmes of study (PoS): the matters, skills and processes which must be taught.
- Attainment targets (ATs): objectives for each subject: knowledge, skill, understanding.
- Statements of attainment (SoA): more precise objectives for each attainment target at each level.
- Profile components: groups of attainment targets brought together for the purposes of assessment and reporting.
- Standard assessment tasks: extended classroom activities within which pupils will be assessed by their teachers through a mixture of oral, written, graphical and practical work.

- How to record and report the progress and standards of individuals and classes.
- How class teachers will be involved in the moderation of assessments.

It is anticipated by government that improved attainment will be achieved by the introduction of the national curriculum, and also by improved self-management by schools. School teachers and their pupils face the timetable shown in Table 9.1 for the introduction of the English attainment targets, statements of attainment and their associated programmes of study (DES and Welsh Office, 1989a, 1989b; DES 1989d). Junior school teachers will be particularly involved in the earlier effects of the national curriculum (English) on pupils who have completed key stage 1, and will be engaged in ensuring the continuing progress of those pupils at key stage 2. For easy reference, the English attainment targets and statements of attainment for key stages 1 and 2 are presented in Appendix 2.

Table 9.1 *Introduction and assessment of core subject: English*

		KS1	KS2	KS3	KS4
Introduction	autumn	1989	1990	1990	1992
Unreported assessment	summer	1991	1994	1993	
1st reported assessment	summer	1992	1995	1994	1994

CURRICULUM DEVELOPMENT PLANS AND THE CLASS TEACHER

In Chapter 2, the relationships between the various aspects of literacy were considered. The importance of objectives, pedagogy and assessment in considering the nature of a school's language and reading programmes was emphasised. Teachers need to know how these elements of the curriculum in their class relate to the school's overall curriculum policy. The staff of each junior school will currently be working on its own curriculum development plan. The key concern is 'How can the school's existing curriculum be brought together with the national curriculum?' The implications for classroom practice are considerable because more explicit and coherent policies will determine practice in, for example, the teaching of reading.

Included in such a curriculum review will be consideration of:

- the existing curriculum;
- availability of resources and their allocation;
- staffing;
- inservice training needs and provisions; and
- shortfalls in existing provisions.

By its very nature, this activity will never be completed.

Schemes of work, described as: 'a written statement which describes the work plans for pupils within a class or group over a specific period', provide the core of such school plans. In addition, these should 'reflect whole-school approaches to teaching and learning' and also 'be a practical guide to teaching a subject within the school's curricular programme' (NCC, 1989c). It is envisaged that existing school curriculum development plans may be revised to take into account the programmes of study, attainment targets and statements of attainment in each subject area. The plans must:

- identify priorities for change;
- set time limits for achieving objectives specified;
- list resources and their uses;
- specify organisational changes to anticipate future requirements.

The plans will be based on a curriculum audit (the process of curriculum review). Such a procedure has been described in *A Framework for the Primary Curriculum* (NCC, 1989b). In December 1989 the School Development Plans Project issued to governors, headteachers and teachers, helpful advice entitled *Planning for School Development* (DES, 1989i). This document is based on the experience of the LEAs and schools that have already undertaken such work. It outlines the reasons for having school development plans, how to carry out a school audit, draw up the plan and make the plan work. Included as an appendix is a case study of how a school audit might be carried out. Interestingly, that example focuses on 'the reading performance of pupils' (ibid., p. 18). This was presented to illustrate the planning process in relation to one of *four* priorities.

An example more relevant to the present book could not have been desired! Readers have here a ready reference to a model that can be adapted to other subjects but which also indicates that reading is a core concern. It is highly likely that illustrative cases are selected for their general appeal and importance in such a document.

Summarising and paraphrasing the content of the three phases involved, it will be seen that the procedure appears straightforward. It requires considerable investment of time and energies by staff. Such plans can be helpful in ensuring that the actions of the class teachers are co-ordinated under the school development plan; a great strength is that no class teacher is left isolated.

Phase 1. Carrying out a school audit (the process of review)

Concern had been expressed by teachers and parents about the reading attainments of first-year pupils in particular. The governors and staff decided to focus on this concern.

Evidence was collected from four major sources: the reading performances of pupils; a short questionnaire to staff concerning their pupils' reading skills and progress; the LEA school adviser's comparison of the pupils' achievements with other schools in the LEA; and the opinions of parents that were expressed at language workshops arranged by the school.

The evidence collected showed that the initial concern was justified and was not confined only to first-year pupils.

'Reading was therefore identified as a strong candidate for a development plan priority' (ibid., p. 18).

Phase 2a. Drawing up the plan (the process of construction)

Target 1. To undertake a more detailed review of the reading of pupils in specified classrooms (time scale – 1 term).

Target 1: tasks

Teachers 'shadow' pupils to identify the variety of reading skills required and the support that pupils need.
Check on resources available and the extent to which they are used in classrooms.
Check the uses made of support staff and parents in assisting the pupils' reading development, and increase their use.

Target 2: increase a wider use of books by pupils (time scale – 3 terms)

Tasks

Inspect the relevance and suitability of the book stock to the pupils.
Remove inappropriate books and order new ones.
Ensure that display and availability of books is improved.
Arrange book-related events such as book weeks; use of Bradford 'Book Flood' reading record forms.

Phase 2b. INSET support

Target 1: provide cover for 'shadowing' team and arrange meetings to discuss findings.

Target 1: Success criteria.

Report by the 'shadowing' team for consideration by all school staff.
Expand awareness of the range and purposes of reading by pupils, the support needed and the effective use of resources.
Staff development concerning programmes of study and attainment targets as a consequence of an INSET day.
Increase parental and support staff involvement in the pupils' reading development.

Target 2: INSET support
Staff involved in a 'training' day devoted to raising awareness of the problem and to devising and arranging special events.

Target 2: success criteria

Adviser's comments on changes in book stock.
Assessment on improvement of the book environment at school.
Increase in use of books by pupils, including borrowing from class libraries.
Pupils' view concerning, and involvement in, special events.

Phase 3. Making the plan work (implementation and evaluation)

The progress of the plan must be kept under review. A timetable for meetings, action and evaluation has to be agreed with the staff.

A checklist of questions can be used to plot the progress of the action plan.

The inevitable difficulties caused, for example, by staff absence or illness may require modifications to the plan.

The weaknesses and strengths of the plan, its successes and failures, should be identified, recorded and discussed. This will enable future developments to evolve from continuing work on the school's development plan.

Central to the curriculum development plan are the concepts of *entitlement* and *access* to the national curriculum for all pupils, including the 'estimated 20 per cent of pupils with s.e.n.' (special educational needs) (NCC, 1989c). It is suggested that curriculum plans for pupils with special educational needs should ensure that all staff *know* which pupils have such needs. As discussed earlier, the very nature of the concept makes this an elusive objective. The plan, and operationally this mainly means the daily endeavours of the class teacher, must make certain that pupils with special educational needs have maximum access to the curriculum, and make satisfactory progress. Of course, this must not adversely affect any other pupils. If it did, one would be creating rather than identifying and alleviating such needs. In practice, professional judgement and balance are, as ever, required. Reflecting on the distinction between the relative ease of saying what is required and doing it, is apposite. Demonstrations of effective teaching and the systematic identification of practices that improve reading attainment could be given the attention characterised by work in the USA described and summarised earlier (see pp. 245–9).

Parents will continue to be deeply interested in the standards and progress in reading that their children are achieving in a particular class at an *unrepeatable* time in their education, irrespective of what planning goes on. The acid test of the reading curriculum will be whether it has resulted in improved standards and progress. Three perennial questions underpin the accountability of the class teacher in relation to this:

- What are the objectives of the reading programme?
- What resources (methods, materials and staff) are available to help the pupils achieve these objectives?
- How can the progress of pupils towards the objectives be assessed?

Because of the national curriculum prescriptions, together with the school's curriculum development plan, these questions will have been addressed in relation to 'Reading' as one profile component in English. Some provisional answers concerning strategies for turning policy into practice have been provided by the National Curriculum Council. These have been disseminated to schools and discussed in INSET meetings (NCC, 1989b, 1989d).

Junior school teachers are still left with many challenges. Focusing on reading only, a major concern is how to teach children in a mixed-ability junior school class whose range of reading attainments can vary from below the 6-year-old level to the 14-year-old level. Classroom organisation and management can make profound differences to the efficacy of the reading programme. The teacher's style is known to affect the learning that takes place. Effects on pupils' reading were discussed in Chapter 2.

TIME ALLOCATION

Time allocation to the activities comprising the junior school curriculum is important. How much time should be spent on reading
and reading-related activities? Although I know of no study specifying an optimum time allocation balance between subjects, guidelines have been recommended in some countries.

A mean age range of suggested time allocations in minutes per
week for years 1 to 7 has been developed based on analyses presented by primary schools (Education Department of Western Australia, 1985). English took 51 per cent of the available time in year 1,
mathematics 13 per cent and science and technology 4 per cent. In
years 3 and 6 respectively, these became 49 per cent, 14 per cent, 4
per cent and 43 per cent, 15 per cent and 6 per cent. Whether this is
either a valid description of current practice or a suspect prescrip-
tion for better practice, is uncertain. In England and Wales the
amounts of time to be allocated to the subjects in the national
curriculum are certainly far vaguer. The term 'a reasonable amount
of time' is more popular. What matters appears to be the outcome
of the national curriculum measured in terms of improved attainments and progress in reading and other areas.

Time is money. LMS is concerned with the efficient management
by schools of restricted financial resources. A school's income will
largely be dependent on the number of pupils attending. Recruit-
ment will, in part, be affected by a school's reputation. In general,
parents want high reading standards at the schools their children
attend. The demands on a school's financial and professional
resources are always greater than what is available. Increasingly,
professionals' time will be costed.

We know that we can help all pupils make progress in relation to
their *own* attainments, i.e. progress in an absolute sense. For some
observers, that is not enough. Questions will be posed such as
'What amount of individual tuition in the teaching of reading is
required to effect a significant improvement in the *relative* reading
attainments of a pupil with reading difficulties?' Then the priority
accorded in a school to such activities will be raised. Underlying
this is 'How much is the ability to read worth?' The author would
argue that the ability is priceless to the individual and to society.
The danger of knowing the cost of everything and the value of
nothing is an ever-present threat. ILEA has produced some
figures. These indicate that 'The amount of remedial help received
was found to be directly related to progress made in reading.
Children who received less than two hours' help each week
showed a relative decline in reading standard but children who
received more than this amount of help showed an increase in

reading standard as the amount of help increased' (Woods, 1979, p. 11).

WHAT WORKS? RESEARCH FINDINGS: HOME; CLASSROOM AND SCHOOL

As mentioned in Chapter 5, the US Department of Education produced a booklet entitled *What Works: Research about Teaching and Learning* (US Department of Education, 1986). The material in it has been assembled by the Department for Research and Improvement. The report does not claim to be comprehensive: in only 65 pages this could hardly be expected. If it appears that many of the findings look obvious, in part this is because research sometimes confirms the self-evident. The findings are none the worse for that, if valid evidence replaces earlier intuitions or common sense. Research findings also challenge accepted 'truths' that often prove less than adequate. Prejudices can be minimised; insights can be achieved; promising practices evaluated and new avenues for exploration identified.

Much of the research reported is concerned with *elementary schools* and with *disadvantaged pupils*, concerns that are central to the present book. The conclusions reported are considered pertinent to the great majority of pupils, but not necessarily to all. The recommendations are *not* intended to be an educational 'recipe' book, more a guide to sound 'nutrition'. Most findings concern parents and teachers, rather than policy-makers and administrators. This is not to deny the importance of officials and politicians in identifying educational priorities and influencing the taxation systems on which the funding of programmes is dependent. Any government that declares a goal such as 'Becoming a Nation of Readers' (the title of the Report of the Commission on Reading: Anderson et al., 1985) but does not provide the financial means to attain that goal when the professional expertise to achieve it is available, is disingenuous. On the other side of the Atlantic, the inadequate spending on books that sadly typifies provision in many state schools in England and Wales is an example in point (Book Trust, 1989).

The booklet is divided into three sections, 'Home', 'Classroom' and 'School'. The following are a selection of key points pertinent to the development of reading:

Home: research-based advice

- Parents are their children's first and most influential teachers. What parents do to help their children learn is more important to academic success than how well-off the family is.

- The best way for parents to help their children become better readers is to read to them – even when they are very young. Children benefit most from reading aloud when they discuss stories, learn to identify letters and words, and talk about the meaning of words.
- Children improve their reading ability by reading a lot. Reading achievement is directly related to the amount of reading children do in school and outside.
- Children who are encouraged to draw and scribble 'stories' at an early age will later learn to compose more easily, more effectively and with greater confidence than children who do not have this encouragement.
- A good foundation in speaking and listening helps children become better readers.

(US Department of Education, 1986)

It is unlikely that any of these points will be a revelation to teachers. The list can be used constructively in the context of a school's development plan, including the reading curriculum development plan. Asking questions such as the following can be helpful:

Are our pupils' parents aware of the points listed?
What are we currently doing (a) to raise pupils' parents' awareness; and (b) to encourage the parents to help their children along the lines indicated?
Should we do more?
If so, what, how, by whom and when?

Classroom: research-based advice

- Parental involvement helps children learn more effectively. Teachers who are successful at involving parents in their children's schoolwork are successful because they work at it.
- Children get a better start in reading if they are taught phonics. Learning phonics helps them to understand the relationship between letters and sound and to 'break the code' that links the words they hear with the words they see in print.
- Children get more out of a reading assignment when the teacher precedes the lesson with background information and follows it with discussion.
- Telling young children stories can motivate them to read. Storytelling also introduces them to cultural values and literary traditions before they can read, write and talk about stories by themselves.
- Teachers who set and communicate high expectations to all their students obtain greater academic performance from those students than teachers who set low expectations.
- How much time students are actively engaged in learning contrib-

utes strongly to their achievement. The amount of time available for learning is determined by the instructional and management skills of the teacher and the priorities set by the school administration.
- When teachers explain exactly what students are expected to learn, and demonstrate the steps needed to accomplish a particular academic task, students learn more.
- Students tutoring other students can lead to improved academic achievement for both student and tutor, and to positive attitudes towards coursework.
- Memorizing can help students absorb and retain the factual information on which understanding and critical thought are based.
- Student achievement rises when teachers ask questions that require students to apply, analyze, synthesize and evaluate information in addition to simply recalling facts.
- The ways in which children study influence strongly how much they learn. Teachers can often help children develop better study skills.
- Student achievement rises significantly when teachers regularly assign homework and students conscientiously do it.
- Frequent and systematic monitoring of students' progress helps students, parents, teachers, administrators and policy-makers identify strengths and weaknesses in learning and instruction.

(US Department of Education, 1986)

Based on extensive research findings, these points contain important messages for the junior school class teacher. They provide a firm basis for effective reading curriculum practice in the classroom. The points concern *all* pupils. They also imply a reading curriculum that is eclectic and interactive.

Asking questions can again be helpful in terms of reading curriculum development:

How many of these points are already incorporated in the class reading programme?
Which aspects of them are (a) best and (b) least well incorporated?
Can the 'good practices' identified in (a) be shared with colleagues?
Can practices identified in (b) be improved?
If so, which *one* should be highlighted for action by the class teacher, how, and by when?

School: research-based advice

- The most important characteristics of effective schools are strong instructional leadership, a safe and orderly climate, school-wide emphasis on basic skills, high teacher expectations for student achievement and continuous assessment of pupils' progress.

- Schools that encourage academic achievement focus on the importance of scholastic success and on maintaining order and discipline.
- Schools contribute to their students' academic attainments by establishing, communicating and enforcing fair and consistent discipline policies.
- Unexcused absences decrease when parents are promptly informed that their children are not attending school.
- Students benefit academically when their teachers share ideas, cooperate in activities and assist one another's intellectual growth.
- Teachers welcome professional suggestions about improving their work, but rarely receive them.
- Students read more fluently and with greater understanding if they have background knowledge of the past and present. Such knowledge is called cultural literacy.
- Advancing gifted students at a faster pace results in their achieving more than similarly gifted students who are taught at a normal rate.
- Business leaders report that students with solid basic skills and positive work attitudes are more likely to find and keep jobs than students with vocational skills alone.

(US Department of Education, 1986)

No man is an Island, entire of it self: every man is a piece of the Continent, a part of the main.

(John Donne, *Meditation XVII*)

Similarly, no classroom or school is an island. All are part of the national curriculum main.

The above research-based points on effective schools can be used in work on each school's development plan. Whilst these points have implications for all aspects of a school's organisation, they can also be directly related to specific areas of curriculum development (such as reading). The following questions merit consideration:

Do the school's educational policies and practices incorporate these points?

Which ones are (a) best and (b) least well incorporated in policy and practice in particular aspects of the curriculum?

Can we disseminate (a) to colleagues in other schools?

Can we learn from other schools where items under (b) have been well developed?

If so, what single issue should be identified for action in this school, by whom and by when?

Conclusion

Research into understanding reading, reducing reading failure and enhancing standards is a continuing challenge. The annual summaries of research in this field indicate the scope of these endeavours (e.g. Weintraub, 1986, 1987, 1988, 1989, 1990). Being aware of, and contributing to, such activities is a key aspect of the continuing professional development of teachers.

PROGRAMMES FOR TEACHING READING

In the teaching of reading one can identify six major orientations. Which are represented in your classroom reading programme? Might some of the suggestions be explored with a view to using them in your classroom?

The orientations are not necessarily mutually exclusive.

Basal reading programmes

It is highly likely that readers of this book themselves learned to read (in part) using materials such as texts, a teacher's manual, supplementary readers, workbooks, and audio-visual materials. Basal reading schemes typically include a wide range of reading skills; the order in which these should be taught is usually suggested in the manual. Such series encourage the use of a variety of pedagogic procedures, which are also described in the manual. The language in the pupils' texts is controlled, and has usually been developed on the basis of word frequency lists. The amount of repetition of words in the texts is also carefully controlled.

The major advantages of such systems are that they are well organised, sequenced, comprehensive, readily available and widely used. Plenty of supplementary materials are also available. The structure and content of such materials can be helpful to the inexperienced teacher. Basal series have a good track record in helping the majority of pupils learn to read and also to develop more advanced reading skills.

Disadvantages include the point that the content and illustrations may not appeal to ethnic minority group pupils, or to pupils from socioculturally deprived communities. As awareness of these criticisms has been raised, authors and publishers have made modifications to meet them in most currently available series. The often unnatural form and content of the language used is also criticised as hindering, rather than helping, reading development. Some series have met this criticism by identifying frequently used *strings* of words, rather than word frequencies, in the construction of texts, for example the Mount Gravatt reading series (Hart et al., 1977).

An excellent critical description of 15 major programmes is available (Aukerman, 1981). A balanced appraisal of the advantages and disadvantages of such reading schemes has been presented by a foremost English expert (Root, 1986b). Aukerman has also developed a checklist of criteria whereby basal reading series can be judged: the teacher is only required to respond 'Yes' or 'No' to the items in the list. The structure of the checklist is presented here, together with the number of major items in each section. An evaluative checklist relating to any materials used in the teaching of reading in the classroom could be a worthwhile facet of a school's curriculum development plan.

How to judge a basal reading series

A. Components of pupils' texts (20)
B. Materials for individual differences (10)
C. Ancillary materials to enhance skills learning (8)
D. Authorship and editorship (9)
E. Relevance and viability of the series (8)
F. Storage of components (5)
G. The instructional programme (9)
H. Would you be happy using the materials? (3)

(Adapted from Aukerman, 1981)

Language experience programmes

The language experience approach to reading contrasts markedly with the basal reader series. Sylvia Ashton-Warner (1963), Russell Stauffer (1969) and Doris Lee and Roach Van Allen (1963) were early proponents of the method. It uses the thinking, feeling and language of individual children as the basis for developing reading materials and reading skills. It is of value to anyone with reading difficulties, irrespective of age or background, because it capitalises on the idiosyncratic interests of the individual. It is based on the following assertions:

'What I think about, I can talk about.'
'What I say, I can write (or someone can write for me).'
'What I can write, I can read (and others can read, too).'
'I can read what I have written, and I can also read what other people have written for me to read.'

The approach is based on the teacher recording the child's spoken material. These texts then become the basis for the pupil's reading. The method can be used either with individuals or groups of pupils. The stories are collected and made into a book. No particular materials are required, although commercially produced materials are available. For example, 'Language Experiences in Reading' (LEIR) was initially developed by Van Allen. The current version also involves work by Venezky and Hahn. The latter carried out a study funded by the United States Department of Education in 1964, which confirmed the effectiveness of the approach in beginning reading. LEIR is published by Encyclopædia Britannica Educational Corporation.

Specific skills are not emphasised. The theoretical basis is a 'top-down' one deriving largely from psycholinguistics. There are some general procedures for eliciting stories from pupils, but means of teaching word recognition skills are given less attention. The sequence and difficulty level of the language is not externally controlled. It derives from the individual pupil's (or group of pupils') stories.

The strengths of the system rest on the firm links between the personal experience of the individual and the texts that are produced, recorded, read and reread. The development of writing and spelling skills can readily be incorporated. From the very start, the importance of reading as a communicative act is highlighted. Words, sentences and stories with high emotional and motivational significance to the individual can be used. Much of this emotionally charged language would never appear in a word frequency count.

(On reflection, when the author was enrolled into the army, a most striking aspect of the language of the barrack room was the increasing frequency with which, over time, certain Anglo-Saxon sexual and anatomical expletives were used, over-used and used without apparent conscious thought. Such vocabulary would appear as high-frequency words in any oral vocabulary frequency count that could have been taken in the barrack room. Such a database could be a useful way of constructing a new basal series. A sample of concurrent graffiti indicated that even four-letter swearwords were often mispelled. Despite this, the messages were frequently clear, albeit somewhat abusive or highly imaginative. Communication did occur.)

A further major strength of the language-experience approach is its extreme flexibility: it can be adapted to pupils of any age and from virtually any background and does not require expensive materials. The fact that some of the spoken language produced by an individual could well be completely idiosyncratic, family specific or having only local currency, is both a strength and a limitation.

The difficulties are that it can be very time demanding. The sequence quoted on p. 317 does not apply to all pupils. The method is reinforcing mainly at the pupil's current level of language use and provides no systematic development of reading skills. Further, it has no inbuilt structure or content of moving the pupil on to higher levels of reading development. It is possible that some of the material the pupil wishes to use could be emotionally intolerable to the tutor (e.g. racist/sexist). Finally, by itself, the language experience approach would be unlikely to be helpful to certain pupils experiencing specific learning difficulties (dyslexia). The ten approaches described in detail in Chapter 6 are likely to be more suitable.

Individualised multisensory programmes

The theoretical basis of these approaches is that all sensory modalities can, to advantage, be used in the teaching and learning of reading. The methodology is usually based on a 'bottom-up' approach to reading development. Visual, auditory, kinaesthetic and tactile modes are often referred to as VAKT in the literature. There are other modalities including the olfactory and the proprioceptive, but the VAKT modes are considered by proponents to be of the greatest educational significance in learning to read. The sequences and combinations made in the uses of these modalities, and the materials to which they are applied, vary considerably. Typically, they claim to capitalise on the pupil's modality strengths and use these to develop competence in the use of weaker modalities.

Currently such methods are frequently advocated as particularly useful for teaching pupils with specific reading difficulties (dyslexia) (Hornsby and Farrer, 1990). Specific skills are emphasised, usually beginning with basic grapho-phonic associations and moving to more complex ones. The content and methodologies are usually highly structured and sequenced. Examples include certain of the specialist approaches described in Chapter 6, such as the Orton–Gillingham Method, the Gillingham–Stillman Alphabetic Method, 'Alpha to Omega' and the Hickey Method. The language used in most of these is also highly controlled. The approaches have been developed so as to introduce the pupil successfully to an increasingly complex sequence of sound–symbol relationships. In most cases it is necessary to purchase the commercially produced materials that comprise the system.

The major strengths of such approaches is that they offer hope.

The underpinning dictum is 'Never let the child lose hope, for once hope is lost, so is everything'. The very small steps involved in the reading programme virtually ensure that the pupil will experience successes, however small. Practice and overlearning make certain that later reading skills are built on firm foundations. Small steps, immediate feedback and reinforcement can help regenerate belief in the ability to learn to read.

One weakness is that the bottom-up, phonics-oriented, multi-sensory method and materials can appear extremely tedious to teachers untrained and inexperienced in this method. It can also be seen as slow and tedious by pupils, unless their teacher can infuse the sessions with enthusiasm and a creative use of the highly structured materials. This is easily advocated, but not as easily achieved consistently and over long periods of time. Theoretically, it has never been unequivocally demonstrated that either speaking or reading comprises hierarchically ordered skills of increasing complexity. The content of the stories used in the early stages is often very contrived, using a restricted range of simple word construction, such as those following the consonant–vowel–consonant (CVC) pattern.

'Real reading' schemes

'Real reading' and 'real books' are terms used to contrast the limitations in text content and structure found in basal reading schemes with the variety in content and form available in the cornucopia of children's literature now available, if the books can be afforded (Book Trust, 1989). Each pupil reads from books of his or her own choice at his/her own rate. The terms 'individualised reading', 'free reading', 'self-selected reading', 'personally selected reading' and 'voluntary reading' are sometimes used as synonyms for 'real reading'. In the UK, advocates have included practitioners, research workers and academics (e.g. Thomson, 1979; Moon and Raban, 1975; Moon, 1986). The centre of the system is the individual conference that the teacher has with each pupil. At this conference, the pupil reads both orally and silently from self-selected material. The teacher makes notes on various aspects of the child's performances in, for example, comprehension and word-attack skills and identifies individual instructional needs. A cumulative record of the child's progress is central to the approach.

'Real reading' requires the availability of a very wide range of reading materials. Variety in both content and genre are essential. The quality of the literature is seen as central. These books must be readily available to pupils in the classroom, and their storage and display are also extremely important: book availability, appeal and access are of the essence. A record has to be kept of each child's chosen books, usually by the pupil supported by the teacher. This work can be managed perfectly adequately by junior school pupils, with the necessary guidance and support. Pupils must also keep their own individual record of what they have read, why they chose the book and what they thought of it. These records can (and should) be used in regular scheduled classroom discussions. In addition to the individual reading conferences, the teacher will work with small groups of pupils on any identified common instructional needs. These could include work on grapho-phonic skills, or on more advanced skills such as skimming and scanning.

Moon has written an extremely popular booklet describing suggested groupings of lists of books suited to this approach. Many of these books have been published in small sets. These can form the basis of the essential book bank on which an individualised approach to reading can be developed. Over a number of years this booklet has regularly been revised and extended. The latest edition is available from the University of Reading's Reading and Language Information Centre (Moon and Ruel, 1990). It is suggested that the books be grouped into 14 stages covering four levels:

- Pure picture books (stage 0)
- Introductory (caption) (stages 1 to 3)
- Developmental readers (stages 4 to 10)
- Bridging readers (stages 11 to 13)

There are many variations on this theme. One called 'Story Chest' is concerned with the early stages of literacy. Story Chest provides materials for nursery and reception, key stage 1 (5–7 years) and key stage 2 (7–11 years) pupils. The Teacher's File describes the philosophy, content and structure of the materials. It also includes many practical suggestions for using the materials as starting points for a wide range of curricular activities (Hutchinson, 1990). The books are '. . . all written in clear, natural language. A strong story line with captivating illustrations makes reading Story Chest books fun and children learn to read as naturally as they learn to speak' (Nelson, 1990). Not all teachers accept that the parallel between speaking and reading development supports this assertion as simply as the publishers indicated (Turner, 1990a, 1990b). In practice, the system is wider than the above quotation suggests.

The system is linked to profile components 1 (Speaking and Listening), 2 (Reading) and 3 (Writing) of the national curriculum. '. . . Story Chest can be your inspiration to fulfilling the requirements of the national curriculum' (Nelson, 1990, p. 4). Without doubt the materials in the system contain sufficient variety and levels to open up many options to the teacher. The materials are grouped in stages from 0 to 20.

Stage 0 is designed to introduce children to Story Chest at a very early age and uses a coloured classroom frieze to portray characters in the series, linked to the upper and lower case letters of the alphabet. Stage 1 begins with the use of very large books ('Big, Big Books'). These are intended to be used for reading together or for 'shared reading'. Discussion, prediction, role-playing and collaborative play provide opportunities for developing a wide range of literacy skills. Cassette recordings include dramatized versions of the stories. These are complemented by 'Read-together' books and books for 'independent reading'. The later material develops a variety of literacy skills up to the standard represented by the end of key stage 2 at the top of the junior school.

Four Evaluation Packs are available to allow teachers to inspect the materials for 30 days before being committed to purchasing anything. These packs cover Story Chest stages 0–2, 2–7, 8–13 and 14–19 respectively.

Special materials are not required for a 'real reading' scheme. Teachers could build up the necessary book bank themselves, over time. Because a suitable and extensive collection of texts is essential, the system requires careful planning and considerable expenditure. Teaching specific reading skills tends not to be emphasised, other than when a need for a particular skill is identified by the teacher. There are no highly specific teaching techniques, but there are a number of key strategies: individual conferences with pupils, record-keeping, flexible grouping and the identification of pupils' instructional needs. The language level of texts is not controlled as in basal reading series. However, as can be seen from the above list, grading of materials can take place.

The strengths of this approach are that the pupils' wide-ranging interests, curiosity and wish to read are engaged. The importance of literature linked to self-directed and motivated learning is emphasised. The content of the texts from which the pupils select is not unduly limited; the forms of language represented are neither restricted nor rigid. The approach encourages sound selection habits and the critical appraisal of literature. It also encourages teachers to extend their knowledge and understanding of children's literature, of the wide range of genres represented, and the varied uses of the information and enjoyment gleaned from books.

The system requires a very generous financial provision for books. LMS is unlikely to release the sums required to establish, maintain and develop such a scheme. Whilst the parent–teacher organisations in some areas will raise money for this and other purposes, in numerous areas of social deprivation raising such additional funds is difficult. It is not impossible; but is it justified? A comprehensive individual record-keeping system is also essential. The class teacher needs to be knowledgeable about children's literature and also about the various skills that characterise the competent reader. Lacking adequate support, pupils may select books that are either too difficult or too easy to provide reading experiences that will optimise their reading development. The class teacher requires a clear idea of the level of reading development of the individual pupil and also of the difficulty and interest levels of the book bank on which the pupil is drawing.

The system also requires a high degree of classroom organisation if it is to work effectively. It is extremely demanding of a class teacher's time and energies to provide sufficient time and opportunities for pupils to browse, to read and for regular individual and group pupil–teacher conferences. In addition, recording individual pupils' progress, identifying skills that require teaching to individuals and groups and ensuring that these are taught and mastered, are some of the management demands. This should not deter the class teacher who, after due consideration, consultation with colleagues and preparation, decides to introduce such a scheme.

In practice, the adoption of this approach is usually agreed for the entire school. An example of some of the difficulties that can occur with a 'real reading' scheme was described in Chapter 2. From that some valuable lessons can be learned by junior school class teachers considering moving in this direction. *All* effective junior school reading programmes have considerable management demands.

Although it is easy to find reading schemes that use restricted vocabularies and language structures that some (not all) experts would criticise, it is *not* the case that all basal reading schemes lack literary merit. The analysis of the reading process and its development, coupled with the explicit structure and methodology of a basal reading scheme, suggests that a combination of the two approaches has much to commend it. In one sense, that is what the class library and supplementary readers were intended to achieve where basal reading schemes were in use.

There is a danger that enthusiasm for 'real reading', in the absence of sound evidence on the superiority of the method for all pupils, can lead to the premature and unjustified abandonment of basal systems that have enabled many pupils learn to read with competence and satisfaction.

A review of research into the efficacy of reading instruction based on 'real' books has been published (Tunnel and Jacobs, 1989). In 40 studies carried out between 1937 and 1971 in which 'core reading schemes' (i.e. basal systems) of teaching reading were compared with 'individualised reading', 24 studies favoured the latter approach, 15 indicated no significant difference, and only 1 favoured the basal approach. A study of 50 classes involving 1,149 8-year-old pupils found 20 statistically significant differences in reading attainments; of these, 14 favoured the literature-based approach (Eldredge and Butterfield, 1986). Perhaps it is unwise to seek very broad generalisations on the relative efficacy of methods!

> Currently the 'experts' are intent on causing confusion and disruption and in so doing all they are achieving is an undermining of teachers' confidence. It is relatively easy to write lucidly in a textbook about the virtues of using 'good children's literature' in the early stages of reading. Such writers reveal a certain arrogance concerning their judgement of what constitutes a 'good' book. And such writers have almost certainly not been exposed to the unremitting daily pressures exerted by a class of mixed-ability lively children. It is totally irresponsible to denigrate teaching techniques which invariably have been found to achieve the required goals.
>
> In any case, it would be naïve for anyone to assume that in reality teachers find themselves with such limited options. For they have always had the wisdom to appreciate that different children need different help at different times. Teachers do need to be conversant with all the alternatives and those with the authority to disseminate this knowledge should extend a greater sense of tolerance and not put forward only one rigid point of view.
>
> (Root, 1986b)

Caveat emptor!

Diagnostic–prescriptive approach

This approach involves a detailed specification of the objectives of the reading programme in operationalised terms, i.e. the reading behaviour and skills under consideration can be observed and measured. Testing of the pupil takes place on entry to, during and on exit from the programme. The diagnostic phase usually involves the use of a battery of tests of various reading and reading-related skills. Pupils who successfully pass criterion tests on some of these go on to work on other skills. What is to be taught has been prescribed on the basis of the diagnosis. Teaching is aimed at enabling the pupil to acquire and demonstrate mastery of the skill, or skills, where weaknesses had earlier been identified. The approach is usually an individualised one, although it is possible to apply it to groups of pupils (Naylor and Pumfrey, 1983). It tends to be used with pupils who have serious difficulties in learning to read, or who appear to make very little progress under the normal classroom programme. It is used in reading clinics and in ordinary schools by support teachers in individual work with pupils.

Special materials are required. These include diagnostic instruments linked to instructional packages, for example workbooks, audio-visual aids and, in the most sophisticated systems, computer-assisted instruction. The Stanford University Computer Assisted Instruction Project has developed such materials. Specific skills are emphasised. These are often word recognition skills, because they are considered important and can readily be programmed. A minority of diagnostic–prescriptive packages addresses a wider range of skills. The effectiveness of the programme is determined by whether or not the pupil reaches the various reading criteria that have been targeted. The skills to be learned are arranged in a carefully sequenced order.

The advantages of this approach are that the materials are well structured and based on an explicit analysis of reading development. Grading of the materials is such that a high level of success by the pupil is ensured and the pupil is allowed to work at his or her own pace. The systems provide for continual assessment. Feedback to the pupil of information on the correctness, or otherwise, of responses to the tasks helps maintain motivation. Pupils who have experienced only failure in their attempts at learning to read by less prescribed approaches can be successful under such a system.

Critics consider that this approach often involves presenting pupils with repetitive, boring and virtually meaningless tasks. The content and format typically do not take into account the interpersonal communicative uses of reading. Only relatively low-level skills lend themselves to this format.

Synthetic phonics programmes

The emphasis is on mastering component phonic skills. These are then combined to form words. A vast variety of materials has been developed to assist both teachers and pupils attain this end. The DISTAR Reading Programme described in Chapter 7 is an example of this approach. The focus is on helping pupils become aware of the importance of, and master, grapho-phonic relationships and word -recognition skills. Many procedures can be used to teach these. The instructional materials are very carefully sequenced.

The strengths of this approach are similar to those of basal reading series. A frequent criticism of synthetic phonics is that competent readers rarely use a synthetic approach to decoding text. This requires qualification. The vast majority of competent readers who meet an unknown word will use whatever context cues they can in their effort to find meaning, including grapho-phonic and/or syntactic cue systems.

A variation of this approach is called *linguistic phonemics* (Hammill, 1987). The vocabulary involved is very strictly controlled and is often based on patterns identified in children's speech, writing and spelling. The importance of grapho-phonic skills is emphasised and the work is finely graded from the very simple to the more complex. The Merrill linguistic readers is one American example. 'Letter Links', a British product by two experts on children's reading and linguistic development, has enjoyed some popularity (Reid and Donaldson, 1980).

COMMENT

It will be clear that these approaches to the teaching of reading have considerable overlap. Consideration by class teachers of their instructional repertoire will usually reveal that many of the approaches are, in varying degrees, already utilised in the class reading programme in different ways.

The information that should be presented in the school's annual curriculum review is described in a government document (DES, 1989i). This has caused considerable concern because the demands appeared too great to be met and, even worse, seemed likely to be of little benefit to interested parties. The Secretary of State for Education spoke to the Society of Education Officers on 25 January 1990 on this topic. He commented that the essential objectives are

> to encourage schools, *particularly primary schools*, to pay more attention to planning the use of lesson time; and to ensure that governing bodies and LEAs receive, or have access to information about the schools' planned use of lesson time, to satisfy themselves that schools have satisfactory arrangements for delivering the National Curriculum.
>
> (My italics.)

The Western Australian analysis of time allocations in the primary school classroom (p. 311) takes on added interest in the light of MacGregor's observations. He then outlined modifications that, without prejudicing the stated objectives, would ease burdens on primary school teachers by reducing the information requirements demanded of school. Further, he also proposed a new and simplified format for reporting the information. Let us hope that time will be found for teaching reading in the primary school classroom, as well as reporting information on when and how it was done. Will the current Secretary of State continue this policy?

TIME MANAGEMENT AND THE CLASS READING PROGRAMME

Under the national curriculum, the importance of management at all levels of education has now been given much greater prominence in both government and LEA thinking and funding. The excellent standards in reading achieved in *many* schools attest to their existing effectiveness and efficiency. By virtue of the requirements of the school development plan outlined earlier, the management, organisation and planning of the curriculum are to be improved. It must not be assumed that management considerations are new to professional practice in schools, but it is worthwhile reflecting on the philosophical bases of management theory and practice. Governments of various hues and also 'big business' all have to their 'credit' blunders of monumental proportions based, in part, on an unquestioning faith in the validity of their collective values and priorities, usually linked to the importance of efficient central management and planning.

There are many chasms between theories of management, ideologies and the real world, whether in politics, business or the classroom. Not all plans can bridge these gaps successfully. 'Groundnuts' and 'Manpower Planning' are salutary reminders of organisational fallibility by government. 'Teacher supply in the 1990s' is another. Why will we face a serious shortage of teachers in the 1990s? In some areas of the country there are already children for whom no teachers can be found. Such a circumstance is unlikely to improve the children's reading skills. The current demographic 'time bomb' was hardly unpredictable. It had fuses that were five and 18 years long, for entrance to primary schools and colleges respectively.

Whilst the author is very sympathetic to the importance of good organisation and planning in any endeavour, including the teaching of reading, it should never be forgotten that a curriculum is *not* merely a combination of programmes of study, schemes of work, attainment targets and statements of attainment. A curriculum is constructed on the basis of continuing negotiations between learners and teachers. A class teacher's reading curriculum is likely to succeed or fail dependent on how the work is negotiated with the pupils.

Because they have always recognised its educational centrality to *any* curriculum, all junior school teachers are keen to improve the reading of their pupils. It has been suggested that the considerable time devoted to such efforts is not always used effectively. We are all aware that 'time is money' and that this is a key consideration in efficient education, according to a market-economy philosophy. Increasingly schools are being asked to account for their expenditure. It is important that limited resources be used efficiently. Classroom observations are reported as showing that, under certain avoidable circumstances, 'the harder the teacher works in reading periods, the less work their pupils do' (Southgate, 1986). This cannot be construed as good classroom practice or management.

In the Bullock Report, *A Language for Life* (DES, 1975) respondents were asked 'How often does the child read to the teacher each week?' The responses showed that great emphasis was given to hearing the poorest achievers read to the teacher. This differential investment of teacher time per pupil in the teaching of reading represents professional concern in primary schools that *all* pupils should be able to read adequately. At the 6-year-old level, more than 50 per cent of teachers listened to all of their pupils at least three or four times weekly. Moving to the second year of the junior school, at the age of 9 some 63 per cent of pupils were reading aloud to their teacher once or twice weekly and 20 per cent of pupils were still reading aloud to teachers three or four times weekly. Despite its age, the Bullock Report contains a wealth of still valuable comment and suggestions. Of its 333 recommendations, 17 were picked out for particular attention. Readers may find it of interest to consider whether these recommendations have been implemented during the intervening 15 years. If not, why not?

An important project, 'Extending Beginning Reading' was completed in the early 1980s (Southgate-Booth et al., 1981). It was a four-year study concerned with pupils aged between 7 and 9+ years of age. Teachers' classroom practices were studied by various techniques, including observation schedules and teachers' logs of activities engaged in during periods when they were teaching reading/writing.

Five major findings of this project are summarised here. Whilst there have certainly been changes in organising the teaching of reading over the last few years, does this list describe current classroom practice?

- The time allocated by teachers for language activities was generally spent on the following activities. In order of importance these were:

  (a) Listening to individual children reading to them from

teacher-selected books at times when the rest of the class was (in theory) engaged in reading/writing activities based on the same or related materials.

(b) Giving assistance to individual pupils engaged in 'free writing' or 'topic work'.

It was quite common to find both activities taking place simultaneously: 'with the teacher supposedly listening to one child reading aloud on her right, while she dealt with queries from a queue of people on her left' (Southgate, 1986).

The earlier discussion of teaching styles (Chapter 1) suggests that many variations on this theme take place. But this practice is still found in many classrooms. There are sound reasons for both activities taking place, but effective management would ensure that they did not do so at the same time.

- The reading sessions usually lasted between 20 and 30 minutes daily. Some extended to an hour. The demands on the teacher were very considerable. The number of switches of attention made by teachers in this situation was recorded. The mean was 15 switches and the maximum noted was 32. The teachers were certainly extremely busy, but the time actually devoted to the individual pupil reading to the teacher was very little; on average it was about 30 seconds.

Southgate argues convincingly that, under such circumstances, the quality of the reading tuition provided was very poor. In addition, the 'on task' reading/writing behaviour of the rest of the class was low. It is reported that the pupils spent one-third of their time on a variety of 'off-task' behaviour. Some engaged in these for up to two-thirds of the time.

As a system of managing reading instruction, the arrangement has relatively little to commend it. It was the style adopted by 25 of the 33 teachers whose work was intensively studied during one year of the project. The other 8 teachers also undertook group work, usually with the more able pupils.

- Only 4 per cent of the reading time was spent on what Southgate calls 'basic skills'. In the junior school, 35 per cent of the 8-year-old pupils and 45 per cent of the 9-year-old pupils knew 'the common rules in the English language'. Of the 200 most commonly used words found in textual materials, only 20 per cent of the younger and 31 per cent of the older pupils could read them all immediately. The research workers observed no teacher test the pupils' recognition of these words or establish a teaching programme that would explicitly encourage their mastery.

- Encouragement of the pupils' interest in books was seen as important by the teachers. However, in the Southgate study, teachers spent longer reading aloud to pupils than the pupils spent on uninterrupted silent reading.
- Pupils spent considerable amounts of time on 'free writing' and project work. Despite this, very little time and attention was devoted to the teaching of reference skills such as the use of dictionaries.

Parallel with the enquiry by Southgate, the Schools Council sponsored research at the University of Nottingham into the reading of 10 to 15-year-old pupils of average and above-average reading attainment (Lunzer and Gardner, 1979). Because this study spanned the junior–secondary range, and contains some important messages for junior school teachers, some of the findings are outlined. The research report, *The Effective Use of Reading*, is a most valuable source of ideas on the development of comprehension skills in various aspects of the curriculum. The advent of the national curriculum gives added point to the report's suggestions for improving reading comprehension in various subject areas.

The report is in three main sections. The first begins with a theoretical analysis of the relationship between spoken and written communication and the problems involved in pupils comprehending textual material. Against this background, an empirical investigation of the characteristics of reading comprehension, based on a small sample of 257 fourth-year junior school pupils, was carried out. On the basis of their findings, the researchers conclude that reading comprehension comprises 'a single aptitude or skill, one which cannot usefully be broken down' (ibid., p. 63). Individual differences in reading comprehension are seen as a function of the pupil's ability and readiness to *reflect* on whatever it is he or she is reading.

A study of the readability of textual materials used in various aspects of the curriculum and of the value of text readability measures led to two main points. Firstly, the texts read by pupils when under the teacher's supervision in class tended to be less difficult than texts studied unaided by pupils. Secondly, that the use of readability formulae is of value to the teacher in organising effective pupil–text matches, provided the teacher is aware of the limitations of the many readability formulae available (e.g. Rye, 1982).

The second section describes the incidence and context of classroom reading, reading done in connection with homework and reading carried out in relation to topic work. Marked differences between the pattern of reading done in the top class of the junior school and in the first year of secondary school were identified. Of considerable importance is the finding that school reading was characterised by 'short bursts' of 1–15 seconds in any one minute in about 50 per cent of all reading across all subjects. Such intermittent reading is seen as incompatible with the reflective reading that the authors consider the essence of reading comprehension, irrespective of whether it takes place in the junior or the secondary school. Although more continuous reading was required in homework tasks, the authors question whether pupils are taught how to do this effectively. They claim that this can be done. Evidence supports their claim.

The final section describes school-based practices that have considerable promise for promoting the more effective use of reading. It includes accounts of pilot work on five related approaches to the improvement of reading comprehension through group discussion techniques. Directed activities related to texts (DARTS) require the teacher to undertake the role of chairman. Their strength is that they link reading to pupil-centred discussion and have been found of value to pupils of below-average reading attainments, not only to those of 'average or above' reading ability. The techniques studied were group cloze, group SQ3R (survey, question, read, recite, review), group sequencing, group prediction and group reading for different purposes (Lunzer and Gardner, 1979). These have been considered elsewhere in the present book (see Chapter 5, pp. 218–23).

Whether or not reading comprehension is as unitary as the Nottingham team believed, is still controversial. Workers who identify different aspects of reading and listening comprehension can also summon research evidence to their support. Lunzer accepts the possibility that the comprehension sub-skills hypothesis might be vindicated, but is dubious of the potential utility of such work. Let us take a parallel. In populations of pupils, reading attainment and attainment in mathematics are quite highly correlated. This may be because both make demands on common intellectual abilities. It is not assumed by teachers that high achievement in one area implies similar attainment in the other, unless specific teaching has been undertaken. Even if reading comprehension skills are highly inter-correlated for groups, this does not imply that they cannot be pedagogically differentiated and do not have to be taught. The fact that someone can skim texts effectively does not necessarily mean that he or she will know when, why or how to scan for information without instruction. 'Learning from the written word' requires sound pedagogy (Lunzer and Gardner, 1984).

COGNITIVE AND AFFECTIVE DIMENSIONS OF READING COMPREHENSION

Goals of reading instruction

Bloom's classification of educational goals is described in two volumes entitled *Taxonomy of Educational Objectives* (Bloom et al., 1956; Krathwohl et al., 1964). The first deals with the cognitive domain. The second analyses the affective domain, which clearly includes pupils' attitudes to reading. Each domain is divided into categories. According to Bloom, these categories can be considered as successive stages in the development of a person's understanding and competence in an area of knowledge (the cognitive domain) and in the growth of emotional involvement in a given area (the affective domain). The categories are as follows.

Cognitive domain	*Affective domain*
1. Knowledge	1. Receiving
2. Comprehension	2. Responding
3. Application	3. Valuing
4. Analysis	4. Organisation
5. Synthesis	5. Characterisation by a value or a value
6. Evaluation	complex

The categories are roughly parallel in the two domains and are of increasing complexity. From the point of view of both assessment and teaching, these categories have considerable advantages as they can provide one basis for a criterion-referenced scale, though this is not their only use. This requires that the categories be translated into operationally defined objectives appropriate to a reading programme. A well-considered reading programme will contain objectives from both domains, although the emphasis accorded to each level will differ dependent on the educational principles guiding the construction of the programme.

It can be argued that the objectives of *any* reading programme can usefully be considered at three levels: global; general and specific.

At the first level (global) these could include the following examples from the cognitive and affective domains:

Cognitive: 'To enable every pupil to become a competent reader'.

Affective: 'To enable every child to obtain pleasure from reading'.

At the next level (general) the main thoughts included in the global objective are given in more detail. For the cognitive domain, these could include the following:

'Knows the relationships between speech and printed language'.
'Develops the skill of decoding text into speech'.
'Understands the meaning of what is read'.

Moving from agreed global objectives to general objectives requires considerable thought, discussion and (almost certainly) compromises between those responsible for planning, organising and 'delivering' the reading curriculum.

The next stage is translating the agreed general objectives into operationally defined specific objectives, which should allow for individual differences in abilities. The specific objectives must also be descriptions of behaviour that can be observed, taught or learned, and assessed. Defining and agreeing these can be a difficult process. Holding the following six criteria in mind helps to make the task more manageable:

A specific objective should:

- be defined in terms of pupils' behaviour;
- be observable;
- be able to be assessed;
- be stated unambiguously so that it means the same to all teachers involved;
- focus on one specified reading activity;
- contain a specific action word such as 'points', 'matches', 'sequences', 'names', 'tells', 'writes', 'spells', 'explains', etc.

In effect, this means that each general objective is analysed into specific observable behaviour. Collectively, mastery of these is expected to lead to development towards the general and global objective.

By analysing the first general objective listed, the following specific objectives could be deduced.
(Knowledge of specifics):

The pupil can *name* flash cards correctly.
The pupil can *match* pictures to printed words, etc.

It is clear that definition of the objectives of a reading curriculum demands that a specific *content* be identified. In terms of the above two specific objectives, 'Which words should be on the flash cards?' and 'Which pictures and words should be matched?'

To help practising teachers, Bloom and his co-workers have produced a handbook. This includes sections by Cazdan on the evaluation of early language development and by Moore and Kennedy on the evaluation of learning in the language arts (Bloom et al., 1971).

The teacher who is interested in the specification of objectives as a means of integrating assessment and teaching in the reading curriculum will find the work of Barrett (1972) of interest.

There are tensions between teachers who consider that the advantages of specific behaviourally defined objectives outweigh their weaknesses, and colleagues who do not. It is one facet of the 'top-down' versus 'bottom-up' controversy considered in Chapters 1 and 2. It is unlikely to end in the near future.

Barrett's taxonomy

One continuing challenge is 'How can pupils be helped to appreciate the difference between questions requiring literal comprehension of a text [the answer is available in the text] and ones demanding inferential comprehension, and deal with them?' This issue highlights the importance of the teacher using questions of various types systematically and consciously to elicit different types of pupil–text interaction. Adroitly phrased closed and open-ended questions, suitably sequenced, can lead pupils from dealing effectively with matters of fact that are readily available in a text to the speculation, conjecture and generation and testing of hypotheses characteristic of creative thinking.

The analysis of cognitive and affective dimensions of reading comprehension skills developed by Barrett has also been influential and has considerable educational value. Barrett's list is not comprehensive, developmental, hierarchical or empirically determined; nor is the Reading national curriculum. The taxonomy was devised by reflective thinking about the nature of the purposes, processes and activities involved in reading comprehension. (The process is similar to the way in which much of the national curriculum has been constructed.) Originally published in 1968, it was adapted in the Bullock Report (DES, 1975). Barrett analyses reading comprehension into five types, each of which is further subdivided. The analysis is shown in the following list. It highlights many possible avenues for teachers to develop particular aspects of pupils' reading comprehension, in all its complexities. When criterion-referenced formative and summative assessments are central to a curriculum, such taxonomies can be very helpful in curriculum development.

Barrett's taxonomy of cognitive and affective dimensions of reading comprehension: summary

1.0 Literal comprehension.

1.1 Recognition
   a. Recognition of details

      b. Recognition of main ideas
      c. Recognition of a sequence
      d. Recognition of comparison
      e. Recognition of cause and effect relationships
      f. Recognition of character traits

1.2 Recall
      a. Recall of details
      b. Recall of main ideas
      c. Recall of a sequence
      d. Recall of comparison
      e. Recall of cause and effect relationships
      f. Recall of character traits

2.0 Reorganisation
2.1 Classifying
2.2 Outlining
2.3 Summarising
2.4 Synthesising

3.0 Inferential comprehension
3.1 Inferring supporting details
3.2 Inferring main ideas
3.3 Inferring sequence
3.4 Inferring comparisons
3.5 Inferring cause and effect relationships
3.6 Inferring character traits
3.7 Predicting outcomes
3.8 Interpreting figurative language

4.0 Evaluation
4.1 Judgements of reality or fantasy
4.2 Judgements of fact or opinion
4.3 Judgements of adequacy and validity
4.4 Judgements of appropriateness
4.5 Judgements of worth, desirability and acceptability

5.0 Appreciation
5.1 Emotional responses to the content
5.2 Identification with characters or incidents
5.3 Reaction to the author's use of language
5.4 Imagery

(Barrett, 1972)

Comment

Because individual tuition for all pupils by the teacher is not always possible, increasingly class teachers are training others to help in teaching their pupils to read. In relation to the class reading programme, Southgate has remarked 'Never do anything yourself which you can train someone else to do for you!' (1986, p. 86). Although this may sound a straightforward and simple solution to an ever-pressing problem, it requires considerable time, energy, enthusiasm, organisational ability and ingenuity. It is not an easy option.

Lunzer and Gardner's work demonstrates that reflective reading can, and should, be developed for pupils of *all* abilities. The techniques exist and their efficacy has been demonstrated; equally importantly, reflective reading is not the prerogative of children with average or above reading attainments. Effective reading for anyone is, *par excellence*, a thinking process. Both objectives and methodologies of the reading curriculum require constant appraisal. A school's curriculum development plan provides an opportunity for such work.

THE READING PROGRAMME AND THE CLASS TEACHER: ATTRIBUTES AND ASPIRATIONS

The following checklist of desirable attributes of the effective classroom reading teacher is intended neither to deter nor depress, but to challenge. Collectively, as yet, we do not understand the nature of reading and its development sufficiently well to conceptualise, predict and control pupils' reading in all its varieties; but we know quite a lot. The teaching profession *does* have sufficient research-based evidence about pupils' abilities and motivations and about methodologies to be able to raise standards of literacy for *all* pupils, given the necessary resources. Because we can only reduce some reading difficulties, rather than obviate them completely in certain cases, this should neither reduce teachers' justifiable pride in their skills nor prevent the profession's aspiration to do better. If there *are* colleagues, anywhere, who meet all of the following criteria, the author would like them to contact him. For mortals, the list can be used to help the class teacher identify aspects of personal professional development that merit attention. The well-prepared class teacher interested in reading has:

- an appreciation of the national curriculum requirements in connection with reading and associated aspects of language;

- a detailed knowledge of how the class reading curriculum plan relates to the school's curriculum development plan;
- an understanding of the complexities of reading as a developmental process;
- an awareness of the importance of physical, psychological, emotional, motivational and socioeconomic factors that affect children's ability to learn to read;
- knowledge of how and where to find information on available methodologies and materials;
- mastery of the pedagogy that will be utilised in the reading programme in the classroom for which he or she is responsible;
- experience in the use of observational procedures, informal reading inventories, normative and criterion-referenced reading tests;
- an appreciation of the respective strengths and weaknesses of various observation and assessment techniques (including SATs);
- the ability to distinguish between formative and summative functions of assessment in the reading curriculum;
- sensitivity to the importance of inter- and intra-individual differences in children's characteristics and the possible effects of these on their learning to read;
- knowledge of research findings concerning the learning and teaching of reading and their implications for the classroom;
- an awareness of what makes an effective class teacher in an effective junior school;
- an appreciation of the professional skills in the teaching and learning of reading possessed by colleagues in the teaching and other professions; and
- organisational ability.

Above all, it is essential that the teacher be able to justify the reading programme in terms of its theoretical bases and its consequences in relation to the attainments, attitudes, progress and motivation of each pupil.

In organising the work in a junior classroom, the teacher has four possibilities for arranging reading activities: work with individual pupils; with groups; with the whole class; or with combinations of these three. The last was recommended in the Bullock Report, and is the class management technique most commonly found in junior schools today. How can the organisation of the reading programme in the classroom be managed?

Children are active learners. The emphasis in the reading curriculum must be placed on the pupil as learner. The teacher's efforts should be devoted mainly to ensuring that systematic plans for successful pupil–text interaction are arranged.

As teachers, we must continue to learn. As the Director of the Dyslexia Institute has put it: 'If the child does not learn the way we teach, can we teach him the way he learns, and then extend and develop his competencies in learning?' (Chastey, 1990).

COMPONENTS OF EFFECTIVE READING PROGRAMMES FOR ALL PUPILS

Pupils coming to primary schools are typically well motivated to learn to read. It is the teacher's responsibility to capitalise on, and enhance, that initial motivation. The research findings reported in the previous section indicate how these ends can be achieved by collaborative action at home, in the classroom and by the school.

Reading should lead to enjoyable, interesting, exciting, pleasurable and useful experiences for the individual, group or class, dependent on the reading activity organised by the teacher. The interests and backgrounds of the pupils are important indicators of what will initially interest them. Though this experiential background should be used by teachers as part of their reading curriculum, pupils' horizons must also be extended by school activities that provide further reading materials.

Experiences of success in reading are a powerful incentive to further reading; experiences of failure rapidly lead to aversion. Inter-individual competitive activities can quickly demotivate individual pupils who find reading more difficult than their peers. The importance of establishing beneficent spirals of reading experiences, leading to enjoyment of the activity cannot be overemphasised. The individual pupil's own endeavours should be the base against which progress is measured. The class teacher must expect forever to be tossed on the horns of the dilemmas posed by normative versus individual expectations of pupils' reading standards and progress. Neither criterion-referenced measurement (formative, summative or evaluative) nor the national curriculum will dehorn the issue.

No single method of teaching guarantees success for all pupils. The style whereby the pupil learns most effectively is crucial and can determine which methodology should be used.

Plenty of opportunities for well-motivated practice are required. The differences between the competent reader and the child just beginning, or experiencing difficulties in making progress, in their uses of grapho-phonic, syntactic and semantic cue systems are described in Chapter 2.

As we saw in Chapter 3, based on the concept of the informal reading inventory and miscue analysis, pupil–text interaction can be categorised as being on one of four levels: 'frustration', 'instructional', 'independent' or 'capacity'. If reading is to become automated so that attention can go directly to the meaning of the text, overlearning is essential. This means providing plenty of opportunities for the pupil to read at the 'independent' level. Practice can make perfect. Work at the 'instructional' level is important to further progress. The avoidance of reading experiences that are seen as at the 'frustration' level by the pupil because the text is inappropriate, is to be sought at all costs.

Providing a large collection of books in the classroom is a first step. These should be graded according to their reading difficulty and interest levels. This has become standard practice in the majority of junior schools. The difficulty level of texts can be calculated using various readability formulae. Nowadays, certain of these formulae are available on disc. Thus a passage of text can be typed into a microcomputer, the difficulty level of the text calculated by the program and displayed on the visual display unit or printed out.

In addition to the 'readability formulae' described in Chapter 4, one helpful scheme for grading reading materials is based on the principle of utilising existing resources and involves using parents, colleagues and pupils (Southgate, 1983). Teachers carry out the initial grading using published lists of books classified by reading age. The NARE book *An A–Z of Reading Books* provides a good start (Atkinson et al., 1985). Increasingly, publishers of children's books provide such information as a matter of course. Many LEA school psychological services have also developed valuable lists. It is suggested by Southgate that groups of pupils of known reading ages act as 'assessment panels' to check on the ascribed levels, simultaneously getting some valuable reading practice. Adults and older pupils can complete the labelling using a colour-coded system such as that in *Individualised Reading* (Moon and Moon, 1985).

Provided one is not averse to the use by pupils of 'technical' language when referring to text, they could be taught the system of grading books for difficulty level using the noun frequency count method developed in New Zealand. The problem of getting pupils to recognise nouns would have to be addressed: the author recalls learning this in the very early years of his junior school education. An alphabetical list of nouns graded in nine difficulty levels is given to the pupils, who then select a prescribed number of nouns from the text whose difficulty level is to be assessed. Each noun is ascribed a number based on its difficulty using the alphabetical list, and a simple calculation is used to estimate text difficulty level

(Elley and Reid, 1974). This estimate is rechecked by taking other samples of nouns from the text. Such a small group activity would certainly cover a number of SoAs in 'Listening and Speaking', 'Reading', 'Writing and Spelling' and 'Mathematics'. Dependent on the text content, SoAs in other subject areas could also be covered simultaneously. The technique can be used on almost any textual materials and can provide children with important insights into what it is that makes text easy or otherwise to read. As a reading activity it can also be useful in vocabulary consolidation and extension.

'USSR in the USA' is the title not of a book on subversion but of an article referring to the importance of Uninterrupted Silent Supervised Reading in American schools (see Rude and Oehlkers, 1984). It was, in part, a reaction against reading systems that had become so reductionist that pupils rarely had opportunity in school to read continuous material for any length of time. It is known that independent reading increases both vocabulary and fluency of reading. Reading books provide practice in the 'whole act' of reading. It is reported that American pupils spend very little time in independent reading. In the average elementary school, pupils spend 7–8 minutes daily in silent reading from books. At home, 50 per cent of 11-year-old children spend only 4 minutes per day on independent reading. These same children spend, on average, 130 minutes per day watching television (US Department of Education, 1986).

The earlier reference to findings in the UK also indicates that a number of British schools are not blameless in this respect (see pp. 327–31). The availability of a good book collection in a class library presents an opportunity for the teacher to ensure that it is well used by pupils. Moves towards this can be furthered by introducing USSR using the following steps:

- Set aside a *regular daily* period for personal USSR.
- Each child must have a personally chosen book at a suitable difficulty level available at the specified time.
- Pupils should have a 'reserve' or continuation book to hand if one is likely to be needed.
- Introduce the USSR period as a treat.
- Introduce the USSR period initially for only a short period.
- Gradually extend the period as the pupils become accustomed to USSR.
- During the USSR period, the teacher should sit facing the class but must not speak to any pupil.
- Non-verbal signals should be used to convey to any pupils who might not be reading what they should be doing.

- Establish the pattern that pupils do not talk or leave their seats during the USSR period.
- The teacher should set an example by also engaging in USSR at the same time as the pupils.
- Ensure that a pupil-prepared notice saying 'Children reading. Please do not disturb' is put on the outside of the door to the classroom.
- Never extend USSR to a point where restlessness become apparent amongst the pupils.

Linked to USSR should be a system of allowing pupils to record which book they had selected, why they chose it and what they thought of it. These recorded opinions can form the basis of discussion periods about books. The activity encourages the development of critical acumen. The records can also be displayed on the wall of the classroom so that classmates can read each others' selections and evaluations. The Ingham–Clift reading record form developed by the Bradford 'Book Flood' experiment provides an admirable format for such records (Ingham, 1982). The accumulation of such documents by each pupil forms an important record of one aspect of the individual pupil's reading development. It also sensitises the class teacher to the appeal of a wide range of books and to how well the available stock meets her pupils' needs.

A strategy for the class teacher

One aim of a whole-school approach is to ensure that help to pupils is provided within the school and, preferably, within the class. Teachers are well aware that, in the vast majority of cases, the progress of such pupils cannot be left solely to the intermittent support provided by specialists attending on a peripatetic basis either within the junior classroom or school; or by pupils attending off-site centres.

An LEA educational psychologist, together with the head of the Reading Service in Stockport LEA, have produced such a strategy in *Learning Difficulties in Reading and Writing: A Teacher's Manual* (Reason and Boote, 1986). Its contents are based on their extensive experience as primary school teachers deeply involved in work in these fields. The manual is not a comprehensive account of teaching methods and materials. It is described by its authors as 'a kind of *survival kit*, an attempt to assemble in one place enough ideas to enable all teachers and parents to give each child some appropriate help' (ibid., p. 1). The theoretically eclectic and pragmatic approach that the authors describe has appealed to many class teachers. In part, this is because its strategy allows the objective of improving the reading of all pupils to be harmonised with that of identifying and alleviating individual pupils' reading difficulties. Their book is one of the many possible syntheses of 'top-down' and 'bottom-up' approaches to the learning and teaching of reading discussed in Chapter 2. The authors reflect the pragmatic concerns of the class teacher rather than adopting a single theoretical position. This is not to say that the manual is atheoretical. It is not. The rationale underpinning it is clearly documented.

The authors emphasise the importance of success to the pupil, the teacher's responsibility for this, and make clear suggestions on how this might be achieved. These are related to a four-stage model of learning to read:

1. Pre-reading;
2. Beginning to read;
3. Intermediate; and
4. Basic reading skills have been mastered.

At each level, three aspects of children's abilities are considered:

- concepts and approaches (reading involves thinking processes);
- visual word recognition; and
- phonics.

Numerous practical suggestions for learning activities and games that can be used in the classroom with individuals and groups, and at home, are clearly described. Coupled with this is valuable and clear advice on the involvement of parents as teachers. The authors' conclusion that 'Children with reading difficulties will not suddenly make miraculous progress as a result of a short reading project' underlines their realistic approach. Such projects can be built upon to the advantage of all involved.

Assessment procedures and the importance of record-keeping are integrated with the sequential teaching suggested. Chapters on spelling and handwriting are also included. The strategy proposed is the stronger because of its clarity and modesty. One of the authors has recently presented an account of how different approaches to intervention can be reconciled (Reason, 1990).

TEACHING READING TO PUPILS WITH SEVERE LEARNING DIFFICULTIES (SLD)

What helpful advice can be given on teaching pre-reading and reading activities to pupils with severe learning difficulties? It is most likely that a formal statement of special educational needs and provision will have been prepared for such a pupil. This is likely to include suggestions for an individual educational programme. Even when additional staff support is available from the LEA, the challenges to the class teacher are considerable, both pedagogically and in terms of time management. A key question is whether the teaching of reading is important to such a pupil. In the author's opinion, the answer is an unequivocal 'Yes'. (If not, issues of disapplication of parts of the national curriculum (English) requirements arise.)

But how can this teaching be done? Teaching reading to children with severe learning difficulties has been very well described in *Let Me Read* (Jeffree and Skeffington, 1980), which is one of a valuable series including *Let Me Speak* (Jeffree and McConkey, 1976) and *Let Me Play* (Jeffree et al., 1977).

The authors firmly assert that the methods they describe are not limited to SLD pupils. The methods of developing pupils' reading described in the first of these books are also considered suitable for pupils whose major, or sole, difficulty is in learning to read. The games and exercises included are deliberately planned so that they can be used by parents, other care-givers and teachers. The teaching suggestions are eminently practical, and derive from the two authors' extensive involvement in research carried out under the aegis of the Hester Adrian Research Centre and also in training teachers on advanced courses leading to the Diploma in the Education of Handicapped Children and the MEd in Special Education at the University of Manchester. According to the authors, their scheme is designed to have 'more the flavour of "fun" than of "lessons", yet it belongs to a carefully thought-out system with appropriate aims and goals'.

Two ideas that have influenced the authors are *symbol accentuation* and *the language experience approach*. Sections deal with reading readiness and the crucial move from 'reading' pictures to reading print. The importance of everyday words of significance to the pupil and of the language experience approach to reading are emphasised. A number of reading-related games are then presented. Word families and phonic analysis games and materials are also included, as are suggestions for building bridges to printed books from established foundations. The appealing simplicity of the authors' plan does not do justice to the imaginative ways in which the themes are developed. (The whole is much more impressive than first impressions of the sum of the parts suggests.)

Foundations
- recognition of words and letters;
- experience of books and stories;

- elementary word-attack skills;
- development of books from their own experience and language.

The Bridge
- games with books familiar because they have been read aloud;
- 'supported' reading of familiar books;
- 'supported' reading of new books;
- independent reading: (a) books, magazines and newspapers; (b) printed messages in the environment.

Suggestions for recording the progress of individuals are presented which could readily be adapted to meet many of the assessment and recording requirements of the national curriculum. The considerable ingenuity shown by the authors and their students is clearly evident. This book can be recommended to all junior school teachers wishing to help pupils with severe reading difficulties and lack of motivation to read. It may be ten years old; it is certainly not out of date.

TEACHER EFFECTIVENESS IN THE TEACHING OF READING

This book is written from the viewpoint that the concept of special educational needs is suspect. It is argued that concern with such needs has led to much misplaced and expensive administrative effort and to a waste of resources. Instead, emphasis has here been placed on the importance of appreciating, identifying and utilising pupils' many individual differences to increase the chances of their learning to read successfully, and with enjoyment. It is not assumed that pupils' inter-individual differences in reading attainments and progress will be eliminated.

It is the author's considered opinion that the reading skills and progress of *all* pupils can be improved, and that the teaching profession has the knowledge and ability available to achieve this goal, in collaboration with parents. Political and financial decisions relating to necessary staffing and material resources are a separate set of issues. Reading for *all*, within the context of a *'whole-school'* approach to meeting individual differences, is the orientation adopted in the present book. Aspiring to such an objective is essential if curricular developments enabling it to be approached are to be created. One danger is that the *ideal* can be the enemy of the *better*. The relatively modest aim is to improve pupils' standards and progress in reading. The means and the ends are equally important: they must be consonant with one another.

It is crucial that within-school curriculum development of the teaching and learning of reading should take place. Currently, one of the biggest growth areas in publishing is in the many fields of national-curriculum-related INSET materials. Schools will select what appears to meet their needs and those of their pupils.

The national curriculum is constructed by negotiation between the class teacher and the pupils, individually and collectively. To identify the reading component of the national curriculum with the specified programmes of study, attainment targets, statements of attainment and standard assessment tasks, is to fail to distinguish its structural *bones* from the *living tissue* of curriculum process. The NCC and SEAC emphasise the importance of both formative and summative assessments of standards and progress in reading. This is an important and constructive pointer towards improved practice.

There are many others. The International Reading Association (IRA) established the Teacher Effectiveness in Reading Committee to review, identify and summarise past and current research on effective teaching of reading. The resulting book is *Effective Teaching of Reading: Research and Practice* (Hoffman, 1986).

The development of a theory capable of integrating the many facets of reading development from the viewpoints of different professions, was highlighted as the top priority:

> Such a theory must account for teacher competencies and decisions, student perceptions and attitudes, and classroom and school reading environments. It should enable us to predict and explain learning outcomes, given varied pedagogical arrangements, which have the teacher, child and reader environment at the center. The development of such a theory is a challenge which remains for the profession, and specifically for the Teaching Effectiveness in Reading Committee.
>
> (Ibid., p. vi)

Whilst such an aspiration may smack of Cloud-cuckoo-land to some readers, the contributors to this book demonstrate clearly that significant steps have been taken towards this still distant theoretical underpinning of classroom practice. In so doing, they open up promising avenues meriting further exploration. Whilst not set within the context of our national curriculum requirements, the issues raised and the findings reported are highly relevant to the improvement of pupils' standards and progress in reading.

A study of the history of research in this area provides the background to the studies in improving teacher effectiveness in the teaching of reading. A further 12 chapters provide details of process–product research, applying research findings in practice, staff development in the teaching of reading, the effects of policy constraints on the specialist reading teacher in relation to effective compensatory reading instruction. From this cornucopia, one item on the principles underpinning effective reading instruction with small groups has been presented in Chapter 5 (pp. 220–3). This work has messages that are likely to be valid for junior school pupils in general, and particularly for those with reading difficulties.

The IRA subsequently published a book aimed at professionals with responsibilities for developing and changing the reading programmes used in schools (Samuels and Pearson, 1988). Theories of change, and the problems of introducing change, are considered. The characteristics of identified exemplary reading programmes are discussed on the basis of research findings. This is followed by descriptions of six effective reading programmes, and discussion of the changes that were required in order to establish them, get them working and continued.

Whatever we do, we must not become isolationist.

TOWARDS THE TWENTY-FIRST CENTURY

To be able to read, and to derive utility and enjoyment from the activity, is to amplify one's human abilities. It is a tribute to many dedicated teachers that such a high proportion of our pupils learn to read well, appreciating the pleasures and utilities of a vast range of genres. Unfortunately, this is not the case for all pupils. Raising pupils' reading standards generally, increasing their progress, identifying and alleviating reading difficulties, are all well within the teaching profession's competence, *given the necessary resources*.

To further extend our collective and individual abilities to understand, predict and control the learning and teaching of reading, requires an active, informed and involved teaching profession. Critical acumen in evaluating innovations is essential.

The creativity, ingenuity and dedication demonstrated by teachers all over the world in this effort have one clear message. We must be open to ideas and practices that colleagues in other countries are developing. We must share our concerns. In these activities, the class teacher is the linchpin.

The profession has much to be proud of in its continuing contribution to the development of literacy. We still have much to do. The national curriculum can be used to this end. The challenges are great. If we truly want a nation of readers, so too must be the responses.

Appendix 1
National sources of information and advice on improving reading

UK AND IRELAND

Adult Literacy and Basic Skills Unit, 229–231 High Holborn, London WC1V 7DA.

Association of Educational Psychologists, 3 Sunderland Road, Durham DH1 2LH.

Book Trust (formerly the National Book League), Book House, 45 East Hill, London SW18 2QZ.

British Psychological Society, St Andrew's House, 48 Princess Road East, Leicester LE1 7DR.

Cambridge Specific Learning Disabilities Group, Department of Education, University of Cambridge, 5 Bene't Place, Cambridge.

Centre for Educational Guidance and Special Needs, School of Education, University of Manchester, Manchester M13 9PL.

Centre for Information on Language Teaching and Research (CILT), 20 Carlton House Terrace, London SW1Y 5AP.

Department of Education and Science, Elizabeth House, York Road, London SE1 7PH.

Education Management Information Exchange (EMIE) (contact via National Foundation for Educational Research in England and Wales).

Godfrey Thomson Unit for Academic Assessment, University of Edinburgh, 24 Buccleuch Place, Edinburgh EH8 9JT.

National Association for Remedial Education (NARE), Central Office, 2 Lichfield Road, Stafford ST17 4JX.

National Association for the Teaching of English (NATE), 49 Broomgrove Road, Sheffield S10 2NA.

National Curriculum Council, 15–17 New Street, York YO1 2RA.

National Educational Resources Information Service, Maryland College, Leighton Street, Woburn MK17 9JD.

National Foundation for Educational Research in England and Wales, 'The Mere', Upton Park, Slough SL1 2DQ.

National Hospitals College of Speech Sciences, Chandler House, 2 Wakefield Street, London WC1N 1PG.

National Oracy Project (NOP), Newcombe House, 45 Notting Hill Gate, London W11 3JB.

Northern Ireland Council for Educational Research, 52 Malone Road, Belfast BT9 5BS.

Publishers Association, 19 Bedford Square, London WC1B 3HU.

Reading Association of Ireland, Educational Research Centre, St Patrick's College, Dublin 9, Republic of Ireland.

Reading and Language Information Centre, University of Reading, Faculty of Education and Community Studies, Bulmershe Court, Woodlands Avenue, Earley, Reading RG6 1HY.

School Bookshop Association, 6 Brightfield Road, Lee, London SE12 8QF.

School Examinations and Assessment Council, Newcombe House, 45 Notting Hill Gate, London W11 3JB.

School Library Association, Liden Library, Barrington Close, Liden, Swindon SN3 6HF.

Scottish Council for Research in Education, 15 St John Street, Edinburgh EH8 8JR.

Special Educational Needs Database, Scottish Council for Educational Technology, 74 Victoria Crescent Road, Glasgow G12 9JN.

Special Educational Resources Information Service (SERIS), 11 Anson Road, Rusholme, Manchester M14 9BY.

United Kingdom Reading Association (UKRA), Administrative Office, c/o Edge Hill College, St Helen's Road, Ormskirk, Lancashire L39 4QP.

Specialist groups and centres concerned with raising awareness and providing help for individuals with literacy-related learning difficulties

Association For All Speech Impaired Children (AFASIC), 347 Central Markets, Smithfield, London EC1A 9NH.

British Dyslexia Association, 98 London Road, Reading, Berkshire RG1 5AU.

Defining Dyslexia, 132 High Street, Ruislip, Middlesex HA4 8LL.

Dyslexia Institute, 133 Gresham Road, Staines, Middlesex TW18 2AJ.

Foundation for the Education of the Underachieving and Dyslexic (FEUD), Maple Hayes Dyslexia School and Research Centre, Abnalls Lane, Lichfield, Staffordshire WS13 8BL.

Helen Arkell Dyslexia Centre, Frensham, Farnham, Surrey GU10 3BW.

Hornsby Dyslexia Centre, 71 Wandsworth Common, Westside, London SW18 2ED.

Invalid Children's Aid Nationwide (ICAN), Allen Graham House, 198 City Road, London EC1V 2PH.

Professional Association of Teachers of Students with Specific Learning Difficulties (PATOSS), 'Sunnybank', Churchill, Oxon. OX7 6NW.

USA

ERIC system (Educational Resources Information Centres)

This is a system of 16 clearing houses established in the USA. Each acquires significant educational literature within its particular area. They represent a major educational resource. The following have been selected as potentially of greatest interest to readers of this book.

The Central Headquarters of the entire ERIC system is: Educational Resources Information Centre (Central ERIC), US Department of Education, Office of Educational Research and Improvement (OERI), Washington, DC 20208, USA.

ERIC Clearinghouse on Reading and Communication Skills, National Council of Teachers of English, 1111 Kenyon Road, Urbana, IL 61801, USA.

ERIC Clearinghouse on Elementary and Early Childhood, University of Illinois, College of Education, 805 West Pennsylvania Avenue, Urbana, IL 61801, USA.

ERIC Clearinghouse on Handicapped and Gifted Children, Council for Exceptional Children, 1920 Association Drive, Reston, VA 22091, USA.

ERIC Clearinghouse on Information Resources, Syracuse University, School of Education, Huntingdon Hall, Room 030, 150 Marshall Street, Syracuse, NY 13210, USA.

ERIC Clearinghouse on Tests, Measurement and Evaluation, Educational Testing Service, Rosedale Road, Princeton, NJ 08541, USA.

The databases of these organisations can be searched electronically at a number of major reference libraries in the UK. The address of the central reference facility is:

ERIC Processing and Reference Facility, ORI Inc., Information Systems, 4833 Rugby Avenue, Suite 301, Bethesda, MD 20814, USA.

International Reading Association (IRA), 800 Barksdale Road, PO Box 8139, Newark, DE 19714–8139, USA.

Appendix 2
Attainment targets and associated statements of attainment: key stages 1 and 2

Key stages 1 and 2 concern pupils aged from 6:00 years (Y 1) to 11:00 years (Y 6).

Levels 1 to 3 of the attainment targets and associated statements of attainment cover key stage 1 for the majority of pupils.

Levels 2 to 5 cover key stage 2 for the majority of pupils.

Materials abstracted, with permission, from *English in the National Curriculum (No. 2)* (Department of Education and Science and the Welsh Office, March 1990)

Note: The statements of attainment at levels 1 to 3 are as specified by Order and published in the statutory Document entitled *English in the National Curriculum* (DES and Welsh Office, 1989b) on 31 May 1989.

Attainment target 1
Speaking and listening

Knowledge, skills and understanding in speaking and listening (AT 1)

The development of pupils' understanding of the spoken word and the capacity to express themselves effectively in a variety of speaking and listening activities, matching style and response to audience and purpose.

Statements of attainment	Example
Level 1	
Pupils should be able to:	
a) participate as speakers and listeners in group activities, including imaginative play.	*Suggest what to do next in a practical activity; tell stories; play the role of shopkeeper or customer in the class shop.*

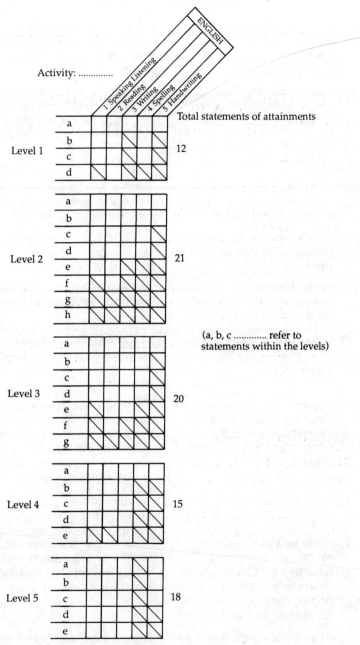

Figure A.1 *Planning grid for statements of attainment at levels 1, 2, 3, 4 and 5*

b) listen attentively, and respond, to stories and poems.

Ask questions about a story or poem; retell a story; enact a poem; draw a picture to illustrate a story or poems.

c) respond appropriately to simple instructions given by a teacher.

Follow two consecutive instructions such as 'Choose some shells from the box and draw pictures of them'.

Level 2

a) participate as speakers and listeners in a group engaged in a given task.

Compose a story together; design and make a model; assume a role in play activity.

b) describe an event, real or imagined, to the teachers or another pupil.

Tell the listener about something which happened at home, on the television or in a book.

c) listen attentively to stories and poems, and talk about them.

Talk about the characters; say what they like or dislike about a story or poem.

d) talk with the teacher, listen, and ask and answer questions.

Talk about events or activities in or out of school – such as a school trip, a family outing or a television programme.

e) respond appropriately to a range of more complex instructions given by a teacher, and give simple instructions.

Follow three consecutive actions such as 'Write down the place in the classroom where you think your plant will grow best, find out what the others on your table think and try to agree on which is likely to be the best place'.

Level 3

a) relate real or imaginary events in a connected narrative which conveys meaning to a group of pupils, the teacher or another known adult.

Tell a story with a beginning, middle and end; recount a series of related incidents that happened at home or in a science activity.

b) convey accurately a simple message.

Relay a simple telephone message in role-play or real life; take an oral message to another teacher.

c) listen with an increased span of concentration to other children and adults, asking and responding to questions and commenting on what has been said.

Listen to the teacher or to a radio programme on a new topic, then discuss what has been said.

d) give, and receive and follow accurately, precise instructions when pursuing a task individually or as a member of a group.

Plan a wall display or arrange an outing together.

Level 4

a) give a detailed oral account of an event, or something that has been learned in the classroom, or explain with reasons why a particular course of action has been taken.

Report on a scientific investigation, or the progress of a planned group activity, to another group or the class.

b) ask and respond to questions in a range of situations with increased confidence.

Guide other pupils in designing something; conduct an interview on a radio programme devised with other pupils.

c) take part as speakers and listeners in a group discussion or activity, expressing a personal view and commenting constructively on what is being discussed or experienced.

Draft a piece of writing, with others, on a word processor; contribute to the planning and implementation of a group activity.

d) participate in a presentation.

Describe the outcome of a group activity; improvise a scene from a story or poem or of the pupils' own devising.

Level 5

a) give a well organised and sustained account of an event, a personal experience or an activity.

Describe a model which has been made, indicating the reasons for the design and the choice of materials.

b) contribute to and respond constructively in discussion, including the development of ideas; advocate and justify a point of view.

Explain the actions taken by a character in a novel; work in a group to develop a detailed plan of action; provide arguments in favour of an approach to a problem.

c) use language to convey information and ideas effectively in a straightforward situation.

Provide an eyewitness account of an event or incident; explain how a personal possession was lost, describing the item in question.

d) contribute to the planning of, and participate in, a group presentation.

Compile a news report or a news programme for younger children; perform a story or poem by means of improvisation, making use of video, or audio recorders where appropriate.

e) recognise variations in vocabulary between different regional or social groups, and relate this knowledge where appropriate to personal experience.

Talk about dialect vocabulary and specialist terms; discuss the vocabulary used by characters in books or on television.

Attainment target 2
Reading

Knowledge, skills and understanding in reading (AT 2)

The development of the ability to read, understand and respond to all types of writing, as well as the development of information-retrieval strategies for the purposes of study.

Statements of attainment   **Example**

Level 1

Pupils should be able to:

a) recognise that print is used to carry meaning, in books and in other forms in the everyday world.

Point to and recognise own name; tell the teacher that a label on a container says what is inside or that the words in a book tell a story.

b) begin to recognise individual words or letters in familiar contexts.

In role-play, read simple signs such as shop names or brand names; recognise 'bus-stop', 'exit', 'danger'.

c) show signs of a developing interest in reading.

Pick up books and look at the pictures; choose books to hear or read.

d) talk in simple terms about the content of stories, or information in non-fiction books.

Talk about characters and pictures, including likes and dislikes.

Level 2

a) read accurately and understand straightforward signs, labels and notices.

Read labels on drawers in the classroom; read simple menus.

b) demonstrate knowledge of the alphabet in using word books and simple dictionaries.

Turn towards the end to find words beginning with 's', rather than always starting from the beginning.

c) use picture and context cues, words recognised on sight and phonic cues in reading.

Use a picture to help make sense of a text; recognise that 'Once' is often followed by 'upon a time'; use initial letters to help with recognising words.

d) describe what has happened in a story and predict what may happen next.

Talk about how and why Jack climbs the beanstalk and suggest what may be at the top.

e) listen and respond to stories, poems and other material read aloud, expressing opinions informed by what has been read.

Talk about characters, their actions and appearance; discuss the behaviour of different animals described in a radio programme.

f) read a range of material with some independence, fluency, accuracy and understanding.

Read something unprompted; talk with some confidence about what has been read; produce craftwork related to reading work.

Level 3

a) read aloud from familiar stories and poems fluently

Raise or lower voice to indicate different characters.

356 *Improving Children's Reading in the Junior School*

and with appropriate
expression.

b) read silently and with
sustained concentration.

c) listen attentively to stories,
talk about setting, story-line
and characters and recall
significant details.

*Talk about a story, saying what
happened to change the fortunes of
the leading characters.*

d) demonstrate, in talking
about stories and poems,
that they are beginning to
use inference, deduction
and previous reading
experience to find and
appreciate meanings beyond
the literal.

*Discuss what might happen to
characters in a story, based on the
outcome of adventures in other
stories.*

e) bring to their writing and
discussion about stories
some understanding of the
way stories are structured.

*Refer to different parts of the story
such as 'at the beginning' or 'the
story ends with'; notice that some
stories build up in a predictable
way, e.g. 'The Three Little Pigs',
'Goldilocks and the Three Bears'.*

f) devise a clear set of
questions that will enable
them to select and use
appropriate information
sources and reference books
from the class and school
library.

*Decide that the wildlife project
needs information about the size
and colour of birds, their food and
habitat, and look it up.*

Level 4

a) read aloud expressively,
fluently and with increased
confidence from a range of
familiar literature.

*Vary the pace and tone of the voice
to express feelings, or to represent
character or mood.*

b) demonstrate, in talking
about a range of stories and
poems which they have
read, an ability to explore
preferences.

*Describe those qualities of the poem
or story which appeal and give an
indication of personal response.*

c) demonstrate, in talking

Recognise and use those clues in a

about stories, poems, non-fiction and other texts, that they are developing their abilities to use inference, deduction and previous reading experience.

text which help the reader predict events.

d) find books or magazines in the class or school library by using the classification system, catalogue or database and use appropriate methods of finding information, when pursuing a line of inquiry.

Use search reading to contribute to an inquiry into health and safety at school or in the home.

Level 5

a) demonstrate, in talking and writing about a range of stories and poems which they have read, an ability to explain preferences.

Make simple comparisons between stories or poems; offer justification for personal preference.

b) demonstrate, in talking or writing about fiction, poetry, non-fiction and other texts that they are developing their own views and can support them by reference to some details in the text.

Discuss character, action, fact and opinion, relating them to personal experience.

c) show in discussion that they can recognise whether subject matter in non-literary and media texts is presented as fact or opinion.

Look for indications which suggest the difference: whether evidence is offered or whether persuasion is used in the absence of facts.

d) select reference books and other information materials and use organisational devices to find answers to their own questions and those of others.

Decide what information is required for a project on a topic of their own choice and locate it by reference to chapter titles, subheadings, typefaces, symbol keys, etc.

e) show through discussion an awareness of a writer's

Recognise puns, word play, unconventional spellings and the choice of particular words and phrases and the effect on the reader.

placing together of pictures and text.

Attainment target 3
Writing

Knowledge, skills and understanding in writing (ATs 3–5)

A growing ability to construct and convey meaning in written language matching style to audience and purpose.

Statements of attainment   **Example**

Level 1

Pupils should be able to:

a) use pictures, symbols or isolated letters, words or phrases to communicate meaning.

Show work to others, saying what writing and drawings mean.

Level 2

a) produce, independently, pieces of writing using complete sentences, some of them demarcated with capital letters and full stops or question marks.

b) structure sequences of real or imagined events coherently in chronological accounts.

An account of a family occasion, a practical task in mathematics or an adventure story.

c) write stories showing an understanding of the rudiments of story structure by establishing an opening, characters, and one or more events.

A story with an opening which suggests when or where the action takes place and which involves more than one character.

d) produce simple, coherent non-chronological writing.

Lists, captions, invitations, greetings cards, notices, posters etc.

Level 3

a) produce, independently, pieces of writing using complete sentences, mainly demarcated with capital letters and full stops or question marks.

b) shape chronological writing, beginning to use a wider range of sentence connectives than 'and' and 'then'.

but   when   after   so   because

c) write more complex stories with detail beyond simple events and with a defined ending.

Stories which include a description of setting and the feelings of characters.

d) produce a range of types of non-chronological writing.

Plans and diagrams, descriptions of a person or place, or notes for an activity in science or design.

e) begin to revise and redraft in discussion with the teacher, other adults, or other children in the class, paying attention to meaning and clarity as well as checking for matters such as correct and consistent use of tenses and pronouns.

Level 4

a) produce, independently, pieces of writing showing evidence of a developing ability to structure what is written in ways that make the meaning clear to the reader; demonstrate in their writing generally accurate use of sentence punctuation.

Make use of titles, paragraphs or verses, capital letters, full stops, question marks and exclamation marks; set out and punctuate direct speech.

b) write stories which have an opening, a setting,

Write, in addition to stories, instructions, accounts or

characters, a series of events and a resolution and which engage the interest of the reader; produce other kinds of chronologically organised writing.

explanations, perhaps of a scientific investigation.

c) organise non-chronological writing for different purposes in orderly ways.

Record in writing an aspect of learning; present information and express feelings in forms such as letters, poems, invitations, posters, etc.

d) begin to use the structures of written Standard English and begin to use some sentence structures different from those of speech.

Begin to use subordinate clauses and expanded noun phrases.

e) discuss the organisation of their own writing; revise and redraft the writing as appropriate, independently, in the light of that discussion.

Talk about content and those features which ensure clarity for the reader.

Level 5

a) write in a variety of forms for a range of purposes and audiences, in ways which attempt to engage the interest of the reader.

Write notes, letters, instructions, stories and poems in order to plan, inform, explain, entertain and express attitudes or emotions.

b) produce, independently, pieces of writing in which the meaning is made clear to the reader and in which organisational devices and sentence punctuation, including commas and the setting out of direct speech, are generally accurately used.

Make use of layout, headings, paragraphs and verse structure; make use of the comma.

c) demonstrate increased effectiveness in the use of Standard English (except in

Understand that non-standard forms for literary purposes might be required in dialogue, in a story

contexts where non-standard forms are needed for literary purposes) and show an increased differentiation between speech and writing.

or playscript; use constructions which reduce repetition.

d) assemble ideas on paper or on a VDU, individually or in discussion with others, and show evidence of an ability to produce a draft from them and then to revise and redraft as necessary.

Draft a story, a script, a poem, a description or a report.

e) show in discussion the ability to recognise variations in vocabulary according to purpose, topic and audience and whether language is spoken or written, and use them appropriately in their writing.

Discuss the use of slang in dialogue and narrative in a published text and in their own writing and comment on its appropriateness.

Attainment target 4
Spelling

Knowledge, skills and understanding in writing (ATs 3–5)

Statements of attainment   **Example**

Level 1

Pupils should be able to:

a) begin to show an understanding of the difference between drawing and writing, and between numbers and letters.

b) write some letter shapes in response to speech sounds and letter names.

Initial letter of own name.

c) use at least single letters or groups of letters to represent whole words or parts of words.

Level 2

a) produce recognisable (though not necessarily always correct) spelling of a range of common words.

b) spell correctly, in the course of their own writing, simple monosyllabic words they use regularly which observe common patterns.

see car man sun hot
cold thank

c) recognise that spelling has patterns, and begin to apply their knowledge of those patterns in their attempts to spell a wider range of words.

coat goat feet street

d) show knowledge of the names and order of the letters of the alphabet.

Name the letters when spelling out loud from a simple dictionary or word book.

Level 3

a) spell correctly, in the course of their own writing, simple polysyllabic words they use regularly which observe common patterns.

because after open teacher
animal together

b) recognise and use correctly regular patterns for vowel sounds and common letter strings.

-ing -ion -ous

c) show a growing awareness of word families and their relationships.

grow growth growing
grown grew

d) in revising and redrafting their writing, begin to check the accuracy of their spelling.

Use a simple dictionary, word book, spell checker, or other classroom resources; make spelling books or picture books.

Level 4

a) spell correctly, in the course of their own writing, words which display other main patterns in English spelling.	*Words using the main prefixes and suffixes.*

Note: At each level of attainment the use of technological aids by pupils who depend on them physically to produce their written work is acceptable.

Attainment target 5
Handwriting

Knowledge, skills and understanding in writing (ATs 3–5)

Statements of attainment	**Example**

Level 1

Pupils should be able to:

a) begin to form letters with some control over the size, shape and orientation of letters or lines of writing.

Level 2

a) produce legible upper and lower case letters in one style and use them consistently (i.e. not randomly mixed within words).	*Produce capital letters and lower case letters which are easily distinguishable.*
b) produce letters that are recognisably formed and properly oriented and that have clear ascenders and descenders where necessary.	*b and d,* *p and b*

Level 3

a) begin to produce clear and legible joined-up writing.

Level 4

a) produce more fluent joined-
up writing in independent
work.

Note: Pupils may be exempted from this target if they need to use
a non-sighted form of writing such as braille or if they have such
a degree of physical disability that the attainment target is
unattainable.

Attainment target 4/5
Presentation
Knowledge, skills and understanding in writing (ATs 3–5)

Statements of attainment	**Example**
Level 5	
Pupils should be able to:	
a) spell correctly, in the course of their own writing, words of greater complexity.	*Words with inflectional suffixes, such as -ed and -ing, where consonant doubling ('running') or -e deletion ('coming') are required.*
b) check final drafts of writing for misspelling and other errors of presentation.	*Use a dictionary or computer spelling checker when appropriate.*
c) produce clear and legible handwriting in printed and cursive styles.	

Appendix 3
What LEAs need to tell parents of children with special educational needs

(Annex 4, DES, 1989e; reproduced by permission)

1 About the 1981 Act procedures, and
2 About the 1988 Education Reform Act and its implications for their children
3 About complaints under the 1944 Act.

1. 1981 ACT

a. *Definitions and Duties*

Definitions of special educational needs, learning difficulties, special educational provision.

Procedures for children with SEN.

Duties of LEA to make and review provision for pupils with SEN.

Duties of LEA to provide for children under age 2 and under 5.

Duties of LEA to make integrated placements, subject to the caveats in Section 2(3).
[Integration in a mainstream school must be compatible with three conditions:
(a) the necessary special educational provision;
(b) efficient education of all pupils; and
(c) efficient use of resources.]

Duties of LEA to make full-time provision up to 19 for all students, whether in school or college.

Duties of LEA under the 1981 Act for young people at school to age 19.

Rights of parents to contribute to assessments and inform discussions.

Rights of parents to have confidentiality.

b. *Assessment*

Rights of parent to request assessment. Need to prepare parents and to explain proposals to assess. The named officer contact.

Parent's right to a minimum period of 29 days within which to comment on the LEA's proposal to assess the child. Translations of procedures and meetings into other languages.

Duty of parent to submit child for assessment, and parent's right to attend such examinations.

c. *Statements*

Parent's right to see all the advice on the assessment of the child following a draft statement.

Significance of proposed (or draft) statement and final statements.

Parent's right to a maximum of 15 days within which to make representations to the LEA on the draft statement.

Content of the statement.

Parent's right to receive a copy of the statement.

Consultation procedures.

Identification of any named persons or key workers.

Annual reviews.

13+ reassessments and their significance for the Disabled Persons (Services, Consultation and Representation) Act 1986.

Parent's right to make representations where the LEA propose to amend or cease to maintain a statement.

Procedures for a child with a statement moving into a new LEA area.

d. *Appeals Procedure*

Explain appeals procedure.

Right of parent to appeal where no statement is made.

Right of parent to appeal against the special educational provision in the statement.

Details of appeals committees.

Details of appeals committees' responsibilities.

Rights of parent to appeal to the Secretary of State.

2. 1988 ACT

National Curriculum

Explanation of: Subjects comprising the national curriculum

Attainment Targets
Programmes of Study
Testing and Assessment

Modifications and/or disapplications to the National Curriculum recorded in the statement and alternative provision being made.

Bibliography

Abrams, J. (1981) 'Dyslexia'. In Harris and Hodges, op. cit.

Adams, F. (ed.) (1987) *Special Education*. London: Councils and Education Press and the Society of Education Officers.

Ainscow, M. and Tweddle, D. (1979) *Preventing Classroom Failure: An Objectives Approach*. Chichester: Wiley.

Ainscow, M. and Tweddle, D. (1984) *Early Learning Skills Analysis*. Chichester: Wiley.

Akerman, T., Gunelt, D., Kenwood, P., Leadbetter, P., Mason, L., Matthews, C. and Winteringham, D. (1983) *DATAPAC: An Interim Report*. Birmingham: Department of Educational Psychology, University of Birmingham.

Anderson, R. C., Heibert, E. H., Scott, J. A. and Wilkinson, I. A. G. (1985) *Becoming a Nation of Readers: The Report of the Commission on Reading*. Washington, DC: United States Government Printing Office.

Arnold, H. (1982) *Listening to Children Reading*. Sevenoaks: Hodder & Stoughton in association with the United Kingdom Reading Association.

Arnold, H. (1984) *Making Sense of It*. London: Hodder & Stoughton.

Ashton, C. J., Stoney, A. H. and Hannon, P. W. (1986) A reading at home project in a first school. *Support for Learning* **1** (1), 43–50.

Ashton-Warner, S. (1963) *Teacher*. London: Secker & Warburg (Penguin Books edn, 1966).

Ashton-Warner, S. (1974) *'Teacher' in America*. London: Cassell.

Atkinson, E. J., Gains, C. W. and Edwards, R. (1985) *An A–Z List of Reading Books*, 5th edn. Stafford: National Association for Remedial Education Publications.

Aubrey, C., Eaves, J., Hicks, C. and Newton, M. (1982) *Aston Portfolio Assessment Checklist*. Wisbech: Learning Development Aids.

Aukerman, R. C. (1981) *The Basal Reader Approach to Reading*. New York: Wiley.

Aukerman, R. C. (1984) *Approaches to Beginning Reading*. Chichester: Wiley.

Bannatyne, A. V. (1967) 'The colour phonics system'. In Money, J. (ed.) *The Disabled Reader*. Baltimore: Johns Hopkins University Press, pp. 193–214.

Bannatyne, A. V. (1971) *Language, Reading and Learning Disabilities*. Springfield, IL: Charles C. Thomas.

Banton-Smith, N. (1970) *American Reading Instruction*. Newark, DE: International Reading Association.

Barker Lunn, J. C. (1970) *Streaming in the Primary School*. Slough: NFER.

Barking and Dagenham LEA, in association with University College,

London (1982) *Barking Reading Project Test Battery*. Barking: Barking and Dagenham Local Education Authority.

Barrett, T. C. (1972) 'Taxonomy of cognitive and affective dimensions of reading comprehension', cited by Clymer, T. 'What is reading?: some current concepts'. In Melnick, A. and Merritt, J. (eds) *Reading Today and Tomorrow*. London: Hodder & Stoughton.

Barrs, M., Ellis, S., Hester, H. and Thomas, A. (1988) *The Primary Language Record*. London: Inner London Education Authority.

Bayliss, S. (1988) Raglan enjoys calm after the storm. *Times Educational Supplement* (29 January), 8.

Beard, R. (1987) *Developing Reading 3–13*. Sevenoaks: Hodder & Stoughton.

Benderson, A. L. (ed.) (1988) Testing, equality and handicapped people. *Focus* **21**. Princeton, NJ: Educational Testing Service.

Bennett, N. (1976) *Teaching Style and Pupil Progress*. London: Open Books.

Bennett, N. (1987) Co-operative learning: children do it in groups – or do they? *Educational and Child Psychology* **4** (3/4), 7–18.

Bentley, D. (1985) *How and Why of Readability*. Reading: Centre for the Teaching of Reading, University of Reading School of Education (now the Faculty of Education and Community Studies).

Beveridge, M. and Edmundson, S. (1989) Reading strategies in good and poor readers in word and phrase presentations. *Journal of Research in Reading* **12** (1), 1–12.

Binkley, M. R. (1986) *Becoming a Nation of Readers: Implications for Teachers*. Washington, DC: Office of Educational Research and Improvement, US Department of Education Programs for the Improvement of Practice.

Binkley, M. R. (1988) *Becoming a Nation of Readers: What Parents Can Do*. Washington, DC: Office of Educational Research and US Department of Education in co-operation with D. C. Heath & Co.

Blackburn, L. (1988) No break for refreshment. *The Times Educational Supplement*, 3755 (17 June), A13.

Blanchard, J. S., Mason, G. E. and Daniel, D. (1987) *Computer Applications in Reading*, 3rd edn. Newark, DE: International Reading Association.

Bloom, B. S., Engelhart, M. D., Furst, E. J., Hill, W. and Krathwohl, D. R. (eds) (1956) *Taxonomy of Educational Objectives, Handbook 1: Cognitive Domain*. New York: McKay.

Bloom, B. S., Hastings, J. T. and Madaus, G. F. (eds) (1971) *Handbook on Formative and Summative Assessment of Student Learning*. New York: McGraw-Hill.

Bobrow, D. G. and Norman, D. A. (1975) 'Some principles of memory schematic'. In Bobrow, D. G. and Collins, A. M. (eds) *Representation and Understanding: Studies in Cognitive Science*. New York: Academic Press.

Boder, E. and Jarrico, S. (1982) *Boder Test of Reading–Spelling Patterns*. New York: Grune & Stratton.

Book Trust (1989) *The Book Check Action File: How to Assess your School's Book Needs. Guidelines for Governors and Teachers in Primary Schools*. London: Educational Publishers Association for the Book Trust.

Booth, T., Potts, P. and Swann, W. (eds) (1987) *Preventing Difficulties in Learning: Curricula for All*. Oxford: Blackwell.

Bradley, L. (1990) 'Rhyming connections in learning to read and spell'. In Pumfrey and Elliott, op. cit., pp. 83–100.

Brannen, B. (1971) 'The evaluation of an in-service course for teachers in the teaching of reading'. Unpublished Diploma in Educational Guidance dissertation, Department of Education, University of Manchester.

Branston, P. and Provis, M. (1986) *CAPER: Children and Parents Enjoying Reading*. London: Hodder & Stoughton.

Branwhite, T. (1986) *Designing Special Programmes: A Handbook for Teachers of Children with Learning Difficulties*. London: Methuen.

Brennan, W. K. (1985) *Curriculum for Special Needs*. Milton Keynes: Open University Press.

Brennan, W. K. (1987) *Changing Special Education Now*. Milton Keynes: Open University Press.

Brewer, W. F. (1976) 'Is reading a letter-by-letter process?' In Singer and Ruddell, op. cit., pp. 536–42.

Bromley Local Education Authority (1989) *Bromley Screening Pack*. Bromley: Bromley Local Education Authority.

Brophy, J. (1986) 'Principles for conducting first grade reading group instruction'. In Hoffman, op. cit., pp. 53–84.

Bryans, T. et al. (1985) 'The Kings Heath Project'. In Topping and Wolfendale, op. cit.

Bryant, P. (1990) 'Phonological development and reading'. In Pumfrey and Elliott, op. cit., pp. 63–82.

Bryant, P. and Bradley, L. (1985) *Children's Reading Difficulties*. Oxford: Blackwell.

Bushell, R. and Cripps, C. (1988) *Specific Learning Difficulties*. Stafford: National Association for Remedial Education.

Bussis, A. M., Chittenden, E. A., Amarel, M. and Klausner, E. (1985) *Inquiry into Meaning: An Investigation of Learning to Read*. Hillsdale, NJ: Lawrence Erlbaum.

Carbo, M., Dunn, R. and Dunn, K. (1986) *Teaching Children to Read Through Their Individual Learning Styles*. Englewood Cliffs, NJ: Prentice-Hall.

Carnine, D. and Silbert, J. (1978) *Direct Instruction Reading*. Columbus, OH: Merrill.

Cashdan, A., Pumfrey, P. D. and Lunzer, E. A. (1971) Children receiving remedial treatment in reading. *Educational Research* 13 (2), 98–105.

Cashdan, A. and Wright, J. (1990) 'Intervention strategies for backward readers in the primary school classroom'. In Pumfrey and Elliott, op. cit., pp. 144–54.

Castle, M. (1990) 'One in three confirms a decline'. *Times Educational Supplement* (6 July), 6.

Cataldo, S. and Ellis, N. (1990) 'Learning to spell, learning to read'. In Pumfrey and Elliott, op. cit., pp. 101–25.

Central Advisory Council for Education in England (1967) *Children and Their Primary Schools*, 2 vols (Plowden Report). London: HMSO.

Chall, J. (1983) *Stages in Reading Development*. New York: McGraw-Hill.

Chapman, L. J. (1983) *Reading Development and Cohesion*. London: Heinemann Educational.

Chastey, H. (1990) 'Meeting the challenge of specific learning difficulties'. In Pumfrey and Elliott, op. cit., pp. 269–88.

Clark, C. R. and Davies, C. O. (1970) *Peabody Rebus Reading Program*. Circle Pines, MA: American Guidance Service.

Clay, M. M. (1979) *The Early Detection of Reading Difficulties: A Diagnostic Survey with Recovery Procedures*. London: Heinemann (2nd edn 1982).

Coltheart, M. (ed.) (1987) *The Psychology of Reading*. Hove: Erlbaum.

Colven, D. and Lysley, A. (1989) Voices of reason: recent products for use in special needs teaching. *Times Educational Supplement* (19 May), B14.

Committee of Enquiry into the Education of Handicapped Children and Young People (1978) *Special Educational Needs* (Warnock Report), Cmnd 7212. London: HMSO.

Committee of Inquiry into the Education of Children from Ethnic Minority Groups (1985) *Education for All* (Swann Report), Cmnd 9453. London: HMSO.

Cornwall, K. F., Hedderley, R. and Pumfrey, P. D. (1983) Specific learning difficulties: the 'dyslexia' versus 'specific reading difficulties' controversy resolved? *British Psychological Society Division of Educational and Child Psychology Occasional Papers* 7 (3), 1–121 (whole edn published December 1984).

Croll, P. and Moses, D. (1985) *One in Five: The Assessment and Incidence of Special Educational Needs*. London: Routledge & Kegan Paul.

Cronbach, L. J. and Furby, L. (1970) How should we measure change – or should we? *Psychological Bulletin* 74, 68–80.

Cutforth, J. A. and Battersby, S. (1962) *Children and Books*. Oxford: Blackwell.

Davies, F. (1986) *Books in the School Curriculum*. London: Educational Publishers Association and the National Book League.

Davies, J. D. and Davies, P. (eds) (1990) *A Teacher's Guide to the Support Services*. Windsor: NFER-Nelson.

Davis, F. B. (1970) 'The assessment of change'. In Farr, R. (ed.) *Measurement and Evaluation of Reading*. New York: Harcourt, Brace & World.

Department of Education and Science (DES) (1967) *Children and Their Primary Schools* (Plowden Report). London: HMSO.

Department of Education and Science (1972) *Children with Specific Reading Difficulties. Report of the Advisory Committee on Handicapped Children* (Tizard Report). London: HMSO.

Department of Education and Science (1975) *A Language for Life* (Bullock Report). London: HMSO.

Department of Education and Science (1978) *Primary Education in England*. London: HMSO.

Department of Education and Science (1981) *Education Act 1981* (Circular 8/81). London: Department of Education and Science.

Department of Education and Science (1982) A classification of local education authorities by additional educational needs. *Statistical Bulletin*. London: Department of Education and Science.

Department of Education and Science (1983a) *Report by HMI on the Effects of*

LEA Expenditure Policies on the Education Service in England, 1981. London: HMSO.

Department of Education and Science (1983b) *Assessments and Statements of Special Educational Needs: Procedures within the Education, Health and Social Services* (Circular 1/83). London: Department of Education and Science.

Department of Education and Science (1987) *The National Curriculum 5–16: A Consultation Document.* London: Department of Education and Science.

Department of Education and Science (1988a) *Report of the Committee of Inquiry into the Teaching of English Language* (Kingman Report). London: HMSO.

Department of Education and Science (1988b) *Local Management of Schools* (Circular 7/88). London: Department of Education and Science.

Department of Education and Science (1988c) *Education Reform Act 1988.* London: HMSO.

Department of Education and Science (1989a) *The Education Reform Act 1988: The School Curriculum and Assessment* (Circular 5/89). London: Department of Education and Science.

Department of Education and Science (1989b) *Education Reform Act: Temporary Exceptions to the National Curriculum* (Circular 8/89). London: Department of Education and Science.

Department of Education and Science (1989c) *Education Reform Act: Temporary Exceptions from the National Curriculum* (Circular 15/89). London: Department of Education and Science.

Department of Education and Science (1989d) *National Curriculum: From Policy to Practice.* London: Department of Education and Science.

Department of Education and Science (1989e) *Revision of Circular 1/83 Assessments and Statements of Special Educational Needs: Procedures within the Education, Health and Social Services* (Circular 22/89). London: Department of Education and Science.

Department of Education and Science (1989f) *A Survey of Pupils with Special Educational Needs in Ordinary Schools, 1988–1989.* A Report by HM Inspectorate. London: Department of Education and Science.

Department of Education and Science (1989g) *Reading Policy and Practice at Ages 5–14.* A report by HM Inspectorate. London: Department of Education and Science.

Department of Education and Science (1989h) Survey of information technology in schools. *DES Statistical Bulletin 10/89.* London: Department of Education and Science.

Department of Education and Science (1989i) *Planning for School Development: Advice to Governors, Headteachers and Teachers (School Development Plans Project).* London: Department of Education and Science.

Department of Education and Science (1990a) *Staffing for Pupils with Special Educational Needs (Draft Circular)* (January). London: Department of Education and Science.

Department of Education and Science (1990b) *Provision for Primary Aged Pupils with Statements of Special Educational Needs in Mainstream Schools.* Report of HM Inspectorate. London: Department of Education and Science.

Department of Education and Science (1990c) *A Survey of the Microelectronics Education Support Unit (MESU)*. Report of HM Inspectorate. London: Department of Education and Science.

Department of Education and Science and the Welsh Office (1987) *National Curriculum: Task Group on Assessment and Testing – A Report* (Black Report). London: Department of Education and Science and the Welsh Office.

Department of Education and Science and the Welsh Office (1988a) *English for Ages 5 to 11. Proposals of the Secretary of State for Education and Science and the Secretary of State for Wales* (Cox Report). London: Department of Education and Science and the Welsh Office.

Department of Education and Science and the Welsh Office (1988b) *National Curriculum Task Group on Assessment and Testing: Three Supplementary Reports*. London: Department of Education and Science and the Welsh Office.

Department of Education and Science and the Welsh Office (1988c) *National Curriculum Task Group on Assessment and Testing Report: a Digest for Schools*. London: Department of Education and Science and the Welsh Office.

Department of Education and Science and the Welsh Office (1989a) *Facsimile of the Educational (National Curriculum) (Attainment Targets and Programmes of Study in English) Order laid before Parliament in May, 1989*. London: Department of Education and Science and the Welsh Office.

Department of Education and Science and the Welsh Office (1989b) *English in the National Curriculum*. London: HMSO.

Department of Education and Science Assessment of Performance Unit (1981) *Language Performance in Schools: Primary Survey Report No. 1*. London: HMSO.

Department of Education and Science Assessment of Performance Unit (1982) *Language Performance in Schools: Primary Survey Report No. 2*. London: HMSO.

Dessent, T. (1987) *Making the Ordinary Schools Special*. Basingstoke: Falmer Press.

Downing, J., Ayers, D. and Schaefer, B. (1983) *Linguistic Awareness in Reading Readiness*. Windsor: NFER-Nelson.

Drever, J. (1964) *A Dictionary of Psychology*. Harmondsworth: Penguin Books.

Drew, D. (1990) From tutorial unit to schools' support service. *Support for Learning* 5 (1), 13–21.

Drillien, C. and Drummond, M. (1983) *Developmental Screening and the Child with Special Educational Needs: A Population Study of 5,000 Children*. London: Heinemann.

Education Department of Western Australia (1985) *Time Allocation in the Primary School*. Perth: W. C. Brown.

Education, Science and Arts Committee (1986) *Achievement in Primary Schools*, Vol. 1. Westminster: House of Commons Report.

Education, Science and Arts Committee (1987) *First Special Report. Special Educational Needs: Implementation of the Education Act 1981. Observations by the Government on the Third Report of the Committee in Session 1986–1987.* London: HMSO.

Edwards, R. P. A. and Gibbon, V. (1964) *Words Your Children Use.* London: Burke.

Ehri, L. C. (1985) 'Sources of difficulty in learning to spell and read'. In Wolraich, M. L. and Routh, D. (eds) *Advances in Developmental and Behavioral Paediatrics.* Greenwich, CT: Jai Press.

Ehri, L. C. and Wilce, L. S. (1983) Development of word identification speed in skilled and less skilled beginning readers. *Journal of Educational Psychology* **75** (1), 3–18.

Eldredge, J. L. and Butterfield, D. (1986) Alternatives to traditional reading instruction. *The Reading Teacher* **40**, 32–7.

Elley, W. B. and Reid, N. A. (1974) '2,000 nouns graded by frequency of usage'. In *Progressive Achievement Tests: UK Supplement to the Teacher's Manual*, appendix 2. London: Hodder & Stoughton.

Engelmann, S. and Bruner, E. C. (1983) *Reading Mastery: Distar Reading I, Presentation Book A.* Chicago: Science Research Associates.

Essen, J. and Wedge, P. (1982) *Continuities in Childhood Disadvantage.* London: Heinemann.

Ewing, J. (ed.) (1985) *Reading and the New Technologies.* London: Heinemann in association with the United Kingdom Reading Association.

Farr, R. and Carey, R. F. (eds) (1986) *Reading: What Can Be Measured?*, 2nd edn. Newark, DE: International Reading Association.

Fawcett, R. (1979) 'Reading laboratories'. In Lunzer and Gardner, op. cit.

Fernald, G. (1943) *Remedial Techniques in Basic School Subjects.* New York: McGraw-Hill.

Fernald, G. and Keller, H. (1921) Effects of kinaesthetic factors in the development of word-recognition. *Journal of Educational Research* **4**, 355.

Foorman, B. R. and Siegel, A. W. (eds) (1986) *Acquisition of Reading Skills: Cultural Constraints and Cognitive Universals.* Hillsdale, NJ: Lawrence Erlbaum.

France, N. and Fraser, I. (1975) *The Richmond Tests of Basic Skills.* London: Nelson.

Francis, H. (1982) *Learning to Read: Literate Behaviour and Orthographic Knowledge.* London: Allen & Unwin.

Fries, C. C. (1962) *Linguistics and Reading.* New York: Holt, Rinehart & Winston.

Frith, U. (1985) 'Beneath the surface of developmental dyslexia'. In Patterson, K. E., Marshall, J. C. and Coltheart, M. (eds) *Surface Dyslexia.* London: Routledge & Kegan Paul.

Fry, E. (1972) *Reading Instruction in Classroom and Clinic.* New York: McGraw-Hill.

Galloway, D. (1985) *Schools, Pupils and Special Educational Needs.* London: Croom Helm.

Galton, M. and Simon, B. (eds) (1980) *Progress and Performance in the Primary Classroom.* London: Routledge & Kegan Paul.

Galton, M., Simon, B. and Croll, P. (1980) *Inside the Primary Classroom*. London: Routledge & Kegan Paul.

Garner, R. (1988) *Metacognition and Reading Comprehension*. Norwood, NJ: Ablex.

Gaskins, I. (ed.) (1988) Teaching poor readers: what works. *The Reading Teacher* (April) (special edn).

Gentile, L. M. and McMillan, M. M. (1987) *Stress and Reading Difficulties: Research, Assessment, Intervention*. Newark, DE: International Reading Association.

Gibson, E. J. and Levin, H. (1975) *The Psychology of Reading*. Cambridge, MA: MIT Press.

Gillham, W. E. C. G. (1986) Paired reading in perspective. *Child Education* **63** (6), 8–9.

Gillingham, A. and Stillman, B. U. (1956) *Remedial Training for Children with Specific Disability in Reading, Spelling and Penmanship*. Cambridge, MA: Educators Publishing Service (5th edn 1969).

Gipps, C. and Gross, H. (1986) 'Children with special needs in the primary school: where are we now?' Paper presented at the 1986 annual conference of the British Educational Research Association.

Gipps, C. and Gross, H. (1987) Children with special needs in the primary school: where are we now? *Support for Learning* **2** (3), 43–7.

Gipps, C., Gross, H. and Goldstein, H. (1987) *Warnock's Eighteen Percent: Children with Special Needs in Primary School*. Basingstoke: Falmer Press.

Gipps, C., Steadman, S., Blackstone, T. and Stierer, B. (1983) *Testing Children: Standardised Testing in LEAs and Schools*. London: Heinemann.

Gjessing, H. J. and Karlsen, B. (1989) *A Longitudinal Study of Dyslexia*. New York: Springer-Verlag.

Glaser, S. M., Searfoss, L. W. and Gentile, L. M. (eds) (1988) *Re-examining Reading Diagnosis: New Trends and Procedures*. Newark, DE: International Reading Association.

Glynn, T., McNaughton, S., Robinson, V., Quinn, M., Wheldall, K., Merrett, F. and Colmar, S. (1987) *Pause, Prompt and Praise Training Pack*. Cheltenham: Positive Products.

Goacher, B., Evans, J., Welton, J. and Wedell, K. (1988) *Policy and Provision for Special Educational Needs: Implementing the 1981 Education Act*. London: Cassell.

Goodman, K. S. (1976a) 'Miscue analysis: theory and reality in reading'. In Merritt, J. G. (ed.) *New Horizons in Reading*, pp. 15–26. Newark, DE: International Reading Association.

Goodman, K. S. (1976b) 'Reading: a psycholinguistic guessing game'. In Singer and Ruddell, op. cit. (first published in *Journal of the Reading Specialist*, May 1967).

Goodman, Y., Watson, D. J. and Burke, C. L. (1987) *Reading Miscue Inventory: Alternative Procedures*. London: Heinemann Educational.

Gorman, T. (1987) *Pupils' Attitudes to Reading at Age 11 and 15*. Windsor: NFER-Nelson.

Gorman, T. and Kispal, A. (1987) *The Assessment of Reading: Pupils aged 11 and 15*. Windsor: NFER-Nelson.

Gorman, T. P., White, J., Brooks, G., Maclure, M. and Kispal, A. (1988)

Language Performance in Schools: Review of the Assessment of Performance Unit Language Monitoring 1979–1983. London: HMSO.

Gorman, T. P., White, J., Hargreaves, M., Maclure, M. and Tate, A. (1984) *Language Performance in Schools: 1982 Primary Survey Report*. London: Assessment of Performance Unit of the Department of Education and Science.

Goswami, U. (1988) Orthographic analogies and reading development. *Quarterly Journal of Experimental Psychology* **40A**, 239–68.

Gough, P. D. (1976) 'One second of reading'. In Singer and Ruddell, op. cit.

Greening, M. and Spencely, J. (1984) Shared reading: a review of the Cleveland project. *Bulletin of the Cleveland County Psychological Service* **11** (2), 10–14.

Gross, H. and Gipps, C. (1987a) Withdrawal symptoms. *Times Educational Supplement* (3 April), 25.

Gross, H. and Gipps, C. (1987b) *Supporting Warnock's Eighteen Percent: Six Case Studies*. Lewes: Falmer Press.

Haas, W. (1970) *Phonographic Translation*. Manchester: Manchester University Press.

Halliday, M. A. K. and Hasan, R. (1976) *Cohesion in English*. London: Longman.

Hammill, D. D. (ed.) (1987) *Assessing the Abilities and Instructional Needs of Students*. Austin, TX: Pro-Ed.

Hammill, D. D., Brown, L. and Bryant, B. (1989) *Consumer's Guide to Tests in Print*. Austin, TX: Pro-Ed.

Hammill, D. D. and McNutt, G. (1981) *The Correlates of Reading: Thirty Years of Correlational Research*. Austin, TX: Pro-Ed.

Hanko, G. (1985) *Special Needs in Ordinary Classrooms*. Oxford: Blackwell.

Hannon, P., Jackson, A. and Weinberger, J. (1986). Parents' and teachers' strategies in hearing young children read. *Research Papers in Education* **1** (1), 6–25.

Harris, T. L. and Hodges, R. E. (1981) *A Dictionary of Reading and Related Terms*. Newark, DE: International Reading Association.

Harrison, C. (1980) *Readability in the Classroom*. Cambridge: Cambridge University Press.

Hart, N. W. M., Walker, R. F. and Gray, B. (1977) *The Language of Children: A Key to Literacy*. Brisbane: Addison-Wesley.

Hegarty, S. (1987) *Meeting Special Needs in Ordinary Schools: An Overview*. London: Cassell.

Henderson, L. (1987) 'Word recognition: a tutorial review'. In Coltheart, op. cit., pp. 171–200.

Hickey, K. (1977) *Dyslexia: A Language Training Course for Teachers and Learners*. Bath: Better Books.

Hicks, C. (1986) Remediating specific reading disabilities: a review of approaches. *Educational Review* **9** (1), 39–55.

Hinson, M. (ed.) (1987a) *Teachers and Special Educational Needs*. London: Longman in association with the National Association for Remedial Education.

Hinson, M. (1987b) 'Assessment and intervention: a key role for S.E.N. support teachers'. In Hinson (1987a) op. cit.

Hoffman, J. V. (ed.) (1986) *Effective Teaching of Reading: Research and Practice*. Newark, DE: International Reading Association.

Hofkins, D. (1990a) Prototype assessment tasks outlined for 641 schools. *Times Educational Supplement* (6 April), 6.

Hofkins, D. (1990b) SAT machinery stripped down. *Times Educational Supplement* 3878 (26 October).

Holly, P. (1987) *The Dilemmas of Low Attainment*. London: Further Education Unit.

Hornsby, B. and Farrer, M. (1990) 'Some effects of a dyslexia-centred teaching programme'. In Pumfrey and Elliott, op. cit., pp. 173–86.

Hornsby, B. and Miles, T. R. (1980) The effects of a dyslexia-centred teaching programme. *British Journal of Educational Psychology* 50 (30), 236–42.

Hornsby, B. and Shear, F. (1975) *Alpha to Omega: The A–Z of Teaching Reading, Writing and Spelling*. London: Heinemann.

House of Commons (1987) *Education Reform: A Bill to Amend the Law Relating to Education*. London: HMSO.

Huey, E. B. (1908) *The Psychology and Pedagogy of Reading*. New York: Macmillan (repr. MIT Press, 1968).

Hunter-Carsch, M., Beverton, S. and Dennis, D. (eds) (1990) *Primary English in the National Curriculum*. Oxford: Blackwell Education.

Hutchinson, P. (1990) *Teacher's File*. Walton-on-Thames: Nelson.

Hynds, J. (1987) Diagnosing dyslexia. *Gnosis* 10 (March), 19–23.

Ingham, J. (1982) *Books and Reading*, 2nd edn. London: Heinemann Educational.

Ingham, J. (1986) *The State of Reading*. London: Educational Publishers Council.

Inner London Education Authority (ILEA) (1982) *Classroom Observation Procedure*. London: ILEA.

Inner London Education Authority (1985) *Educational Opportunities for All? Research Studies*. London: ILEA Research and Statistics Branch.

Inner London Education Authority (1986a) *The Junior School Project: A Summary of the Main Report*. London: ILEA Research and Statistics Branch.

Inner London Education Authority (1986b) *The Junior School Project. Part A: Pupils' Progress and Development*. London: ILEA Research and Statistics Branch.

Inner London Education Authority (1986c) *The Junior School Project. Part B: Differences between Junior Schools*. London: ILEA Research and Statistics Branch.

Inner London Education Authority (1986d) *The Junior School Project. Part C: Understanding School Effectiveness*. London: ILEA Research and Statistics Branch.

Inner London Education Authority (1986e) *The Junior School Project. Technical Appendices*. London: ILEA Research and Statistics Branch.

James, W. (1899) *Talks to Teachers*. London: Longman, Green.

Jeffree, D. M. and McConkey, R. (1976) *Let Me Speak*. London: Souvenir Press (Academic and Educational).

Jeffree, D. M., McConkey, R. and Hewson, S. (1977) *Let Me Play*. London: Souvenir Press (Academic and Educational).

Jeffree, D. M. and Skeffington, M. (1980) *Let Me Read*. London: Souvenir Press (Academic and Educational).

Johnson, M. S., Kress, R. A. and Pikulski, J. J. (1987) *Informal Reading Inventories*. Newark, DE: International Reading Association.

Johnston, P. H. (1983) *Reading Comprehension: A Cognitive Basis*. Newark, DE: International Reading Association.

Jorm, A. F. (1983) *The Psychology of Reading and Spelling Difficulties*. London: Routledge.

Kamil, M. L. (1978) 'Models of reading: what are the implications for instruction in comprehension?' In Pflaum-Connor, S. (ed.) *Aspects of Reading Education*. Berkeley, CA: McCutchan Publishing.

Kanji, G. (1990) Growing concerns. *Times Educational Supplement* (2 March), 44.

Kavale, K. A. and Forness, S. R. (1985) *The Science of Learning Disabilities*. Windsor: NFER-Nelson.

Kay-Shuttleworth, J. (1873) 'Memorandum on the influence of the "Revised Code" on popular education' (written in 1868). In *Thoughts and Suggestions on Certain Social Problems*. London: Longman, Green (repr. 1973, Scholar Press, Menston).

Kelly, T. A. (1981) *Evaluation of Reading Books: A Teacher's Guide*. Sandwell: Child Psychology Service.

Kennedy, A. (1984) *The Psychology of Reading*. London: Routledge.

Krathwohl, D. R., Bloom, B. S. and Masia, R. B. (1964) *Taxonomy of Educational Objectives, Handbook 2: Affective Domain*. New York: McKay.

Laberge, D. and Samuels, S. J. (1974) Towards a theory of automatic information processing in reading. *Cognitive Psychology* 6, 293–323.

Lane, C. (1990) 'ARROW: alleviating children's reading and spelling difficulties'. In Pumfrey and Elliott, op. cit.

Laskier, M. (1986) 'Word-recognition attainments in infant school pupils: identification and modification'. Unpublished MEd thesis, Department of Education, University of Manchester.

Lee, D. M. and Allen, R. V. (1963) *Learning to Read through Experience*. New York: Appleton-Century-Crofts.

Levy, P. and Goldstein, H. (eds) (1984) *Tests in Education*. London: Academic Press.

Lindsay, G. (ed.) (1984) *Screening for Children with Special Needs*. London: Croom Helm.

Lindsay, G., Evans, A. and Jones, B. (1985) Paired reading and relaxed reading: a comparison. *British Journal of Educational Psychology* 55 (3), 304–9.

Littler, M. (1990) *Northwest SEMERC Software Survey*. Oldham: Northwest SEMERC.

Lunzer, E. A. and Gardner, K. (eds) (1979) *The Effective Use of Reading*. London: Heinemann Educational Books for the Schools Council.
Lunzer, E. A. and Gardner, K. (1984) *Learning from the Written Word*. Edinburgh: Oliver & Boyd.

Mabey, C. (1981) Black British literacy: a study of reading attainment of London black children from 8–15 years. *Educational Research* **23** (2), 83–95.
Maccoby, E. E. and Jacklin, C. (1980) 'Psychological sex differences'. In Rutter, M. (ed.) *Scientific Foundations of Developmental Psychiatry*. London: Heinemann.
Mackay, D., Thompson, B. and Schaub, P. (1979) *Breakthrough to Literacy: Teacher's Manual*, 2nd edn. London: Longmans for the Schools Council.
Mackintosh, N., Mascie-Taylor, C. N. and West, A. M. (1988) 'West Indian and Asian children's educational attainments'. In Verma and Pumfrey, op. cit.
McNally, J. and Murray, W. (1962) *Key Words to Literacy*. London: Schoolmaster Publishing.
McNally, J. and Murray, W. (1984) *Key Words to Literacy and the Teaching of Reading*. Kettering: Teacher Publishing.
McNaughton, S., Glynn, T. and Robinson, V. M. (1981) *Parents as Remedial Reading Teachers*. Wellington: New Zealand Council for Educational Research.
Marsh, G., Friedman, M., Welch, V. and Desberg, P. (1980) 'The development of strategies in spelling'. In Frith, U. (ed.) *Cognitive Processes in Spelling*. London: Academic Press.
Marzano, R. J. and Marzano, J. S. (1988) *A Cluster Approach to Elementary Vocabulary Instruction*. Newark, DE: International Reading Association.
Mathews, M. M. (1966) *Teaching to Read: Historically Considered*. Chicago: University of Chicago Press.
May, F. B. (1986) *Reading as Communication: An Interactive Approach*. Columbus, OH: Merrill.
Melck, E. (1986) *Finding out about Specific Learning Difficulties/Dyslexia*. Rugby: Melck.
Miles, T. R. (1970) *On Helping the Dyslexic Child*. London: Methuen.
Miles, T. R. (1983) *Dyslexia: The Pattern of Difficulties*. London: Collins Educational.
Miles, T. R. and Miles, E. (1975) *More Help for the Dyslexic Child*. London: Methuen.
Miles, T. R. and Miles, E. (1983) *Help for Dyslexic Children*. London: Methuen.
Montgomery, D. (1990) *Children with Learning Difficulties*. London: Cassell.
Moon, C. (1986) 'Spot and Pat: living in the best company when you read'. In Root (1986a) op. cit.
Moon, C. and Raban, B. (1975) *A Question of Reading*. London: Ward Lock Educational (2nd edn, Macmillan, 1980).
Moon, C. and Ruel, N. (1990) *Individualised Reading*. Reading: Reading and Language Information Centre, University of Reading.

Morgan, R. (1986) *Helping Children Read: The Paired Reading Handbook.* London: Methuen.

Morris, J. (1986) 'Appraising phonic resources'. In Root (1986a) op. cit.

Morris, J. M. (1984) Phonics 44 for initial literacy in English. *Reading* **18** (1), 13–23.

Morris, R. (1973) *Success and Failure in Learning to Read*, revised edn. Harmondsworth: Penguin Books.

Mortimore, P., Sammons, P., Stoll, L., Lewis, D. and Ecob, R. (1988) *School Matters – The Junior Years.* Exeter: Open Books.

Morton, J. (1969) The interaction of information in word-recognition. *Psychological Review* **76**, 165–78.

Moseley, D. (1990a) 'Suggestions for helping children with spelling problems'. In Pumfrey and Elliott, op. cit., pp. 255–68.

Moseley, D. (1990b) 'Lit-oracy: a technological breakthrough'. Duplicated paper, School of Education, University of Newcastle.

Moss, P. (1990) Assessment. *Head Teachers Review* (Summer), 30–1.

Muncey, J. (1986) *Meeting Special Needs in Mainstream Schools.* Coventry: Coventry Education Department.

Naidoo, S. (ed.) (1988) *Assessment and Teaching of Dyslexic Children.* London: Invalid Children's Aid Nationwide.

National Curriculum Council (NCC) (1989a) *English Key Stage 1: Non-statutory Guidance.* York: National Curriculum Council.

National Curriculum Council (1989b) *Curriculum Guidance 1: A Framework for the Primary Curriculum.* York: National Curriculum Council.

National Curriculum Council (1989c) 'Implementing the national curriculum – participation by pupils with special educational needs': Comments on DES Circular No. 5/89. *Circular Number 5.* York: National Curriculum Council.

National Curriculum Council (1989d) *A Curriculum for All: Special Educational Needs in the National Curriculum.* York: National Curriculum Council.

National Curriculum Council (1989e) 'Publications on the national curriculum from the NCC, DES, HMI and SEAC'. *Circular Number 7.* York: National Curriculum Council. (Update issued December 1990.)

National Curriculum Council (1989f) *English 5–11 in the National Curriculum.* York: National Curriculum Council.

National Diffusion Network (1990) *Educational Programmes That Work*, 16th edn. Longmont, CO: Sopris West in co-operation with the National Dissemination Study Group.

National Foundation for Educational Research (1989) *Touchstones.* Slough: NFER-Nelson.

Naylor, J. G. and Pumfrey, P. D. (1983) The alleviation of psycholinguistic deficits and some effects on the reading attainments of poor readers: a sequel. *Journal of Research in Reading* **6** (2), 129–53.

Nelson Ltd (1990) Primary and middle school catalogue. Walton-on-Thames: Nelson.

Neville-Brown, E. (1990) Children with spelling and writing difficulties: an alternative approach'. In Pumfrey and Elliott, op. cit., pp. 289–304.

Newell, P. (1985) *ACE Special Education Handbook: the New Law on Children with Special Needs*, 2nd edn. London: Advisory Centre for Education.

Newell, P. (1988a) Marching backwards. *Times Educational Supplement* 3755 (17 June), A2.

Newell, P. (1988b) *ACE Special Education Handbook: the New Law on Children with Special Needs*, 3rd edn. London: Advisory Centre for Education.

Newton, M. J. and Thomson, M. E. (1982) *Aston Index (Revised)*. Wisbech: Learning Development Aids.

Norrie, E. (1960) *Edith Norrie Letter Case*. English version obtainable from The Helen Arkell Centre, Frensham, Farnham, Surrey GU10 3BW.

Obrist, C. and Stuart, A. (1990) 'The Family Reading Groups Movement'. In Hunter-Carsch et al., op. cit., pp. 197–206.

Office of Educational Research and Improvement (1986) *Becoming a Nation of Readers: Implications for Teachers*. Washington, DC: US Department of Education.

Orton, J. L. (1967) 'The Orton–Gillingham approach'. In Money, J. (ed.) *The Disabled Reader*. Baltimore: Johns Hopkins University Press, pp. 119–45.

Orton, S. T. (1925) Word-blindness in schoolchildren. *Archives of Neurological Psychiatry* 14 (5), 581–615.

Orton, S. T. (1937) *Reading, Writing and Speech Problems in Children*. London: Chapman & Hall.

Paired Learning Project (1989) *Paired Learning: Tutoring by Non-Teachers*. Kirklees: Paired Learning Project.

Patterson, K. and Coltheart, V. (1987) 'Phonological processing in reading: a tutorial review'. In Coltheart, op. cit., pp. 421–48.

Pearson, L. and Lindsay, G. (1986) *Special Needs in the Primary School: Identification and Intervention*. Windsor: NFER-Nelson.

Perera, K. (1984) *Children's Writing and Reading: Analysing Classroom Language*. Oxford: Blackwell.

Platt, G. (1975) 'Some effects of the in-service training of teachers in the teaching of reading'. Unpublished MEd thesis, Department of Education, University of Manchester.

Potton, A. (1983) *Screening*. London: Macmillan Education.

Prentice, J. (1987) Real books and paired reading in context. *Reading* 21 (3), 159–68.

Pryke, D. (1987) *Read to Me with Me. A Guide to Parents Who Are Helping Children to Enjoy Reading at Home*. Telford: Shropshire Language Centre.

Publishers Association (1986) 'Expenditure on books by LEAs in England and Wales, 1984/5', Duplicated summary table. London: Educational Publishers Council.

Pumfrey, P. D. (1971) Effects of a selection procedure on the placement of children in special schools. *Research in Education* 5, 10–24.

Pumfrey, P. D. (1977) *Measuring Reading Abilities: Concepts, Sources and Applications*. London: Hodder & Stoughton.

Pumfrey, P. D. (1978) 'Accountability: theoretical and practical issues related to reading'. In Chapman, L. J. and Czerniewska, P. (eds) *Read-

ing: From Process to Practice. London: Routledge & Kegan Paul in association with the Open University.

Pumfrey, P. D. (ed.) (1980) *O. C. Sampson: Child Guidance. Its History, Provenance and Future.* Leicester: British Psychological Society.

Pumfrey, P. D. (1985) *Reading: Tests and Assessment Techniques,* 2nd edn. Sevenoaks: Hodder & Stoughton in association with the United Kingdom Reading Association.

Pumfrey, P. D. (1986a) 'Measuring attitudes to reading'. In Vincent and Pugh, op. cit.

Pumfrey, P. D. (1986b) Paired reading: promise and pitfalls. *Educational Research* **28** (2), 89–94.

Pumfrey, P. D. (1988a) 'Monitoring the reading attainments of children from minority groups: LEA practices'. In Verma and Pumfrey, op. cit.

Pumfrey, P. D. (1988b) A three-year longitudinal study of children's reading behaviours: what has been learned? *Research in Education* **30** (3), 163–76.

Pumfrey, P. D. (1990a) 'Teaching and testing pupils with reading difficulties'. In Pumfrey and Elliott, op. cit., pp. 187–208.

Pumfrey, P. D. (1990b) 'Literacy and the national curriculum: the challenge of the 1990s'. In Pumfrey and Elliott, op. cit., pp. 3–13.

Pumfrey, P. D. (1990c) 'The reading attainments and examination results of British West Indian pupils: challenges of, and responses to, underachievement'. In Pumfrey, P. D. and Verma, G. K. (eds) *Race Relations and Urban Education: Contexts and Promising Practices.* Basingstoke: Falmer Press.

Pumfrey, P. D. and Elliott, C. D (eds) (1990) *Children's Difficulties in Reading, Spelling and Writing: Challenges and Responses.* Lewes: Falmer Press.

Pumfrey, P. D. and Fletcher, J. (1989) Differences in reading strategies among 7:00 to 8:00 year old children. *Journal of Research in Reading* **12** (2), 114–30.

Pumfrey, P. D. and Laskier, M. (in preparation) *Early Words Test Battery.*

Pumfrey, P. D. and Mittler, P. D. (1989) Peeling off the label. *Times Educational Supplement* (13 October), 29–30.

Pumfrey, P. D. and Reason, R. in association with Allan, B., Bartlett, R., Coleman, J., Dean, M., Forrester, A., Gregory, M., Hedderly, R., Webster, D. and Wilkins, J. (1991) *Specific Learning Difficulties (Dyslexia).* Windsor: NFER-Nelson.

Pumfrey, P. and Ward, J. (in press) Term of birth and special educational placement: the impact of assessment procedures in an LEA. *Research in Education.*

Quin, V. (1988) 'New medical aspects of reading and spelling difficulties'. Paper presented at the University of Manchester Department of Education (November).

Quin, V. and MacAuslan, A. (1986) *Dyslexia: What Parents Ought to Know.* Harmondsworth: Pelican Books.

Reason, R. (1990) 'Reconciling different approaches to intervention'. In Pumfrey and Elliott, op. cit., pp. 40–59.

Reason, R. and Boote, R. (1986) *Learning Difficulties in Reading and Writing: A Teacher's Manual.* Windsor: NFER-Nelson.

Reason, R., Rooney, S. and Roffe, M. (1987) Co-operative learning in the infant school. *Educational and Child Psychology* **4** (3&4), 40–8.

Reason, R., Farrell, P. and Mittler, P. (1989) 'Changes in assessment'. In Entwistle, N. E. (ed.) *Handbook of Educational Ideas and Practices.* London: Croom Helm.

Reid, J. and Donaldson, M. (1980) *Letter Links.* Edinburgh: Holmes McDougall.

Roberts, G. R. (1989) *Teaching Children to Read and Write.* Oxford: Blackwell.

Robertson, A. H., Henderson, A., Robertson, A., Fisher, J. and Gibson, M. (1983) *Quest: Screening, Diagnosis and Remediation Kit.* Leeds: Arnold-Wheaton.

Robinson, F. P. (1961) *Effective Study*, 4th edn. New York: Harper & Row.

Root, B. (ed.) (1986a) *Resources for Reading: Does Quality Count?* London: Macmillan.

Root, B. (1986b) 'In defence of reading schemes'. In Root (1986a), pp. 3–6.

Rozin, P. and Gleitman, L. R. (1977) 'The structure and acquisition of reading II. The reading process and the acquisition of the alphabetic principle'. In Reber, A. S. and Scarborough, D. L. (eds) *Towards a Psychology of Reading.* Hillsdale, NJ: Lawrence Erlbaum.

Rude, R. T. and Oehlkers, W. J. (1984) *Helping Students with Reading Problems.* London: Prentice-Hall International.

Rupley, W. H. (1976) Effective reading programmes. *The Reading Teacher* (March), 616–20.

Rutter, M., Tizard, J. and Whitmore, K. (1970) *Education, Health and Behaviour.* London: Longman.

Rye, J. (1982) *Cloze Procedure and the Teaching of Reading.* London: Heinemann Educational.

Salvia, J. and Ysseldyke, J. E. (1985) *Assessment in Special and Remedial Education.* Boston: Houghton Mifflin.

Sampson, O. C. (1975) *Remedial Education.* London: Routledge & Kegan Paul.

Samuels, S. J. and Laberge, D. (1983) 'Critique of a theory of automatic information processing in reading looking back: a retrospective analysis of the Laberge–Samuels Reading Model'. In Gentle, L. M., Kamil, M. L. and Blanchard, J. S. (eds) *Reading Research Revisited.* Columbus, OH: Charles E. Merrill.

Samuels, S. J. and Pearson, P. D. (eds) (1988) *Changing School Reading Programs: Principles and Case Studies.* Newark, DE: International Reading Association.

Scarr, S., Carparulo, B. K., Ferdman, B. M., Tower, R. B. and Caplan, J. (1983) Developmental status and school achievements of minority and non-minority children from birth to 18 years in a British Midlands town. *British Journal of Developmental Psychology* **1** (1), 31–8.

Schonell, F. J. and Wall, W. D. (1949) Remedial education centre. *Educational Review* **2**, 3–30.

School Examinations and Assessment Council (SEAC) (1989) *A Guide to*

Teacher Assessment. Pack A: Teacher Assessment in the Classroom. Pack B: Teacher Assessment in the School. Pack C: A Source Book of Teacher Assessment. London: Heinemann Educational on behalf of the School Examinations and Assessment Council.

Schwartz, S. (1984) *Measuring Reading Competence: A Theoretical–Prescriptive Approach.* New York: Plenum Press.

Science Research Associates (SRA) (1985) *Direct Instruction: A Review.* Henley-on-Thames: Science Research Associates.

Searls, E. F. (1985) *How to Use the WISC-R Scores in Reading/Learning Disability Diagnosis.* Newark, DE: International Reading Association.

Secretary of State for Education and Science (1988) Text of speech to the Annual Conference of the National Association of Head Teachers, Eastbourne. London: Department of Education and Science.

Seddon-Johnson, M., Kress, R. A., and Pikulski, J. J. (1987) *Informal Reading Inventories*, 2nd edn. Newark, DE: International Reading Association.

Sewell, G. (1986) *Coping with Special Needs: A Guide for New Teachers.* London: Croom Helm.

Seymour, P. H. K. (1986) *Cognitive Analysis of Dyslexia.* London: Routledge & Kegan Paul.

Simm, T. (1986) The long-term results of remedial teaching of reading. *Educational Psychology in Practice* **1** (4), 142–7.

Singer, H. and Ruddell, R. B. (eds) (1976) *Theoretical Models and Processes of Reading*, 2nd edn. Newark, DE: International Reading Association.

Singer, H. and Ruddell, R. B. (eds) (1985) *Theoretical Models and Processes of Reading*, 3rd edn. Newark, DE: International Reading Association.

Slavin, R., Sharan, S., Kagan, S., Hertz-Lazarowitz, R., Webb, C. and Schmuck, R. (eds) (1985) *Learning to Co-operate: Co-operating to Learn.* New York: Plenum Press.

Smith, F. (1973) *Psycholinguistics and Reading.* New York: Holt, Rinehart & Winston.

Smith, F. (1979) 'Conflicting approaches to reading research and instruction'. In Resnik, L. B. and Weaver, P. A. (eds) *Theory and Practice of Early Reading*, Vol. 2. Hillsdale, NJ: Lawrence Erlbaum.

Smith, F. (1982) *Understanding Reading*, 3rd edn. New York: Holt, Rinehart & Winston.

Snowling, M. J. (ed.) (1985) *Children's Written Language Difficulties: Assessment and Management.* Windsor: NFER-Nelson.

Snowling, M. J. (1990) 'Dyslexia in childhood: a cognitive-developmental perspective'. In Pumfrey and Elliott, op. cit., pp. 126–43.

Solity, J. and Bull, S. (1987) *Special Needs: Bridging the Curriculum Gap.* Milton Keynes: Open University Press.

Southgate, V. (1983) *Children Who Do Read.* London and Basingstoke: Macmillan Education.

Southgate, V. (1986) 'Teachers of reading: planning for the most effective use of their time'. In Root (1986a) op. cit., pp. 80–98.

Southgate-Booth, V., Arnold, H. and Johnson, S. (1981) *Extending Beginning Reading.* London: Heinemann Educational for the Schools Council.

Spache, G. D., McIlroy, K. and Berg, P. C. (1981) *Case Studies in Reading Disability*. New York: Allyn & Bacon.

Spache, G. D. and Spache, E. B. (1986) *Reading in the Elementary School*, 5th edn. Boston: Allyn & Bacon.

Statutory Instruments (1989) *Statutory Instrument No. 1181. The Education (National Curriculum) (Temporary Exceptions for Individual Pupils) Regulations 1989*. London: HMSO.

Stauffer, R. G. (1969) *Teaching Reading as a Thinking Process*. New York: Harper & Row.

Stierer, B. (1985) School reading volunteers: results of a postal survey of primary school headteachers in England. *Journal of Research in Reading* **8** (1), 21–31.

Sumner, R. (1987) *The Role of Testing in Schools*. Windsor: NFER-Nelson.

Sutcliffe, J. (1988) The PACT that led to hostilities. *Times Educational Supplement* (8 January), 8.

Tansley, P. and Panckhurst, J. (1981) *Children with Specific Learning Difficulties*. Windsor: NFER-Nelson.

Thomas, D. (1990) 'Reading between the lines'. *Times Educational Supplement* (6 April), 21.

Thomson, B. (1979) *Reading Success: A Guide for Parents and Teachers*. London: Sidgwick & Jackson.

Tomkow, E. M. (1984) 'A survey of the testing of reading in Manchester primary schools'. Unpublished MEd (Reading) dissertation, School of Education, University of Manchester.

Tomlinson, S. (1981) *Educational Subnormality – A Study in Decision-making*. London: Routledge & Kegan Paul.

Topping, K. (1983) *Educational Systems for Disruptive Adolescents*. London: Croom Helm.

Topping, K. (1986) *Parents as Educators*. London: Croom Helm.

Topping, K. (ed.) (1987a) *The Paired Reading Bulletin No. 3*. Huddersfield: Paired Reading Project.

Topping, K. (1987b) *The Peer Tutoring Handbook: Promoting Co-operative Learning*. London: Croom Helm.

Topping, K. (ed.) (1988) *Paired Reading Bulletin No. 4*. Huddersfield: Paired Reading Project.

Topping, K. (1990) 'Outcome evaluation of the Kirklees Paired Reading Project'. Unpublished PhD thesis, Division of Education, University of Sheffield.

Topping, K. and McKnight, G. (1984) Paired reading – and parent power. *Special Education: Forward Trends* **11** (3), 12–15.

Topping, K. and Whiteley, M. (1990) Participant evaluation of parent-tutored and peer-tutored projects in reading. *Educational Research* **32** (1), 14–32.

Topping, K. and Wolfendale, S. (eds) (1985) *Parental Involvement in Children's Reading*. London: Croom Helm.

Tough, J. (1981) *A Place for Talk*. Schools Council Communication Skills Project: Children with Moderate Learning Difficulties. London: Schools

Council in association with Ward Lock Educational and Drake Educational Associates.

Tracey, R. J. and Rankin, E. F. (1970) 'Methods of computing and evaluation of residual gain scores in the reading programme'. In Farr, R. (ed.) *Measurement and Evaluation of Reading*. New York: Harcourt, Brace & World.

Trickey, G. E. F. (1986) Letter names and the teaching of reading. *Educational and Child Psychology* **3** (2), 103–10.

Trisman, D. A., Waller, M. I. and Wilder, G. (1976) *A Descriptive and Analytic Study of Compensatory Reading Programmes*. Princeton, NJ: Educational Testing Service.

Tunnel, M. O. and Jacobs, J. S. (1989) Using 'real' books: research findings on literature based instruction. *The Reading Teacher* **43**, 470–7.

Turner, M. (1990a) Positive responses. *Times Educational Supplement* (19 January), 24.

Turner, M. (1990b) 'A closed book?'. *Times Educational Supplement* (20 July), 12.

Turner, M. (1990c) *Sponsored Reading Failure*. Warlingham: Independent Primary and Secondary Education Trust.

Tyler, S. (1990) 'Subtypes of specific learning difficulty: a review'. In Pumfrey and Elliott, op. cit., pp. 29–39.

Tyler, S. and Elliott, C. D. (1988) Cognitive profiles of groups of poor readers and dyslexic children on the British Ability Scales. *British Journal of Psychology* **79**, 493–508.

Tyre, C. and Young, P. (1984) 'An action research project for dyslexic pupils'. In *Report of a Seminar Held by the Department of Education and Science on 12th May, 1984, to Disseminate the Findings of Four Research Projects on Specific Learning Difficulties*. London: Department of Education and Science.

United States Department of Education (1986) *What Works: Research about Teaching and Learning*. Washington, DC: United States Department of Education.

Verma, G. K. and Pumfrey, P. D. (eds) (1988) *Educational Attainment: Issues and Outcomes in Multicultural Education*. Basingstoke: Falmer Press.

Vernon, M. D. (1977) Varieties of deficiency in reading process. *Harvard Educational Review* **47** (3), 87–100.

Vincent, D. (1985) *Reading Tests in the Classroom*. Windsor: NFER-Nelson.

Vincent, D., Green, L., Francis, J. and Powney, J. (1983) *A Review of Reading Tests*. Windsor: NFER-Nelson.

Vincent, D. and Pugh, A. (eds) (1986) *The Testing and Evaluation of Reading*. London: Macmillan in association with the United Kingdom Reading Association.

Walker, C. (1974) *Reading Development and Extension*. London: Ward Lock Educational.

Waterland, E. (1985) *Read with Me: An Apprenticeship Approach to Reading*. Stroud: Thimble Press.

Watts, P. (1990) Changing times: changing services? *Support for Learning* **5** (1), 6–12.

Webster, A. and McConnell, C. (1987) *Children with Speech and Language Difficulties.* London: Cassell.

Webster, A. and Wood, D. (1989) *Children with Hearing Difficulties.* London: Cassell.

Weintraub, S. (ed.) (1986) *Annual Summary of Investigations Relating to Reading: July 1st 1985–June 30th 1986.* Newark, DE: International Reading Association.

Weintraub, S. (ed.) (1987) *Annual Summary of Investigations Relating to Reading: July 1st 1986–June 30th 1987.* Newark, DE: International Reading Association.

Weintraub, S. (ed.) (1988) *Annual Summary of Investigations Relating to Reading: July 1st 1987–June 30th 1988.* Newark, DE: International Reading Association.

Weintraub, S. (ed.) (1989) *Annual Summary of Investigations Relating to Reading: July 1st 1988–June 30th 1989.* Newark, DE: International Reading Association.

Weintraub, S. (ed.) (1990) *Annual Summary of Investigations Relating to Reading: July 1st 1989–June 30th 1990.* Newark, DE: International Reading Association.

Welch, J. (1987) The individual needs of gifted children. *Support for Learning* **2** (4), 19–26.

Wellington, J. and McDonald, G. (1989) TES survey: computers in the classroom. *Times Educational Supplement* (17 March), B21–7.

Wells, G. (ed.) (1985) *Language, Learning and Education.* Windsor: NFER-Nelson.

Wheldall, K. and Metten, P. (1985) Behavioural peer tutoring: training 16-year-old tutors to employ the 'pause, prompt and praise' method with 12-year-old remedial readers. *Educational Psychology* **5** (1), 27–44.

White, A. (1982a) *Reading and Remedial Reading Resources: Primary.* Leicester: Leicester Schools' Psychological Service.

White, A. (1982b) *Reading and Remedial Reading Resources: Secondary.* Leicester: Leicester Schools' Psychological Service.

Wijk, A. (1959) *Regularised Inglish.* Stockholm: Almquist & Wiksell.

Williams, P. (1988) *A Glossary of Special Education.* Milton Keynes: Open University Press.

Wiltshire County Council Education Department (1988) *Early Identification of Special Needs.* Trowbridge: Wiltshire County Council.

Wolfendale, S. (1987) *Primary Schools and Special Needs: Policy, Planning and Provision.* London: Cassell.

Woods, J. (1979) *Literacy Survey: The Relationship between Reading Progress and Extra Help in Reading.* London: ILEA Research and Statistics Branch.

World Federation of Neurology (1968) *Report of Research Group on Dyslexia and World Illiteracy.* Dallas: WFN.

Young, P. and Tyre, C. (1983) *Dyslexia or Illiteracy? Realising the Right to Read.* Milton Keynes: Open University Press.

Zakaluk, B. L. and Samuels, J. S. (1988) *Readability: Its Past, Present and Future.* Newark, DE: International Reading Association.

Name Index

Subject Index